Kingship and Justice in the Ottonian Empire

THE OTTONIAN DYNASTY
A Basic Genealogy

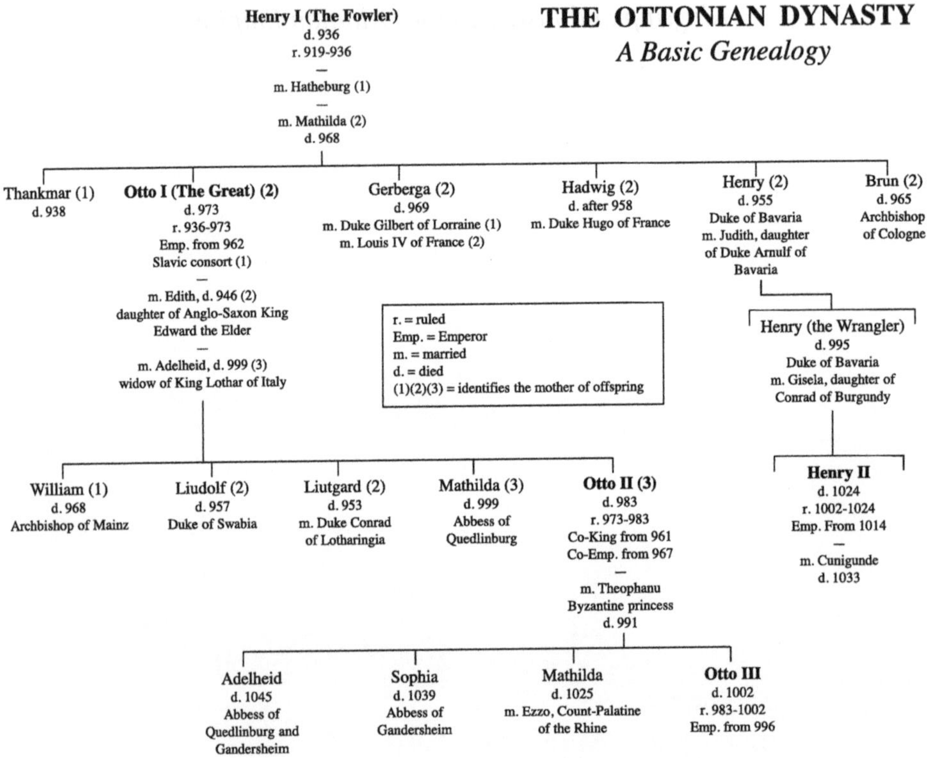

Kingship and Justice in the Ottonian Empire

Laura E. Wangerin

University of Michigan Press

Ann Arbor

Published in the United States of America by the
University of Michigan Press
Printed and bound by CPI Group (UK) Ltd, Croydon, CR0 4YY

First published May 2019

A CIP catalog record for this book is available
from the British Library.

Library of Congress Cataloging-in-Publication data
has been applied for.

ISBN: 978-0-472-13139-6 (Hardcover : alk paper)
ISBN: 978-0-472-12528-9 (ebook)

To my mother
Donna Eggers
and
In loving memory of my father
Gene Eggers

Acknowledgments

Over the many years that this book has been in the making, I have accumulated too many debts of gratitude to adequately acknowledge them all here, though I will try to convey my thanks to as many people as possible in this small space. I owe thanks first to the many people who read part or all of the manuscript of this book throughout its development. The anonymous readers at the University of Michigan Press provided many thoughtful comments and helpful suggestions. The kind invitations to share my work in various workshops and seminars resulted in generous feedback, and thanks are extended to the Seton Hall History Department Faculty Workshop; the University of Chicago Medieval Colloquium; the University of New Hampshire Dunfey Conference on Legitimacy, Lordship and Government in the Post-Carolingian World; and the University of Wisconsin-Madison Institute for Legal Studies Workshop.

Institutional support has been crucial for the completion of this book. The Seton Hall University Summer Writing Retreats organized by Mary Balkun provided dedicated writing time that was very much appreciated. The Honorary Fellowship in the Department of History at the University of Wisconsin-Madison has been especially helpful in providing access to resources without which this book could not have been written. Thanks are also extended to the many libraries, and their librarians and staff members, who facilitated the research for this volume and granted permission to reproduce images from their collections, including those at Seton Hall University, the University of Wisconsin-Madison, the University of Chicago, the Warburg Institute, the British Library, the John Rylands University Library at the University of Manchester, the Bayerische Staatsbibliothek, and the Bamberg Staatsbibliothek.

This project could not have been accomplished without the support of a small army of family members, friends, colleagues, teachers, and mentors. At the University of Wisconsin-Madison, Karl Shoemaker was my graduate advisor, and I am grateful for his unfailing support of my research, then and now. Leonora Neville and Thomas Dale provided critical feedback as well as ongoing support of this project. Mark Kleijvek and Ivy Corfis offered commentary on my dissertation that was helpful in reenvisioning it as a book. Ellen Bauerle at the University of Michigan Press deserves thanks for seeing the potential of this project and helping to make it become a reality. Thanks also go to Gordon Thompson, who drew the maps for this volume. In the History Department at Seton Hall University, I am fortunate to have found warm and welcoming colleagues who have been incredibly supportive of my work. The same can be said of many other people across the university.

I am continually humbled by the generosity of the people I have met in academia who have shared ideas, offered suggestions, and provided encouragement; many of these encounters have developed over the years into valued friendships. At risk of inadvertently neglecting to include someone or an unfortunate lapse of memory, the following people nonetheless deserve a special mention. David Bachrach, Robert Berkhofer III, John Bernhardt, Candace Pryor Brown, Michael Clanchy, Bill Connell, Valerie Garber, Laura Gathagan, Patrick Geary, Paul Hyams, Nathaniel Knight, Ada Kuskowski, Amy Livingstone, Jonathan Lyon, David MacDonald, Sara McDougall, Bill North, Levi Roach, Tom Rzeznik, Jim Sweet, and Angela Weisl are among those who have listened, encouraged, read, commented, suggested, and shared. People such as these define what I always envisioned an ideal scholarly community could be like. It is a privilege to be a part of it.

The unwavering support and enthusiasm of friends and family throughout the course of this journey just shows how fortunate I am. Thanks to all of our friends in Wisconsin, Michigan, Illinois, New Jersey, and scattered through the rest of the United States and around the world. Thanks to my parents, Gene and Donna Eggers, for everything. Thanks to our four-legged friends who reminded me how important it is to walk away from the computer periodically to get out and play. Not all of them are still with us, but this project would have been much less joyful without the presence of Lucy, Dakota, Skyler, and Zor. And thanks most of all to my husband Bill. This book would not exist without him. So Bill, for all of the many ways you have helped make this possible—thank you.

Contents

Abbreviations

Af	Laws of Alfred. In *Die Gesetze der Angelsachsen*, edited by Felix Liebermann, vol. 1. Halle: Max Niemeyer, 1903, 16–88.
As	Laws of Æthelstan. In *Die Gesetze der Angelsachsen*, edited by Felix Liebermann, vol. 1. Halle: Max Niemeyer, 1903, 146–83.
ASC	Swanton, Michael, ed. *The Anglo-Saxon Chronicle*. New York: Routledge, 1998.
Atr	Laws of Æthelred. In *Die Gesetze der Angelsachsen*, edited by Felix Liebermann, vol. 1. Halle: Max Niemeyer, 1903, 218–70.
BL	British Library, London.
Cn	Laws of Cnut. In *Die Gesetze der Angelsachsen*, edited by Felix Liebermann, vol. 1. Halle: Max Niemeyer, 1903, 278–371.
Cn 1020	Cnut's letter to England, 1020 CE. In *Die Gesetze der Angelsachsen*, edited by Felix Liebermann, vol. 1. Halle: Max Niemeyer, 1903, 273–275.
Cn 1027	Cnut's letter to England, 1027 CE. In *Die Gesetze der Angelsachsen*, edited by Felix Liebermann, vol. 1. Halle: Max Niemeyer, 1903, 276–77.
Eg	Laws of Edgar. In *Die Gesetze der Angelsachsen*, edited by Felix Liebermann, vol. 1. Halle: Max Niemeyer, 1903, 192–215.
EHD	Whitelock, Dorothy. *English Historical Documents*. Vol. 1, *500–1042*. 1955. Reprint, London: Routledge, 1979.
Em	Laws of Edmund. In *Die Gesetze der Angelsachsen*, edited by Felix Liebermann, vol. 1. Halle: Max Niemeyer, 1903, 184–91.
KJV	King James Version of the Bible.

HR	Arnold, Thomas, ed. *Symeonis Monachi Opera Omnia*. Vol. 2, *Historia Regum*. Cambridge: Cambridge University Press, 1885.	
MGH	*Monumenta Germaniae Historica*	
	DD CI	Diplomas of Conrad I. In *Diplomata Regum et Imperatorum Germaniae*. Edited by Theodor Sickel. Hanover: Hahn, 1879–84, 2–36.
	DD CII	Diplomas of Conrad II. In *Diplomata Regum et Imperatorum Germaniae*. Vol. 4. Edited by Harry Bresslau. Hanover: Hahn, 1909, 1–417.
	DD HI	Diplomas of Henry I. In *Diplomata Regum et Imperatorum Germaniae*. Vol. 1. Edited by Theodor Sickel. Hanover: Hahn, 1879–84, 39–79.
	DD HII	Diplomas of Henry II. In *Diplomata Regum et Imperatorum Germaniae*. Vol. 3. Edited by Harry Bresslau, Hermann Bloch, and Robert Holtzmann. Hanover: Hahn, 1900–1903, 1–692.
	DD OI	Diplomas of Otto I. In *Diplomata Regum et Imperatorum Germaniae*. Vol. 1. Edited by Theodor Sickel. Hanover: Hahn, 1879–84, 89–638.
	DD OII	Diplomas of Otto II. In *Diplomata Regum et Imperatorum Germaniae*. Vol. 2. Edited by Theodor Sickel. Hanover: Hahn, 1893, 10–384.
	DD OIII	Diplomas of Otto III. In *Diplomata Regum et Imperatorum Germaniae*. Vol. 2. Edited by Theodor Sickel. Hanover: Hahn, 1893, 393–875.
	MGH BDKz 2	*Die Briefsammlung Gerberts von Reims*. Edited by Fritz Weigle. Die Briefe der deutschen Kaiserzeit 2. Weimar: Hermann Bohlaus Nachfolger, 1966.
	MGH Capit	*Capitularia Regum Francorum*. 2 vols. Edited by Alfred Boretius and Victor Krause. Capitularia, Legum Sectio II. Hanover: Hahn, 1883–97.
	MGH Conc	*Die Konzilien Deutschlands und Reichsitaliens, 916–1001*. 2 vols. Edited by Ernst-Dieter Hehl. Concilia 6. Hanover: Hahn, 1987–2007.
	MGH Const	*Constitutiones et Acta Publica Imperatorum et Regum*. Vol. 1. Edited by L. Weiland. Hanover: Hahn, 1893.
	MGH Epist IV	*Epistolae Karolini Aevi*. Vol. 2. Edited by Ernest Duemmler. Berlin: Weidmann, 1895.

MGH Leges — *Legum*. 2 vols. Edited by G. H. Pertz. Hanover: Hahn, 1837.

MGH SRG — Scriptores rerum Germanicarum in usum scholarum.

MGH SS — *Scriptores*. Vols. 3, 4, and 6. Edited by G. H. Pertz. Hanover: Hahn, 1839–44.

NCMH — *The New Cambridge Medieval History*. 7 vols. Cambridge: Cambridge University Press, 1995–2005.

RI — *Regesta Imperii*. http://www.regesta-imperii.de/en/startseite.html

s.a. (pl. s.aa.) — *sub anno*

S 000 — Catalog number in *The Electronic Sawyer Online Catalogue of Anglo-Saxon Charters*, http://www.esawyer.org.uk

Map 1. The Ottonian Empire at the time of Otto the Great

Introduction

The Saxon Ottonian dynasty lasted barely a century. It was comprised of five rulers: Henry I (r. 919–36) and his son Otto I the Great (r. 936–73), grandson Otto II (r. 973–83), great-grandson Otto III (r. 983–1002), and great-grandson (through a different line) Henry II (Otto III's second cousin, r. 1002–24). The brevity of this dynasty belies its importance in the shaping of medieval Europe. The empire they ruled extended far beyond the lands that comprise present-day Germany, incorporating areas that are today parts of the Netherlands, France, Italy, and Switzerland.[1] The accomplishments of the Ottonians were significant. Not only was Henry I able to bring the other German dukes under some semblance of control, but he also kept the Magyar invaders on the eastern frontiers at bay, eventually converting them into tributaries. He is credited with building fortified burgs across his realm and restructuring Saxon society.[2] His son, Otto I, decisively defeated the Magyars at the Battle of the Lech and pursued an active policy of expansion. Anointed as Roman emperor by the pope in 962, Otto's realm became the foundation for what would later be known as the Holy Roman Empire. With a flow of wealth from tributaries and newly discovered silver veins in the Harz Mountains,[3] the Ottonians

1. See map 1 at the beginning of this book. The various terms employed by scholars to discuss the Ottonian Empire are treated below, under "A Note about Terminology."

2. The term *burg* can refer to any number of kinds of fortified sites, including castles, walled towns, forts, and manors. Widukind of Corvey provides our only contemporary explicit textual reference for Henry's supposed *Burgenbauordnung* (castle-building order), although there is archaeological evidence of active fortification throughout the realm, if not of an actual edict. See Widukind of Corvey, *Res gestae Saxonicae* 1.35, in *Widukindi monachi Corbiensis rerum gestarum Saxonicarum libri tres*, ed. Paul Hirsch and H.-E. Lohmann after G. Waitz and K. A. Kehr, MGH SRG 60 (Hanover: Hahnsche Buchhandlung, 1935), 48–51; Günter P. Fehring, *The Archaeology of Medieval Germany: An Introduction*, trans. Ross Samson (New York: Routledge, 1991), 137–38; David S. Bachrach, "Henry I of Germany's 929 Military Campaign in Archaeological Perspective," *Early Medieval Europe* 21.3 (2013): 307–37.

3. See Widukind, *Res gestae Saxonicae* 3.63, 138: "terra Saxonia venas argenti aperuerit"; Thietmar of Merseburg, *Chronicon*, 2.13, in *Thietmari Merseburgensis Episcopi Chronicon*, ed. Robert Holtzmann, MGH SRG 9 (Berlin: Weidmannsche Buchhandlung, 1935), 53: "apud nos inventa est primum vena argenti." See also Helen Boyce, *The Mines of the Upper Harz from 1514 to 1589* (Mena-

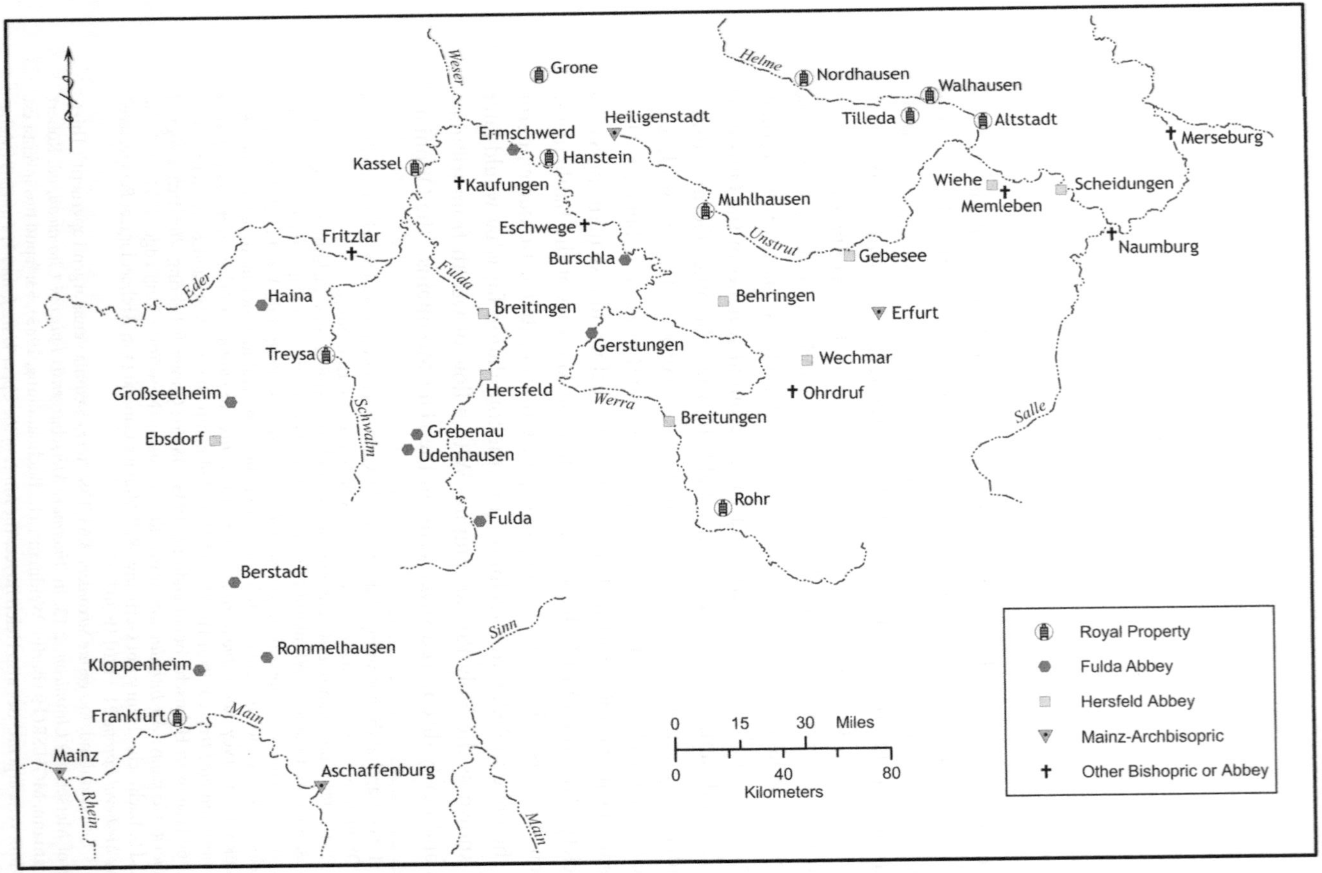

Map 2. Itinerary stations in parts of Thuringia, Franconia, and southern Saxony. Adapted from John Bernhardt, *Itinerant Kingship and Royal Monasteries in Early Medieval Germany c. 936-1075* (Cambridge: Cambridge University Press, 1993), 329 and Wolfgang Metz, "Quellenstudien zum Servitium regis (900–1200)," part 1, *Archiv für Diplomatik* 22 (1976): 226.

built thriving cross-cultural contacts with other Western European cultures as well as with Byzantine, Eastern European pagan, and Arab societies. An active program of building churches, abbeys, burgs, and palaces was undertaken, accompanied by a great flourishing of art and culture. Additionally, the Ottonians reconceptualized what it meant to be kings. Under the Ottos especially, the idea of sacral kingship was cultivated and embraced, and this conceptualization permeated royal art, architecture, ritual, and rulership. That they were the envy of their contemporaries is borne out by the conscious imitation of their rituals by other rulers.[4]

Yet there remains much about the Ottonians that we do not know, despite the richness of the sources—which include contemporary histories and chronicles, diplomas and charters, hagiographies and religious writings, and material objects. For example, we know little about Ottonian lawmaking and enforcement. Scholars have recognized the importance of ritual and symbolic behaviors in the Ottonian political sphere while puzzling over the apparent lack of administrative organization,[5] a contradiction between what we know about the

---

sha, WI: George Banta, 1920), 6. Boyce notes that mines in the south of the Ottonian Empire were active before the tenth century but that the Rammelsberg mines near Goslar in the Harz were first worked during the reign of Otto I ca. 970. She also remarks that "the date of discovery of ore in the Hartz is a disputed question" and that the generally accepted testimony is that of Thietmar (14–15).

4. We can see something of the influence and awe their court inspired in the adaptation of imperial symbolism by the Anglo-Saxon king Edgar and in descriptions of his coronation at Bath in 973. The Roman origins of Bath, with ruins of an amphitheater that might still have existed in the twelfth century, carried with it imperial connotations, as did the suggestion of contemporary chronicles that kings from around Britain came to pay homage to Edgar (Ann Williams, "An Outing on the Dee: King Edgar at Chester, AD 973," *Mediaeval Scandinavia* 14 (2004): 229–43; Williams's note 11 discusses the ruins and their significance). The twelfth-century chronicler John of Worcester reports that after being crowned and anointed at Bath, Edgar "boarded a skiff," and "having set them [the lesser kings] to the oars, and having taken the helm himself, he skilfully steered it through the course of the River Dee" (*The Chronicle of John of Worcester*, ed. and trans. Patrick McGurk [Oxford, 1995], II:424/5). One cannot mistake the similarity of this description with the coronation of Otto I the Great, in 936, when he succeeded his father as Duke of Saxony and king of Germany. The coronation ceremony took place at Aachen, a location also heavy with imperial associations, this time both Roman and Carolingian, and Widukind of Corvey reports that Otto was attended at table at the banquet afterward by the dukes of the four other duchies of the kingdom (Widukind, *Res gestae Saxonicae* 2.1-2.2, 63–67).

5. Timothy Reuter, "The Making of England and Germany, 850–1050: Points of Comparison and Difference," in *Medieval Polities and Modern Mentalities*, ed. Janet Nelson (Cambridge: Cambridge University Press, 2006), 292. See also Karl Leyser, "Ottonian Government," *English Historical Review* 96.381 (1981): 721–53; Henry Mayr-Harting, *Church and Cosmos in Early Ottonian Germany: The View from Cologne* (Oxford: Oxford University Press, 2007), 3; Hagen Keller, "Zum Charakter der 'Staatlichkeit' zwischen karolingischer Reichsreform und hochmittelalterlichem Herrschaftsausbau," *Frühmittelalterliche Studien* 23 (1989): 248–64; Gerd Althoff, *Die Ottonen: Königsherrschaft ohne Staat*, 2nd ed. (Stuttgart: W. Kohlhammer, 2005). David Bachrach offers a critique of and corrective to the idea that the Ottonians lacked an administrative apparatus ("Exercise of Royal Power in Early Medieval Europe: The Case of Otto the Great, 936–73." *Early Medieval Europe* 17.4 (2009): 389–419).

Ottonians as successful rulers and their traditional characterization as rulers of a disorganized polity. Trying to account for the apparent disparity between their political and military achievements, cultural and artistic efflorescence, and relative dynastic stability, which seemingly accompanied a disinterest in writing law or creating a centralized hierarchical administration, is a tension that continues to persist in the scholarship. This book argues that far from being accidental successes or employing primitive methods of governance, the Ottonians were shrewd rulers and administrators who exploited traditional methods of conflict resolution and delegated jurisdictional authority to keep control over their vast empire. Thus, one important aim of this book is to challenge our preconceived notions of what successful government looks like.

Historiography

Historical interpretations and understandings of German medieval history have been colored by early modern and modern assumptions about how Germany transitioned from the Middle Ages to modern statehood. The problem for historians was how to account for an early modern historical development that did not match the path taken by France and England. In their narratives, they perceived that the German kings wantonly gave away power and authority to their magnates, who adhered to practices like royal election to ensure their own positions. By their assessment, the Germans were thus less politically progressive than their French and English neighbors, whose governments were pushing toward centralized power and administration.[6] To account for any appearance of backwardness suggested by this model, nineteenth-century historians asserted that Germany's path to modernity not only was different but set Germany on a special path toward its own modern state idiom. This *Sonderweg*, an approach to understanding the Ottonian era and its successor kingdoms under the Salians and Hohenstaufens, is inherently teleological and assumes that the medieval mind appreciated modern governmental apparatuses as superior to their own state, a questionable proposition at best.[7] German historians of the nineteenth and twentieth centuries often struggled with what are now generally considered to be flawed methods of inquiry, and alternative approaches

6. David A. Warner, "Reading Ottonian History: The *Sonderweg* and Other Myths," in *Challenging the Boundaries of Medieval History: The Legacy of Timothy Reuter*, ed. Patricia Skinner (Turnhout: Brepols, 2009), 81–114. For a summary of the historiographic tradition of Ottonian Germany, see Laura Wangerin, "The Governance of Ottonian Germany in Historiographical Perspective," *History Compass* 15.1 (2017): e12367. https://doi.org/10.1111/hic3.12367

7. Warner, "Reading Ottonian History," 98.

introduced in Germany in the 1930s and 1940s were often influenced by the ideologies of the National Socialist regime. Since the mid-twentieth century, however, key scholars have challenged our perceptions of the Middle Ages as a whole and have presented work influential enough to encourage others to open new areas of inquiry. These new approaches and methodologies have stimulated lively debate in the field, not only challenging historians to reconsider long-held assumptions, but also suggesting new and exciting ways to engage with the tenth-century German empire.

While exhibiting the influence of the National Socialist era, the period immediately preceding World War II and the decades that followed found historians engaging German medieval history with revolutionary new approaches, and their work and its subsequent responses had a profound impact on the field.[8] Especially Otto Brunner's methodology in *Land und Herrschaft* (1939)—with its overt rejection of historians' bias toward modern state structures, either consciously or unconsciously employed as models in their investigations into the medieval past or set up as desirable historical outcomes toward which the Middle Ages proceeded—continues to influence scholarship today.[9] Through his insights about how the various functions that today would be considered state or government prerogatives were distributed between and among a variety of individuals from various social levels, Brunner demonstrated that the traditional divisions between political history and social history were often meaningless when applied to Ottonian history and had important ramifications for the study of medieval history in other parts of Europe.[10] Historians responsible for building on this understanding and positively reshaping the field of Ottonian studies in the 1970s and 1980s include, for example, Hagen Keller, Gerd Althoff, Henry Mayr-Harting, and Karl Leyser.

An additional break with traditional historiography and methodology came in the late 1990s, when an interest in ritual behavior in the Middle Ages suggested new ways of understanding conflict and using primary sources that described conflict and conflict resolution. The idea that the behaviors and actions recounted in these texts were as important as the reported speech or documents produced in the course of these conflicts has influenced all aspects of medieval political history, including that of the Ottonians, suggesting that conflicts between kings and nobles in medieval Germany were not treasonous attempts to

8. Charles R. Bowlus, "The Early Kaiserreich in Recent German Historiography," *Central European History* 23.4 (1990): 350–51. These historians include Gerd Tellenbach and Otto Brunner.

9. Otto Brunner, *Land und Herrschaft: Grundfragen der territorialen Verfassungsgeschichte Südostdeutschlands im Mittelalter* (Baden bei Wien: Rohrer, 1939).

10. Brunner, 145–46, 241; Bowlus, 355.

seize power as much as carefully structured political dramas with subtle and complex rules understood by those involved. These "rules of the game" allowed nobles and kings a means of conflict resolution that can be inferred by the historian from descriptions of the nonverbal communications in records of these conflicts, which can potentially provide a more accurate idea of what was actually happening than can reliance on reported speech. In addition to providing a new approach to understanding Ottonian history, this scholarship on ritual behavior has stimulated lively debate, continuing today, over the use and interpretation of sources.[11]

Scholars have also opened new possibilities by probing the relationships between kings and their nobles in other innovative and exciting ways, such as suggesting that the Ottonian rulers exploited feuds between nobles to promote their own personal agendas.[12] These investigations have foreshadowed work in other areas of medieval history by approaching violence as normative and stressing the tenth century's *differentness* from our own world. These concerns with the interactions and relationships between the medieval *Reich* and its society form a recurring theme and have had a lasting and continuing impact on the field. By forcing a view of the era "with rather more sharp edges and uncomfortable questions" and by pushing for new perspectives, it may be possible to achieve "a powerful rethinking of early German history."[13]

Early modern and modern historians of medieval German history have often been accused of arguing for German exceptionalism. While this book argues that the Ottonians' approach to governing was different and uniquely suited to the social, cultural, and political milieu that they ruled, it is specifi-

11. While not dealing with the Ottonians, Geoffrey Koziol's *Begging Pardon and Favor* (Ithaca, NY: Cornell University Press, 1992) started the debate in favor of using public political ritual behaviors to understand the past. Philippe Buc, while writing in response to Koziol, uses the Ottonians as his exemplars (and takes Althoff to task as well) in *The Dangers of Ritual: Between Early Medieval Texts and Social Scientific Theory* (Princeton, NJ: Princeton University Press, 2001). But Gerd Althoff, in *Spielregeln der Politik im Mittelalter: Kommunikation in Frieden und Fehde* (Darmstadt: Wissenschaftliche Buchsgesellschaft, 1997), was the first to suggest that this new approach to understanding ritual could provide insights into the ubiquitous conflicts described in the medieval German *Reich* and that the behaviors and gestures described were an important means of communication in conflict resolution in the public arenas of politics and feud. See also Gerd Althoff, "The Variability of Rituals in the Middle Ages," in *Medieval Concepts of the Past: Ritual, Memory, Historiography*, ed. Gerd Althoff, Johannes Fried, and Patrick Geary (Cambridge: Cambridge University Press, 2002), 71–87.

12. Karl Leyser, *Rule and Conflict in an Early Medieval Society: Ottonian Saxony* (Bloomington: Indiana University Press, 1979), 9–47.

13. Len Scales, "Beyond the *Regnum Teutonicum*," *German History* 27.1 (2009): 147, referencing the impact of Timothy Reuter on the field. The entries included in the present study's bibliography supply a representative list of Reuter's considerable scholarship.

cally not arguing that the Ottonians were more precocious or exceptional than any other medieval system. By pushing for a rethinking of how we traditionally have thought about medieval government in general and German government in particular, I am here arguing for an appreciation of the different approaches that medieval rulers utilized in governing their kingdoms and empires. Exceptionalism is tricky, but so is the tendency to generalize. Trying to generalize from trends across the geographic and temporal breadth of the Middle Ages must necessarily create outliers, which historians must then accommodate. The present study is an effort to challenge both the impulses to generalize and the impulses to account for differences as precocious or regressive. I hope that the governing system of Ottonian Germany can be appreciated on its own terms, as a way that intelligent rulers dealing with circumstances that often were unique to their territory were able to create and control an empire. Other governments faced different challenges and responded to them in their own ways.

A Note about Terminology

The terminology used by scholars to describe the Ottonian realm is varied and confusing. The Ottonian Empire was complex. Its kingdom comprised East Francia, the kingdom of the Eastern Franks that had formed the bulk of Charlemagne's eastern empire, as opposed to West Francia, or the kingdom of France. In the tenth century, Germany did not yet exist as a state or even as a clearly defined region, though such terms are useful for designating the geographic region where the Ottonians were active. Saxony was the region from which the Ottonians came, where they spent much of their time, and where they enjoyed the greatest support. Additionally, the borders of their realm were greatly expanded by the conquests of Otto I. The term *Holy Roman Empire* did not come into use until long after the Ottonians, in the twelfth century. In the tenth century, the Ottonian realm was simply called the "Western Roman Empire," to distinguish it from the Eastern Roman Empire of the Byzantines. This medieval *Reich* encompassed not only Germanic regions such as Saxony, Franconia, Swabia, and Bavaria but also significant portions of Italy and areas that are today parts of the Netherlands, France, and Switzerland. Throughout this study, the terms *East Francia*, *Western Roman Empire*, and *Reich* are used synonymously to designate the Ottonian Empire.

Historians refer to the members of the dynastic line that includes Otto I the Great as the Ottonians or the Liudolfings, referring to the family name of these kings and emperors. In this study, the terms *Ottonian* and *Liudolfinger* should be understood to refer to the same noble Saxon family, the one from which Henry I and his successors came.

Medieval historians must determine how best to describe the subjects, activities, and structures of a world that is very foreign to our own. Many elements of that world often misleadingly seem familiar to us or similar to elements of our own, and their interpretation is further complicated by the use of "loaded" terminology that carries with it implications and assumptions that are invalid when considering the distant past. That some of these terms are part of the everyday parlance we employ to describe how we ourselves experience the modern world further dulls our awareness of the free use of such terms and of the implications such usage might hold for our understanding of the past, as well as for how history and historic inquiry are communicated and understood by others.

Many of the terms we use to understand and describe types of governance and states derive from early modern ideas about state-building and how governments ought to look. After all, in this period of Enlightenment, governments were torn down and re-created, as in revolutionary France, or built new, as in the United States. With the concurrent development of new sciences that studied different kinds of human societies, such as anthropology and sociology, as well as early modern intellectuals' expression of an inherent sense of superiority and manifest destiny of progress, the perception of governments as progressive or regressive, as precociously modern or persistently backward, tinged how the past was viewed, studied, and judged. While scholars today are much more self-conscious about how they approach their subjects, several of those early modern holdovers of terminology persist. Dichotomies such as centralized/decentralized, public/private,[14] or legal/extralegal[15] suggest distinctions and imply a worldview that quite simply did not exist in the tenth-century world this book explores. How can we best describe a government that had no geographic capital, that freely delegated or franchised authority, and to which "law" meant not written legislation but customary self-help conflict resolution operating alongside a complex and sophisticated court system that judged pleas

14. See Fredric L. Cheyette "Some Reflections on Violence, Reconciliation, and the 'Feudal Revolution,'" in *Conflict in Medieval Europe: Changing Perspectives on Society and Culture*, ed. Warren Brown and Piotr Górecki (Burlington, VT: Ashgate, 2003), 256–57; Max Weber recognized the inapplicability of a public/private distinction with what he calls "traditional" governments, including those of the Middle Ages, in *The Theory of Social and Economic Organization*, trans. A. M. Henderson and Talcott Parsons (New York: Oxford University Press, 1947), 341–42. See also Talcott Parsons' introduction to Weber, 58, 61.

15. For a discussion on what is "law" in the Middle Ages, see Frederic L. Cheyette, "Suum cuique tribuere," *French Historical Studies* 6.3 (1976): 287–99.

on a case-by-case basis? If the preceding dichotomies are inadequate, what language should replace them?[16] There is no easy or quick answer, of course, but terms that merit a more considered and thoughtful assessment, especially as their employment (as terms and as topics) are central to this study, are *power*, *decentralization*, and *success*.

Obviously, understanding power is important to understanding relationships. To gauge by the sheer number of monographs on medieval history that use the word *power* in their titles, this significance has not been lost on historians. But what exactly does that term mean? Several titles have sought to define it, while others have quite deliberately not. Some point out that since power relationships exist at all levels of society, the study of power could quite simply encompass the entire study of history; others suggest that power has its own history. For some, the term *power*, used explicitly or implicitly in their writing, refers to a specific element of rulership.[17] Additionally and significantly, any discussion of power and what it means ends up drawing in larger and equally complex concepts, such as law or conflict. Since its publication, Frederic Cheyette's article that began with the simple question "What is 'Law'?" has prompted, within the circles of medieval law and conflict studies, "a persistent uncertainty of just what 'law,' or 'conflict,' or related words 'mean,' in their essence, and within the context of this particular different and exotic society."[18] Other words have been subject to debate and reappraisal as well—perhaps most notably *feudalism*.[19] But defining the term *power* presents additional problems. What is power? What exactly does it mean to have power? Is power the ability to coerce? Is it the act of coercion itself?[20]

In *The Sources of Social Power*, Michael Mann defines power as "the ability

16. Warren Brown and Piotr Górecki wrangle with these kinds of tensions—regarding the use of modern terminology to explain past structures, reification of concepts or terms, and problems with nominalism and referents—in "What Conflict Means: The Making of Medieval Conflict Studies in the United States, 1970–2000," in Brown and Górecki, *Conflict in Medieval Europe*, 1–35.

17. See, for example, introduction to *The Experience of Power in Medieval Europe, 950–1350*, ed. Robert Berkhofer, Alan Cooper, and Adam J. Kosto (Burlington, VT: Ashgate, 2005), 1–7; introduction to *Representations of Power in Medieval Germany, 800–1500*, ed. Bjorn Weiler and Simon MacLean (Turnhout: Brepols, 2006), 1–14; Brown and Górecki, "What Conflict Means," esp. 10–18.

18. Cheyette, "Suum quique tribuere," 287; Brown and Górecki, "What Conflict Means," 4. Cheyette was playing with the new self-consciousness about terms and their use in historic writing that arose in the 1970s, which was perhaps best illustrated by Paul Veyne, who asked the question "Qu'est-ce que l'histoire?" (What is history?) at the beginning of his influential essay "Comment on écrit l'histoire" (*Comment on écrit l'histoire suivi de Foucault révolutionne l'histoire* [1971; repr., Paris: Éditions du Seuil, 1978], 9).

19. Elizabeth A. R. Brown, "The Tyranny of a Construct: Feudalism and Historians of Medieval Europe," *American Historical Review* 79.4 (1974): 1063–88.

20. Máire A. Dugan, "Coercive Power," *Beyond Intractability*, September 2003, http://www.beyondintractability.org/essay/threats

to pursue and attain goals through mastery of one's environment."[21] He further clarifies that his approach to a study of power rests on two fundamental ideas: first, that "societies are constituted of multiple overlapping and intersecting sociospacial networks of power";[22] second, that the best way to examine the structure and history of a society is by looking at the interactive relationships between the "four sources of social power: ideological, economic, military, and political."[23] The key, according to Mann, is to recognize that these are "*overlapping networks of social interaction*, not dimensions, levels, or factors of a single social totality"; that they are "also *organizations, institutional means of attaining human goals*"; and that "their primacy comes not from the strength of human desires for ideological, economic, military, or political satisfaction but from the particular *organizational means* each possesses to attain human goals, whatever these may be."[24] A decade earlier than Mann, Michel Foucault was experimenting in his writings with the meaning of power. While much of his speculation focused on power relative to the state, he incorporated many similar ideas about power into his oeuvre, including the importance of viewing power as networked relationships, "power networks that invest the body, sexuality, the family, kinship, knowledge, technology, and so forth."[25] One might understand Mann's emphasis on organizational means to parallel Foucault's ideas that power is a "management of possibilities" achieved through government, understood in the very broad early modern definition of government as "the way in which the conduct of individuals or groups might be directed," including tools and methods of statecraft as well as the direction of families, souls, communities, or children.[26] A notable distinction regarding Foucault's ideas about power is that he saw violence as one of many tools of power but not as power in and of itself: "What defines a relationship of power is that it is a mode of action that does not act directly and immediately on others. Instead, it acts upon their actions: an action upon an action, on possible or actual future or present actions."[27] For the purposes of the present study, power should be understood as encompassing the related ideas of networked social relationships, the ability to govern or direct behaviors, and the ability to do so indirectly as well as directly, by means of tools such as legislation, force, or consent.

21. Michael Mann, *The Sources of Social Power*, vol. 1 (1986; repr., New York: Cambridge University Press, 2012), 6.
22. Ibid., 1.
23. Ibid., 2.
24. Ibid.; Mann's italics.
25. Michel Foucault, "Truth and Power," in *Power*, ed. James D. Faubion (1994; repr., New York: New Press, 2000), 111–33, 123.
26. Michel Foucault, "The Subject and Power," in *Power*, 326–48, 341.
27. Ibid., 340.

Like *power*, the terms we have come to use to understand how governments are organized are also problematic. The traditional dichotomy of centralized/decentralized, which seems fairly straightforward at first glance, embodies early modern and modern conceptions of how an effective government ought to look. This road is fraught with peril. Precisely this conception has led scholars to consider the Anglo-Saxon government of the early Middle Ages, with its hierarchical courts and administrative apparatuses overseen by the king and his high court, to be precociously modern, for that government resonates, perhaps more than any other medieval one, with Western cultural expectations for good, effective governance. Likewise, decentralized governments have been characterized as primitive, as less modern, or even as part of failed state infrastructures, which is one reason why traditional historical narratives have reflected puzzlement over how the Ottonians were able to successfully govern for over a century, despite their lack of governmental apparatuses such as we see with the Anglo-Saxons or even the direct predecessors of the Ottonians, the Carolingians. These perceptions, often unconsciously employed, do a disservice to the study of medieval government, to systems of rule characterized as centralized or decentralized. By comparing, even unconsciously, the centralized systems and our modern states, we run the risk of oversimplification, of missing key elements that made those governments unique and particular to their very different, very foreign worlds. By dismissing decentralized governments as backward or primitive, we focus on the results of successful governing without understanding the mechanisms that made those successes possible and without appreciating their own sophisticated apparatuses that—though different—were no less effective. In the case of the Ottonians, who are the subject of this study, it is clear that a "decentralized" government did not mean a fragmentation of power. But what terminology could we use instead? The dichotomy of "fixed" versus "localized" seems unsatisfactory to describe the Ottonian system, as does discussing "symmetrical" versus "asymmetrical" patterns of power. In the present study, then, the term *centralized* refers to a hierarchical administrative structure of monarchial governance, and the term *decentralized* indicates an administrative structure dependent on delegated or franchised authority, without any implied dilution of regnal power.

The last term that it is necessary to deal with here is *success*. How is successful governance measured? How do we know if the Ottonians were successful? Did they consider themselves successful as a dynasty or as rulers? My use of the term *success* as a way of defining Ottonian governance is my own. I consider the Ottonians to have been successful because they enjoyed relative dynastic stability and were able to quash internal unrest, maintain and expand their spheres of influence, and defend and expand their borders. They acquired fabulous wealth and were able to sponsor building programs and artistic output of an exceptional nature. Additionally, later generations of scholars, lyricists, poets, and painters looked back on the Ottonians as the epitome of an imperial court. Success indeed.

This Book

Originally, this book was conceived as an extended comparative study of the Ottonians and Anglo-Saxons. While its current form now focuses on the Ottonians, it seemed helpful to make comparisons to the Anglo-Saxons and/or other polities in some chapters or sections. The intent of these comparisons is not to suggest that any one system was better than another but to show that multiple systems (i.e., West Francia, East Francia, Anglo-Saxon England, Italy) operated perfectly well alongside each other while being nothing alike. At the same time, all these polities were, in some degree, inheritors of the Carolingian tradition. While each of the individual chapters of this book deals with a different aspect of Ottonian governance, I hope that the reader will come away with an overall sense of the complexity, the sophistication, and the functionality of the Ottonian method of rule, to which the Ottonians owed their success.

Chapter 1 explores governing structures in Ottonian Germany, arguing that key elements of the Ottonians' style of rulership were strengths, not, as has often been suggested, weaknesses that detracted from their authority. In fact, these elements, which included such things as an emphasis on the royal *iter*, rule by consensus, and a significant degree of delegated authority, comprised a highly developed political system. It served the needs of its kings and emperors and created a stable infrastructure of government able to withstand the rebellions and power struggles that were normal among the medieval nobility. This system stood in stark contrast to the situations in France and Italy and bears closer examination as an example of a successful model of governance.

Chapter 2 investigates the relationship between royal and ecclesiastical power. In Ottonian Germany, ecclesiastical jurisdictions were important, often contentious components of the system of royal governance. In Germany, in contrast to other areas, ecclesiastical jurisdictions resembled those of great lords both in their scope and in their obligations to the emperor. Whereas bishops could, like their secular counterparts, operate with great autonomy in the administration of law and justice over their lands, they were also responsible for such duties as military service. The conflicts that would arise later in the eleventh century, as part of the Investiture Controversy, no doubt found their inception in the disputes that arose over episcopal and abbatial elections. Throughout the medieval world, kings tried to place *fideles*, lords who owed them allegiance, in these positions, but bishops in the Ottonian Empire were more like great princes, with substantial revenues and powers. There was still significant fluidity between the concepts of secular and sacred spheres, and episcopal elections could be highly charged events. The effectiveness of the Ottonian system lay largely in its ability to control its magnates and command their loyalty, through force if necessary. When the Ottonian dynasty ended, it was perhaps inevitable that great lords, both secular and ecclesiastical, would attempt to assert or expand their influence. The first Salian rulers had to deal with a certain measure of turmoil, reminiscent of the magnate rebellions and struggles that Henry I and Otto I faced when establishing their dynasty and that challenged Henry II after the sudden death of Otto III. That bishops were among those rebellious magnates should not surprise us. The Investiture Controversy ended up substantially redefining the relationship between the church and the German emperors, and the present study suggests that it was a conflict over patronage and resource allocation, foregrounded in the Ottonian efforts to create and maintain control over imperial bishoprics and monasteries.

Legislative activity, the subject of chapter 3, is another area of Ottonian rule that bears reconsideration. While the dearth of legislative materials from the Ottonians has been remarked on but never really investigated, the prolific production of legislation by the Anglo-Saxons in a period when the rest of the medieval West was producing little, if any, has been held up as one example of Anglo-Saxon precociousness. But the intensely violent and endemic feuding culture of the Anglo-Saxon kingdoms was potentially the source of their prolific legislative activity, and the Ottonians were not trying to bring feuding behaviors under royal control. This distinction reflects two very different approaches to governing in the two realms. While the Anglo-Saxons were actively trying to claim a royal monopoly on blood justice, the Ottonians were content to limit their involvement to cases where feuding became too disruptive to ignore. Feud behavior was allowed by the Ottonians because it served their purposes for peacekeeping in the realm. Of the very little legislation that was written, much of it addressed out-of-control feuding activities in specific localities. This focus further suggests that attempts to control feud behaviors drove legislative activity in both realms. It also supports the idea that to maintain order in their realm, the Ottonians relied on traditional methods of conflict resolution in jurisdictions delegated to local authorities.

Chapter 4 examines Ottonian symbols of authority and looks at how ruler images, relics, and rituals reinforced the development of a ruling ideology. Not only do the pictorial representations of Ottonian rulers demonstrate how they used images as part of their efforts to legitimize their rule as sacral, but these representations also help show the evolution of a distinctive political philosophy. The legitimization of this claim to sacral kingship was reinforced by the use of symbols and rituals. Chapter 4 argues not only that the representations of Ottonian rulers can be used to understand how they were developing an ideology of kingship but also that these visual images and rituals were important with regard to their affective power in helping to enforce this concept of kingship.

Chapter 5 looks at the administration of justice and how the Ottonians' ideas about justice reflected their ruling ideologies. In their development of an ideology of sacral kingship, the Ottonians positioned themselves as the imitators of Christ on earth. They saw themselves not merely as kings who promulgated God's law but as anointed emperors who inhabited the sacral sphere and whose judgments directly mediated divine will. This version of kingship is articulated in a case-by-case petition-based royal process, as opposed to a royal legislative program, and reflects the distinctive way in which justice was administered in the Ottonian Empire. The petition-based nature of imperial law, with its dependence on intercessors, has a certain logic to it when considered in the context of liturgical kingship. Just as one communicated with God by petition and intercession—via prayers and the intercession of priests—a similar process was required when pleading for justice before the *christomimetes*.

Additionally, the Ottonian kings' reliance on trial by combat reinforces the idea of sacral kingship.[28] Karl Leyser once commented that it must have been easier for recalcitrant nobles to submit to a sacral king than to a nonsacral one,[29] and this was surely true for the outcome of judicial duels as well. Even when the outcome was unclear or disputed, it provided both a terminus to a conflict and peace between factions. Like their reliance on feuds, these other elements of Ottonian rulership provided a strong and effective system that did not need to rely on efforts toward legal consistency across their realm.[30]

As we have seen, one element that contributes to the continued misunderstanding of the Ottonians is that the traditional narratives and vocabulary used to

28. Like the difference between the Anglo-Saxon proliferation of legislation and the nearly complete absence of Ottonian legislation, the frequent use of trial by combat by the Ottonians stands in stark contrast to its complete absence in Anglo-Saxon England.

29. K. Leyser, *Rule and Conflict*, 95.

30. These elements include the development of an ideology of liturgical kingship, the success of the Ottonian system of delegated jurisdictional authority with a petition-based imperial court, and the use of the bilateral ordeal to help adjudicate certain cases.

describe Ottonian government suggest that its structure, conventionally described as decentralized, was anomalous to its success.[31] Again for lack of better vocabulary, the term *decentralized*, used to describe organizational patterns in other kinds of systems, is used throughout this book as a synonym for a distributed system, without carrying any value-laden implications. The Ottonian system of governance and legal authority is foreign to our modern worldview and in many ways more tied to the eras that preceded it, with little obvious impact on modern institutions. We should take care not to fall into the trap of considering various models of premodern governance as either precocious or regressive. The Ottonian model of governance provided a framework for rule that withstood significant pressures, including the stresses of dealing with rebellion or dynastic change, as well as allowed expansion of territory and influence, significant cultural output and achievement, and ongoing investment in infrastructure, including fortifications, monasteries, and churches.

The Ottonians had no political center or capital and maintained a complex itinerary that kept the royal court almost continually mobilized. There was a strong sense of the need for the actual presence of the king to ensure stability throughout the realm. The Ottonian governing model was indeed decentralized (to use our definition), and its key strengths were features of that decentralized, distributed infrastructure, including such things as an emphasis on the royal *iter*, rule by consensus, and a significant degree of delegated authority. Far from being indicative of a dilution of power or ineffectual kingship, these elements formed the foundation of a highly developed political system. It served the needs of its kings and emperors and created a stable infrastructure of government able to withstand the rebellions and power struggles that were normal among the medieval nobility. This infrastructure stood in stark contrast to the situations in England, France, and Italy and bears closer examination as an example of a successful model of premodern governance.

The essential structure of Ottonian authority was hierarchical and consisted of an extension of the king's rule over his *familiares* from his household to others less close in kinship, *amicitia*, and proximity. Magnates who were further removed from court circles were still his *fideles*, but obligations were imposed on

31. While itinerance in early medieval Europe was not unique to the Ottonians, both their commitment to it as a central feature of their government and the sheer distances covered by the court stand in contrast to other medieval polities. For example, the tenth-century Anglo-Saxon kings maintained an itinerary but were only perambulating a geographic area the size of a single Ottonian county. Additionally, their government was distinguished by a hierarchy of institutions that seem, especially in the English-speaking world, much more tangibly tied to modern ideas about governance. That many of these institutions persist today reinforces that perception.

them less frequently.[32] That irregularity in intensity of government throughout the Ottonian *Reich* is one of its significant features. Regnal authority weighed more heavily in Saxony than in regions where the Ottonian influence was less entrenched, such as Bavaria, Carinthia, Swabia, and Lotharingia.[33]

While many aspects of Ottonian government consciously emulated that of the Carolingians, much of the Ottonian version depended on traditional means of political conduct and peacekeeping, such as a reliance on *amicitia* networks (family, friends, and kinship relationships), the commonly understood rules for feud negotiations, and public rituals to communicate negotiated settlements.[34] These well-attested elements of Ottonian government do not suggest anything that supports a "royal technology of power"[35] or strength of government with the ability to enforce the royal will. But the Ottonians did indeed have a "royal technology of power," although it has not been understood as such thus far.

32. K. Leyser, "Ottonian Government," 733; see also Gerd Althoff, *Family, Friends, and Followers: Political and Social Bonds in Early Medieval Europe*, trans. Christopher Carroll (Cambridge: Cambridge University Press, 2004), esp. 65–101.

33. K. Leyser, "Ottonian Government," 733.

34. Regarding the importance of ritual behaviors in dispute resolution, see Koziol, *Begging Pardon and Favor*; Althoff, *Spielregeln der Politik im Mittelalter*, 21–56. For discussion of other political rituals specific to Ottonian Germany, see Buc, *Dangers of Ritual*, 15–50; David A. Warner, "Ritual and Memory in the Ottonian *Reich*: The Ceremony of *Adventus*," *Speculum* 76.2 (2001): 255–83.

35. Paul Hyams uses this phrase when arguing against a maximalist interpretation of Anglo-Saxon legal institutions to refer to the governmental apparatuses needed to carry out a king's orders when he is not physically present, that is, the crucial difference between aspirational law and the ability to enforce it (*Rancor and Reconciliation in Medieval England* [Ithaca, NY: Cornell University Press, 2003], 101).

CHAPTER 1

Governing Structures in Ottonian Germany

The Ottonians produced almost no legislation. But to assume that there was no sense of a law or imperial order in their empire would be a mistake. The Ottonian chancery produced "technically accomplished and beautiful" diplomas,[1] which provide us the best documentary evidence of the Ottonians. Like the literary sources, these documents "proclaimed the ritual and homiletic functions of kingship if only to lend the greatest possible weight and force to the legal and fiscal changes enjoined in their dispositive clauses."[2] That there were legal changes indicated in the diplomas is key, and these documents have been greatly underestimated by those seeking evidence of written legislative activity in East Francia during the Ottonian era.

But questions arise regarding the large number of Ottonian diplomas that are extant today, especially considering the lack of legislative documents. Were diplomas used as a tool of governance? Were they used in lieu of legislation? Evidence for imperial interest in the administration of justice throughout the realm includes documents that address feuding activities, trade policies, and dispute resolution, as well as synodal decrees.[3] The German royal court was conceived of as the general guardian of justice and judicial rights.[4] The idea of the king as the supreme magistrate, whose duty it was to provide peace and justice for all his subjects, evolved under the Carolingians in their capitularies but harked back to even older, traditional Germanic ideas about kingship.[5] From the *Annals* of Flodoard of Reims, we know that even from the rule of Henry I,

1. Karl Leyser, "Ottonian Government," *English Historical Review* 96.381 (1981): 725.

2. Ibid., 724.

3. For documents addressing feuding activities, see DD HII 501, 507. The connection between Ottonian diplomas and imperial trading policies is noted by Peter Johanek ("Merchants, Markets, and Towns," in *NCMH* 3:81). For dispute resolution, documents are extant for the reigns of Otto I to Henry II and include DD OI 269, 340, 342, 375, 398–99, 400, 405, 416; DD OII 266, 282, 298, 315; DD OIII 193, 227, 270, 278, 339, 396, 411; and DD HII 299, 461, 465, 467.

4. Benjamin Arnold, *Medieval Germany, 500–1300: A Political Interpretation* (Toronto: University of Toronto Press, 1997), 146.

5. Ibid., 151–52.

administering justice and maintaining peace was a matter of concern for the Ottonian kings, who were actively involved in negotiating peace within their realm and in neighboring kingdoms, pursuing recalcitrant lords who refused to come to justice, and convening synods to resolve conflicts involving ecclesiastical lords.[6]

Ottonian courts were itinerant. This method of rulership, which kept the king and his household perpetually on the move, still had all the administrative needs of sedentary courts. While the chancery was utilized in a different way than under the Carolingians, its importance in the Ottonian governmental structure must not be underestimated. The continuity between the Carolingian and Ottonian chanceries and the model of having chancery officials perform double duty as court chaplains are the most notable elements of this administrative arm.[7] The Ottonians staffed their chapel and chancery with *capellani*, clerical elites who were usually talented noblemen, although there were less prominent notaries who did not become part of the capellanate. They were often utilized for missions outside of the court, followed the court as part of the king's *comitatus*, were expected to attend and occasionally preside over Italian *placita* (public assemblies), were sent on diplomatic missions, mediated between disputing parties, and, as the emperor's emissaries, acted as principals in local assemblies.[8]

Much about Ottonian administrative functionaries remains unknown to historians, including the degree to which the Ottonians emulated their Carolingian predecessors in their structure and methods of governance. In particular, the Ottonians' lack of *missi dominici*, royal or imperial messengers, has been

6. For example, Henry I sent one of his magnates into Lotharingia to resolve conflict among the Lotharingians (926), vigorously pursued Count Boso to bring him to justice and try to gain his allegiance (928–29), and intervened with King Raoul on behalf of Heribert to negotiate a peace (934). Otto I busily negotiated peace between Louis and Hugh the Great and between Heribert and Heribert's son in 942 and again between Louis and Hugh the Great in 947. Otto also convened a *placitum* (965) and synods (962, 965). Not only were the synods summoned by Otto and not by ecclesiastical authorities, but the *Annals* report that at least one synod heard legal cases and was a venue for lawmaking (Flodoard of Reims, *Annales*, s.a. 948, in MGH SS 3, 395–98; this synod is also recorded in MGH Conc 6.1, 135 and MGH Const 1, 8–16). These events are recorded in multiple chronicles; even in cases where there is clearly borrowing from earlier texts, their inclusion speaks to the perceived importance of these activities as regnal and imperial duties.

7. K. Leyser, "Ottonian Government," 725. Josef Fleckenstein's *Die Hofkapelle im Rahmen der ottonisch-salischen Reichskirche*, vol. 2 of *Die Hofkapelle der deutschen Könige* (Stuttgart: Anton Hiersemann, 1966), remains the classic study on the role of the chapel and *capellani* within the Ottonian court.

8. K. Leyser, "Ottonian Government," 725–26. Timothy Reuter refers to *capellani* as "clerical vassals of the king," calling attention to both their function and their relationship to the king ("The 'Imperial Church System' of the Ottonian and Salian Rulers: A Reconsideration," in *Medieval Polities and Modern Mentalities*, ed. Janet Nelson [Cambridge: Cambridge University Press, 2006], 330–31).

a puzzle. We know very little about the various administrative functionaries of the Ottonian court. The diplomas that follow Carolingian formulae and list *judices*, *vicarii*, and *exactores* after counts and other lords in their immunity clauses do not reveal who held these roles or what their precise duties might have been. We see no return to Carolingian practices like capitularies to instruct *missi dominici*, special envoys of the king who were sent out to handle royal affairs when the ruler himself was unable to be physically present. The usefulness of written administrative and legal instructions and of royal agents such as the *missi* in a geographically broad realm with a peripatetic royal court seems self-evident. Yet we see no use of *missi* outside of Italy at all by the Ottonians, no inclination to keep administrative records, and no development of archival processes—all practices followed by the Carolingians.[9] While many aspects of Carolingian rule were borrowed by the Ottonians, the *missi* are missing. This omission has perplexed historians, who have struggled to understand why such an obviously useful tool of governance, of which the Ottonians certainly were aware, was not utilized.[10]

It is time to rethink the *missi dominici* and their role in Ottonian governance. The Ottonians did employ *missi*, although their presence is perhaps not always as obvious as it was in Carolingian government. The model of *missi* employed by the Ottonians more closely resembled that of Frankish kings before Charlemagne, rather than the reforms of the institution that were initiated in the course of his reign. The use and implementation of *missi dominici* in the Ottonian *Reich* was a thoughtful and deliberate adaptation of a Carolingian insti-

9. K. Leyser, "Ottonian Government," 727; see also Gerd Althoff, *Family, Friends, and Followers: Political and Social Bonds in Early Medieval Europe*, trans. Christopher Carroll (Cambridge: Cambridge University Press, 2004), 117. Regarding the Carolingians' use of writing as an essential component of their government, see Rosamond McKitterick, *The Carolingians and the Written Word* (Cambridge: Cambridge University Press, 1989), 23–77. Regarding the specific lack of written instruments in Ottonian government, especially compared to the Carolingians, see John Bernhardt, *Itinerant Kingship and Royal Monasteries in Early Medieval Germany, c. 936–1075* (Cambridge: Cambridge University Press, 1993), 51. David Bachrach has pushed for a reassessment of the importance of written instruments to the Ottonians as a tool of their rule, asserting the continuity of practice with their Carolingian predecessors ("Exercise of Royal Power in Early Medieval Europe: The Case of Otto the Great, 936–73," *Early Medieval Europe* 17.4 [2009]: 396–97). Tantalizing fragments such as the *Indiculus Loricatorum*, a conscription list for armed contingents during the reign of Otto II, suggest that while the Ottonians may have lacked the archival practices of the Carolingians, written documents may have been equally ubiquitous (MGH Const 1, 632–33).

10. For example, in his study of Ottonian government, Karl Leyser noted, "The capellani did not feel prompted to suggest to their royal masters even a return to Carolingian practices like the issue of capitularies for the instruction of *missi* or the despatch of such *missi* north of the Alps" ("Ottonian Government," 727). In a discussion of imperial efforts to exert control over the counts, Timothy Reuter likewise noted, "The Carolingians had made some attempt to do this through capitularies and *missi dominici*, but even then it was almost unknown for a count to be deposed for maladministration, and this is *a fortiori* true of the Ottonian Reich, which had neither capitularies nor *missi dominici*" ("Imperial Church System," 341–42).

tution that, like other aspects of Ottonian rule, provided a flexible tool of governance that could be used in different ways to serve different needs throughout their realm. In concert with other institutions of governance particular to the Ottonians, such as the *iter regis*, and broadly delegated jurisdictional authority, the *missi* demonstrate how Ottonian kings co-opted or adapted a variety of means in their efforts to assert royal authority throughout their realm.

The Missing *Missi*

The use of *missi dominici* as court officials predated Charlemagne (ca. 742–814 CE), but under his rule, they developed into an essential institution of his empire and one of the key distinguishing features of his government.[11] The Merovingians had used *missi* as royal legates, dispatching *missi* when needed to address specific tasks or missions within their realm.[12] The key innovation under Charlemagne was the transition from *missi ad hoc*, or occasional *missi*, to regular or ordinary *missi* with assigned geographic areas within which they exercised their authority (*missatica*) and a broad range of duties attendant with their position, in addition to being charged with specific tasks as the need arose.[13]

---

11. The literature dealing with Charlemagne's government in general and the *missi dominici* in particular is extensive. See F. L. Ganshof, *Frankish Institutions under Charlemagne*, trans. Bryce Lyon and Mary Lyon (Providence: Brown University Press, 1968); Jürgen Hannig, "Zur Funktion der karolingischen 'missi dominici' in Bayern und in den südöstlichen Grenzgebieten," *Zeitschrift der Savigny-Stiftung für Rechtsgeschichte* 101 (1984): 256–300; Hannig, "Zentral Kontrolle und regionale Machtbalance: Beobachtungen zum System der karolingischen Königsboten am Beispiel des Mittelrheingebietes," *Archiv für Kulturgeschichte* 66 (1984): 1–46; Karl F. Werner, "Missus—marchio—comes: Entre l'administration centrale et l'administration locale de l'Empire carolingien," in *Histoire comparée de l'administration (IVe–XVIIIe siècles): Actes du XIVe colloque historique franco-allemand, Tours, 27 mars–1er avril 1977, organisée en collaboration avec le Centre d'Études Supérieurs de la Renaissance par l'Institut Historique Allemand de Paris*, BdF 9 (Munich: Artemis, 1980), ed. Werner Paravicini and Karl F. Werner, 191–239. For a basic overview of the literature, see Reinhold Kaiser, "Les évêques de Langres dans leur fonction de 'missi dominici,'" in *Langres et ses évêques, VIIIe–XIe siècle: Aux origines d'une seigneurie ecclésiastique; Actes du colloque Langres-Ellwangen, Langres, 28 Juin 1985,* edited by Josef Semmler (Langres: Société historique et archéologique de Langres, 1986), 93–96. The significance and efficacy of Charlemagne's efforts to overhaul and institutionalize the office of the *missi* has begun to be reassessed in more recent literature. See, for example, François Bougard, *La justice dans le royaume d'Italie de la fin du VIIIe siècle au début du XIe siècle* (Rome, 1995), 177–89, 296–99; Rosamond McKitterick, "Charlemagne's *Missi* and Their Books," in *Early Medieval Studies in Memory of Patrick Wormald*, ed. Stephen Baxter et al. (Burlington, VT: Ashgate, 2009), 253–67; Jennifer R. Davis, *Charlemagne's Practice of Empire* (Cambridge: Cambridge University Press, 2015).

12. Rosamond McKitterick, *The Frankish Kingdoms under the Carolingians* (New York: Longman, 1983), 93; Davis, 33.

13. Ganshof, *Frankish Institutions*, 24; Davis, 33; Kaiser, "Les évêques de Langres," 94.

In Charlemagne's government, the primary officials were the counts, bishops, and *missi*. Prior to 802, the use of *missi* had been intermittent and could designate persons acting as ambassadors or messengers or engaging in political negotiations on behalf of the king. After 802, however, the office became more formal.[14] *Missi* were assigned in pairs of one lay *missus* and one clerical *missus*, who were expected to act together. *Missatica*, jurisdictional boundaries for each pair of *missi*, were defined, as were the many specific duties they were expected to perform as carriers of royal authority. These responsibilities included a variety of judicial functions, receiving oaths, overseeing counts, inspecting the behavior of clergy and laity, enforcing the king's *bannus*, and serving as the conduit for communication between the king and his subjects.[15] Other, more specific directives with which Charlemagne charged various *missi* included settling disputes and conducting inquests, mobilizing troops and keeping records of who was required to provide military service, and compiling a survey of the Holy Land.[16] The focus of debate among Carolingian scholars seems to center on two key issues that are paramount for an understanding of *missi* in the Carolingian era: (1) the importance of *missi* as a way of asserting local control and (2) the degree to which *missi* served as a means of communication throughout Charlemagne's Frankish Empire.[17] *Missi* were generally appointed to serve areas in which they already had some degree of local influence, they were instructed to work closely with the counts, and there is evidence of active communications back and forth between the king and *missi*, the latter seeking clarification of instructions, reporting on their activities, and giving updates regarding specific projects.[18]

---

14. In 802, Charlemagne issued his so-called administrative capitulary, which comprehensively outlined the various expected duties of his *missi*. See Ganshof, *Frankish Institutions*, 6–7; McKitterick, "Charlemagne's *Missi*," 256–60; *Capitulare Missorum Generale*, MGH Capit 1, 91–99.

15. McKitterick, "Charlemagne's *Missi*," 259–60; Davis, 34, 50; Bougard, *La justice dans le royaume d'Italie*, 178.

16. Matthew Innes, *State and Society in the Early Middle Ages: The Middle Rhine Valley, 400–1000* (Cambridge: Cambridge University Press, 2000), 193–94; Davis, 292.

17. Regarding local control, see Hannig, "Zentrale Kontrol," 36; Hannig, "Zur Funktion," 271–72, 275–77, 298–99; Innes, 193–94; Davis, 80–84; Kaiser, "Les évêques de Langres." For lengthy discussions of how the aspect of communications is directly related to the use of writing in Charlemagne's government, see F. L. Ganshof, "The Use of the Written Word in Charlemagne's Administration," in *The Carolingians and the Frankish Monarchy*, ed. F. L. Ganshof (London: Longman, 1971), 125–42; McKitterick, "Charlemagne's *Missi*"; Janet Nelson, "Literacy in Carolingian Government," in *The Uses of Literacy in Early Medieval Europe*, ed. Rosamond McKitterick (Cambridge: Cambridge University Press, 1990), 258–96; Davis, 311–14. There is little doubt that Charlemagne expected his *missi* to communicate his will to the people, whether through oral or written instructions, and to report back to him regarding their activities as his agents acting as an arm of the crown.

18. See, for example, Davis, 73–77, discussing Arn of Salzburg's career as *missus* to Bavaria; Kaiser, "Les évêques de Langres," 101–5, regarding Bishop Isaac of Langres; Innes, 193–94, describing the *missus* Count Rupert, a descendant of the founders of Lorsch.

Much of what we know about how the office of *missi* changed under Charlemagne, as well as about how he wanted these officials to function, is revealed in his capitularies. Carolingian capitularies, comprised of *capitula*, short topical sections addressing a variety of issues, were essentially administrative documents that were developed in the course of Charlemagne's reign and enjoyed continued use by his successors. The format was not new; Roman and canon law often appeared in it, and there are extant capitularies from Pippin's reign as well. Charlemagne adopted and adapted the format for his own administrative purposes. His capitularies covered a broad array of issues and purposes, including instructive documents, *leges*, agendas, admonitions, and even sermons.[19] These documents sometimes formed the record of decisions made at assemblies composed of both ecclesiastical and secular lords, so it is no surprise that they addressed matters of both spiritual and secular concern.[20] As with the capitularies, Charlemagne adopted and adapted the office of *missi dominici* to his own ends. Capitularies were sent out to each count or *missus*, who would read them aloud to the people in his jurisdiction and assure that their directives were followed.[21] Some of these documents were programmatic, like efforts of Charlemagne to provide for uniform rule and enforcement throughout his realm, and some were regional, addressed to specific new territories of his empire as a part of his process of consolidation.[22] The *missi* were a way for Charlemagne to keep a check on the counts and ensure their compliance with his expectations of their office and the duties associated with it.[23] A central tenet of the capitularies was the impetus toward centralization and the institution of royal influence at the local level throughout his realm. The *missi* under Charlemagne were ubiquitous royal officials, appearing everywhere throughout his kingdom as they perambulated their assigned *missatica*, supervised counts, or were dispatched on specific royal business.

The system of *missi* and *missatica* envisioned and institutionalized by Charlemagne persisted as a feature of Frankish government under his successors. Louis the Pious (778–840 CE) overhauled the *missatica* in 825, and the subse-

19. Rosamond McKitterick, *Charlemagne: The Formation of a European Identity* (Cambridge: Cambridge University Press, 2008), 233–34; R. C. van Caenegem, *An Historical Introduction to Private Law*, trans. D. E. L. Johnston (Cambridge: Cambridge University Press, 1992), 21–24.

20. Judith Herrin, *The Formation of Christendom* (Princeton, NJ: Princeton University Press, 1987), 432–33; Thomas F. X. Noble, "Secular Sanctity: Forging an Ethos for the Carolingian Nobility," in *Lay Intellectuals in the Carolingian World*, ed. Patrick Wormald and Janet Nelson (Cambridge: Cambridge University Press, 2007), 9.

21. McKitterick, *Carolingians and the Written Word*, 28. A capitulary of Louis the Pious of 825 ("Admonitio ad Omnes Regni Ordines," capit. 26, MGH Capit 1, 307), which is repeated by Charles the Bald in 864 ("Edictum Pistense," capit. 36, MGH Capit 2, 327), outlines these instructions.

22. McKitterick, *Charlemagne*, 237–45. Saxony was one of these regional capitulary recipients.

23. Davis, 97.

quent division of his kingdom suggests further redistribution of *missatica*, but he and his sons Charles the Bald (823–77 CE) and Louis the German (806–76 CE) continued to utilize the *missi dominici* as a practical and effective tool of government.[24] Since the *missatica* system had only been instituted in the region at the center of Carolingian royal power—that is, in the Frankish heartlands between the Loire and Meuse—Louis the German did not have the tradition of *missatica* as an organizing principal for his government. But he did use the institutions of itinerant kingship and *missi dominici* to assert his authority throughout East Francia. Under Louis the German, *missi dominici* were used in much the same way as they had been under Charlemagne and Louis the Pious: to supervise the counts, act as royal agents, and dispense justice.[25] Knowing that *missi*—albeit *missi ad hoc*, not ordinary *missi*—were used as effective agents of government in the East Frankish realm through the late ninth century, we are left to wonder why they are absent in the tenth.

The apparent utility of the office of *missus dominicus* in the service of Charlemagne's empire and its continued use in the governments of his successors have puzzled Ottonian scholars. If the office was so useful, why did the Ottonians not use it in the administration of their empire? Even if the Carolingian model was less effective than their capitularies would have us believe, it was successful enough that Charlemagne's immediate successors continued to use it in much the same way as he had. Louis the German, as we already noted, used *missi ad hoc* to perform all kinds of business on behalf of the king: their investment as royal officers extended the range and authority of the king through activities that included a variety of legal and judicial actions, as well as supervisory roles.[26] The *missi* allowed the king to enforce his will without having to be physically present. In a large imperial realm, the ability to delegate royal authority—indeed, to have the force of royal command far from wherever the king's person actually might be—would clearly be advantageous. Especially because the Ottonians sought to legitimize their imperial dynastic claims by modeling their empire after that of the Carolingians, historians have puzzled over the lack of evidence of any regular use of *missi* by the Ottonian kings. But there are clues to this puzzle.

Missi dominici are mentioned in several Ottonian diplomas as one of the many kinds of authorities from whom immunists were granted exemption. It is

24. Kaiser, "Les évêques de Langres," 98, 100; McKitterick, *Frankish Kingdoms*, 95.

25. Eric Goldberg, *Struggle for Empire: Kingship and Conflict under Louis the German, 817–876* (Ithaca, NY: Cornell University Press, 2009), 222.

26. Goldberg, 222–23. Under Louis the Pious, *missi* "acted as ambassadors, received oaths of loyalty, punished criminals, investigated property right disputes, invested recipients with royal lands, supervised land transactions, and brought judicial appeals before the king."

likely, especially regarding confirmations of privileges granted in the past, that these mentions were just part of the formulaic language of these documents, often repeated in subsequent confirmations to emphasize continuity of the grants. For example, in 938, Otto I confirmed an immunity for the bishopric of Osnabrück, specifying

> that no one, neither public judge nor the power of other courts or counts or *missi dominici*, now or in the future, should presume to restrain [anyone] in the place of that bishopric, neither holding *placita* or [imposing] judicial fines or public duties or giving orders or designating *fideiussores* [men who stood as surety], either servile or free or half-free and the rest.[27]

A diploma issued to Bishop Drogo of Osnabrück in 960 seems to reconfirm the same grant of immunity and adds to the formula specific mention of protection from dukes, counts, and viscounts.[28] That addition, plus the notification that the confirmation was being reissued because of abuses, could suggest that certain lords of those ranks had been infringing on episcopal rights.[29] The parallel designation of *legatus dominicus* also appears in an immunity diploma of Otto the Great, in a rather long confirmation for Gembloux in 946: "And throughout the abbey's own environs, not anyone, count or *legatus dominicus,* employs any power without permission of the abbot and his advocate."[30] *Legatus dominicus* appears again in the confirmation diploma for Gembloux issued by Otto II in 979,[31] further supporting the idea that these titles in lists of officials from whom charter recipients have immunity were included as holdovers from the texts of earlier charters.[32]

But even if these titles are included pro forma in the formulae employed

27. DD OI 20: "ut nullus iudex publicus neque alia iudicaria potestas aut comites vel missi dominici per tempora discurrentes in locis illius episcopatus placita habenda vel freda exigenda aut parafreda aut paratas faciendas vel fideiussores tollendos aut servos vel liberos sive liddones et ceteros aut eos qui censum persolvere debent quod muntscat vocatur, a nemine praesumatur constringere."

28. DD OI 212: "ut nullus iudex publicus neque alia iudicaria potestas, duces comites aut vicecomites vel missi dominici per tempora discurrentes, in locis illius episcopatus placita habenda."

29. DD OI 212: "ut eidem aecclesiae suae iam per multos retro annos decimis ad eandem sanctam sedem debite pertinentibus iniuste deprivate aliquo modo iusticiam fieri decrevissemus et nostrae immunitatis et libertatis praeceptum per quod res et potestates quae suo episcopio iure debentur firmius ac plenius habere valuisset, conscribi praeciperemus."

30. DD OI 82: "Nec per gyrum ipsius abbathie quislibet comes sive legatus dominicus ulla utatur potestate sine permissione abbatis et advocati."

31. DD OII 187.

32. Examples can be found scattered throughout the diplomas. For other examples of this formulaic use, see DD OI 4, 259, 335, 462; DD OII 277, 249; DD OIII 394.

in these diplomas, we cannot discount the possible use of *missi* by the Ottonians, especially since we see *missi* included in other ways in Ottonian diplomas. While *missi* may not have been employed by the Ottonians in exactly the same way that the Carolingians utilized them, they were indeed used. The names of several of these officials, both secular and ecclesiastical, appear in a variety of ways in diplomas. Numerous documents identify specific men as *missi*, and several documents record the appointment of a *missus*, as well.

Missi appear in numerous documents as witnesses and signatories, listed in both the text and the authentication of the documents. Under Otto I, for instance, Hubert of Parma, "ecclesiae episcopus et missus domni imperatoris," presided alongside Otberto, "marchio et comes palacii," at a *placitum* in Lucca, to notarize and strengthen a confirmation issued by Otto I in 964.[33] In a document issued at Monte Veltrajo in 967, Hubert is a signatory: "Hubertus episcopus et missus subscripsit."[34] At Chiassa in 970, "Otbertus marchio et comes palatio," presided over an assembly including "Siefredus qui et Sicco vocatur, missus domni imperatoris,"[35] and in Cremona in 998, "Otto dux et missus domni ipsius Ottonis imperatoris" presided over a legal proceeding.[36] Also in 998, in Rome, Archdeacon Leo oversaw a judicial proceeding and signed the resulting diploma, "Leo sacrosancti palatii archidiaconus et missus interfui et subscripsit."[37] In 1001, a *missus* was listed among those present at a judicial assembly at Pavia, in the text of the document recording attendees: "Albericus iudex et missus idem domni imperatoris."[38] Albericus shows up again in documents of Henry II, such as one from Pavia where he is listed in the text naming those present: "Albericus iudex et missus ipsius domni imperatoris."[39] Henry II presided over a *placitum* near Verona in 1021 that lists a "Tado missus domni imperatoris subscripsi" among its signatories.[40] At Chieti in 1022, "Armannus vassus et missus domni imperatori" is listed among attendees at an imperial *placitum*, and signatories at an imperial *placitum* at Campo di Pietra in 1022 include a "Leo servus Eusebii episcopus et missus imperatoris affuit."[41]

33. DD OI 269.

34. DD OI 342.

35. DD OI 400.

36. DD OIII 270. Duke Otto also indicated his office as *missus* in his signature: "Otto dux et missus subscripsi."

37. DD OIII 278.

38. DD OIII 411. His office was noted in his signature as well: "Albericus iudex et missus domni imperatoris interfui."

39. DD HII 299. Albericus is also listed as a signer: "Albericus iudex et missus domni imperatoris interfui."

40. DD HII 461.

41. DD HII 465, 467. There are other examples as well. For instance, the text of an undated charter of Otto II emphasizes the office of a certain Iring, "Iring missus domni" and "predictus

In addition to named *missi* within the text of documents, which testifies to their presence at various proceedings, we also see several instances of documents recording imperial appointments of *missi*. Otto I, for example, appointed a certain Adalgis as *missus dominicus* for the county of Milan.[42] In 962, Otto I granted to Bishop Wido of Milan and Bishop Hubert of Parma the powers of a *missus dominicus* over their ecclesiastical jurisdictions.[43] Another diploma from the reign of Otto I describes a 972 *placitum* in Milan that was presided over by two imperial officials, the palatine count Adalbert and Ezico, "missus domni imperatoris."[44] Similar diplomata are extant for Otto III and Henry II. In 1001, Otto III awarded Bishop Hieronymus the entire county of Vicenza and gave him the powers and responsibilities of a *missus* over all the people of his church.[45] Henry II created a family of *missi dominici* in the counties of Milan, Pavia, and Seprio, when he made Amizo, son of Herlembald, and Amizo's son Herlembald *missi*.[46]

These references to *missi* in Ottonian diplomata are all Italian or, in the case of the few that were issued at *placita* held in Germany, deal with Italian matters. Why do we see "real" *missi* only in Italy? It is not coincidental that Italy is also the only place the Ottonians issued capitularies. Unlike among the Carolingians, we do not see any impulse by Ottonian emperors to create written legislation. Writing and promulgating capitularies, as well as the explicit use of *missi*, was something the Ottonians did in Italy, but not north of the Alps. François Bougard notes the importance of *missi* to the Ottonians as they tried to consolidate their control in Italy.[47] But Italy was not "home" to the Ottonians. Their efforts to exert their authority by using institutions that already existed, especially in a region only infrequently visited relative to the intensity with which they perambulated throughout their territories north of the Alps, should not be surprising.

Important differences between Italy and the Germanic areas of the *Reich*

dominicus missus videlicet Iring" (DD OII 325). One from 981 mentions "Gibertus episcopus de Terdona missi sacri palatii" (DD OII 255). In 1000, a *placitum* noted the presence of a certain Benzo among other imperial officials: "Benzo missus domni imperatoris interfui" (*Codex diplomaticus Langobardiae*, ed. Giulio Porro-Lambertenghi, Historiae patriae monumenta edita jussu regis Caroli Alberti 13 [Augustae Taurinorum, 1873], no. 984, col. 1729). A small portion of this diploma is DD OIII 195.

42. DD OI 347.

43. DD OI 248 (Bishop Wido), 239 (Bishop Hugo). The immunity for Parma, including the powers of a *missus* over episcopal estates, was subsequently confirmed by Otto III in 989 (DD OIII 54) and by Henry II in 1004 (DD HII 71).

44. DD OI 416.

45. DD OIII 406.

46. DD HII 308: "elegimus Amizonem Herlembaldi filium, militem sancti Ambrosii, et Herlembaldum eius filium, ut sint imperiales missi."

47. François Bougard, "La justice dans le royaume d'Italie," in *La giustizia nell'alto medioevo (Secoli IX–XI)* (Spoleto: Presso la Sede del Centro, 1997), 1:166.

gesture to why certain Carolingian institutions, like the *missi*, were adopted or adapted by the Ottonians. All of the documents that mention Italian *missi* emphasize the role of these men in the administration of justice, documenting their presence in their capacities as presider, judge, or witness to judicial or legal proceedings. In the diplomata that record the appointments of imperial *missi*, their roles in administering justice are explicitly emphasized. In the German *Reich* north of the Alps, the Ottonians relied not on the centralized control emphasized by the Carolingians but, instead, on local ecclesiastical and secular authorities that formed a network of jurisdictions, with autonomous or semi-autonomous authorities responsible for dispute resolution. These authorities operated in concert with the royal courts—where disputes could be brought before the king in a *placitum* or synod—and worked alongside the extralegal recourse of waging feuds. The full embracing of the two systems, legal and extralegal, operating in tandem, with secular or ecclesiastical lords acting as local jurisdictional authorities, was the foundation of the Ottonian justice system.

The Ottonians were shrewd rulers, able to allow nobles and others to work out their own disputes through legitimate feud activity so long as the disruptions did not threaten imperial interests. By granting their margraves, counts, and bishops broad autonomy in handling their own affairs, they were able to respond independently and quickly to threats that appeared—internal or external. Key elements of Ottonian success included having numerous local rulers able to govern with a fair degree of autonomy assured by the broad immunities granted by the king (with the king intervening or sending reinforcements only as needed to respond to specific situations), as well as the ability of those semiautonomous authorities to respond to situations on the ground and react effectively. The vast majority of comital, episcopal, and even lesser noble estates in tenth-century Germany were noncontiguous; though every lord controlled his own realm, that realm might be broadly distributed within a patchwork of jurisdictions controlled by other lords, each with their own evaluation of potential threats or opportunities. Given the size of the Ottonian Empire, this dispersal of agents allowed resources to be allocated according to need in situations where threats necessitated royal intervention or support, rather than wasting energy and resources on futile attempts to predict and respond to the unrealized and unpredictable possibility of future threats.[48] In Italy, the political situation was much different, and the Ottonians struggled to impose their

48. For more information on how attempts to predict future events can weaken an organization through the squandering of resources and by lessening its ability to defend itself, see Nassim Nicholas Taleb's treatment of uncertainty theory in *The Black Swan: The Impact of the Highly Improbable* (New York: Random House, 2007).

authority in the peninsula. In that situation, they followed the lead of the Carolingians, who used *missi* and issued capitularies that introduced new legal ideas or methods of administering justice, a practical way to assert their authority at a local level in newly acquired territories.

The Ottonian realm in Germania also differed from Italy (and the Carolingian heartland) in the sense that royal authority in East Francia, in contrast to France, had direct fiscal interests in nearly every part of the domain. Where the *missatica* outlined clear geographic territories where Carolingian *missi* and the counts were supposed to cooperate, those territories were contiguous. Rosamond McKitterick has suggested that Charlemagne's reforms that included the creation of *missatica* and the institution of regular *missi* were reflective of a more sedentary kingship—that Charlemagne was adopting a less energetic royal itinerary. The use of the *missi* (ordinary and ad hoc) made travel by the king less necessary.[49] The Ottonians, by contrast, used their itinerancy as a way of asserting their authority. Thus, their royal itinerary, fragmented fiscal estates, and systems of maintaining power and control by cultivating *amicitia* networks and delegating jurisdictional authority worked directly in the interests of Ottonian kings.

As with the Carolingians, the nobility featured prominently in Ottonian government, and control over their realm was intimately tied to control over their magnates. But unlike the Carolingians, the Ottonians did not create a system of calculated redundancies in their administration in order to check the power of their counts, and they did not require or request a continuing flow of communications back and forth from all of their agents. Instead, the Ottonian kings went out of their way to place trusted men in positions of authority throughout their realm, as secular lords, as ecclesiastical lords, or sometimes invested with both lordships simultaneously, as in the case of Otto I's brother Brun of Cologne (Duke of Lotharingia and archbishop of Cologne). Loyalty was cultivated through carefully maintained *amicitia* networks extending throughout the realm, and *Königsnähe*, or proximity to the king, was how one won prestige, privileges, and offices.[50]

We can see that, at least in Italy, the system of *missi dominici* as instituted by Charlemagne did survive under the Ottonians, albeit in a form that resembled

49. McKitterick, *Charlemagne*, 213.

50. On the importance of these personal relationships in the Ottonian Empire, see, for example, Althoff, *Family, Friends, and Followers*; Sean Gilsdorf, *The Favor of Friends: Intercession and Aristocratic Politics in Carolingian and Ottonian Europe* (Leiden: Brill, 2014); Hagen Keller, "Grundlagen ottonischer Königsherrschaft," in *Reich und Kirche vor dem Investiturstreit: Vorträge beim wissenschaftlichen Kolloquium aus Anlass des 80. Geburtstags von Gerd Tellenbach*, ed. Karl Schmid (Sigmaringen: Thorbecke, 1985), 17–34.

the jurisdictional delegations of their German territories. While we do not see *missatica*, the areas assigned to *missi* are geographically well defined—often urban centers and their outskirts, an episcopal parish, or a county. By appointing *missi* in Italy and specifying their role in the administration of justice, these officials paralleled the local jurisdictional authority granted to secular and ecclesiastical lords and court functionaries elsewhere in the *Reich*. While the Ottonians did not have a centralized hierarchical bureaucracy, they did achieve a degree of consistency in how justice was administered throughout their empire.

Liudprand of Cremona as a *Missus ad Hoc*

Although there are few examples of Ottonian imperial officials with the titles *missi dominici*, there could very well have been officials filling the same role for the tenth-century imperial court that the Carolingian *missi* satisfied in the eighth and ninth centuries.[51] The importance of such officials is not in what they were or were not called but rather in what they did. The roles of *missi* were extensive, but as Rosamond McKitterick has pointed out, their key purpose was to provide a means of communication throughout the empire.[52] It was noted above that perhaps the most important thing the *missi* provided was an extension of the person (and power) of the emperor himself.[53] Were there people in the Ottonian Empire who, though they did not perhaps carry the title of *missi*, did just that? While we do not have extensive information about most of the courtiers and their specific duties to the emperor, the background we have for one man, Liudprand of Cremona, suggests that looking at the roles of officials, rather than at their titles, might be a more effective approach to the problem of *missi* in Ottonian governance.

Liudprand of Cremona, a tenth-century cleric from a family in the northern Italian region of Lombardy, provides us with some of the most important and entertaining narrative sources for the tenth century. Many of his writings record his own experiences or observations of events. As a youth and young

51. This view is supported by the use of *missi*-type officials by Charles the Fat. A certain Ruodbert, custodian of the royal chapel, is identified in the dating clauses of charters from 882 and 887 as "*missus* of the emperor in place of the count" (Simon MacLean, *Kingship and Politics in the Late Ninth Century: Charles the Fat and the End of the Carolingian Empire* [Cambridge: Cambridge University Press, 2003], 87, referencing DD St. Gall 620 and 657). Even if the title *missus* was not being used by the Ottonians, the persistence of the title in late Carolingian circles and the use of imperial functionaries in *missi*-type ways would certainly have demonstrated the utility of that kind of office to an emperor.

52. McKitterick, "Charlemagne's *Missi*," 261.

53. Goldberg, 222.

man, he served in the Italian courts of Hugh of Arles and Berengar II. Sometime shortly after 949, after falling out of favor with Berengar, he fled Italy to seek refuge at the court of Otto I. Of most importance for the present discussion is the period Liudprand spent in exile at Otto's court before returning to Italy in 962, years for which we have the least amount of information about him. Liudprand's writings, many of which date from that period, tell us little about the day-to-day activities of a member of the imperial court. That those were busy years for him is without question.[54] Other men likewise had fled Lombardy to seek service at Otto's court,[55] which attracted talented men from across Europe and was a place where those who feared Otto's enemies—in this case, Berengar—could find refuge and be rewarded for their talents.[56]

Liudprand's talents were many. While there has been considerable speculation about how well he actually knew Greek,[57] there is no doubt that he was familiar, at least to a degree, with both secular and canon law. By the standards of the tenth century, he was very well educated.[58] His mastery of the classics, the bit of Greek he had picked up on his trips to Byzantium, the practical knowledge he had gained from having firsthand experience at the Byzantine court, and a familiarity with the ideas and traditions of the late Carolingian world would have made him a useful acquisition for Otto's court.[59] It has been remarked, based on his education, experiences, and broad interests, that not until Gerbert of Aurillac (ca. 946–1003), later Pope Sylvester II, did a similar intellect appear.[60] Other than constant laments about his exile, Liudprand records nothing of his experiences in Germany. But the fact that we know little about his time north of the Alps does not negate the importance that he was traveling with the Ottonian court, active as a functionary in that court, and performing duties for which he was later rewarded with an episcopal see. Bishops were key administrative figures in the Ottonian court, and Liudprand continued to serve Otto I while overseeing his bishopric at Cremona.

Many of the functions that Liudprand performed are very like those as-

54. Jon N. Sutherland, *Liudprand of Cremona, Bishop, Diplomat, Historian: Studies of the Man and His Age* (Spoleto: Centro Italiano di Studi sull'Alto Medioevo, 1988), 8–9.

55. Ibid., 15.

56. Ibid., 10.

57. Liudprand's *Antapodosis* is littered with Greek references and comments, but they usually seem to be more in the service of impressing the reader than of complementing his history. Even given that many of Liudprand's quotes are from authors he was unlikely to encounter outside of Byzantium, Sutherland expresses doubt that the cleric's "knowledge was extensive as he would lead us to believe"; Sutherland notes that on Liudprand's second trip to the Byzantine court, "he apparently still had need of a translator—a fact which he seems to have tried to conceal" (ibid., 23).

58. Ibid., 41.

59. Ibid.

60. Ibid., 25.

cribed to the Carolingian *missi*.[61] He was part of the imperial retinue, named in imperial diplomata, and attended *placita* and synods presided over by the emperor.[62] He was sent as an imperial proxy to oversee an episcopal synod.[63] His trip to the Byzantine court as an imperial ambassador to negotiate for a bride for Otto II is well attested by his own account.[64] In the *Historia Ottonis*, he recorded his official presence at the trial of Pope John XII in 963.[65] The same source suggests, too, that messengers were regularly dispatched from the imperial court not only to relay communications between parties but also to look into matters of concern to the court and to investigate reports of unrest.[66] That we see Liudprand most visibly in Italian affairs, and that there is no record of the same sort of systematic deployment of imperial representatives or titular *missi* that we saw under the Carolingians, is to miss the point. Especially given the extent to which the Ottonians emulated the Carolingians in other ways, it is not a stretch to suggest that even though they did not mirror the *missi dominici* of the Carolingians exactly, the Ottonian functionaries were fulfilling the same kinds of roles in the Ottonian imperial court. Liudprand's deployment by the court seemed to take into consideration geographic areas where he might have had personal expertise or influence, including his earlier embassy to Byzantium under Berengar II or his family connections in Lombardy and Italy. It further suggests the likelihood that the Ottonian emperors made use of their functionaries in the most practical manner possible, employing those who might have local influence to represent them in their various territories.

Liudprand specifically named himself as one of the representatives of the imperial delegation at the *placitum* hearing testimony on the fiasco involving Popes John XII and Leo VIII in 963,[67] he appears in diplomata of 967 recording a *placitum* at Ravenna and a grant of immunity,[68] and he was sent as ambassador to Constantinople.[69] An affiliation with the imperial chancery conferred great prestige—so much so that Otto I revived the Carolingian practice of des-

61. See McKitterick, "Charlemagne's *Missi*"; Janet Nelson, "Kingship and Royal Government," in *NCMH* 2:412–15.

62. DD OI 340–41.

63. DD OI 374 (in MGH DD, vol. 2, "Nachträge und Berichtigungen," 879–80).

64. Liudprand of Cremona, *Relatio de Legatione Constantinopolitana*, in *Liudprandi Cremonensis Opera Omnia*, ed. Paolo Chiesa, Corpus Christianorum (Turnhout: Brepols, 1998), 185–218.

65. Liudprand of Cremona, *Historia Ottonis* § 9, in *Opera Omnia*, 173–74.

66. Liudprand of Cremona, *Historia Ottonis* §§ 4, 5, and 7, 170–73.

67. Liudprand of Cremona, *Historia Ottonis* § 9, 174.

68. DD OII 340–41.

69. Liudprand of Cremona, *Relatio de Legatione Constantinopolitana*, 185–218. The descriptions of many of the duties of these Ottonian court officials parallel those fulfilled by the *missi dominici* under the Carolingians.

ignating archbishops as honorary chancellors.[70] Like the archbishop of Canterbury, who served as chancellor in Anglo-Saxon England, leading archbishops in the Western Roman Empire were recognized as arch-chancellors. The archbishop of Mainz was normally recognized from 965 as archchancellor, and the archbishop of Cologne received the same designation over Italy from 1031.[71]

The missing *missi* in Ottonian government have been one of many puzzling aspects of that dynasty's rule. But perhaps they have been there all along. The Ottonian uses of governing functionaries, such as Liudprand of Cremona, as *missi ad hoc* harks back to a pre-Carolingian use of *missi* that is perhaps more traditional than the innovative model instituted by Charlemagne. But an adaptation of Charlemagne's creation of regular *missi* was also utilized extensively in Italy by the Ottonian emperors, where the political climate was significantly different than in Germany. This evidence suggests that the Ottonians were thoughtful and considerate in determining what tools they deployed in the service of their rule. Their deliberate utilization of the pre-Carolingian models of *missi ad hoc* in a wide variety of tasks, in combination with adaptations of Charlemagne's overhaul of the role of *missi* for specific regions, points to an intelligent and considered approach to rulership. It is worth noting, too, that the diplomata of Henry I, the first of the Ottonian kings, do not seem to mention *missi*. *Missi dominici* were perhaps a tool best suited for use in an established kingdom and its new territories, rather than by a warrior king who had yet to establish dynastic stability. At any rate, it seems clear that how we conceive of the use of *missi dominici* in Italy by Ottonians, as well as the possibility that *missi dominici* were used as a tool of Ottonian government generally, bears reconsideration.

Kings and Nobles

Under the Ottonians, Germany did not yet exist as we know it today; the empire was comprised of smaller territories with their own cultural identities. The duchies of Bavaria, Saxony, Franconia, Alemannia, Swabia, and Carinthia were augmented, by conquest or expansion, to include Lotharingia (modern-day Lorraine), Bohemia, and other territories ruled by powerful local dukes, counts, and margraves. The duchies served three key purposes under the Ottonians: they were a way to recruit for armies, they had an important role as

70. Arnold, *Medieval Germany*, 146.
71. Ibid.

peacekeepers,[72] and the ruling groups in them provided interconnected *amicitia* networks that extended throughout the secular and ecclesiastical aristocracy of East Francia, a network that rendered essential duties as well as opportunities to leverage personal connections and relationships.[73] The duties that adhered to the landowning magnates were key for imperial control.[74]

The Carolingians had employed *amicitia* relationships in their dealings with the rulers of the lesser kingdoms they incorporated into their empire. Such relationships became typical of Henry I's interactions with his own magnates, as well as with foreign kings.[75] Even in the ninth century, offices such as duke, margrave, or count carried with them juridical, military, and fiscal responsibilities to the crown.[76] By the tenth century, East Frankish secular nobles had established holdings consisting of estates, fortifications, and military retinues that could be used for their own support as well as in fulfilling obligations to the king. Additionally, these secular lords had authority over various kinds of jurisdictions, including advocacy over ecclesiastical ones, which Benjamin Arnold suggests was probably one of the more lucrative forms of jurisdictional authority for secular lords.[77] But the military aspect of these lordships was a crucial factor for the Saxon Liudolfings' ducal acceptance as the rightful rulers.[78] The Magyar invasions and the successes of Henry I and Otto I against them were central to the Ottonians' rise to power and ability to spread their authority across Germany and then into Italy.[79] This constant need to be warrior kings made imperative the acquisition of martial resources—namely, men, led by margraves, bishops, and magnates—as well as the effective delegation of authority.

Prior to the eleventh century, the nobility in Germany were loosely organized assemblages linked by real or mythological kinship ties with a distant

72. Ibid., 52. Arnold notes that there was "a legal dimension in which the duke took responsibility for keeping the peace. But except in a few cases, he was not lord over the comital jurisdictions." The importance of these various jurisdictional distinctions is discussed below.

73. As an example of how these *amicitia* networks functioned, Bishop Ulrich of Augsburg presented his young nephew to Otto I to serve at court, offering at the same time his military forces to the king's service.The goal was that his nephew would gain experience and network in the royal court, with the hope of a future royal appointment to a bishopric as his skills and interaction with the king and his court drew him favorable notice (Gerhard von Augsburg, *Vita Uodalrici* 3, in *Vita Sancti Uodalrici: Die älteste Lebensbeschreibung des heiligen Ulrich*, ed. Walter Berschin and Angelika Häse [Heidelberg: Universitätsverlag C. Winter, 1993], 112).

74. Arnold, *Medieval Germany*, 52.

75. Bernhardt, *Itinerant Kingship*, 12.

76. These responsibilities also adhered to ecclesiastical lords; see chapter 2.

77. Arnold, *Medieval Germany*, 129.

78. Ibid., 46.

79. Benjamin Arnold, *Power and Property in Medieval Germany: Economic and Social Change, c. 900–1300* (Oxford: Oxford University Press, 2004), 27.

ancestor, whereas in the eleventh century and later, we see noble families forming well-defined groups with clearly delineated family trees.[80] The key features that set apart the nobility of Germany from other classes were the right to exercise judicial authority, as well as specific legal differences.[81] In a tenth-century world where the aristocracy was more loosely defined across kinship associations and was less dependent on birth with a specific pedigree, it was the proximity to great men that occasioned opportunities to improve one's state, status, and wealth. Familiarity with the king, *Königsnähe*, could bring a person offices, titles, and lands.[82] It might also result in a person being entrusted with imperial business or other tasks of government, such as military duties, including leading armies. The career of Liudprand of Cremona, discussed above, demonstrates this system at work. As a member of the imperial court, he was entrusted with a variety of duties, including an embassy to Byzantium, and was eventually rewarded with his own bishopric in return for his service. Liudprand's example shows how clerics, as well as secular nobility, stood to gain from *Königsnähe*, which could bring a person power, honor, and wealth.[83] But with each new king, the ranks of the *familiares* closest to the king could change, increasing the uncertainty and the stakes of the already highly charged situation surrounding each succession. Yet it was crucial for the king to be able to place trustworthy allies in key positions throughout the kingdom.[84]

80. Leopold Genicot, "Recent Research on the Medieval Nobility," in *The Medieval Nobility: Studies on the Ruling Classes of France and Germany from the Sixth to the Twelfth Century*, ed. Timothy Reuter (New York: New Holland, 1979), 27. It is quite likely that the English nobility were similarly less organized prior to the eleventh century (Peter A. Clarke, *The English Nobility under Edward the Confessor* [Oxford: Clarendon, 1994], 141).

81. Clarke, 142.

82. For a list of other sources that discuss *Königsnähe* in detail, see Lars Hermanson, introduction to *Rituals, Performatives, and Political Order in Northern Europe, c. 650–1350*, ed. Wojtek Jezierski et al. (Turnhout: Brepols, 2015), 24n71.

83. Gerd Tellenbach, "From the Carolingian Imperial Nobility to the German Estates of Imperial Princes," in Reuter, *Medieval Nobility*, 207. *Königsnähe* was also tied to the royal *iter* and the delegation of local authority as a way of both legitimizing local rulers and maintaining a royal presence. Bernhardt connects this to royal sacrality, noting that on the *iter*, "the king's presence served to document his relationship with those having nearness to him (the concept of *Königsnähe*), and it thereby also legitimized the nobility" (*Itinerant Kingship*, 50). Stephen Jaeger notes how *Königsnähe* functioned in episcopal appointments and featured as a key theme in episcopal *vitae* after Otto I ("The Courtier Bishop in *Vitae* from the Tenth to the Twelfth Century," *Speculum* 58.2 [1983]: 315).

84. Germany was not the only place where *Königsnähe* existed; it could be found among the Anglo-Saxon kings, too (Clarke, *English Nobility*, 143). Two examples are the relatively sudden and complete turnover of one kin group of leading nobles in favor of another late in the reign of Æthelred and again during the reign of Cnut (Robin Fleming, *Kings and Lords in Conquest England* [Cambridge: Cambridge University Press, 1991], 36–38). Asserting that a "community of interests fostered by English kings and their closest associates" provided the scaffolding for running the kingdom, Fleming notes that "until c. 1000 it appears that the friends and kinsmen who fostered or sponsored one another's children, who were buried in the same sacred grounds, and who left bequests to one another in their wills, formed the backbone of a successful secular administration"

Beginning with Henry I, Ottonian rulers treated ducal appointments as a royal office, even while continuing to recognize dynastic succession among the lower nobility. This had the dual benefit of creating dukes as royal officials—and thus access points to the royal court—while simultaneously ensuring the continuity and position of noble families within those duchies.[85] Otto I further established royal control of the dukes and their territories, using his authority to depose and replace dukes, as well as to exercise his prerogative to bring duchies under direct royal jurisdiction when an office was vacated.[86] The control of ducal appointments by the Ottonians points to the authority wielded by their kings. Conrad I had tried to restrict the hereditary rights of Duke Henry of Saxony, the future Henry I, even attempting an assassination to prevent him from achieving the same scope of powers as his father, though Conrad did not (or could not) depose and replace Henry. Under Henry I and Otto I, ducal positions were distributed to loyal magnates, and the king had the authority to appoint and depose dukes.

It is possible that the success of *Königsnähe* under Henry I and Otto I led the magnates to consent to elect minor co-kings or co-emperors (Otto II and Otto III). If *amicitiae* cohorts were likely to change with the succession of a new king, the election of a minor coruler could potentially help entrench an existing *amicitia* network. The magnates who were *familiares* under the older king would be more likely to remain in favor under the new king once he succeeded as sole ruler. Thus, the dynastic stability that the Ottonians enjoyed by pressing their magnates for endorsement of their minor sons also provided an opportunity for their magnates to perpetuate their own influence at court and extend that influence to their own networks of kin. This opportunity is perhaps best illustrated by the election of the minor Otto III, who was only three years old when Otto II died. Henry the Wrangler assumed control of the regency, which was clearly going to be a long one, given Otto's youth. Otto's mother, Theophanu, also had supporters for her claim to be regent, as demonstrated in a letter written by Gerbert of Aurillac to an Ottonian lady at court soon after Henry the Wrangler assumed control.

> Approach my Lady Theophanu in my name to inform her that the kings of the French [Lothar and Louis V] are well disposed towards her son

(36–37). This description of what is essentially Anglo-Saxon *Königsnähe* depicts the same kind of *amicitia* network of friends and family that we see the Ottonians utilizing with such efficacy.

85. Bernhardt, *Itinerant Kingship*, 13; Gerd Althoff and Hagen Keller, *Heinrich I. und Otto der Große: Neubeginn und karolingischem Erbe* (Göttingen: Muster-Schmidt, 1985), 80–81, 223.

86. Bernhardt, *Itinerant Kingship*, 20.

[Otto III], and that she should attempt nothing but the destruction of Henry's tyrannical scheme, for he desires to make himself king under the pretext of guardianship.[87]

The considerable support that Theophanu had, evidenced here and elsewhere, suggests that she had earned the respect and trust of many from among church leaders and the aristocracy. But it could also suggest that Theophanu was a known entity who would continue the policies of her husband regarding those who had influence under Otto II at court, since they were her and Otto III's *familiares* as well.[88] If Henry had gained the throne, there is little doubt that he would have rewarded his own circle of loyal nobles with positions and privileges, at the expense of those who had attempted to prevent his election.[89]

The importance of these networks and of a king's ability to build them up, tear them down if they presented threats, and use them as tools in the successful administration of his kingdom was critical to the Ottonians. These systems were also so effective because the men in them owed allegiance to only one lord; a man might change his allegiance but could not serve multiple lords, which might lead to conflicting alliances.[90] This model of lordship stood in stark contrast to the French model, where it was common for men to claim allegiance to more than one lord.[91]

The distinction between allegiance to one lord in Germany and the model of multiple lordship common in France might be more than just an academic observation. It is possible that allegiance to multiple lords exacerbated the trend toward the "feudal revolution" in France, when powerful lords successfully challenged the authority of the king, leading to issues that simply did not

87. Harriet Pratt Lattin, ed. and trans., *The Letters of Gerbert, with His Papal Privileges as Sylvester II* (New York: Columbia University Press, 1961), 67–68; Gerbert of Aurillac, letter to Lady Imiza, January–February 984, in MGH BDKz 2, ep. 22: "Dominam meam Theuphanu imperatricem meo nomine convenite. Reges Francorum filio suo favere dicite nichilque aliud conari nisi tyrannide Heinrici velle regem se facere volentis sub nomine advocationis destruere."

88. The additional presence of the former empress Adelheid, Otto III's grandmother, who worked with her daughter-in-law Theophanu to secure his succession, no doubt greatly strengthened the young king's position in relation to Henry's challenge.

89. An Anglo-Saxon example demonstrates the importance of these groups of *familiares* and allies to the king. Edward the Confessor returned to England in 1041. After having been in exile for over twenty-five years—effectively an entire generation—he had no power base in England when he returned, no networks of political allies and friends. Witness lists in his diplomas clearly suggest that Edward was trying to create a group of men who literally owed him everything, whose positions were due entirely to him, and who would thus form the foundation of an *amicitia* network (Clarke, *English Nobility*, 143–44).

90. This model of lordship, where men served only one lord, was practiced in late Anglo-Saxon England as well.

91. Clarke, *English Nobility*, 150.

exist in Germany or were more easily dealt with there.[92] Loyalty to a single lord might have provided a better organizational model for the regnal allocation of authority among multiple agents, and it would have prevented conflicts of interest leading to the escalation of feuds if loyalty were owed to two lords who became enemies. Loyalty to one lord also might provide a structure where, if *Königsnähe* was the best way to enhance one's position, a noble might be less likely to reject a succession in favor of predation and attempts to enhance personal authority through violence, instead allying himself with a lord whose loyalty to the king could result in an enhancement of his own status. The alternative possibility, resulting from multiple loyalties, might lead to the rise of small, independent lordships with varying levels of commitment to the crown.[93]

While magnates were essential to the Ottonian kings in administering their government, the aristocracy in Germany—in contrast to the situation in England and France—also played a key role in determining the succession of kings. Ottonian kingship at the beginning of the tenth century continued to be based on traditional Germanic ideals of election. In the post-Carolingian era of imperial fragmentation and under pressure from Magyar invasions from the East, being a strong warrior able to muster necessary forces to defend the frontiers and keep the nobility in check was not the least of the important qualities necessary for leadership. When the Ottonians came to power with the election of Henry I (the Fowler) in 919 after the death of Conrad I, a non-Carolingian king who had been elected by the German dukes to succeed Louis the Child, kingship in tenth-century East Francia was anything but secure and, indeed, was a highly dangerous affair. Rebellious magnates wrought widespread destruction in retribution for perceived assaults on their dignity or honor. Thietmar of Merseburg, a chronicler writing in the late tenth and early eleventh centuries, alludes to the numerous times Conrad's and Henry's forces battled before they were reconciled, emphasizing this constant threat of violence, as well as the normalcy of it.[94] Fritz Kern emphasizes the election of a Germanic king as a "formal legal" act, whether it be to elect a successor to a deceased king or to formally depose and replace a sitting king.[95] But a legally elected king did not mean an unchallenged succession.

---

92. Thomas N. Bisson, "The 'Feudal Revolution,'" *Past & Present* 142 (1994): 6–42.

93. While this was the situation exhibited in France, I am in no way endorsing the idea of France during the "feudal revolution" as a failed state narrative. I am trying to emphasize the differences between kingdoms that defy explanation by a single model or paradigm.

94. See the below discussion of issues of succession during Henry I's lifetime.

95. Fritz Kern, *Kingship and Law in the Middle Age*, trans. S. B. Chrimes [New York: Frederick A. Praeger, 1956], 86. This forms part of Kern's argument that Germanic kingship—whether Anglo-Saxon, Frankish, or Lombard—was a legal kingship based on law that both ruler and ruled were required to follow.

Henry the Fowler, a magnate who had rebelled against King Conrad I, was nonetheless designated by Conrad to be his successor.[96] The sources show that Conrad recognized the potential for the same sort of problem with powerful predatory lords that arose in France. According to Widukind of Corvey in his tenth-century *Res Gestae Saxonicae*, when Henry's father, Duke Otto of Saxony, died, Conrad was afraid to grant Henry the same scope of powers and so did not, a move that was perceived as a deliberate affront by Henry. Realizing that a resentful Henry was as dangerous as a powerful one, Conrad conspired to kill him, but the plot unraveled.[97] Henry openly rebelled, occupying lands throughout Saxony and Thuringia with his army, seizing properties, and expelling the king's supporters.[98] This story is repeated by Thietmar of Merseburg, who hints at the wide-scale disruption caused by the frequent armed encounters between the two men.

> But on to other things, as it would take me a long time to tell, how often having engaged with each other they [i.e., the king and Duke Henry] were defeated or victorious, and how, finally, at the instigation of good men they came together as friends.[99]

Although the sources make it sound like the election of Henry after the death of Conrad was a fairly straightforward affair, they also report that Henry had to deal with Arnulf of Bavaria, who felt that he, too, had a legitimate claim to the crown.[100] Henry and Arnulf rode to confront each other with their armies but, according to Liudprand's account, ultimately reached an agreement without engaging in battle.[101] As Benjamin Arnold wryly observes, "It is obvious that

---

96. Liudprand of Cremona, *Antapodosis* 2.19 (rebellion), 2.20 (Conrad's exhortation to elect Henry as his successor), in *Opera Omnia*, 43–44.

97. Widukind of Corvey, *Res gestae Saxonicae* 1.22, in *Widukindi monachi Corbiensis rerum gestarum Saxonicarum libri tres*, ed. Paul Hirsch and H.-E. Lohmann after G. Waitz and K. A. Kehr MGH SRG 60 (Hanover: Hahn, 1935), 30–32.

98. Ibid.

99. Thietmar of Merseburg, *Chronicon* 1.7, in *Thietmari Merseburgensis Episcopi Chronicon*, ed. Robert Holtzmann, MGH SRG 9 (Berlin: Weidmannsche Buchhandlung, 1935), 12: "Sed mihi ad alia properanti longum est enarrare, quocies congressi mutuo cederent vel vincerent, et quod postremo bonorum instinctu in amiciciam convenirent."

100. These sources were written *ex post facto* and in service to the legitimization of the Ottonian dynasty. Philippe Buc points out that the "German annals produced in the first third of the tenth century (as opposed to entries written later into annalistic manuscripts) do not mention the accession of Henry I" (*The Dangers of Ritual: Between Early Medieval Texts and Social Scientific Theory* [Princeton, NJ: Princeton University Press, 2001], 15–16). The Ottonian myth of Henry's humility in declining a formal coronation was likely a later invention to account for his accession as king, perhaps against the expectations of contemporary observers.

101. Liudprand of Cremona, *Antapodosis* 2.21–23, in *Opera Omnia*, 44–46. Widukind of Corvey gives a slightly different account of Henry's succession and the encounter with Arnulf, stating

no German king had ever been elected by the whole eligible body; only a representative few would actually have made the journey to the place of election, traditionally upon Franconian soil, to make known the wishes of their own *gens* or to listen to the debate and then come to a decision."[102] It is obvious, too, that each vote would take into account the personal needs, wants, and desires of that particular magnate. While some things, like security, might be of common concern, there were doubtless nobles, like Arnulf, who aspired to improve their position and put forth their own claims to the throne and who had the support of followers hoping to find an improvement in their own status by linking their fortunes to the rise of their lords.

Issues of succession were always flash points for high emotion and divisiveness. During Henry I's lifetime, in 936, the question of succession was already an issue. One faction (backed by Henry) wanted Otto I as king; another, reportedly with the support of Mathilda (Henry I's wife), wanted Otto's younger brother Henry to be the designated successor, arguing that Henry's birth during his father's kingship (not before Henry I became king, like Otto) gave the younger brother a superior claim.[103] Thankmar, Henry I's son by his first marriage, rebelled against Otto I and was killed in battle during the hostilities. Henry ultimately became Duke of Bavaria and father of Henry the Wrangler, who pursued his own claim to the throne, first against Otto II and then by kidnapping the minor Otto III.[104]

When Otto III died unexpectedly without an heir in Italy in 1002, the nobility was fiercely divided between competing claims to the throne. Thietmar of Merseburg, while not an impartial reporter of events,[105] gives us some indica-

---

that after he was elected, Henry had to do battle with Burchard of Alemania; after Burchard wisely saw that it was better to subject himself to Henry, the latter proceeded to Bavaria, where Arnulf had taken refuge in the fortress at Regensburg; only after being besieged and realizing he could not prevail did Arnulf yield himself to the new king (*Res gestae Saxonicae* 1.27, 39–40). The differences in the stories likely reflect the different agendas of the authors. Widukind is emphasizing the military prowess of Henry and the submission of the other powerful dukes to him. Liudprand is more concerned with emphasizing consensus. Essential here is not what actually happened but what is portrayed as the ideal of kingship by the chroniclers.

102. Arnold, *Medieval Germany*, 177. Widukind of Corvey gives a description of consensual acclamation of Otto I at his coronation ceremony at Aachen (*Res gestae Saxonicae* 2.1, 65).

103. *Vita Mathildis Reginae* § 9, in MGH SS 4, 289 (quoted in Kern, 18n10): "Quia natus esset in aula regali."

104. Fritz Kern suggests that the succession of Edgar in England when he died in 975 offers "an exact parallel to the German throne-contest of 936." When Edgar died, each of his two minor sons had their cadre of supporters, but those against the elder Edward argued, "Quia matrem eius, licet legaliter nuptam, in regnum tamen non magis quam patrem eius, dum eum genuit, sacratam fuisse sciebant" (Eadmer, *Vita Dunst* 35, quoted in Kern, 18n10).

105. Since Thietmar's reporting of events serves as a legitimizing strategy for the succession of Henry II, the chronicler extols the virtues of Henry as a kingly person and emphasizes the unkingly actions of his rivals.

tion of both the degree of concern among the nobility and the potential for violence that such competition could engender.

> Meanwhile, having learned of their lord's [Otto III's] premature death, the leading men of the Saxons sadly convened at the royal estate of Frohse, held as a benefice from the emperor by the then Count Gunzelin. Giselher, archbishop of Magdeburg, along with his suffragan bishops, Duke Bernhard, the margraves Liuther, Ekkehard, and Gero, and the great men of the region pondered the condition of the realm.[106]

This meeting, however, quickly became ugly. The assembled nobility and ecclesiasts soon became aware that Margrave Ekkehard was pushing his claim to the throne. Alarmed, the archbishop and the higher-ranking nobles went outside to discuss this turn of events privately, and all swore an oath that none of them would elect anyone until a later convention at Werla. Ekkehard, who, according to Thietmar, "reckoned on the support of the eastern counts and therefore of the duchy,"[107] believed he would have sufficient support for his claim, and after a disastrous encounter at Werla with the daughters of Otto II (and sisters of Otto III), abbesses Adelheid and Sophia, he nonetheless continued on with Bishop Bernward to Hildesheim, "where he was received as king and treated with honour," but shortly thereafter was brutally murdered and dismembered.[108] Duke Herman of Swabia, the candidate supported by Archbishop Heribert of Cologne, had the backing of "the majority of the nobles who attended the funeral procession [of Otto III]," men who "promised Duke Herman their support in acquiring and securing the royal dignity and falsely declared that Henry was not suitable for this for a variety of reasons."[109] Duke Henry of Bavaria, the

106. David A. Warner, ed. and trans., *Ottonian Germany: The* Chronicon *of Thietmar of Merseburg*, Manchester Medieval Sources (Manchester: Manchester University Press, 2001), 188–89; Thietmar, *Chronicon* 4.52, 190: "Interim principes Saxoniae, comperta senioris sui nece inmatura, ad Frasam curtem regiam, quam tunc Guncelinus comes ex parte inperatoris in benefitium tenuit, tristes conveniunt, Gisilerus archiepiscopus Magadaburgiensis cum coepiscopis, Bernhardus dux, Liutharius et Ekkihardus ac Gero marchiones cum optimatibus regni, de statu rei publice tractantes."

107. Warner, *Ottonian Germany*, 210–11; Thietmar, *Chronicon* 5.7, 228: "Comites vero orientales paucis tantum exceptis regnumque in spe habuit."

108. Warner, *Ottonian Germany*, 208; Thietmar, *Chronicon* 5.4, 5.6, 225–26. Warner (208n18) notes, "The absence of a male heir made the princesses the most visible representatives of the Liudolfing/Ottonian house. It has been suggested [by Karl Leyser, "Ritual, Ceremony and Gesture: Ottonian Germany," in *Communications and Power in Medieval Europe: The Carolingian and Ottonian Centuries*, ed. Timothy Reuter (London: Hambledon, 1994), 203] that Ekkehard's provocative actions were intended to demonstrate that direct descent from the traditional ruling house was no longer a prerequisite for the throne."

109. Warner, *Ottonian Germany*, 190; Thietmar, *Chronicon* 4.54, 193: "Maxima pars procerum,

son of Henry the Wrangler, was ultimately acclaimed king at Werla by the assembled nobles, but he spent the early years of his reign suppressing rebellion and garnering support. Thietmar's descriptions of the political maneuvering after the death of Otto III give a sense of how secular and ecclesiastical magnates might align themselves with different factions, especially when no clear line of succession—even one that might be contested—had been determined before the king's death.

Adalbert of Magdeburg, writing around 960, frequently used language concerning stability, peace, and unification as desirable outcomes of kingship.[110] Henry I remained a Germanic king in the old sense—a *primus inter pares* (first among equals) and, first and foremost, a warlord. Under the Ottos (Otto I the Great, 912–73 CE; Otto II, 955–83 CE; and Otto III, 980–1002 CE), who reshaped the idea of kingship over the course of their reigns, we also see a reshaping of governance.[111] By melding ideals of Frankish and Germanic rulership with their own style of leadership, they created a unique system of succession and established a kingship that was strong, stable, and resilient. They created a system for regulating and legitimating claims to power in such a way that succession crises could be resolved in favor of a claimant without the potential of chaos ensuing from divisiveness. This does not mean that successions proceeded uncontested, but there was an honorable resolution for failed claimants and their supporters, who, having been deselected, needed to demonstrate support for their former rivals. After he was elected, Henry I battled with Burchard of Alemania until Burchard prudently saw that it was better to subject himself to Henry, and Arnulf, too, ultimately yielded himself to the new king.[112] When it became clear that Henry II was intending to subdue him by force, Duke Herman likewise petitioned for peace on behalf of himself as well as his supporters.[113]

---

qui hiis exequiis intererant, Heirimanno duci auxilium promittunt ad appetendum regnum, Henricum mencientes ad hoc non esse ydoneum propter multarum causarum qualitates."

110. See Adalbert of Magdeburg, *Continuatio Reginonis*, s.aa. 919 (Conrad's efforts toward peacekeeping, which wore him out), 921, 923–25, 936, 939, 953, 956; in *Reginonis abbatis Prumiensis Chronicon cum continuatione Treverensi*, ed. F. Kurze, MGH SRG 50 (Hanover: Hahn, 1890), 156-61, 166-69. Timothy Reuter has remarked that the rhetoric of security "was widespread in the Middle Ages, especially where legitimation was called for" ("The Insecurity of Travel in the Early and High Middle Ages: Criminals, Victims, and Their Medieval and Modern Observers," in *Medieval Polities and Modern Mentalities*, 42–43). Adalbert's comments are unique in this context, in that he emphasizes not just the peace rhetoric referenced by Reuter but the specific quality of unification.

111. Evidence of the development of this new way of thinking about kingship lies in the imagery produced throughout the reigns of the Ottonians. See chapter 4.

112. Widukind, *Res gestae Saxonicae* 1.27, 39–40.

113. Thietmar, *Chronicon* 5.20, 245.

Iter Regis: The Royal *Iter*

The kings themselves were the conduit for royal authority, and the royal *iter* provided a means of distributing that authority. The Ottonian court was continuously on the move, and its perambulations throughout the empire formed an important communication network between the king and his magnates. The periodic presence of the king provided opportunities to convene assemblies, formal venues for communication between the king and his lords.[114] The late Carolingian era provided precedents for this style of kingship. While itinerant rule is sometimes perceived as less effective than polities governed from a single geographic locus, itinerancy could be a highly effective form of rule.[115] The royal *iter* also exemplifies how hard it is to clearly separate the sacred and the secular in the medieval world. The itinerary of the Ottonian kings, like that of the Carolingians, was partly economic and partly political but was also sacral in nature.[116] The *iter* was essential to the Carolingians' success in governing, by facilitating formal meetings with secular and ecclesiastical lords and promoting its military agenda.[117] The *Annals of Fulda*, which give a distinctly king-

114. K. Leyser, "Ottonian Government," 746–47; Bernhardt, *Itinerant Kingship*, 56–57. Regarding assemblies as vehicles for communication between kings and their magnates, see Stuart Airlie, "Talking Heads: Assemblies in Early Medieval Germany," in *Political Assemblies in the Earlier Middle Ages*, ed. P. S. Barnwell and M. Mostert (Turnhout: Brepols, 2003), 29–46; Timothy Reuter, "Assembly Politics in Western Europe from the Eighth Century to the Twelfth," in *The Medieval World*, ed. P. Linehan and J. Nelson (London: Routledge, 2001), 432–50; and Heinz Wolter, *Die Synoden im Reichsgebiet und in Reichsitalien von 916 bis 1056* (Paderborn: Schöningh, 1988).

115. Eckhard Müller-Mertens's development and application of new methodologies spurred new considerations of the *iter* as a highly effective method of governance (*Die Reichsstruktur im Spiegel der Herrschaftspraxis Otto des Großen* [Berlin: Akademie-Verlag, 1980]). See also Bernhardt, *Itinerant Kingship*, 56–57; K. Leyser, "Ottonian Government," 746–77; Carlrichard Brühl, *Fodrum, Gistum, Servitium Regis: Studien zu den wirtschaftlichen Grundlagen des Königtums im Frankenreich und in den fränkischen Nachfolgestaaten Deutschland, Frankreich und Italien vom 6. bis zur Mitte des 14. Jahrhunderts*, 2 vols. (Cologne: Böhlau, 1968); Thomas Zotz, "Präsenz und Repräsentation: Beobachtungen zur königlichen Herrschaftspraxis im hohen und späten Mittelalter," in *Herrschaft als soziale Praxis: Historische und sozial-anthropologische Studien*, ed. Alf Lüdtke, Veröffentlichungen des Max-Planck-Instituts für Geschichte 91 (Göttingen: Vandenhoeck und Ruprecht, 1991), 168–94; Caspar Ehlers, "Having the King—Losing the King," *Viator* 33 (2002): 1–42. A. Kränzle suggests that the absence of the king was as important as his presence in effective itinerant governance ("Der abwesende König: Überlegungen zur ottonischen Königsherrschaft," *Frühmittelalterliche Studien* 31 [1997], 120–57).

116. Henry Mayr-Harting, *Church and Cosmos in Early Ottonian Germany: The View from Cologne* (Oxford: Oxford University Press, 2007), 3–4; Buc, *Dangers of Ritual*, 39; David A. Warner, "Henry II at Magdeburg: Kingship, Ritual and the Cult of Saints," *Early Medieval Europe* 3.2 (1994): 136; John W. Bernhardt, "'On the Road Again': Kings, Roads and Accommodation in High Medieval Germany," in *Every Inch a King: Comparative Studies on Kings and Kingship in the Ancient and Medieval Worlds*, ed. Lynette Mitchell and Charles Melville (Leiden: Brill, 2013), 305.

117. Arnold, *Medieval Germany*, 130. Arnold explains that the military business of the crown "was very demanding considering the advance of the Northmen and the Slavs, the rivalries with

centered view of events from 838 to 901, show how very important the *iter* was to the ninth-century Frankish rulers.[118] Adalbert of Magdeburg's continuation of Regino of Prüm's *Chronicle*, covering events through 967, shows that it was no less important to the Ottonians. Thietmar's *Chronicon*, recording events through 1018, emphasizes the importance of this aspect of Ottonian rule into the reign of Henry II. Through the *iter*, the kings personally channeled royal authority directly to the areas they ruled.[119]

When Henry I became king, he was preoccupied with the conflicts that besieged his realm. He first assembled his army and subdued the Duke of Swabia and the Duke of Bavaria, who ultimately pledged their support to the new king.[120] Gaining allies who could augment his military forces and putting an end to the civil wars that were disrupting the kingdom were essential first steps to addressing external conflicts on two fronts, from Lotharingia in the West and from the Hungarian Magyars in the East. Through a combination of military force and marriage diplomacy, Henry added Lotharingia to his kingdom. Military force and hostage taking facilitated a negotiation of a nine-year peace with the Magyars.[121] Henry spent those years consolidating his support and fortifying the frontiers of his kingdom. In this kind of environment, the impetus toward itinerant rule would have been necessary to reinforce the bonds of loyalty that Henry was trying so hard to establish. Indeed, his efforts to consolidate his position are evidenced by the locations from which he was issuing diplomata—mostly areas comprising his old ducal territory of Saxony, but also

---

the other Carolingian kingdoms, and the internal predilection for major feuds to work out regional political rivalries."

118. *Annales Fuldenses sive Annales Regni Francorum Orientalis*, ed. Friedrich Kurze, MGH SRG 7 (Hanover: Hahn, 1891).

119. Mayr-Harting, *Church and Cosmos*, 3–4. The importance of itinerant rule did not make it any less grueling for the royal family and members of the court. Gunther Wolf assembled the itinerary for Empress Theophanu, the wife of Otto II. It attests not only to the continuance of the imperial itinerary by Theophanu, Adelheid, and the young Otto III after Otto II's death but also to the necessary grit of the queens throughout their tenures. According to Wolf's outline, Theophanu likely had her first child, her daughter Adelheid, in Magdeburg around July 30, 977, was in Grone on August 1 and in Passau a week later. While Wolf is not as sure about the birth dates of her other children, their placements in the itinerary give no indication of significant periods for recovery or "lying in" (Wolf, "Das Itinerar der Prinzessin Theophanu / Kaiserin Theophanu 972–991," in *Kaiserin Theophanu, Prinzessin aus der Fremde: Des Westreichs Grosse Kaiserin*, ed. Gunther Wolf [Weimar: Böhlau, 1991], 8–10).

120. Widukind, *Res gestae Saxonicae* 1.27, 39–40; Liudprand of Cremona, *Antapodosis* 2.21–23, 44–46.

121. Widukind, *Res gestae Saxonicae* 1.30, 1.32, 42–43, 45. Liudprand of Cremona does not mention the peace negotiated but adds other details that, like Widukind's and even if not strictly accurate, suggest the possibilities that arose when there was a regime change. For example, Liudprand suggests that the Hungarians attacked Merseburg because they were specifically testing the new king—both his willingness to abide by the old tribute arrangements and his ability to resist them in battle (*Antapodosis* 2.24, 46).

Franconia and Thuringia—as well as the diplomas' subject matter. Most of the diplomata are confirmations of immunities for ecclesiastical institutions, but there are also significant grants of lands to ecclesiasts, institutions, and *fideles*. The production of diplomata attests to particular aspects of governance, such as the maintenance of a chancery and the holding of assemblages where business with the court could be conducted. Henry did not issue many diplomas over his seventeen-year reign, nor did he hold many assemblies, and the issuance locations indicated in his diplomata suggest that for matters of royal business, he did not venture far from the areas where he could be assured of support. Even in this abbreviated fashion, he was practicing the art of kingship in an idiom that would have been recognizable and legitimizing to those he was ruling. But his perambulations were not yet a fully developed *iter regis*. What Henry had begun, his son, Otto I, was able, during the first half of his reign, to finish, managing the feuds among the nobility and pacifying the pagans in the East. In his far-flung kingdom, the borders of which would expand even further over the course of his reign, Otto seized on the *iter* as a legitimizing element of empire—with, after all, Carolingian precedents—and as an effective way to govern and dispense justice.

The *iter* provided opportunities for a petition-based system of royal justice. Louis the German, a grandson of Charlemagne and king of Bavaria before becoming king of all East Francia, was known to intervene personally in disputes and to allow disputants in conflicts to appeal to him directly. This ninth-century practice did not look backward to his grandfather Charlemagne's methods as much as it foreshadowed the kind of personal kingship that the Ottonians would practice in the tenth century.[122] This kind of kingship does not become evident in the sources until the rule of Otto I. We see this kind of king as the conduit for royal authority with the Ottos, but not with Conrad I and Henry I. While we do not see any extant diplomata dealing with dispute resolution for either Conrad or Henry, this type of diploma seems to have been a normal product of the rule of the Ottos and Henry II south of the Alps.[123] Since Italy was only acquired by Otto I through his marriage to Adelheid in 951, it is perhaps unfair to judge Conrad I and Henry I for their lack of diplomata regarding dispute resolution. But narrative evidence also suggests as much.[124] It is

122. Warren Brown, *Unjust Seizure: Conflict, Interest, and Authority in an Early Medieval Society* (Ithaca, NY: Cornell University Press, 2001), 198. For a discussion of late Carolingian government in East Francia, see Goldberg, *Struggle for Empire*, 206–30.

123. See, for example, DD OI 340, 398–99, 416; DD OII 282, 315; DD OIII 193, 278, 339; DD HII 465.

124. For example, Widukind, *Res gestae Saxonicae* 3.29, 117; Thietmar, *Chronicon* 5.13, 235–36; 6.32, 312; 6.98, 391; 7.62, 475–76.

possible that activities such as dispute resolution were dependent on a relative degree of political stability, which would have been fairly elusive to Conrad and Henry while they were wrangling with internal feuds and external threats like the Magyars, both of which were brought under control by Otto I. The actual presence of the king was requisite for asserting his authority.

If we look at the writings of Adalbert of Magdeburg (ca. 910–81) and Thietmar of Merseburg (975–1018), we can see something of this transformation. After having served the Ottonians in various ways at court and then in ecclesiastical offices, Adalbert was made the first archbishop of Magdeburg. His chronicle is a continuation of a chronicle by Regino of Prüm (d. 915), probably written in 967 or 968 and covering the years from 909 to Otto II's Christmas visit to Rome in 967.[125] While Adalbert tries to record Henry I's location for each year he writes about, little in the chronicle reflects an itinerary operating as a function of government. Since most of Henry's activities that Adalbert describes are martial, concerned with subduing internal and external threats to his realm, this is hardly surprising. The initial entries concerning Otto I read similarly, but beginning around 942, the recording of Otto's locations suggest administrative travel of a planned nature, rather than sudden or urgent military activity. For example, Otto celebrated Christmas in Frankfurt in 942, held an assembly at Duisburg in 944, attended a synod at Ingelheim in 948, celebrated the Feast of the Purification of the Virgin Mary at Frankfurt in 950, and so on. These types of activities reflect an enhanced concern with formalized governance and ritual, public ceremonials in which Otto had time to engage because of his military successes and the elimination or diminution of internal and external threats.

During his reign, Otto I greatly expanded the territory under his rule. As he subdued recalcitrant dukes and extended his influence, he expanded the royal jurisdiction and absorbed former Carolingian properties into the royal fisc.[126] Otto's *iter* encompassed a broader area than had his father's. Though, like

125. Simon MacLean, ed. and trans., *History and Politics in Late Carolingian and Ottonian Europe: The "Chronicle" of Regino of Prüm and Adalbert of Magdeburg*, Manchester Medieval Sources (Manchester: Manchester University Press, 2009), 55. Adalbert is also sometimes referred to as Adalbert of Saint Maximin at Trier.

126. Bernhardt, *Itinerant Kingship*, 20. For example, after the death of Eberhard of Franconia, Otto absorbed the duchy into the royal demesne, as Ekkehard of St. Gall notes in *Casus Sancti Galli* (chap. 11, in Ekkehard IV, *Casus Sancti Galli*, ed. Hans F. Haefele, Ausgewählte Quellen zur deutschen Geschichte des Mittelalters 10 [Darmstadt: Wissenschaftliche Buchgesellschaft, 1980], 42). See also Bernhardt, *Itinerant Kingship*, 20n62; Johannes Laudage, *Otto der Große: Eine Biographie* (Regensburg: Verlag Friedrich Pustet, 2001), 260–61; Hagen Keller, *Ottonische Königsherrschaft: Organisation und Legitimation königlicher Macht* (Darmstadt: Wissenschaftliche Buchgesellschaft, 2002), 65–71.

Henry, he was most at home in Saxony and Franconia, Otto was visibly more engaged further afield. He spent a significantly larger proportion of his time in Franconia than had Henry, and perambulations between and within Saxony, Franconia, and Lotharingia accounted for 83 percent of Otto's time.[127] But his itinerary also reflected the shape of his developing empire, and incorporated places of particular importance at particular times. For example, in 951, Otto marched into Lombardy against Berengar II, was crowned king of Italy, and married his second wife, Adelheid. He remained in Pavia for several months, arranging his affairs there before turning his attention back north to Saxony. A decade later, he returned to Italy to deal with new political challenges and seize the opportunity to be crowned Roman emperor. This time, his time in Italy stretched to several years before he again gravitated to the north.[128] Sojourns in Italy figured in the imperial itinerary from then on.

The perambulations of the Ottonian court were not just an administrative necessity. The ability of a king to travel throughout his realm and govern from the various places where he chose to stop was effectively an assertion of the king's authority.[129] The royal *iter* and the *adventus*, a formal ceremony celebrating the arrival of the emperor, served as means of communication and legitimization and as reminders of his royal prerogative.[130] The areas that the royal court traveled to and through were not necessarily intended to cover all parts of the realm in any given time frame but formed an important network of communication throughout the *Reich*.[131] John Bernhardt, adapting a model devised by Eckhard Müller-Mertens, defines the sociopolitical geography of the Otton-

127. Bernhardt, *Itinerant Kingship*, 20–21; Müller-Mertens, 269.

128. The events described by Liudprand of Cremona in the *Historia Ottonis* suggest the new emperor's direct involvement in Italian affairs for the years immediately following his imperial coronation; the diplomas issued by Otto are consistent with this interpretation, designating Italian locales from early in 962 through the beginning of 956 (DD OI 235–74).

129. Levi Roach, *Kingship and Consent in Anglo-Saxon England, 871–978* (Cambridge: Cambridge University Press, 2013), 46; K. Leyser, "Ottonian Government," 746–47; Bernhardt, *Itinerant Kingship*, 56–57.

130. David A. Warner, "Ritual and Memory in the Ottonian *Reich*: The Ceremony of *Adventus*," *Speculum* 76.2 (2001): 257; Ernst H. Kantorowicz, "The 'King's Advent' and the Enigmatic Panels in the Doors of Santa Sabina," *Art Bulletin* 26.4 (1944): 210; Peter Wilmes, *Der Herrscher -"Adventus" im Kloster des Frühmittelalters* (Munich: Wilhelm Fink Verlag, 1976), 140; David A. Warner, "Thietmar of Merseburg on Rituals of Kingship," *Viator* 26 (1995): 56.

131. This was also the case in England, where the itineraries of Anglo-Saxon kings functioned as "part of the broader communication network which helped hold the kingdom together, designed to facilitate meetings between rulers and their followers at strategically chosen locations" (Roach, *Kingship and Consent*, 46). Compare with Susan Reynolds's ideas about networked relationships as crucial to understanding medieval towns (*Kingdoms and Communities in Western Europe, 900–1300* [Oxford: Oxford University Press, 1997]). She asserts that it is only possible to really understand medieval society by looking at the bonds between people and groups and their collective activities (3–5). The *iter* and *Königsnähe*, as well as the networks of delegated authority discussed below, can all be understood in this context.

ians by zones.[132] The "central zone" comprises the traditional homeland of the Ottonians, in Eastern and Southern Saxony and Northern Thuringia. Here the Ottonians felt most at home and spent most of their time, especially early in their dynastic tenure.[133] Bernhardt identifies as "core zones" areas where the Ottonians received high levels of political and economic support, held most of their properties, and chose to spend much of their time; these territories were concentrated around Eastern and Southern Saxony, as well as parts of the Rhineland and Lower Lotharingia that could be roughly triangulated within key royal centers (Gandersheim-Magdeburg-Merseburg, Frankfurt-Ingelheim-Worms, and Aachen-Nijmegen-Cologne).[134] The central and core areas were connected to each other via "transit zones," areas that the kings needed to pass through to get from one core zone to the next.[135] The frequency of royal visits and the intensity of rule in all of these areas varied. The Saxon heartlands were where the early Ottonians spent much of their time, the central and core zones were important areas for governance and conducting royal and imperial political business, and the transit zones experienced brief but frequent visits as the kings traveled along the royal roads connecting the various royal and imperial centers. Map 2 at the beginning of this book identifies itinerary stations within one of these transit zones.[136] Not only does it clearly mark how the density of royal properties in Southern Saxony disappears through the transit area, but it also marks the great number of properties that were utilized as itinerary stops by the royal court. Part of the strategy of such travel must have been to help disperse the obligation of hospitality, not only among different ecclesiastical institutions, but also between different properties held by each of those institutions. While the actual size of the royal entourage traveling with the king varied, its requirements could pose a significant burden.[137]

132. See Müller-Mertens's *Reichsstruktur*.

133. Bernhardt, *Itinerant Kingship*, 63.

134. Ibid., 62.

135. Ibid., 66–67.

136. Map 2 was adapted from maps of itinerary stations published by Bernhardt (*Itinerant Kingship*, 329) and Wolfgang Metz ("Quellenstudien zum Servitium regis (900–1200)," part 1, *Archiv für Diplomatik* 22 [1976]: 226).

137. Estimates about the numbers of people who traveled with the king's court vary widely and, of course, were not static, but it is probably fair to assume that his entourage generally included at least several hundred people. For debates regarding the sizes of these entourages, see Bernhardt, *Itinerant Kingship*, 58; Brühl, 168–71; Hans Conrad Peyer, *Von der Gastfreundschaft zum Gasthaus: Studien zur Gastlichkeit im Mittelalter*, MGH Schriften 31 (Hanover: Hahn, 1987), 156–57. The requirements of the court could be enormous; the anonymous twelfth-century author of the *Annalista Saxo* suggests that Otto I had daily need of a thousand swine and sheep and ten cartloads each of wine and beer, supplemented by additional provisions: "Iste inperator singulis diebus habuit huiusmodi cibum, sicut scriptum invenitur; Mille porcos et oves, 10 carradas vini, 10 cervisie, frumenti maltra mille, boves 8 preter pullos et porcellos, pisces, ova, legumina, aliaque quam plura" (MGH SS 6, 622).

Early Ottonians tended to keep their perambulations close to home, in territories where they enjoyed the highest degree of support and the most resources at their disposal, traveling to less friendly areas only infrequently. Ecclesiastical and secular lords from outside the core and central zones needed to travel to the court when they had business with it. Over time, as the kings consolidated their power, their itineraries came to include areas such as Swabia and Bavaria; that Otto III issued charters in those regions demonstrates that he was conducting business there directly.[138] Imperial visits continued under Henry II and into the early Salian period.[139] The Ottonians show how an itinerant system could effectively assert authority over a far-flung geographic region, with built-in flexibility to accommodate either the needs of the moment or an expansion of their sphere of influence.

In Germany, secular and ecclesiastical lords also toured throughout their estates and holdings, taking advantage of stopping points to hold assemblies or administer justice.[140] Thus, we see the same general method of itinerant government practiced in smaller geographic areas by local lords.[141] These travels between properties at lower levels of government and between and among properties and zones at higher levels of government formed important communication networks, which operated both independently (e.g., among estates

138. Bernhardt, *Itinerant Kingship*, 66. See, for example, DD OIII 22, 47–49, 125, 153–54, 157, 159–61, 190, 344, 346–48, 370–73, 480.

139. Bernhardt, *Itinerant Kingship*, 66; Caspar Ehlers, "Bayern und Sachsen im Itinerar Heinrichs II: Ein Beitrag zur Bearbeitung Bayern im Repertorium der deutschen Königspfalzen," *Zeitschrift für bayerische Landesgeschichte* 65.3 (2002): 799–838. For Henry II, see DD HII 21–35, 51, 54, 59, 76–78, 115, 130–32, 192–93, 207–8, 211–17, 228–32, 273, 315–18, 355, 394–95, 399, 400, 454, 458, 460, 494, 496–99; for Conrad II, DD CII 24–26, 28–29, 38–40, 49, 51, 58–59, 103–9, 133–39, 142, 146, 179, 186, 206–12, 214, 224–26, 281. The patterns of travel and stays in Swabia and Bavaria seem to coincide with the need for transit to Italy. Initially, under Otto III, singular surviving diplomas in these regions between the Ottonian heartland and Italy suggest imperial stopovers en route to extended stays in Italy. We begin to see more extended stays in both Swabia and Bavaria throughout the reign of Henry II. Given the tendency of kings to spend time where they felt most at home, Henry's comfort in traversing these regions, particularly Bavaria, doubtless derived from his former position as Duke of Bavaria.

140. Regarding itineracy among bishops, see Warner, "Ritual and Memory," 265; H. E. J. Cowdrey, "The Structure of the Church, 1024–1073," in *NCMH* 4.1:247. Rather of Verona emphasizes, among other duties of bishops outlined in his *Praeloquia*, the importance of bishops traveling throughout their sees (Rosamond McKitterick, "The Church," in *NCMH* 3, 135). Regarding itineracy of secular lords, see Bernhardt, *Itinerant Kingship*, 45; Peyer, 146–99.

141. As noted above, the *iter* was also a feature of Anglo-Saxon government (Roach, *Kingship and Consent*, 45). Levi Roach has gestured to the Anglo-Saxon *iter regis* as a method of rulership in tenth-century England, observing the essential roles of feasting with one's magnates and asserting the royal prerogative for the king, while providing opportunities for nobles to demonstrate their *Königsnähe* and gain access to the king's presence (Levi Roach, "Hosting the King: Hospitality and the Royal *Iter* in Tenth-Century England," *Journal of Medieval History* 37 [2011]: 40). For the Ottonians and the Anglo-Saxons, the *iter* was an important social and political ritual as well as a function of rule for the kings and their nobles.

owned by a single monastery) and in concert with each other. These local area networks created the foundations for larger, wider networks of communications throughout the *Reich*, ensuring that governance at local and regnal levels was a presence throughout the kingdom.

Decentralization and Power

Among the distinctive features of Ottonian governance, we have seen a network of communications facilitated by royal and imperial *missi*-type officials, as well as *missi* from bishops and nobles that facilitated communication throughout the realm, between each other, and between themselves and the king.[142] The pattern of noncontiguous landholding was another essential feature of the Ottonians and prevented any single person from being able to accumulate a contiguous minikingdom like those amassed by French dukes. Additionally, having personal and fiscal interests throughout the realm necessitated the *iter regis* to assert the royal prerogative and administer business of the realm, such as the hearing of petitions and the dispensation of justice. The Ottonians recognized the potential advantage and danger that large consolidated land parcels could offer, as evidenced by the future Henry I's efforts to accumulate land around Magdeburg and by Conrad I's alarm at his activities. Thietmar of Merseburg records that Henry I was responsible for Merseburg's consolidation into a single property.[143] Thietmar implies that this consolidation was deliberate, though he does not indicate a military end for such a plan (Henry was not yet king).[144] That Henry was an "ambitious man," as Thietmar characterizes him, seems without doubt. After Henry's father died, leaving him well positioned, Conrad

142. Regarding the importance of assemblies in providing a venue for communication between the king and his magnates, see K. Leyser, "Ottonian Government," 746–47; Bernhardt, *Itinerant Kingship*, 56–57; Airlie; Reuter, "Assembly Politics." Wolter (*Die Synoden*) discusses these same issues with regard to synods, which also created a formal venue for communication.

143. Thietmar, *Chronicon* 1.3, 7: "Ab Henrico sumatur exordium, qui predicte civitatis adpertinencia multorum ius tunc respiciencia univit, maioraque hiis multum sua virtute et industria subegit." Warner (*Ottonian Germany*, 68n9) remarks that one of Henry's methods for attempting to unify the city's properties was through marriage to Hatheburg, the daughter of Count Erwin; the count was one of these "owners."

144. Thietmar, *Chronicon* 1.5, 8: "Interim cuiusdam matronae famam, quae Hatheburch dicebatur, Heinricus comperiens, qualiter eam sibi sociaret, iuvenili exarsit amore. Haec erat filia Ervini senioris, qui in urbe predicta, quam Antiquam civitatem nominamus, maximam tenuit partem, et quia is filium non habuit, geminis filiabus suis e medio decedens reliquit. Ob huius pulchritudinem et hereditatis divitiarumque utilitatem internuntios Heinricus quam propere misit, et quamvis hanc esse viduam et sciret velatam, suae tamen ut satis faceret voluntati, eam fide promissa petivit." These properties that Henry was so eager to acquire may also have included a monastic foundation (Warner, *Ottonian Germany*, 70n17).

first declined to grant the scope of powers Henry's father had to the new duke. Conrad then conspired with the bishop of Halberstadt to kill Henry. When Henry discovered the plot, he confiscated all of Halberstadt's holdings in Saxony and Thuringia and expelled the king's supporters.[145] According to Thietmar's account, Henry was deliberately consolidating holdings, and Thietmar's comment about the duke's ambitiousness, "quia vir fuit industris,"[146] indicates that Henry was a man who had the potential to be a significant threat to Conrad's authority, a threat of which we can assume Conrad was aware, since he tried to limit Henry's scope of powers and then conspired to eliminate him. The involvement of the bishop of Halberstadt in the plot is not surprising, as bishops were often complicit in plots with or against Ottonian lords and kings, but it speaks to Conrad's need for support in such an action; he did not act on his own, though it is unclear whether he needed the bishop's support for military reasons, logistical reasons, or to demonstrate that he had ecclesiastical support or some small degree of consensus. The import of a king killing a new but legitimate duke without any justifiable cause would not be lost on the other magnates. Henry's conscious attempt to establish a fortified burg with consolidated territories and local landowners willing to acknowledge him as lord sounds very like the organization of lords in France that Bisson identifies as hallmarks of the "feudal revolution."[147] That Conrad took steps to ensure that such power did not attenuate to a single lord suggests that he and his advisors were aware of the potential problems that could arise from such arrangements and kept a careful eye on the activities of their magnates.

Agents were used throughout the empire, to represent the king, of course, and also bishops, abbots, and noblemen. No one person could effectively supervise all of one's land parcels throughout a kingdom as widespread as that of the Ottonians. The necessity of administering justice throughout the poten-

145. Thietmar, *Chronicon* 1.7, 12. Shortly thereafter, Henry put aside Hatheburg and pursued Mathilda, allegedly for her wealth (Thietmar, *Chronicon* 1.9, 14).

146. Thietmar, *Chronicon* 1.5, 10; Holtzmann gives "quia vir fuit illustris." Warner (*Ottonian Germany*, 70n18) adheres to the original textual "industris" as opposed to the more common correction "illustris." He notes that the decision to translate it as "ambitious" as opposed to "industrious" is his own, reflecting how he interprets the gist of Thietmar's story, and I am inclined to agree with Warner's interpretation.

147. Bisson, "Feudal Revolution," 9. Bisson's article invigorated the "feudal revolution" debate, a scholarly discussion that took place in subsequent issues of *Past & Present*, between Bisson, Dominique Barthélemy, Stephen White, Timothy Reuter, and Chris Wickham. See "Debate: The 'Feudal Revolution,'" *Past & Present* 152 (1996), for Barthélemy and White's contributions; "Debate: The 'Feudal Revolution,'" *Past & Present* 155 (1997), for Reuter and Wickham's contributions; "The 'Feudal Revolution': Reply," *Past & Present* 155 (1997), for Bisson's response. Bisson develops his thesis more fully in *The Crisis of the Twelfth Century: Power, Lordship, and the Origins of European Government* (Princeton, NJ: Princeton University Press, 2009).

tially broad areas where one held jurisdictional authority, as well as personal fondness for particular properties, lent itself to a peripatetic court, and itinerancy by bishops, nobles, and the king himself ensured the periodic presence of authority. The delegation of authority among nobles throughout the empire did not dilute the authority of the king but, rather, assured that it was a ubiquitous presence. That positions were not necessarily hereditary and that fiscal properties granted to beneficiaries reverted back to the crown upon death emphasizes the importance of *Königsnähe* and *amicitia* networks in the overall communications and governing apparatuses of the Ottonian Empire. The distribution of authority may have also worked to preserve a kind of balance of power among the great men of the kingdom, as they navigated their relationships with each other and with the king.

Historians have struggled with how to account for the success of the Ottonians' rule despite the noncentralized organizational structure of their government. Timothy Reuter, for example, asserts that Ottonian Germany cannot be considered a highly organized polity, because of the loose nature of its law and order, the importance there of ritualized and symbolic actions (especially those with political implications), and the absence there of clear administrative structures.[148] This position is problematic on multiple levels. It appears that Reuter is privileging centralization and teleology.[149] His position also demonstrates the difficulty of trying to visualize systems of governance on their own terms and disentangle one's sensibilities, at least in the post-Enlightenment West, from privileging centralized bureaucratic structures. What if a noncentralized state was the best way to address the threats that faced the Ottonian *Reich*? The Ottonian system provided a flexible matrix of structured control over its territories, one as reflective of East Frankish political idiosyncrasies as of the Ottonians' ability to adapt those idiosyncrasies to their own purposes.

Royal authority in the Ottonian Empire had direct fiscal interests in nearly every part of its domain. The itinerancy, the fragmented fiscal estates, and the systems of maintaining power and control despite feuds and rebellions of mag-

---

148. Timothy Reuter, "The Making of England and Germany, 850–1050: Points of Comparison and Difference," in *Medieval Polities and Modern Mentalities*, 284–99. Bernhardt notes that itinerant rulership is not unique to the European Middle Ages, pointing to the fourteenth-century Javanese kings, Hawaiian and Tahitian kings, and kings in several African countries in the early modern period (*Itinerant Kingship*, 45–46).

149. For these views, see Reuter, "Making of England and Germany," 292n29; Gerd Althoff, *Amicitia und Pacta: Bundnis, Einung, Politik und Gebetsgedenken im Beginnenden 10. Jahrhundert* (Hanover: Hahn, 1992); Timothy Reuter, "Peace-Breaking, Feud, Rebellion, Resistance: Violence and Peace in the Politics of the Salian Era," in *Medieval Polities and Modern Mentalities*, 355–87; Karl Leyser, "From Saxon Freedoms to the Freedom of Saxony: The Crisis of the Eleventh Century," in *Communications and Power in Medieval Europe: The Gregorian Revolution and Beyond*, ed. Timothy Reuter (London: Hambledon, 1994), 51–67.

nates worked directly in the interests of royal authority, helping it to avoid getting caught in massive power struggles like we see in France. Noncontiguous territories were less susceptible to fragmentation of the kind suffered by France in the tenth and eleventh centuries.

The extensive holding of noncontiguous territories was another distinctive feature in East Francia that influenced Ottonian governance. The Ottonian kings had a vested interest in properties in every province, which intensified the importance of the *iter* and their *amicitia* networks throughout their realm.[150] For example, in the wedding charter for Otto II and Theophanu, the gifts to Theophanu included unspecified properties in Italy, along with named properties north of the Alps located in what are today the Netherlands, Belgium, and several locations in Germany.[151] While two of these properties, Nordhausen and Tilleda, are only about 30 kilometers apart, the distance between Nordhausen and Boppard is about 370 kilometers. This landholding pattern contrasts sharply with that of France, whose king held very little land personally throughout his realm and instead held a small contiguous territory. In Germany, the king's holdings were vast and spread throughout the entire kingdom. The holdings of their magnates and the properties of bishoprics and abbeys followed similar patterns of dispersal over noncontiguous territories.[152] These kinds of landholding patterns likely contributed to England and Germany's resistance to the "political disarray" exhibited during the "feudal revolution" in France, where kings held a relatively small portion of the kingdom and where a lord's lands tended to be compact but relatively absolute—that is, all lords held power within a rather well-defined geographical area but had little or no authority outside those boundaries. This geographical limitation to where a lord exercised power even held true to a certain degree for the French kings.[153] Thus, in England and Germany, though every lord controlled his own realm, that realm might be broadly distributed within a patchwork of jurisdictions controlled by other lords, each with his own evaluation of potential threats or opportunities. Especially given the size of the Ottonian Empire, this dispersal of holdings allowed resources to be allocated according to need in situations where threats necessitated royal intervention or support, rather than wasting

150. Arnold, *Medieval Germany*, 55.

151. The named properties are Walcheren and Tiel in the Low Countries, Wichelen with the Abbey of Nivelle and its holdings, Boppard in the Middle Rhine, Herford, Tilleda, and Nordhausen: "Uualacra, Uuigle cum abbatia Niuelle, quattuordecim milibus eó pertinentibus mansis, imperatoris quoque curtes nostras propria maiestate dignas: Bochbarda, Thiela, Heriuurde, Dullede, Nordhuse" (DD OII 21).

152. Map 2 at the beginning of this book shows how properties belonging to several major houses in the area connecting Saxony and Thuringia were distributed.

153. Clarke, *English Nobility*, 147–48.

energy and resources on futile attempts to predict and respond to the unrealized and unpredictable possibility of future threats.[154]

Key elements to Ottonian success included having numerous local rulers able to govern with a fair degree of autonomy assured by the broad immunities granted by the king (with the king intervening or sending reinforcements only as needed to respond to specific situations), as well as the ability of those semiautonomous authorities to respond to situations on the ground and react effectively. These local lords can be seen as "multiple sensors," an especially apt metaphor here since the vast majority of comital and episcopal estates and even lesser noble ones in tenth-century Germany were noncontiguous. These provided an infrastructure for communication networks, as property holders managed estates by traveling between them or engaged others to manage them on their behalf; negotiated and engaged with other landholders via messengers, assemblies, or at court; and communicated with the king, who was himself engaged in the aforementioned activities as well as following a careful itinerary throughout his realm. These networks are hinted at in surviving narrative sources from the tenth century but can only be speculated about, because there are no written records attesting to them. Perhaps, by focusing only on the existence or lack of written evidence of communication networks, the extent to which these networks existed or were utilized has been underestimated.

The potential advantage to the Ottonian kings of having agents widely dispersed throughout patchworks of estates—whether ecclesiastical or secular lords or their representatives—far outweighed the risks of the periodic conspiracies and rebellions. We must assume that the Ottonians were aware of centralization as a way of governing. Such a strategy had been attempted under Charlemagne, and their contemporaneous Anglo-Saxons ruled via a hierarchy of bureaucratic institutions staffed by royal officials. But we cannot assume that the Ottonians' rule by a different model meant that they were less sophisticated in governing. Their decentralized government incorporated elements of traditional Germanic kingship and adopted various Carolingian institutions north

154. For more information on how attempts to predict future events can weaken an organization through the squandering of resources and by lessening its ability to defend itself, see Taleb's treatment of uncertainty theory in *The Black Swan*. With those who might argue that Henry I's *Burgenbauordnung* was an attempt to predict and respond to future attacks by the Magyars, I disagree. The defenses built on the eastern frontier served more as a deployment of additional sensors and a means of attempting to maintain the upper hand in the violent give-and-take that defined the relationship between the Magyars and the *Reich*. Leyser describes the fortress system as a "network of burgwards and *burgbanns* which bound both Saxon and Slav populations to castlework, dues and watch services" and a "systemic and contiguous network of fortifications, of labor services, and an organization to maintain them," a network that sounds much more like a sustainable sensory system with the ability to react defensively if threatened ("Ottonian Government," 734, 736).

of the Alps, and in Italy, they generally ruled according to preexisting customs and law while asserting their primacy in local affairs.

The "rejection of centralized control in favor of multiple semi-independent agents that individually solve problems as they arise in the environment" is a recurrent pattern in nature, where centrally controlled organizational schemes tend to be the ones least likely to thrive;[155] instead, "the job of sensing the environment is farmed out to multiple agents that have a great deal of power to respond on behalf of the larger organism."[156] This biological model sounds very much like the Ottonian method of delegating authority and jurisdiction. By granting their margraves, counts, and bishops broad autonomy in handling their own affairs, the Ottonians were able to respond independently and quickly to threats that appeared—internal or external. Rafe Sagarin, who has written extensively on decentralized security systems in nature, gives three key reasons why decentralized and distributed organizations are so adaptable and successful.

> First, multiple sensors all looking or experiencing the environment from their own perspective provide more opportunities to identify unusual changes and unexploited opportunities. . . . Second, multiple agents committed to the security mission in their own local area create opportunities to specialize tasks, so energy isn't wasted in having every part of the organism doing the same thing. . . . Those doing the most important things get the resources to replicate their activities. . . . Third, distributed sensors respond to the most immediate environmental conditions in time and space—they see the environment for what it "is" rather than what it "should" be according to some preconceived notion.[157]

Sagarin's description of a dispersed sensory network sounds very like the Ottonian system.[158] As with successful natural security systems, the Ottonians were adaptable, able to manipulate uncertainty and maintain redundant and multifunctioning security. They also actively developed symbiotic relationships with real or potential rivals—for example, in their relationship with the papacy or their efforts to Christianize the Slavs and, perhaps most strikingly, in Otto I's

155. Rafe Sagarin, *Learning from the Octopus: How Secrets from Nature Can Help Us Fight Terrorist Attacks, Natural Disasters, and Disease* (New York: Basic Books, 2013), 18.

156. Ibid., 64.

157. Ibid., 67.

158. See Laura Wangerin, "Octopuses and Ottonians: Biological Systems as Models for Decentralized Medieval Government," *Annalen des Naturhistorischen Museums in Wien*, ser. A, 120 (2018): 31–49.

efforts in Northern Italy, culminating with his marriage to Adelheid.[159] The true value and adaptive capacity of decentralized biological systems are beginning to be exploited by modern organizational strategists. Perhaps by using this lens as a way of understanding Ottonian government, we can gain a better appreciation of the Ottonians' style of rule as a strategically organized system.

The Ottonians did not wantonly give away authority and jurisdictions, as many historians have claimed.[160] Instead, they created a system that reflected the careful development of a policy that evolved from practical considerations and applications of justice in their kingdom and empire. The kings delegated extensive authority, depending on their ecclesiastical and secular lords to maintain order and hold courts for their own demesnes. Only if matters got beyond the control of the local lord would the king be compelled to intervene. Though decentralized, this was a coherent legal ideology, organized around unifying principles and overseen by the monarchy. A model of governance blending delegation and itinerancy perfectly suited the real political and invasive threats that faced the Ottonian realm. These characteristics have caused the Ottonians to be perceived as more organizationally primitive, but it is more likely that these factors made them particularly resilient to threats that arose, both inside and outside the empire.

159. Even Benjamin Arnold has a chapter titled "The Symbiosis of the German Church and Medieval Kingship" in his *Medieval Germany* (137–39).

160. For perhaps the best overview of the problems inherent in traditional approaches to German medieval history, see David A. Warner, "Reading Ottonian History: The *Sonderweg* and Other Myths," in *Challenging the Boundaries of Medieval History: The Legacy of Timothy Reuter*, ed. Patricia Skinner (Turnhout: Brepols, 2009), 82–114. Warner discusses how historical interpretations and understandings of the Middle Ages in Germany "have been affected by assumptions regarding Germany's historical passage from the Middle Ages to modernity." The problem for German historians has been "the fact that Germany did not develop the characteristics commonly associated with the modern state, or at least with the latter's early modern prototype. . . . While English and French kings were centralizing power and administration, German kings surrendered power and independence to the aristocracy whose position was ensured by the archaic practice of the royal election" (96). This approach to understanding the Ottonian era and its successor kingdoms under the Salians and Hohenstaufens (called "the medieval German *Sonderweg*" by Timothy Reuter) is inherently teleological and assumes that the medieval mind appreciated modern governmental apparatuses as superior to their own state, a proposition Warner identifies as questionable at best (98).

CHAPTER 2

Ecclesiastical Jurisdictions and Royal Authority

In Ottonian Germany, ecclesiastical jurisdictions were important—but often contentious—components of the system of royal governance.[1] German ecclesiastical jurisdictions resembled those of great lords both in their scope and in their obligations to the emperor. While bishops could operate, like their secular counterparts, with great autonomy in the administration of law and justice over their lands, they were also responsible for duties that included military service. The conflicts that would arise later in the eleventh century, as part of the Investiture Controversy, doubtless found their inception in the disputes that arose over episcopal and abbatial elections. Throughout the medieval world, kings tried to place *fideles*, lords who owed them allegiance, in these positions, but bishops in the Ottonian Empire were more like great princes in their own right, with substantial revenues and powers. There was significant fluidity between the concepts of secular and sacred spheres, and episcopal elections could be highly charged events. The effectiveness of the Ottonian system lay largely in its ability to control its magnates and command their loyalty, through force if necessary. When the Ottonian dynasty ended, it was perhaps inevitable that great lords, both secular and ecclesiastical, would attempt to assert or expand their influence. The first Salian rulers had to deal with a certain measure of turmoil, reminiscent of the magnate rebellions and struggles that Henry I and Otto I faced when establishing their dynasty and that challenged Henry II after the sudden death of Otto III. That bishops were among those rebellious magnates should not surprise us. The Investiture Controversy in the late eleventh and twelfth centuries ended up substantially redefining the relationship between

1. For discussion framing the network of bishops against the political map of European kingdoms ca. 950–1050, see Timothy Reuter, "A Europe of Bishops: The Age of Wulfstan of York and Burchard of Worms," in *Patterns of Episcopal Power: Bishops in Tenth and Eleventh Century Western Europe*, ed. Ludger Körntgen and Dominik Wassenhoven (Berlin: De Gruyter, 2011), 17–38. Regarding the importance of monasteries to governing institutions such as the royal *iter*, see John W. Bernhardt, *Itinerant Kingship and Royal Monasteries in Early Medieval Germany, c. 936–1075* (Cambridge: Cambridge University Press, 1993).

the church and the German emperors, but it was fundamentally a conflict over patronage and resource allocation, foregrounded in the Ottonian efforts to create and maintain control over imperial bishoprics and monasteries.

In Ottonian Germany, we see a high degree of interaction between ecclesiastical and royal spheres of influence. Ecclesiastical lords and institutions were crucially important in ensuring that the reach of the government extended to all of their subjects.[2] Likewise, the power accrued by ecclesiastical authorities could not have developed without the gifts of land and the delegation of secular authority by the crown. The overlap between secular and ecclesiastical jurisdictional concerns is manifested in the Ottonian Empire in a model where ecclesiastical lords were granted broad jurisdictional authorities over their *familiae*, the people under their rule, and acted as dispensers of secular justice as well as religious law.

The Ottonians' relationship with the pope was unique among tenth-century rulers. Whereas their imperial status designated a special relationship between the German emperors and Rome, tensions arose over authority and the Ottonian involvement in the Holy See. The pope was necessary to anoint them as emperors, but they clearly viewed him as a subordinate power, subject to their authority and serving at their pleasure. In France and England, kings treated the pope as a foreign dignitary of equal status, albeit over the spiritual realm, rather than the secular. The Ottonians, in contrast, considered the pope the most important of their many bishops. The Ottonians were keenly involved in episcopal appointments within their empire, including that of the pontiff. The conjunctions of royal and ecclesiastical power in negotiating these appointments often led to conflict between opposing factions.[3,4] This relationship between ecclesi-

2. Encouraging close cooperation between their bishops also proved to be a powerful legitimizing strategy, as well as a way to emphasize the cohesiveness of the empire. See Wolfgang Huschner, "Erzbischof Johannes von Ravenna (983–998), Otto II. und Theophanu," *Quellen und Forschungen aus Italienischen Archiven und Bibliotheken* 83 (2003): 1–40.

3. As noted in the introduction to the present study, the term *power* should be understood as encompassing the related ideas of networked social relationships, the ability to govern or direct behaviors, and the ability to do so indirectly as well as directly, by means of tools such as legislation, force, or consent.

4. These key differences set the stage for the Investiture Controversy in the post-Ottonian *Reich*, and the descriptions of disputed abbatial and episcopal elections by chroniclers such as Thietmar of Merseburg became fodder for the fight, but the context for these Ottonian episcopal appointments predates the eleventh-century Gregorian reforms and canon law revolution. The Gregorian reforms, dating from the mid-eleventh century and named for Pope Gregory VII, addressed issues including clerical abuses such as simony and lay investiture. The Investiture Controversy was born out of these reform efforts, when Henry IV of Germany (king from 1056, Holy Roman Emperor from 1084 to 1105) opposed Pope Gregory VII's assertion that kings and emperors had no authority to appoint bishops in their realms. See Uta-Renate Blumenthal, *The Investiture Controversy: Church and Monarchy from the Ninth to the Twelfth Century* (Philadelphia: University of Pennsylvania Press, 1982), for a comprehensive treatment of the reforms and their sociopolitical context.

astical lords or institutions and royal authority was not always contentious, but the persistent tension between church and ruler was a dynamic that defined their interactions throughout the Ottonian period.

The *Reichskirchensystem* and Ecclesiastical Jurisdictional Authority

While there is general acknowledgment of the importance to the Ottonians of the networks of royal monasteries, abbeys, and churches, as well as the people who led those institutions, the degree to which these institutions' establishment was a deliberate application of royal and imperial policy has been the subject of debate in recent decades. Scholarship in the nineteenth century and for much of the twentieth accepted the idea of an Ottonian-Salian *Reichskirchensystem* as a de facto component of German government in the tenth and eleventh centuries. This traditional view of an imperial church system held that the network of royal bishoprics, abbeys, and monasteries formed a system, that is, that it was the articulation of a deliberately deployed imperial policy, conceptualized and developed over the course of the tenth century. Not until 1982, when Timothy Reuter challenged the existence of a *Reichskirkensystem* and some of the necessary conclusions it embodied, did scholars enter into serious debate over whether or to what degree such a system existed.[5] By no means has Reuter's dismissal of a *Reichskirkensystem* been met with universal acceptance; some have responded to his argument by reasserting their commitment to the concept as a valid description of governing practice by Ottonian and Salian emperors.[6] Whether and to what degree an imperial church system was developed by the Ottonians and their successors remains an unresolved point of contention, but

For elements of this reform that relate to the canon law revolution, see Kathleen Cushing, *Papacy and the Law in the Gregorian Revolution* (New York: Oxford University Press, 1998); Uta-Renate Blumenthal, "The Papacy and Canon Law in the Eleventh-Century Reform," *Catholic Historical Review* 84 (1998): 201–18; John T. Gilchrist, "Canon Law Aspects of the Eleventh Century Gregorian Reform Programme," *Journal of Ecclesiastical History* 13 (1962): 21–38.

5. Timothy Reuter, "The 'Imperial Church System' of the Ottonian and Salian Rulers: A Reconsideration," in *Medieval Polities and Modern Mentalities*, ed. Janet Nelson (Cambridge: Cambridge University Press, 2006), 325–54.

6. Josef Fleckenstein, "Problematik und Gestalt der ottonisch-salischen Reichskirche," in *Reich und Kirche vor dem Investiturstreit: Vorträge beim wissenschaftlichen Kolloquium aus Anlass des 80. Geburtstags von Gerd Tellenbach*, ed. K. Schmid (Sigmaringen: Thorbecke, 1985), 83-98; Rudolf Schieffer, "Der ottonische Reichsepiskopat zwishen Königtum und Adel," *Frühmittelalterliche Studien* 23 (1989): 291–301. In "Origins of Courtliness after 25 Years" (*Haskins Society Journal* 21 [2009]: 200–201), C. Stephen Jaeger gives a concise summation of the current state of the debate (noting that for both the Ottonian and the Salian periods, "very little ground has shifted in the concept 'Reichskirche'" since Reuter's article [201n52]).

these debates have forced scholars to address Reuter's criticisms and further define the parameters of what, exactly, a *Reichskirkensystem* entailed.

The reality was probably somewhere between the two positions: that a *Reichskirkensystem* existed, or did not. As important as ecclesiastical appointments and the political roles of bishops, abbots, and other church officials were to the successful governance of the Ottonian *Reich*, it is clear that the Ottonian rulers were very deliberate in their administration of such positions, doing their best to appoint officials who would best serve the interests of the king as well as the interests of their sees. Yet the degree to which these positions functioned as imperial offices varied widely, as did the impunity with which the king or emperor could appoint his own men to those positions. Conflict between local and imperial interests are evidenced through controversies such as that reported by Thietmar of Merseburg regarding the appointment of archbishops at Magdeburg by Henry II (discussed at length below). Local politics and powerful families influenced such decisions, as did the ruler's desire to place his own *familiares* into these positions. Regardless of their original relationship to the king or any indebtedness they might owe him for their elevation, once bishops or abbots were in place, they often found their loyalty to the king to be in conflict with their new local or ecclesiastical interests. Shortly after being named archbishop of Mainz in 954, Otto I's illegitimate son William sent an alarmed letter to Pope Agapetus II, complaining that Otto's plans to elevate Magdeburg to an archbishopric impinged on William's own metropolitan authority (and complaining, too, about the appointment of William's uncle Brun as archbishop of Cologne).[7]

Traditionally, the frequency with which the Ottonians' granted immunity has been perceived as a sign of the inherent weakness of their government. Following that line of argument, the Ottonians franchised their authority, giving away their power. Yet immunities were ably employed as tools of a strong rulership. The importance of immunities in medieval kingship has begun to be reassessed, and the picture that emerges is one of continuity, adaptability, and the performance of power.[8] Immunities were not a new development under the Ottonians; they were a common way to allocate jurisdictional authority and privileges under the Merovingian and Carolingian kings as well. But much of the scholarship assumes that the need to rely on immunities was both a sign of

7. Philipp Jaffé, ed., *Bibliotheca Rerum Germanicarum*, vol. 3, *Monumenta Moguntina* (Berlin: Weidmann, 1866), 347–50.

8. See, for example, Barbara Rosenwein, *Negotiating Space: Power, Restraint, and Privileges of Immunity in Early Medieval Europe* (Ithaca, NY: Cornell University Press, 1999), especially 1–23; David S. Bachrach, "Immunities as Tools of Royal Military Policy under the Carolingian and Ottonian Kings," *Zeitschrift der Savigny-Stiftung für Rechtsgeschichte* 130 (2013): 1–36.

and remedy to an inherently weak kingship.[9] The earliest immunity known to us, issued by Theuderic III in 688, demonstrates attributes of regnal stability—what Barbara Rosenwein identifies as "continuity, amity, and cooperation."[10] Grants of immunities may not have been concessions made by the crown to buy the fidelity of or pacify their lay and ecclesiastical lords, nor were they signs of royal or imperial weakness. Instead, as David Bachrach has argued, immunities were "practical tools" that the kings had at their disposal "for the purpose of allocating the resources of the government in ways that furthered royal policies."[11] Bachrach further distinguishes between the use of immunities "as a tool of politics rather than as a tool of government or administration";[12] that is, immunities were not distributed solely as a reward or enticement to secure political support but, instead, were an essential institution of the Ottonian governing apparatus. In its use by the Merovingian and Carolingian rulers, Rosenwein demonstrates, the immunity evolved into a political instrument, its malleability in the face of changing situations being one of its most important features.[13] For the Ottonians, arguing for an either-or position (immunities being used to manipulate political situations or immunities being used as a method of governance) places too many restrictions on a kind of charter that presented a wide array of potential uses. Seen in this light, the ability to grant immunities signals strong kingship and an administrative strategy to organize administration of royal and imperial resources, as well as an imaginative and flexible rulership that seized opportunities to exploit the various methods at their disposal. By the ninth century, the issuance of immunities had become such a basic component of Carolingian government that their use was essentially inevitable under the Ottonians. That the Ottonians, like their Carolingian predecessors, were able to use the immunity to serve their own widely varied political needs and purposes speaks to the innovative spirit of their rulership.

Beginning in the tenth century, grants of immunity in areas under the control or influence of the Ottonian *Reich* often included full judicial authority and the rights to incomes from those lands.[14] However, these immunities were

9. See D. Bachrach, "Immunities," 2–6, for a historiography of the debates and evolution of our understanding regarding immunities.

10. Rosenwein, *Negotiating Space*, 84–85.

11. D. Bachrach, "Immunities," 7; here, Bachrach is mainly interested in the use of immunities as a way of improving the efficiency of military support and mobilization by the kings, but their importance in providing delegated authority and the *servitium regis* is not diluted by that emphasis.

12. D. Bachrach, "Immunities," 35.

13. Rosenwein, *Negotiating Space*, 5, 96–97, 213.

14. Wendy Davies and Paul Fouracre, eds., *Property and Power in the Early Middle Ages* (Cambridge: Cambridge University Press, 1995), 13. For a good summary of the development of immunities in the early medieval Western legal tradition, see Katherine Fischer Drew, "Public vs. Private Enforcement of the Law in the Early Middle Ages: Fifth to Twelfth Centuries," *Chicago-Kent Law Review* 70 (1994–95): 1583–92.

granted almost exclusively to ecclesiastical institutions. While we know of some such grants to laity, they existed on a much smaller scale.[15] Grants of juridical immunity protected ecclesiastical lords—such as bishops and abbots—from the potential meddling of local counts, dukes, or margraves, and these grants included forests and towns with the jurisdictions that attenuated with them, although the actual exercise of justice within these jurisdictions was delegated to aristocratic advocates.[16] Ecclesiastical institutions in Ottonian Germany were concerned about making sure they received written confirmations of their privileges from reigning kings and emperors. These diplomas, which generally specified that the king was issuing them at the request of an abbot or bishop, confirmed landholding, immunities, and privileges. In a rather typical example, Henry I's 920 confirmation for the Abbey of Fulda, we see the confirmation had been issued at the request of the abbot and cast as following the tradition of previous kings.

> And the aforementioned abbot asked that likewise we should take the same monastery into our protection with the monks there serving God and with the things and men legally belonging to it and that we should join our diploma to the diploma of the aforesaid kings, and since we have judged his petition to be eminently just and reasonable, we have freely accommodated and have given assent to the benefice which he asked for.[17]

This diploma mentions that the immunities were to be valid for "ecclesias villas loca vel agros" (churches, villas, dwellings, and fields) and specifies jurisdictional privileges, forbidding any royal officers or judiciaries from hearing legal cases, exacting fines, raising oath helpers, or compelling any of the monastery's men, free or unfree, to be judged. The administration of justice is an economic privilege for ecclesiastical communities: the king conceded to Fulda all proceeds generated from the administration of justice as it would have been administered had it belonged to the royal fisc.[18]

---

15. Davies and Fouracre, *Property and Power*, 13.

16. Benjamin Arnold, *Medieval Germany, 500–1300: A Political Interpretation* (Toronto: University of Toronto Press, 1997), 129–30.

17. Boyd Hill, *Medieval Monarchy in Action: The German Empire from Henry I to Henry IV* (New York: Allen and Unwin, 1972), 111; DD HI 1: "Obsecravit namque prescriptus abba ut similiter ipsum monasterium cum monachis ibidem deo militantibus et cum rebus et hominibus sibi legaliter aspicientibus sub nostra constitueremus defensione ac prefatorum regum auctoritati nostram inngeremus auctoritatem, cuius petitionem, quia iustam immo rationabilem esse iudicavimus, et beneficio quod postulavit assensum prebuimus."

18. DD HI 1: "quicquid de supradictis rebus ius fisci exigere poterat, pro aeterna remuneratione prefato monasterio et monachis concessimus."

A variety of immunities and privileges were granted to the German ecclesiastical institutions by their kings. The *ius fisci* concerned rights of the fisc, and appears to be one of the more lucrative and least often granted privileges.[19] The person or institution that received *ius fisci* was entitled to all (or sometimes a specific part) of the revenues generated from properties or fiscal revenues, such as fees and tolls. Monasteries and institutions that received these fiscal privileges tended to be great houses, such as Fulda, or strategically important bishoprics, such as Chur.[20] The *ius fisci* and the additional privileges of immunity, including the right to a tithe of their own goods and the right to elect their own abbots, were successively confirmed. The courts at which these immunities would be acknowledged and formally confirmed by the king were doubtless a ceremonial part of the royal *iter*.[21] Trier, Tours, and Utrecht also were the fortunate recipients of similar immunities that included the *ius fisci*.[22] The East Frankish bishops engaged professional advocates to administer their secular courts, lay magnates who were thus able to enjoy a share of these royal concessions. These administrative functionaries were in attendance at *placita*, synods, and other court gatherings. A *placitum* held by Otto I and Pope John XIII to adjudicate a conflict between Archbishop Peter of Ravenna and a certain deacon, Rainerius, had in attendance—besides the emperor and the pope—a great crowd of counts, bishops and archbishops, judges, appointed functionaries, notaries, and advocates (the *placitum* is discussed in chapter 5).[23] The public ritual that accompanied the conferral of a confirmation was no less important than the document that recorded it. Gerd Althoff and Geoffrey Koziol have noted how performance and ritual comprised important elements of medieval court culture and interactions, especially with regard to dispute resolution.[24]

19. See D. Bachrach, "Toward an Appraisal of the Wealth of the Ottonian Kings of Germany, 919–1024," *Viator* 44.2 (2013): 1–28 (regarding the potential scale and royal management of the royal fisc); Bernhardt, *Itinerant Kingship*, 30–31 (on the connection between the integrity of the royal fisc and royal control over churches as Otto I consolidated power by means of immunities).

20. DD OI 209, discussed in D. Bachrach, "Immunities," 21.

21. Diplomas from Conrad I (912), Henry I (920), Otto I (936), and Otto II (975) use identical wording to that given above, with small scribal variations, all specifying the place of issue as Fulda (DD CI 6; DD HI 1; DD OI 2; DD OII 103).

22. Trier: DD OI 320; DD OII 52; DD OIII 51. Tours: DD OII 233; DD OIII 289. Utrecht: DD HI 27; DD OII 19.

23. DD OI 340. Davies and Fouracre note, "Ecclesiastical immunists, since they were clerics, were not supposed to operate their immunities themselves, so far as this meant holding or appearing in courts; instead, they were to have a lay advocate to do this for them" (*Property and Power*, 14). Arnold notes that these aristocratic advocates "all too often abused their powers" (*Medieval Germany*, 130).

24. Gerd Althoff, *Spielregeln der Politik im Mittelalter: Kommunikation in Frieden und Fehde* (Darmstadt: Wissenschaftliche Buchgesellschaft, 1997); Geoffrey Koziol, *Begging Pardon and Favor: Ritual and Political Order in Early Medieval France* (Ithaca, NY: Cornell University Press, 1992).

Christina Pössel suggests that ritualized performances were not merely one-off kinds of mediated interaction but needed to be constantly reperformed.[25] The physical reperformance of the issuance of an immunity, for example, was not only a reminder of the relationship between a king and institution but also an opportunity to re-create the relationship based on changed circumstances or new understandings of an arrangement or an agreement that may have evolved over time. Barbara Rosenwein has gestured to the issuance of immunities as a declaration of the power of the issuing party, a way to demonstrate control over access to resources.[26] The confirmation of immunities was not merely an administrative formality but, instead, an important opportunity to publicly demonstrate the relationship between the king and an ecclesiastical institution, to proclaim its privileges and obligations, and to emphasize the king's power to confer and revoke.

The various kinds of donations arranged by the East Frankish kings to sustain their ecclesiastical foundations included lands, villages, portions of tithes or revenues, and so forth. Occasionally, entire counties were placed under the jurisdiction of bishoprics. While Timothy Reuter asserts that these donations seem to have been concessions demanded by bishops as opposed to intentional asset distributions by the king, there were practical reasons that the king might want to consolidate resources under episcopal control.[27] One such grant given by Otto I to Bishop Hartbert of Chur in 951 and confirmed by Otto III conceded fiscal revenues from the county of Chur to the bishopric.[28] In the eighth century, Chur had been ruled by its bishops, until Charlemagne consolidated his control over the region by turning it into a county. By the early tenth century, the county of Churraetia had been incorporated into the duchy of Swabia. The grant thus transferred revenues from the county and ducal coffers to those of the bishopric. This grant would have been highly desirable and presumably lucrative.[29] While we occasionally see men who held both secular and ecclesias-

25. Christina Pössel, "The Magic of Early Medieval Ritual," *Early Medieval Europe* 17.2 (2009): 124. Rosenwein notes that "the *gesture* of giving out immunities could be continually renewed," a public display of largesse that in no way depleted a king's resources (*Negotiating Space*, 216; Rosenwein's italics).

26. Rosenwein, *Negotiating Space*, 216.

27. Reuter, "Imperial Church System," 339–40. See Leo Santifaller, *Zur Geschichte des ottonisch-salischen Reichskirchensystems* (Vienna: Akademie der Wissenschaften, 1964), 105–15, for a list of these kinds of grants (cited in Reuter, 339n77).

28. DD OI 139: "concedimus donamus atque offerimus eclesiae sanctae dei genitricis Mariae beatique Lucii confessoris Christi que est caput Curiensis episcopii, cui preest venerabilis episcopus Hartbertu[s noste]r fidelis, in comitatu predicti ducis Recia omnem fiscum de ipso Curiense comitatu." The confirmation diploma is DD OIII 48.

29. Chur was the episcopal seat of a region of intensive agricultural production, as well as mining, minting, and fish farming. Its position on a strategic pass through the Alps made it a vital

tical offices (e.g., Otto I's brother Brun, who was both Duke of Lotharingia and archbishop of Cologne), granting an ecclesiastical lord the judicial revenues from a duchy or county without the secular office was not a usual practice. Otto expanded Chur's privileges in 958, with a grant of additional properties and the mint at Chur.[30] These privileges and incomes would have been a substantial move toward establishing the bishops of Chur as powerful local rulers. They also would have helped ensure control over a transalpine route to Italy at a point when Otto I's interests were drawn in that direction, as several routes through the Alps converged at Chur. Shoring up the bishopric of Chur was an important strategy from a defensive position. Its location at the point where passes through the Alps emerged above the Rhine would have been logistically important defensively and as a base for practical provisioning and support of Otto I's armies for his campaigns in Italy.[31]

The peacekeeping power of regional jurisdictional authorities in the form of ecclesiastical and secular lords was important in Germany. Following a trend begun by the Carolingians, immunities were commonly granted and broad in scope. In the tenth-century Ottonian Empire, grants of immunity often included full regalian and judicial rights.[32] One result of this was that ecclesiastical institutions and immunists looked and acted more like counts: the exemptions suggested proximity to imperial power, not removal from it.[33] The imperial system of judges and advocates operating under the authority of great ecclesiastical lords appears to have worked. Local disputes were handled locally, by some combination of legal and extralegal means, including negotiation, mediation, or adjudication by the local lord or his court. If this system ceased to be effective or if altercations reached a degree of disruption beyond the ability of local lay or ecclesiastical lords to control them, a *placitum* would be called, and the king would then intervene. Far from diminishing imperial power, the generous granting of immunities freed the emperor to deal only with matters that concerned the greatest of his magnates or that were most likely to cause disruption to his empire. Despite the lack of Ottonian legislative

conduit for trade, as well as giving it military importance. In the 940s and 950s, Chur withstood several attacks from the Saracens who had established at Fraxinetum, so it is likely that whatever Otto I's intentions were regarding these endowments, securing the frontiers of his empire against invaders was a part of them. See Reinhold Kaiser, *Churrätien im frühen Mittelalter: End 5. bis Mitte 10. Jahrhundert* (Basel: Schwabe, 1998).

30. DD OI 191.

31. D. Bachrach, "Immunities," 19. Bachrach gives a detailed time line of the expansion of privileges and immunities at Chur, specifically linking the enlargement of its influence and increase of its revenues to Otto I's efforts to create an administrative body to support his military campaigns (19–22).

32. Davies and Fouracre, *Property and Power*, 13.

33. Ibid., 15.

activity, the system of jurisdictional immunities that the Ottonians inherited from their Carolingian predecessors was an effective way of managing law and justice throughout the realm.

The Interdependence of Ecclesiastical and Royal Authority in Germany

The successions of confirmations issued for ecclesiastical communities reflected those communities' worries about the revocation of jurisdictional rights. Evidence of engagement in the administration of law and justice also suggests a different kind of problem—namely, outright challenges to episcopal authority. The late Carolingian chronicler Regino of Prüm suggests just such a concern. In 895, "a great synod was celebrated at Tribur against the very many laypeople who were trying to diminish episcopal authority. Twenty-six bishops together with the abbots of monasteries gathered there and made strong in writing many decrees concerning the state of the Holy Church."[34] King Arnulf, who would be anointed as emperor later that same year, was present at this synod and held a public assembly at Worms afterward, "with leading men who came to him from all the kingdoms which were under his command."[35] If Regino and his continuator, Adalbert of Magdeburg, are to be believed, it would appear that church officials had authority over crimes committed against their own. For example, in 903, Archbishop Fulk of Reims was murdered by one of Count Baldwin's men, ostensibly over a disputed piece of land. The culprit was excommunicated by Fulk's successor, "along with many other bishops."[36] In 913, Bishop Einhard of Speyer was blinded by two counts, a case that was dealt with at the Synod of Hohenaltheim in 916, where Bishop Richwogo of Worms was charged with investigating the crime and bringing those responsible to justice.[37] When Bishop

34. Simon MacLean, *History and Politics in Late Carolingian and Ottonian Europe: The "Chronicle" of Regino of Prüm and Adalbert of Magdeburg* (Manchester: Manchester University Press, 2009), 218–19; Regino of Prüm, *Chronicon*, s.a. 895, *Reginonis abbatis Prumiensis Chronicon cum continuatione Treverensi*, ed. F. Kurze, MGH SRG 50 (Hanover: Hahn, 1890), 143: "Anno dominicae incarnationis DCCCXCV. sinodus magna celebrata est apud Triburias contra plerosque seculares, qui auctoritatem episcopalem inminuere temptabant; ubi XXVI episcopi cum abbatibus monasteriorum residentes plurima decreta super statum sanctae ecclesiae scripto roboraverunt."

35. MacLean, 219; Regino of Prüm, *Chronicon*, s.a. 895, 143: "Post haec Arnulfus Wormatiam venit ibique optimatibus ex omnibus regnis suae ditioni subditis sibi occurrentibus conventum publicum celebravit."

36. MacLean, 227; Regino of Prüm, *Chronicon*, s.a. 903, 149.

37. Adalbert of Magdeburg, *Continuatio Reginonis*, s.a. 913, in *Reginonis abbatis Prumiensis Chronicon cum continuatione Treverensi*, ed. F. Kurze, MGH SRG 50 (Hanover: Hahn, 1890), 155; MacLean, 233n10; MGH Conc 6.1, 1–41.

Benno of Metz was blinded by the people of the town, all of the perpetrators were excommunicated at a synod held in the same year at Duisburg.[38] More telling, perhaps, is the synod held in 948 at Ingelheim. In addition to thirty-four bishops, King Otto I and King Louis both attended. Adalbert notes that "many things of use to the Church were promulgated," but the one case he gives details about involves an attack on church property: "The case of Heribert's son Hugh, who had invaded the see of the church of Rheims and expelled Archbishop Artoldus, was also aired, and he was condemned by the judgment of all the bishops who were there."[39] Justice for these great crimes does not appear to fall to the ecclesiastical lord of the district or see or to the landholders against whom they were committed. Rather, it is determined by groups of bishops. The convention of synods, with the hearing and judgment of crimes, was clearly a significant piece of episcopal business.

The case of Bishop Benno of Metz deserves a bit more attention as an example of the interaction of secular and ecclesiastical concerns at a local level. While Adalbert provides few details about the reason the people of Metz attacked Benno, Flodoard of Reims outlines the events that led up to the assault. In describing the events of 927, Flodoard notes that "at that time [King] Henry gave the diocese of Metz to Benno, God's servant, despite an election [of another] by the people of Metz."[40] Although he does not suggest any causation between events, Flodoard states, in the entry for 928, that "Bishop Benno of Metz was the victim of a plot and was castrated and blinded,"[41] so it is difficult not to make that connection. This incident provides an example, perhaps, of what Regino of Prüm was referring to when he mentioned the laypeople who were trying to diminish episcopal authority. The actions of the townspeople of Metz suggest that they felt they had a voice in the episcopal election, even when Henry conferred the office onto his own candidate. Clearly, there was some-

38. Adalbert, *Continuatio*, s.a. 927, 158.

39. MacLean, 249; Adalbert, *Continuatio*, s.a. 948,163–64: "DCCCCXXXXVIII. sinodus in Inglenheim a XXXIIII episcopis habetur; cui presidente Marino episcopo, Romanae ecclesiae legato, incliti reges Otto et Ludowicus affuerunt. In qua multis ecclesiasticae utilitatis rebus promulgatis causa quoque Hugonis filii Heriberti, qui Artaldum archiepiscopum expellens sedem ecclesiae Remensis invaserat, ventilatur; et omnium, qui affuerant, iudicio episcoporum dampnatur."

40. Steven Fanning and Bernard S. Bachrach, eds. and trans., *The* Annals *of Flodoard of Reims, 919–966* (Toronto: University of Toronto Press, 2008), 16; Flodoard of Reims, *Annales*, s.a. 927, 377: "Ibi etiam Heinricus episcopium Mettensium, contempta electione ipsorum, cuidam, ut ferebatur, Dei servo dedit, cognomento Bennoni." The *Vita S. Uodalrici* also provides an example, albeit a less colorful one, of Henry installing his own candidate when faced with multiple episcopal aspirants to the see of Augsburg (Gerhard von Augsburg, *Vita Sancti Uodalrici* 1.1, in *Vita Sancti Uodalrici: Die älteste Lebensbeschreibung des heiligen Ulrich, mit der Kanonisationsurkunde von 993*, ed. Walter Berschin and Angelika Häse [Heidelburg: Universitätsverlag C. Winter, 1993], 96).

41. Fanning and Bachrach, 18: Flodoard, *Annales*, s.a. 928, 378: "Benno Mettensis episcopus, insidiis appetitus, eviratus luminibusque privatus est."

times tension between local and royal favorites in episcopal appointments. Since the townspeople would have been effectively under the rule of the bishop as their lord, there may have been real concern about who would hold that position. These events are doubtless related to some of the difficulties King Henry experienced in trying to control internal conflict and opposition. Metz, in the troublesome duchy of Lotharingia, was a particularly volatile region, prone to revolt.[42] The attack against Benno was a way of defying the authority of the king. The excommunication of the townspeople involved would have effectively demonstrated the king's right to make episcopal appointments and would have shown the interconnectedness of royal will and ecclesiastical authority.[43]

Thietmar of Merseburg does not reference this incident at all in his *Chronicon*, perhaps because it was geographically somewhat removed from his sphere of influence, but he wrote about other episcopal elections in great detail. The example of Bishop Benno emphasized royal prerogative in episcopal appointments, and Thietmar also asserts that kings and emperors were the only ones who had the right to make such appointments.[44] This may have been rhetoric employed in Thietmar's efforts to portray the actions of the Ottonian kings in an admirable light. In the context in which the remark was made, it might have been a genuine concern that kings and not lesser nobles be involved in episcopal elections. Either way, the circumstances under which episcopal appointments were made greatly concerned Thietmar. He devoted a significant amount of his *Chronicon* to describing them. Despite his assertion about the

42. Otto I finally brought some semblence of order to the region with the dual appointment of his brother Brun as archbishop of Cologne and Duke of Lotharingia. This appointment established a strong imperial ally at the heart of both secular and ecclesiastical concerns in Lotharingia.

43. The potential dangers that a king faced in rejecting a locally elected candidate and placing his own man as bishop is demonstrated in the trouble Henry II ran into at Trier. He refused to accept the nomination of Adalbero, installed his own candidate as bishop, and provoked a rebellion led by Adalbero's brothers Duke Henry of Bavaria and Bishop Dietrich of Metz (Sean Gilsdorf, *The Favor of Friends: Intercession and Aristocratic Politics in Carolingian and Ottonian Europe* [Leiden: Brill, 2014], 84).

44. Thietmar of Merseburg, *Chronicon* 1.26, in *Thietmari Merseburgensis Episcopi Chronicon*, ed. Robert Holtzmann, MGH SRG 9 (Berlin: Weidmannsche Buchhandlung, 1935), 34. This statement is made in reference to his observation that Duke Arnulf of Bavaria enjoyed the unique privilege of being able "to distribute all the bishoprics in his territories on his own initiative" (David A. Warner, ed. and trans., *Ottonian Germany: The* Chronicon *of Thietmar of Merseburg* [Manchester: Manchester University Press, 2001], 86; Thietmar, *Chronicon* 1.26, 34: "qui omnes episcopatus in hiis partibus constitutos sua distribuere manu singularem habuit potestatem"). According to Thietmar, this prerogative sounds hereditary, but that Arnulf, as an example of his virtue, chose not to "leave this great honour to his successors. Rather, this right pertains to our kings and emperors alone who have been placed in this world as representatives of the highest ruler. Only they rightly take precedence above all other pastors" (Warner, *Ottonian Germany*, 86; Thietmar, *Chronicon* 1.26, 34: "sed cum hic post varios virtutum suimet ornatus vitam hanc finisset, non successoribus suis tantum reliquit honorem. Quin potius reges nostri et imperatores, summi rectoris vice in hac peregrinacione prepositi, hoc soli ordinant meritoque pre caeteris pastoribus suis presunt").

right of kings and emperors to make episcopal appointments, that Otto II and Theophanu granted Magdeburg the right to elect their own archbishop clearly made an impression, which he attempts to convey to his readers: "By imperial decree, and in the presence of Archbishop Adalbert, he [Otto II] granted the brothers serving God at Magdeburg the right to elect their archbishop. He confirmed this gift with a book which included splendid portraits in gold, of himself and the Empress Theophanu."[45] Archbishop Adalbert also threatened anyone who attempted to infringe on this liberty with excommunication.

The right to elect their own bishops or abbots, as well as benefices of lands placed under their control, were grants that were greatly valued by ecclesiastical institutions. As in the case of grants of jurisdictional authority, we see confirmations of these kinds of grants being issued by subsequent kings. These confirmations were important not only for the institutions to which they were issued but also in demonstrating continuity of rulership and the legitimacy of the confirming king. Among the extant diplomas for the monastery of Stavelot-Malmedy, a diploma issued in 950 by Otto I confirms the decrees of his predecessors. The lengthy body of the document lists the specific landholdings of the monastery, but of interest here is the promulgation.

> It was becoming [for] the imperial majesty of our predecessors not only to conserve inviolably pious acts but also to confirm their judgment by swift production [of a confirming diploma]. Therefore, that all faithful know our diligence, because Abbot Odilo from the monastery of Stavelot and Malmedy and also the monks living in the same cloister brought before us the decree of Emperor Louis and King Childeric in which it is comprised, just as the man, Saint Remaclus by name, to be sure, who now rests in the same monastery, might have presented the order by King Childeric in which the commands of King Sigebert were inserted . . . [46]

45. Warner, *Ottonian Germany*, 127; Thietmar, *Chronicon* 3.1, 97: "Insuper licenciam archiepiscopum eligendi confratribus Magadaburg Deo famulantibus precepto imperiali presenti archiepiscopo Atelberto dedit et cum uno libro, qui hodie ibidem est, in quo sua et imperatricis Theophanu ymago auro splendet formata, munus affirmavit." DD OII 207 (November 19, 979) grants this privilege and threatens anathema to anyone violating it.

46. DD OI 118: "Imperialem celsitudinem decet predecessorum suorum pie facta non solum inviolabiliter conservare, sed etiam censure sue alacriter auctoritate confirmare. Idcirco notum sit omnium fidelium nostrorum industrie, quia Odilo abba ex monasterio Stabulaus et Malmundario nec non et monachi in eisdem cenobiis consistentes detulerunt nobis preceptum Lodouici imperatoris et Hilderici regis in quo continebatur, qualiter vir sanctus Remaclus scilicet nomine qui nunc in eodem monasterio requiescit, detulisset prefato Childerico regi preceptiones Sigiberti regis in quibus erat insertum . . ." This confirmation was not an innovation by Otto I, of course, as many of the diplomas mention the kings whose privilege is being renewed. But given that the Ottonians

The mention of the specific kings whose traditions and pious acts are being confirmed and continued by Otto not only provides a measure of reassurance for the monastic institution but also legitimizes Otto's claim to kingship, as he is the most recent in a catena of confirming kings. But this is not the end of Stavelot-Malmedy in extant diplomas. In a document dating probably from between 952 and 954, Otto I confirmed the right of free elections for the monks.[47] About a decade later, in 966, Otto I issued a diploma in which he pledged imperial protection and again granted the right of free elections to the brothers.[48] In 980, Otto II granted the right of free election to the monks of Stavelot-Malmedy, with the further clarification that they were to choose candidates from the cloister of Stavelot unless there were none suitable, in which case they could elect an abbot from Malmedy.[49] In this diploma, Otto II also listed the kings and emperors whose orders he was perpetuating by this decree and in whose line he fell: "according to the custom of our predecessors, that is, of Sigebert, Childeric, Clovis, and Dagobert, the kings who had built these same monasteries, and not only [according to the custom] of the emperors Charles and Louis, but also of the most serene august emperor Otto, our father of blessed memory . . ."[50] In 987, Otto III issued a diploma asserting the right of the monks to elect an abbot from among their own ranks.[51] This right was asserted again by Henry II.[52]

These diplomas explicitly emphasized the intent that grants of land and privileges be perpetual. Formulae attested to this intent, often with the signature of the king adding emphasis: "And that these precepts remain inviolable and corroborated in perpetuity, by our own hand we sign at the bottom of this record."[53] But the perpetuality of these grants was more or less at the whim of the reigning monarch. Thietmar was very much aware of this, and his concern is evident throughout his descriptions of episcopal elections. Where the right of election had not been granted to a bishopric or archbishopric, Thietmar reports the emperor's appointment of candidates with an occasional snide

were obsessed by the legitimation of their dynasty as well, the specific pedigrees could have served a dual purpose.

47. DD OI 167.

48. DD OI 319.

49. DD OII 219.

50. DD OII 219: "secundum praedecessorum nostrorum morem, id est Sigiberti, Hilderici, Chlodouei, Dagobercti regum qui et eorundem monasteriorum fuere constructores, nec non et imperatorum Karoli, Hludovuici, sed et serenissimi beatae memoriae [Ott]onis genitoris nostri augusti imperatoris concederemus . . ."

51. DD OIII 33.

52. DD HII 238.

53. DD OI 167: "Et ut haec praeceptio maneat inviolata et in perpetuum corroborata, manus nostrae descriptione subter eam signavimus."

comment about the candidate but without ever questioning the emperor's right to make the appointment.[54] The political aspect of episcopal appointments was an accepted reality. But in cases where the right of election had specifically been granted to an ecclesiastical institution, as at Magdeburg, Thietmar's concern about imperial interference is evident. As an archiepiscopal diocese, Magdeburg was far more important than the royal monastery of Stavelot-Malmedy, and the way in which the right of election had been conferred to Magdeburg—in a public ceremony, with the precious gilded book presented as confirmation of the gift—emphasized that importance. But despite having been granted that privilege, an institution of that significance also seemed to necessitate imperial intervention. The result was constant imperial meddling in Magdeburg's appointments, to the concern and distress of its canons. The diploma specified that they had the right to their "exclusive decision in electing a leader from among themselves, which no king or imperial power that comes after can take away by their own judgment without suffering anathema, this privilege we firmly concede."[55] In addition, the writ's threat of excommunication for any who might infringe on this right was publicly announced by Archbishop Adalbert at the ceremony where the book was presented.

In 981, two years after this privilege was awarded to Magdeburg, Archbishop Adalbert died. According to Thietmar, the clergy and the people of Magdeburg elected a certain Ochtrich and sent a representative "in the company of brothers and warriors, to announce the result to the king and to remind him of his promise."[56] When they reached the emperor in Italy, they asked one of the emperor's faithful men, Giselher, to intercede for them and explain their mission to him. Giselher instead asked the emperor that he be granted the arch-

54. For examples, see Thietmar, *Chronicon* 1.23, 2.24 (Cologne, 31, 68), 2.26 (Regensburg, 70–72), 6.40 (Merseburg, 323–24); for the contested appointments at Magdeburg, see 3.12–16 (110–19), 5.40–41 (267–68), 6.62 (351–52), 6.66–67 (356–59), 6.74 (362–65), 6.79 (368–69), 6.81 (370–73), 6.89 (380–81). The control over episcopal elections was one way that the Ottonians were able both to maintain a network of imperial agents throughout the empire and to farm out the royal fisc without risk of alienation (Reuter, "Imperial Church System," 326). For a discussion of Thietmar's canonical and professional understanding of episcopal elections, see David Warner, "Thietmar of Merseburg: The Image of the Ottonian Bishop," in *The Year 1000: Religious and Social Responses to the Turning of the First Millennium*, ed. Michael Frassetto (New York: Palgrave Macmillan, 2002), 94–97.

55. DD OII 207: "singulare arbitrium eligendi inter se pastorem, quod rex nullus aut imperialis deinceps potestas nisi sub anathemate a suo iure demere possit, hoc privilegio firmiter concessimus."

56. Warner, *Ottonian Germany*, 137; Thietmar, *Chronicon* 3.13, 113: "Universus autem clerus et populus, ut supramemoravimus, completa electione, miserunt Ekkihardum, qui dicebatur Rufus, cum consorcio aliorum fratrum et militum, qui hanc imperatori nunciarent et de promissis admonerent."

bishopric for himself.[57] The emperor agreed, and the pope pledged his support if the senate agreed. Giselher distributed bribes among the emperor's leading men, "especially among the Roman judges." If Thietmar is to be believed, these bribes were substantial. He reports that Bishop Dietrich of Metz accepted one thousand talents of gold and silver from Giselher.[58] In a synod held at Rome, Giselher's appointment was confirmed. When, in 1004, Giselher died, the tensions about elections rose again. Henry II accompanied the bishop's body back to Magdeburg but sent his chaplain ahead "to secure the canons' unanimous agreement to the election of Tagino," the emperor's candidate. Anxiety about the situation at Magdeburg is palpable: "Meanwhile, the provost of this church, Walthard, assembled the brothers and, after announcing both the death of their lord and the imminent arrival of the king, begged them to find a successor so that they might retain their ancient right of electing. Everyone responded that they wanted him to be their lord, God willing."[59] The "ancient right of electing," since being granted and assured by Otto II in 979, had yet to be exercised by the canons at Magdeburg. The king sent another representative, Bishop Arnulf, to a meeting with the canons and the prelate's (i.e., Giselher's) warriors, to convince them to elect Tagino. Walthard tried again, reportedly affirming Magdeburg's ostensible electoral right and putting forth his own candidacy. The result was a private consultation between Walthard and the king, in which, "after promising many things," the king secured "both his and the chapter's agreement to the election of Tagino."[60]

57. Gerd Althoff references this incident specifically, noting the custom of using an intercessor to approach the Ottonian kings, usually an advisor or relative (*Spielregeln Der Politik im Mittelalter: Kommunikation in Frieden und Fehde* [Darmstadt: Wissenschaftliche Buchgesellschaft, 1997], 193–94). Use of intercessors was a normal way of presenting petitions to Frankish and Ottonian kings, although the case of Giselher demonstrates the importance of choosing the right person to represent one's case. Thietmar's report, while obviously promoting the side of the Magdeburg canons, "nonetheless suggests the potential conflicts of interest facing powerful and well-placed advocates" (Gilsdorf, *Favor of Friends*, 82). Giselher and his appointment have drawn a lot of scholarly attention. See Gerd Althoff, "Magdeburg-Halberstadt-Merseburg: Bishöfliche Repräsentation und Interessenvertretung im ottonischen Sachsen," in *Herrschaftsrepräsentation im ottonischen Sachsen*, ed. Gerd Althoff and Ernst Schubert, Vorträge und Forschungen 46 (Stuttgart: Thorbecke, 1998), 267-93; Wolfgang Huschner, *Transalpine Kommunikation im Mittelalter: Diplomatische, kulturelle und politische Wechselwirkungen zwischen Italien und dem nordalpinen Reich (9.–11. Jahrhundert)*, MGH Schriften 52 (Hanover: Hahnsche Buchhandlung, 2003), 2:728–94.

58. Thietmar, *Chronicon* 3.16, 116. Such descriptions of bribery and corruption in Rome would have been especially valuable to pro-imperial forces during the Investiture Controversies that arose in the late eleventh and twelfth centuries.

59. Warner, *Ottonian Germany*, 232; Thietmar, *Chronicon* 5.40, 267: "Quo audito rex corpus archiantistitis precedens usque Magadaburg subsequitur, premittens eo capellanum suum Wigbertum, ut de electione Taginonis unanimem fratrum voluntatem impetraret. Prepositus quoque eiusdem civitatis Waltardus nomine, convocatis in unum fratribus universis, obitum presulis et adventum regis indicavit illis, obsecrans, ut aliquem inquirerent invicem, cum quo consuetudinem antiquam electionis retinerent."

60. Warner, *Ottonian Germany*, 232; Thietmar, *Chronicon* 5.41, 268: "Qui mox prepositum vocans multumque ei promittens, et sui licentiam ac consotiorum in eleccione Taginonis gratiam

When Tagino died in 1012, the canons and the *milites* again deliberated, since Henry II indicated that the brothers at Magdeburg were not to hold an election but were merely to present him with the name of a unanimously agreed-on candidate.[61] Walthard again was put forth as the candidate. This time, acting as the brothers of Magdeburg hoped, the intercessor with the king "achieved the desired result though not without difficulty."[62] Walthard finally was installed as archbishop of Magdeburg at the king's command. Unfortunately, Walthard died only a few months later. The canons again attempted to put forth a candidate, Thietmar's cousin Dietrich. They knew Dietrich was unlikely to be approved, but they "elected him nonetheless . . . to preserve [their] right to do so."[63] The results of the election were sent to the king in the care of Bishop Erich. But Thietmar reports, "The king had returned from his western campaign and was trying to appoint his chaplain, Gero, to the now vacant office of archbishop. Bishop Erich came to him, but got no hearing for the message he had brought. Then, [Thietmar's] cousin Dietrich was summoned to Grone where the king accepted him into his service in Gero's place."[64] The bishops and canons felt compelled to put forth a candidate, even an unqualified one, just to try to preserve their right to do so. The reaction from the king suggests that he saw things differently, though he was willing to appoint Dietrich to a position at court. We have seen Giselher, one of the king's men, gaining such an appointment as a reward for service, and Gero, the king's chaplain, being likewise rewarded. Dietrich, admittedly too young to be granted a bishopric, was then made the king's chaplain. Thietmar was bitterly disappointed that the canon's right to election was not preserved, but the king did seem, by his actions, to take into consideration Dietrich's candidacy as a possibility for a later appointment.

While the frustration of the canons of Magdeburg in attempting to exercise their right of election was substantial according to Thietmar's reports, these

acquisivit." Tagino himself had been a victim of imperial meddling in episcopal elections. Ten years earlier he had been unanimously elected to be bishop of Regensburg, but when he went to the emperor to present himself and "receive what had been promised," the emperor gave that bishopric to his chaplain Gebhard (Thietmar, *Chronicon* 5.43, 270).

61. Thietmar, *Chronicon* 6.62, 351–52.

62. Warner, *Ottonian Germany*, 282; Thietmar, *Chronicon* 6.66, 357: "Redingus ad regem veniens legacionem suam suppliciter profert et, quamvis ardue, tamen desiderata impetrans."

63. Warner, *Ottonian Germany*, 286; Thietmar, *Chronicon* 6.74, 363: "Nos igitur fratres omnes ad capitulum convenientes, nepotem meum excepto quodam Bennone elegimus, non hoc ob iuventutem eius impleri posse sperantes, sed pro conservande electionis gracia et caritate archiepiscopi Thaginonis hoc maxime facientes."

64. Warner, *Ottonian Germany*, 291; Thietmar, *Chronicon* 6.81, 370: "Interim rex ab expeditione occidentali rev[er]titur et Geronem suimet capellanum ponere [in va]cuum conatur. Huic presul Hericus occurren[s et] legationem suam aperiens non exauditur. Thiedricus nepos meus [tunc] ad Gronam vocatus venit et a rege per manus [succi]pitur et in vice Geronis deinceps habetur."

maneuverings all make sense from the standpoint of normal patterns of patronage. Henry II did not want to accept Dietrich as the episcopal candidate, and Thietmar seemed aware that this candidacy was unlikely to be confirmed.[65] The emperor created a compromise, whereby he was able to promote his own candidate—his chaplain—and named Dietrich in the chaplain's place. It is likely, however, that there was more going on here and that Henry's decision was based on more than just rewarding his own men with key posts. Henry II was unique among the Ottonian rulers in the sheer numbers of local candidates he refused to confirm (not just at Magdeburg, but in all bishoprics), preferring to place his own chaplains or those of his close associates in episcopal positions.[66] These appointments were not necessarily just rewards for his *fideles* but may have been decisions driven by larger political issues. The see of Magdeburg had been at the heart of a feud between the counts of Wettin and the counts of Walbeck. Walthard was an *amicus* of the Wettin family; Thietmar and his cousin Dietrich were descended from the counts of Walbeck.[67] By refusing both candidates and placing his own men as bishops, it is likely that Henry was attempting to defuse local political rivalries.

The episcopal elections at Magdeburg speak to the highly complex relationships between the Ottonian kings and their bishops. Generally, bishops and archbishops were appointed from among the king's leading men and seem to have spent a considerable time not only at court but also acting as trusted messengers or *missi* within the realm and as ambassadors without. The importance of being known at court and having allies there for the purpose of securing episcopal appointments cannot be understated. Thietmar reports that Sigismund, the bishop of Halberstadt, advised his desired successor Bernhard, "Go to the king's court, taking with you anything of mine which might be necessary for this. And there, you should acquire the favor and aid of powerful men so that you will be allowed to succeed me without opposition."[68] But the knife cut two ways, as kings and emperors made episcopal and archiepiscopal selections

---

65. There is always the possibility that Thietmar reverse engineered this story. Presenting Dietrich as a candidate that the canons knew was a long shot and unlikely to be approved saves face for both the canons and the emperor. The canons had attempted to preserve their right to elect, and the emperor had placed a more qualified candidate in the position.

66. Reuter, "Imperial Church System," 350–51. John Bernhardt discusses the succession at Magdeburg as part of a pattern of Henry II's increasing insistence on control over royal ecclesiastical foundations ("King Henry II of Germany: Royal Self-Representation and Historical Memory," in *Medieval Concepts of the Past: Ritual, Memory, Historiography*, ed. Gerd Althoff, Johannes Fried, and Patrick Geary [Cambridge: Cambridge University Press, 2002], 52–55).

67. Gilsdorf, *Favor of Friends*, 83, 83n127. Thietmar's father was Count Siegfried of Walbeck.

68. Warner, *Ottonian Germany*, 83; Thietmar, *Chronicon* 1.22, 28: "Vade ad curtem regiam, sumens ex mea parte, quae tibi sint ad haec necessaria, et acquire gratiam et auxilium ibi optime valentium, ut tibi liceat sine omni offensione mihi succedere."

that would shore up support among families or regions as necessary. For example, Henry II selected Bavarians to be archbishops of Magdeburg, Cologne, and Mainz. It is not a coincidence that he "relied heavily on Bavarian support."[69] His episcopal appointments reflected that reliance and his need for continued loyalty among the Bavarian magnates. Ottonian bishops also served as military leaders and were expected to provide military support when needed as well as serve in a military capacity themselves.[70] We saw above how the *milites* of Magdeburg were engaged in the discussions regarding the elections of new bishops. Like secular magnates, ecclesiastical lords maintained military households.[71] Ecclesiastical lordships mirrored secular lordships in their structure, importance, and utility to the emperor, both in the ways the men holding them fulfilled the obligations that accompanied those positions and in the value they had as gifts to be bestowed, either as rewards for services rendered or in expectation of future services. Sometimes, a candidate was removed from monastic life and granted a bishopric against his will.[72] But it was clearly to the advantage of the emperor and the dioceses to be in agreement regarding the disposition of the bishoprics. An election, or at least discussion about it, seems to have involved the various clergy affiliated with an institution, the *milites* who owed their loyalty to its ecclesiastical lord, the people of the town, and other bishops. All of these people had keen vested interests in the appointment, and even

69. Arnold, *Medieval Germany*, 59.

70. For example, Thietmar had been required to go to Meissen for garrison duty while he was bishop of Merseburg (Thietmar, *Chronicon* 7.53, 465).

71. See, for example, David S. Bachrach, *Warfare in Tenth-Century Germany* (Woodbridge, UK: Boydell, 2012), 88n89; in this lengthy footnote regarding narrative sources in which we can see *milites* supported within households, all Bachrach's examples and descriptions are of bishops' households. We see other hints of episcopal military households in Thietmar's *Chronicon*. For example, as a youth, Count Ansfrid was sent to two episcopal courts for instruction, first to his uncle Robert, archbishop of Trier, to be "instructed in all earthly law and then especially in divine law," and then "to the vigorous Lord Brun, archbishop of Cologne, to be educated in military matters" (Warner, *Ottonian Germany*, 174–75; Thietmar, *Chronicon* 4.31, 169: "dum adhuc esset alto progenitorum germine puerulus, cum omni lege mundana a patruo suo Rutperto, Treverice civitatis episcopo, tum divina adprime est institutus; inde a patruo suo, scilicet suo equivoco, XV comitatuum comite, strennuo dompno Brunoni archiepiscopo Agrippinensi traditur ad res militares"). A less subtle example occurs in Thietmar's report of the election of Walthard as archbishop of Magdeburg. Immediately following the consecration, "since he wished to launch another attack on his brother-in-law, [the king] asked those of his leading men who were present how things stood in their campaign against Boleslav. The king committed the entire issue to the newly installed bishop" (Warner, *Ottonian Germany*, 283; Thietmar, *Chronicon* 6.67, 357–59: "Cumque generum suum rex iterum cum exercitu petere voluisset, cum presentibus suis principibus, qualiter Bolizlaus ab hiis invaderetur, tractavit. Hec omnia archiepiscopo noviter constituto et suas curias positas in Saxonia commisit").

72. More than once, the emperor forced the award of a bishopric on a candidate whether the candidate wanted it or not. For example, Flodoard of Reims reports that Otto I gave the bishopric of Tongres to Abbot Hugh of Saint Maximin at Trier, who did not want it but was forced to accept it anyway (*Annales*, s.a. 945, in MGH SS 3, 391–92).

though a bishop spent significant time away from his see while attending to the emperor and his needs, the local impact of an appointment could be significant. Even the Ottonians' treatment of the papacy suggests that they viewed it as the most important among the sees in their sphere of influence, which were all at their disposal to intervene with as they saw fit.[73]

Thietmar's *Chronicon* gives us a sense that no matter the reassurances in charters, like the assurance of free abbatial elections, grants made in perpetuity were subject to political forces that could render them moot. The dissolution of the bishopric of Merseburg serves as a case in point. After Giselher had been appointed archbishop of Magdeburg in 981—perhaps even at the same synod at which he was confirmed and installed—the bishopric of Merseburg, "whose lord previously had been independent, ceased to be the seat of a bishopric and was subjected to the church at Halberstadt."[74] The many properties of Merseburg were then divided among other dioceses, with Otto II's permission. Giselher kept nine burgs for the see of Magdeburg and then deliberately destroyed or altered documents to ensure the permanent destruction of the see of Merseburg.

> Documents which conveyed royal or imperial gifts he [Giselher] either burned or, by altering the name of the recipient, made them refer to his own church [Magdeburg]. Payers of tribute, and everything that was supposed to belong to Merseburg, he intentionally scattered so that they might never be gathered together again.[75]

This passage must be read remembering that Merseburg was Thietmar's bishopric and that its subjugation to Halberstadt and the dispersal of its properties—the loss of which was probably part of the imperial rationale behind requiring

73. For example, the diploma known as the *Privilegium Ottonianum*, a document produced after Otto I's imperial coronation, is an imperial confirmation of papal territories (DO I 235). As we have seen, such confirmations were issued to subject institutions.

74. Warner, *Ottonian Germany*, 139; Thietmar, *Chronicon* 3.14, 115: "Mersburg, que usque huc libera dominabatur, ecclesie Halverstadensi, sede episcopali destructa, subditur."

75. Warner, *Ottonian Germany*, 140; Thietmar, *Chronicon* 3.16, 117–19: "Pars episcopatus nostri, que iacebat inter Salam et Elstram ac Mildam fluvios et Plisni, Vedu et Tuchurini pagos, cum villis Passini et Piscini Frederico Cicensi episcopo datur. Folcoldo autem Misnensis ecclesie antistiti pars illa conceditur cum atpertinentibus villis Wissepuig et Lostatawa, que ad Gutizi orientalem pertinet ac fluviis Caminizi Albiaque distinguitur; sibi autem retinuit urbes novem, quarum hec sunt nomina: Scudici, Cotug, Wurcin, Bichni, Ilburg, Dibni, Pauc, Luibanici et Geserisca. Precepta, que munera regalia seu imperialia detinebant, aut igne comburebat aut ecclesie sue mutato nomine designari fecit. Mancipia et totum, quod Mersburg respicere debuit, ne umquam colligeretur, sponte dispergit."

Thietmar's own inheritance to be promised as a prerequisite to his appointment as bishop, and which also no doubt stimulated his complaints about the diminishment of his see—would have merited the harsh accusations expressed here.[76] Deliberate forgery like that described by Thietmar was not necessarily perceived to be criminal in nature or even morally and ethically dubious. Ecclesiastical institutions, like secular landholders, often found their lands and jurisdictional privileges challenged, as evidenced by the above discussion regarding confirmation of immunities. In an effort to secure and strengthen their claims, these institutions sought and acquired royal confirmations of grants and property transactions. Where the records or memory of acquisitions were thin or unconvincing, they would often produce new documents to support their claims. Michael Clanchy notes that although forgeries may be spurious, that does not necessarily mean they were inaccurate. Charters were often derived from other, earlier documents. Sometimes they were created to turn oral memory into a written record. A forgery was not necessarily intended to cheat or defraud; instead, the goal might be "to produce a record in a form which was acceptable, particularly in courts of law, at the time it was made. . . . Forgers re-created the past in an acceptable literate form."[77] In other words, forged documents were designed to represent a specific reality, which might not by definition be a false reality. The majority of forgeries were not intended to be deliberately deceptive, as the modern usage of the term *forgery* tends to connote. They were intended to represent reality as it was supposed to be or should have been. While Thietmar's complaints about forging and destroying documents sounds modern in its condemnation of Giselher's actions, we should not forget that if the result of this activity had been an augmentation of Merseburg's holdings, we likely either would not have heard of it or would have heard of it framed as a legitimate activity.

The making and unmaking of bishoprics was a matter of imperial concern. As examples, we have, of course, the foundations of Magdeburg and Merseburg by Otto I, the former of which was to become a key seat of power in the realm. This could only have happened by severely diminishing the existing diocese of Halberstadt, which lost much of its territory to the new bishopric of Magdeburg. In 965, Otto I ordered Hildeward, bishop of Halberstadt, to Rome, where he unveiled his plans to establish an archbishopric at Magdeburg.

76. See Thietmar, *Chronicon* 6.40, 322–24 (regarding contributing his inheritance to the bishopric); 1.1, 5 and 6.62, 350–52 (regarding the diminishment of the see of Merseburg).

77. Michael T. Clanchy, *From Memory to Written Record: England, 1066–1307*, 3rd ed. (Malden, MA: John Wiley and Sons, 2013), 319–20.

> With him, the emperor discussed the plan he had long concealed in his heart, namely, that in the hope of eternal reward and for the defense of their common fatherland, he had always wanted to establish an archbishopric in the city of Magdeburg. He promised that he was ready to grant whatever Hildeward might ask if he would agree to the fulfillment of this oath. Being a wise man, he went along with this pious request and conceded to God, St Maurice, and the emperor that part of his diocese situated between the rivers Ohre, Elbe, and Bode, and also the road known as Friedrichsweg. Furthermore, at the emperor's affectionate request, he gave to God and St Lawrence the parish located between the flow of the Wilderbach, the salt lake, the Saale, Unstrut, Helme and the ditch near Wallhausen.[78]

In exchange for his cooperation, Otto awarded Hildeward the new archbishopric.[79] There was a lot of horse-trading in the establishment of new bishoprics, as well as a dependence on new bishops to provide part of those foundational properties. Thietmar, for example, reports that prior to his election as archbishop of Merseburg, he was summoned by the archbishop of Augsburg and "at the king's command, questioned as to [his] willingness to aid [his] church with [his] hereditary property."[80] Only once

78. Warner, *Ottonian Germany*, 106–7; Thietmar, *Chronicon* 2.20, 63: "cum quo, quod diu absconderat, secretum mentis revolvit, scilicet se facturum in urbe Parthenopolitana archiepiscopatum semper studuisse ob spem remuneracionis eterne defensionemque communem patrie, seque ad omnia, quecumque umquam ab eo expetisset promisit paratum, si sibi consentiret hoc perficere votum. Hic autem, ut erat vir sapiens, pie annuebat peticioni; partemque parrochie, que sita est inter Aram et Albiam et Bodam fluvios, et insuper viam, que Fritherici dicitur, Deo concessit sanctoque Mauricio ac imperatori. Insuper idem caritative rogatus a cesare augusto, dedit Deo sanctoque Laurencio parrochiam iacentem inter fluvios Willerbike et Salsum mare et Salam ac Unstrod et Helmana et foveam, que est iuxta Valehusen."

79. Episcopal foundations did not always proceed as smoothly as Thietmar depicts here. When Henry II was trying to establish a new bishopric at Bamberg, he "constantly entreated Bishop Henry of Würzburg, one of his familiares, that he might agree to this heartfelt plan and, in return for compensation, surrender parochial rights over" a specific district. Bishop Henry agreed, with the understanding that he would receive the pallium for the new bishopric and that the Bamberg prelate would be subject to him. When he realized that "he absolutely would not receive the archepiscopal dignity, he refused to fulfill his promise and rejected his summons to the council meeting" at which the episcopal foundation would be established (Warner, *Ottonian Germany*, 257–58; Thietmar, *Chronicon* 6.30, 311: "Cum vero archipresulatum se nullatenus adipisci posse sentiret, promissa complere rennuit et ad predictum concilium vocatus venire noluit").

80. Warner, *Ottonian Germany*, 265; Thietmar, *Chronicon* 6.40, 323: "Postera die vocatus interrogabar ab eo iussu regis, si aliqua ex parte hereditatis mee ecclesiam meam vellem adiuvare." For an example of how a bishop might be expected to augment a see's landholdings once in office, besides bringing his own wealth to the diocese, see Timothy Reuter's analysis of the *Vita Meinwerci episcopi Patherbrunnensis*. Reuter notes that Meinwerk was expected by Henry II to use his own inheritance to endow the foundation of a new bishopric at Paderborn but was also actively managing relations between Paderborn and the magnates of his see to increase its holdings via gifts and

this matter had been settled did the king present Thietmar with the pastoral staff.

Thietmar notes the creation of a bishopric at Gniezo in 999, "as I hope legitimately, but without the consent of the aforementioned bishop [Eid] to whose diocese the whole region is subject."[81] Ideally, territorial claims of bishops, on whom the emperor relied as an essential arm of his government, were to be taken into consideration before diminishing their authority. Thus, Thietmar observes that Henry II had always dreamed of establishing a bishopric at Bamberg and "constantly entreated Bishop Henry of Würzburg, one of his *familiares*, that he might agree to this heartfelt plan and, in return for compensation, surrender parochial rights over that district which is named after the river Regnitz." According to Thietmar, "The bishop took a favourable view of his beloved lord's request and gave his consent, with the understanding that he would receive the pallium for his church and that the pastor of Bamberg would be subject to him."[82] Thietmar's own bishopric, Merseburg, is a case for how these makings and unmakings of episcopal sees could be a source of political tensions beyond the bishops themselves. Empress Theophanu favored restoring the bishopric at Merseburg and had a dream in which Saint Lawrence appeared to her and urged her to do so. She left this obligation to Otto III to fulfill, "for the eternal salvation of his father's soul."[83] Adelheid, her mother-in-law, favored the formation of a bishopric at Halberstadt, which could not happen if Merseburg was restored. After Theophanu's death, Otto III, still a minor and likely under the guidance of Adelheid, participated in a public ritual consecrating the cathedral at Halberstadt in 992, during which he laid a golden staff on the altar of Saint Stephen, an act that essentially comprised a public promise not to reestablish the bishopric at Merseburg. Once he came of age, however, he reversed his decision and reestablished the bishopric, following his mother's wishes.[84] This

donations, some of which Reuter suggests were acquired by coercion ("Property Transactions and Social Relations between Rulers, Bishops, and Nobles in Early Eleventh-Century Saxony: The Evidence of the *Vita Meinwerci*," in *Property and Power in the Early Middle Ages*, ed. Wendy Davies and Paul Fouracre [Cambridge: Cambridge University Press, 1995], 165–99).

81. Warner, *Ottonian Germany*, 183; Thietmar, *Chronicon* 4.45, 184: "Nec mora, fecit ibi archiepiscopatum, ut spero legitime, sine consensu tamen prefati presulis, cuius diocesi omnis haec regio subiecta est."

82. Warner, *Ottonian Germany*, 257–58; Thietmar, *Chronicon* 6.30, 310: "Heinricum Wirciburgiensem episcopum sibi multum familiarem, ut proposito animi suimet asspirare voluisset parrochiamque in pago, qui a Radinzca fluvio nomen sortitur, positam concederet sibi concambio vendicandam, sepe rogavit. Dilecti senioris iustas peticiones presul benigne suscipiens, ea racione consensit, ut pallium suae permittens aecclesiae Bavenbergiensem sibi subderet pastorem."

83. Warner, *Ottonian Germany*, 157–58; Thietmar, *Chronicon* 4.10, 143: "redintegrato episcopatu patris sui animam in novissimo die ad eternam requiem."

84. Gerd Althoff, *Otto III*, trans. Phyllis G. Jestice (University Park: Pennsylvania State University Press, 2003), 51.

demonstrates two very different positions with regard to whether a bishopric at Merseburg should exist or not, as two empresses represented different factions with different aspirations. As Archbishop Giselher of Magdeburg was active at court between 991 and 994,[85] he was one of the many bishops who participated in the Halberstadt consecration. He had a vested interest in seeing the bishopric of Halberstadt succeed and that of Merseburg remain defunct. Thus, we can see how the emperor's bishops and ecclesiastical lords were able to press for their own interests when they had gained positions of trust and favor while serving as advisors to the emperor.

Warrior Bishops and Bishops with Secular Lordships

When reading the contemporary chroniclers of the Ottonian era, one is struck by the degree to which their bishops were expected to both provide armored contingents and be fully engaged as leaders in battle. While organizing the defense of one's own city might not seem too far afield of medieval episcopal activities, the active engagement of bishops as leaders and warriors in battle was an expected part of their duties to the emperor.[86] The *Indiculus Loricatorum* of 981 provides insight into this phenomenon, as it comprises a mustering order from the reign of Otto II. Not only do the numbers of troops specified from ecclesiastical lords (bishops and abbots) outnumber lay troops by more than two and a half times, but it is clearly stated that many of the ecclesiasts—though not all—were expected to lead their contingents.[87]

85. Althoff, *Otto III*, 51.

86. Bishops regularly organized the military defense of their sees or cathedral cities and led their *milites* alongside secular forces in battles. One of the central events of the *Vita Sancti Uodalrici* is the defense of the city of Augsburg in 955 against the Magyars, although Saint Ulrich is said to have commanded the defense on horseback without himself holding a weapon (Gerhard, *Vita Sancti Uodalrici* 1.12). Thietmar of Merseburg reports numerous incidences of bishops defending (or attempting to defend) cities and fighting in battles (e.g., *Chronicon* 2.27, 3.19, 5.21). The "commitment of bishops to the military purposes of the new German imperium on a regular basis" was a key achievement of Otto I in imperial organization (Benjamin Arnold, "German Bishops and Their Military Retinues in the Medieval Empire," *German History* 7.2 [1989]: 163). David Bachrach makes a compelling case for grants of ecclesiastical immunities being central to Frankish and Saxon military strategies, an argument that emphasizes the importance of bishops to imperial defense ("Immunities," 1–36). David Warner notes that military activity was expected among the secular duties of bishops ("Image of the Ottonian Bishop," 85–110). See also Timothy Reuter, "*Episcopi cum sua militia*: The Prelate as Warrior in the Early Staufer Era," in *Warriors and Churchmen in the High Middle Ages: Essays Presented to Karl Leyser*, ed. T. Reuter (London: Hambledon, 1992), 79–94; John France, "War and Sanctity: Saints' Lives as Sources for Early Medieval Warfare," *Journal of Medieval Military History* 3 (2005): 14–22.

87. *Indiculus Loricatorum*, in MGH Const 1, 632–33.

The dispute over the bishopric at Reims provides one such example of warrior bishops on the Continent. Archbishop Artoldus, who, as we saw above, was reported by Flodoard to be a monk before his promotion to the bishopric, besieged Chausot on behalf of King Louis IV, who arrived on the fifth day of the siege. From there, Artoldus accompanied Louis to recapture Châtillon-sur-Marne. Artoldus was also active in trying to defend the *urbs* of Reims from its siege.[88] Despite his background as a monk, Artoldus's role as a bishop came with the expectation that he would be actively involved in warfare when the need arose. His adversary, Archbishop Hugh, is reported to have captured and destroyed a *castrum* and besieged a *munitio*, both while holding his bishopric.[89] Many other instances can be found. The *vita* of Ulrich of Augsburg stresses the importance of bishops as military leaders and in defense of cities during periods of rebellion.[90] Ulrich was one of Otto I's supporters during the rebellion of Otto's son Liudolf and Duke Conrad the Red of Lotharingia. Ulrich's *milites* fought alongside those of his brother, Duke Dietpald, an army which was decisive in defeating the rebels and their supporters in Swabia. He also defended Augsburg against Magyar attacks in 955, fortifying the city and leading his *milites* in battle.[91] The extended *amicitia* network is invoked as well, as when Ulrich presented his young nephew to Otto to serve in his court, simultaneously offering his military forces to the king's service.[92] Ottonian kings needed to have men who were loyal to them in positions of both secular and ecclesiastical authority.[93] The normalcy of this as an episcopal enterprise is emphasized by the inclusion in the bishop's *vita* of his military activity and direct engagement in fighting for the king. Ulrich was the first saint to be canonized by the pope instead of by local authorities, and the inclusion of actions as appropriate to a *gesta* as a *vita* attests to these activities as normal ones in which bishops engaged, even if an appropriate degree of justification for military engagement seemed necessary.[94] Liudprand of Cremona's *Antapodosis* contains several reports to this effect, mentioning bishops who abandoned their sees

88. Flodoard, *Annales*, s.a. 940, 386.

89. Flodoard, *Annales*, s.a. 943, 390.

90. Gerhard, *Vita Sancti Uodalrici* 1.10, 172–74.

91. Gerhard, *Vita Sancti Uodalrici* 1.10, 174–76, 192.

92. Gerhard, *Vita Sancti Uodalrici* 1.3, 112.

93. Gerhard, *Vita Sancti Uodalrici*, 1.10, 177–80. For a summary of the revolt and its implications, see D. Bachrach, *Warfare*, 47–54.

94. Walter Berschin, "Realistic Writing in the Tenth Century: Gerhard of Augsburg's *Vita S. Uodalrici*," in *Aspects of the Language of the Latin Prose*, ed. Tobias Reinhardt, Michael Lapidge, and J. N. Adams, Proceedings of the British Academy 129 (Oxford: Oxford University Press, 2005), 377–82.

and attempted to take others by force, as well as archbishops who conspired and joined their forces with rebellious magnates.[95] Thietmar's *Chronicon* abounds with examples of bishops being called into military action or voluntarily siding with rebellious lords and engaging in battle against the king. He reports that in 1017, several years after his election as archbishop of Merseburg, he himself was required to report to Meissen for garrison duty.[96] Military service seems to have been a norm with regard to expectations for the bishops of tenth-century Frankish kings in both East Francia and West Francia, a norm that reinforced the need for those kings to have the right candidates in key episcopal positions.[97] Less important institutions, like Stavelot-Malmedy, were less likely to have imperial meddling in their elections. But in important positions, which, by definition, would include all archbishoprics, emperors had a keen interest to place candidates who would be both loyal (an important characteristic, but one that was often changeable, judging by the number of bishops and archbishops who initiated or joined insurrection), and capable to fulfill whatever needs the emperor had, whether that be as advisor, ambassador, or warrior.

Part and parcel of this culture of warrior bishops of the Ottonians was the appointment of men to both ecclesiastical and secular lordships.[98] Otto I's brother Brun serves as perhaps the best example. Brun succeeded to the archbishopric of Cologne in 953 and "along with the bishopric received the *ducatus* and rule over the whole of the Lotharingian kingdom."[99] This kind of concentration of

95. Liudprand of Cremona, *Antapodosis* 4.6, 4.27, 4.32, in *Liudprandi Cremonensis Opera Omnia*, ed. P. Chiesa, Corpus Christianorum (Turnhout: Brepols, 1998), 98, 115–16, 120.

96. Thietmar, *Chronicon* 7.53, 465.

97. In France, counts attempted control of episcopal elections as often as kings, to the same ends, including consolidating family power, creating a powerful loyal ally, or increasing their abilities to personally help enrich a bishopric with wealth and personal influence. Regarding bishops and their elections in tenth-century France, see William Ziezulewicz, "Abbatial Elections at Saint Florent-de-Saumur (ca. 950–1118)," *Church History* 57.3 (1988): 289–97; Constance B. Bouchard, "The Geographical, Social and Ecclesiastical Origins of the Bishops of Auxerre and Sens in the Central Middle Ages," *Church History* 46.3 (1977): 277–95; Jacques Boussard, "Les évêques en Neustrie avant la Réforme grégorienne (950–1050 environ)," *Journal des savants*, 1970, 161–96.

98. From the tenth century, French cities such as Reims and Langres had bishops who were also counts, but this phenomenon was not nearly as common elsewhere as in Germany (Constance B. Bouchard, *Strong of Body, Brave and Noble: Chivalry and Society in Medieval France* [Ithaca, NY: Cornell University Press, 1998], 159). For how bishops could become the heads of German principalities in the twelfth and thirteenth centuries, well after the Investiture Controversy, see Benjamin Arnold, *Count and Bishop in Medieval Germany* (Philadelphia: University of Pennsylvania Press, 1991). Regarding the development of episcopal lordship in our period, see John Eldevik, *Episcopal Power and Ecclesiastical Reform in the German Empire: Tithes, Lordship, and Community, 950–1150* (Cambridge: Cambridge University Press, 2012).

99. MacLean, 255; Adalbert, *Continuatio Reginonis*, s.a. 953, 167: "cui Brun frater regis succedens totius Lothariensis regni ducatum et regimen cum episcopatu suscepit." See also Thietmar, *Chronicon* 2.23–24, 65–68; Flodoard, *Annales*, s.a. 953. Widukind defends Brun's holding of both ecclesiastical and secular lordships by referencing 1 Samuel 7:15: "Ac ne quis eum culpabilem super hoc dixerit, cum Samuelem sanctum et alios plures sacerdotes pariter legamus et iudices"

secular and ecclesiastical power in the hands of one person was not unheard of in continental politics. Archbishop Robert of Rouen and Bishop Yves of Seez are examples of contemporary Norman bishops who also held secular titles. In Germany, Brun's dual titles notwithstanding, counties were commonly placed under episcopal control, with laymen continuing to administer them. The key difference in these situations was that those administrators, essentially fulfilling comital duties, answered to the bishop instead of the king.[100]

The joining of the secular and ecclesiastical lordships in Lotharingia corresponds with the tendency of Ottonian rulers to place family members in positions of episcopal power whenever possible. The decision to place Brun as both archbishop of Cologne and Duke of Lotharingia—Lotharingia being notorious for its tendency toward rebellion—was clearly a strategic move on the part of Otto I to ensure that he had a strong ally positioned to quash both secular and episcopal plotting against him.[101] Brun reportedly was responsible for providing military training for one of his cousins, Ansfrid, who served as Otto I's sword-bearer in 962 and eventually became bishop of Utrecht.[102] Brun was able to extend his influence beyond episcopal protégés and into Lotharingian monastic reform as well.[103] He is the most extreme example, but selections for imperial bishoprics seem to have been granted to family members when possible. Bishop Poppo of Würzburg—some sort of relation to the Ottonians[104] and "very dear to the king"—was succeeded in the bishopric by a kinsman also called Poppo.[105] Bishop Dietrich of Metz was Otto I's cousin. Archbishop Henry of Trier was said, by Flodoard of Reims, to be a relative of the king.[106] The story of Otto I's eldest (but illegitimate) son, William, also demonstrates the strategic nature of these appointments. Adalbert reports, "Archbishop Frederick [of

(Widukind of Corvey, *Res gestae Saxonicae* 1.31, in *Widukindi monachi Corbiensis rerum gestarum Saxonicarum libri tres*, ed. Paul Hirsch and H.-E. Lohmann after G. Waitz and K. A. Kehr, MGH SRG 60 [Hanover: Hahnsche Buchhandlung, 1935], 44). See also Warner, "Image of the Ottonian Bishop," 86–87.

100. Reuter, "Imperial Church System," 339–41.

101. Brun had been sent as a young child to Utrecht to study with the bishop there; even though he was summoned to Otto's court as a teenager a decade or so later, the contacts and relationships that he established could only have helped him as he worked to establish his rule over Lotharingia, even if only by giving him a good sense of the various factions that existed there.

102. Thietmar, *Chronicon* 4.31, 209; Henry Mayr-Harting notes that Ansfrid was a nephew of Queen Mathilda, the mother of Brun and Otto I (*Church and Cosmos in Early Ottonian Germany: The View from Cologne* [Oxford: Oxford University Press, 2007], 26n89).

103. Anne Wagner, "L'image du pouvoir épiscopal aux Xe–XIe siècle: l'exemple lorrain," in *Hagiographie, idéologie et politique au Moyen Âge en Occident: Actes du colloque international du Centre d'Études supérieures de Civilsation médiévale de Poitiers, 11–14 septembre 2008*, ed. Edina Bozóky (Turnhout: Brepols, 2012), 233–41.

104. MacLean (261n162) notes that "Otto II referred to Poppo II as his *nepos*."

105. Adalbert, *Continuatio Reginonis*, s.a. 961, 170. See also Thietmar, *Chronicon* 7.26, 430–31.

106. Flodoard, *Annales*, s.a. 956, 403.

Mainz] died. He was vigorous in holy religion and very praiseworthy, if only he had not seemed so reprehensible in this alone: that wherever even a single enemy of the king sprang up he immediately placed himself at his side. The king's son William succeeded him, after he was harmoniously elected by the clergy and the people at Arnstadt."[107] Replacing a problematic archbishop prone to rebellion with a family member was not a foolproof method against revolt—Liudolf and Thankmar demonstrated that even sons could incite rebellion—but it was an important way for the king to extend the authority of the royal family into troublesome areas.

What are we to make of the continued efforts to justify the appropriateness of military activity by the German bishops? In his *Vita Sancti Brunonis*, Ruotger expends tremendous effort to justify Brun's military activity as essential to that bishop's peacekeeping mandate.[108] In analyzing a redaction of Gerhard's *Vita Uodalrici*, John Eldevik notes that the copyist "was uncomfortable with certain aspects of Ulrich's relationship with the imperial court and army," downplaying or omitting references to military obligations and service.[109] How might we account for the differing ideals expressed between the canonical view of clerical nonengagement in military activities and the lived reality of military bishops? I suggest that the dichotomy, while evident and necessarily justified in *vitae* (which are, after all, prepared statements in support of sanctity), was not necessarily problematic for Ottonian bishops. Bishops that needed to engage in military activity did. In trying to account for the very different positions adopted by Burchard of Worms in his *Decretum*, outlining canonical principles, and his *Lex familia*, a practical list of crimes and punishments by which to rule those under his jurisdiction, Greta Austin proposes that Burchard was, in essence, able to successfully wear two hats: that of canonist, and that of ruler of the

---

107. Adalbert, *Continuatio Reginonis*, s.a. 954, 168: "Fridericus archiepiscopus obiit, vir in sancta religione strennuus et valde laudabilis, nisi in hoc tantum videbatur reprehensibilis, quod, sicubi vel unus regis inimicus emersit, ipse se statim secundum apposuit. Cui successit regis filius Willihelmus, a populo et clero in Arnestat concorditer electus." See also Thietmar, *Chronicon* 2.35, 82–83. Thietmar's comments regarding Frederick are only complimentary, that as bishop he "pleased both God and the world" and that "at the end of his life he gave thanks to God that he had never acquired anything unjustly for his church or lost anything" (Warner, *Ottonian Germany*, 117; Thietmar, *Chronicon* 2.34, 81: "Hic in fine suo gracias egit Deo, quod ecclesie sue nil umquam iniuste acquisierit seu perdiderit"). As Thietmar's family seems to have frequently been at odds with the emperors, this is perhaps unsurprising, as is his snide remark, revealing something of his elitist tendencies, that William is "the offspring of a captured Slavic noblewoman and the king" (Warner, *Ottonian Germany*, 118; Thietmar, *Chronicon* 2.35, 82: "de matre quamvis captiva et Sclavonica tamen nobili et ex rege predicto genitus." Here, Thietmar does not refer to any election, merely to a succession.

108. Ruotger, *Vita Sancti Brunonis, Coloniensis Archiepiscopi*, in MGH SS 4, 252–56.

109. Eldevik, 59.

laypeople of his see.[110] What worked within the broader philosophical theory of canon law was not useful in the day-to-day rule of his people. This position seems reasonable. It seems, too, that Germanic bishops would have been able to adopt a similar approach to their military activities. Military obligations were part and parcel of bishoprics in the Ottonian Reich and were a necessary component of the resources on which the Ottonians were able to call in service to their rule. That military activity was not sanctioned by the scope of duties the church prescribed for its bishops was merely academic and did not reflect the realities of daily life.

Bishops engaging in military training and action, however controversial that might be within the scope of Gregorian pastoral activities, was not an unknown practice throughout the medieval West. What does seem to have been new is the degree to which the Ottonians were able to demand military service from their bishops and regularly depend on them as a part of their armed forces.[111] Defending one's own bishopric or seizing the properties of political rivals would not have been outside the scope of episcopal actions—whether condoned or condemned—that we see across Europe. Under Charlemagne, we see episcopal or monastic requirements to provide armed knights, as well as participation in military campaigns.[112] This trend accelerated under the Ottonians, who counted on forces from bishoprics and archbishoprics to augment their armies, had those troops led by their episcopal leaders, and instituted the warrior bishop as the episcopal norm in Germany. The advantage of this military service in a distributed, networked system is evident. When considered alongside the armies of the traditional military class (dukes, counts, and margraves), requiring military service of the bishoprics and their bishops multiplies the troop options for the king. A broadly dispersed scattering of small armies of various sizes that could be deployed in any number of combinations acts as another layer to the kind of distributed security network that was discussed in chapter 1, a network comprised of semiautonomous agents who can act with a wide degree of latitude in assessing and responding to risk. A militarized episcopal structure provided not so much a counterpoint as a complement to ducal and comital power.

---

110. Greta Austin, "Vengeance and Law in Eleventh-Century Worms: Burchard and the Canon Law of Feuds," in *Medieval Church Law and the Origins of the Western Legal Tradition*, ed. Wolfgang P. Müller and Mary E. Sommar (Washington, DC: Catholic University of America Press, 2006), 68.

111. Arnold, "German Bishops," 163.

112. For example, the abbot of Fulda maintained a large personal military and provided substantial support in Charlemagne's Saxon campaigns (Bernard S. Bachrach, *Charlemagne's Early Campaigns (768–777): A Diplomatic and Military Analysis* [Leiden: Brill, 2013], 225–26).

Clearly, there was a high degree of interaction between ecclesiastical and royal spheres of influence in the Ottonian *Reich*. The intersection of royal and ecclesiastical authority began with the kings and their courts. The delegation of judicial and jurisdictional authority to their ecclesiastical lords, preferably men with strong ties to the court, ensured the promulgation and enforcement of the peace through the monasteries' and bishoprics' governance of lands under their control. Since the East Francians were successors to the Carolingians, with their complex administrative systems, it is possible that much of this authority was understood, leaving little need to commit law to writing, especially given the great numbers of diplomas and cartulary documents that record the outcomes of grants, privileges, synods, and *placita*.[113] These outcomes, which could provide the foundation, if needed, for adjudicating future disputes, may have been perceived as being more important than written law.

113. See David S. Bachrach, "Exercise of Royal Power in Early Medieval Europe: The Case of Otto the Great, 936–73," *Early Medieval Europe* 17.4 (2009): 389–419, where Bachrach argues for the extensive use of written documents by Otto I in the administration of his realm.

CHAPTER 3

Feud and Legislative Activity

That the Ottonians produced essentially no legislation throughout their tenure as kings and emperors has long puzzled historians, who have tried to work out how the Ottonians functioned successfully as rulers despite leaving no real evidence of an imperial legislative tradition.[1] This legislative deficiency is especially confounding when one considers the prevalence of feud as a means of conflict resolution in the tenth and eleventh centuries. Particularly among the nobility, violence that accompanied feuding behaviors presumably would have needed to be curbed to maintain order over a vast empire.

Now fallen out of favor, the long-lived positivist perspective on feud cast the practice as one primitive step on the path toward an enlightened and rational system of justice. But the feuding mentality has been demonstrated to have persisted well into the early modern period in much of Europe.[2] It stands to reason that such a "durable phenomenon"[3] would have served some fundamental purpose. Indeed, anthropological reassessment of violence during the Middle Ages has suggested that feuds were not anarchic in nature but, rather, performed an ordering function in society.[4] Thanks to the work of scholars

1. Parts of this chapter were presented at the 2013 International Medieval Congress at the University of Leeds, in a paper entitled "Royal Saints and Royal Feuds in the East and West Saxon Kingdoms," and at the 2017 International Congress on Medieval Studies at Western Michigan University, in a paper entitled "Lawless Order and Functional Feuding: Bloodfeud and Lawmaking in Anglo-Saxon England and Ottonian Germany." The earlier paper was subsequently revised and published as "Royal Feuds and the Politics of Sanctity in Anglo-Saxon England and Ottonian Saxony," *Mirabilia* 18.1 (2014): 78–94.

2. Otto Brunner, *Land and Lordship: Structures of Governance in Medieval Austria*, trans. Howard Kaminsky and James van Horn Melton (Philadelphia: University of Pennsylvania Press, 1992), 55, 63.

3. Jeppe Büchert Netterstrøm, "Introduction: The Study of Feud in Medieval and Early Modern History," in *Feud in Medieval and Early Modern Europe*, ed. Jeppe Büchert Netterstrøm and Bjorn Poulsen (Aarhus: Aarhus University Press, 2007), 12.

4. Stephen D. White, "Feuding and Peace-Making in the Touraine around the Year 1100," *Traditio* 42 (1986): 195–263, esp. 260–61.

such as J. M. Wallace-Hadrill, feuding can be seen as a way to negotiated peaceful conflict settlement.[5]

The Ottonians were the successors, as well as conscious emulators, of the Carolingians, who were responsible for recording the laws of the many Germanic kingdoms they incorporated into their empire as well as producing legislation of their own. The Ottonians also imitated aspects of Byzantine culture, another society with a strong legislative tradition. Clearly, their lack of legislation did not result from a lack of understanding how law functioned as part of a ruling ideology. We also have canonical handbooks from Ottonian Germany, written as manuals to be referred to by bishops and other ecclesiastical rulers who wanted to follow canonical procedures for dealing with real situations or problems.[6] These books were not intended to be aspirational visions of law, grand pronouncements that had little chance of enforcement. They were intended for use by local lords—albeit ecclesiastical ones—in governing the peoples in their jurisdictions. Thus, these texts that predominantly concern canon law should be considered in a discussion of secular government, peacekeeping, and justice.

We know that synods served as forums where legal cases were heard and where lawmaking took place.[7] We also know that the canonical legislative texts circulated widely, intended for use by ecclesiastical lords in ruling their local jurisdictions, and that there was a perceived need for these texts, not least because feud was a complex issue for medieval lords and their subjects. Regino of Prüm compiled his *Libri duo de synodalibus causis et disciplinis ecclesiasticis* at the request of the archbishop of Trier and dedicated it to the archbishop of Mainz.[8] That it was the foundation of much of Burchard of Worms's *Decretum* attests to the *Libri duo*'s importance as a working text.[9] It is about the administration of ecclesiastical justice by ecclesiastical lords managing both secular and clerical communities. The inclusion of matters that are distinctly secular in nature, such as feud, further demonstrates its use by ecclesiastical lords governing both lay and clerical communities.[10] The importance of the *Libri duo* as a source for Burchard of Worms was not solely its use in his *Decretum*; Burchard also pro-

5. J. M. Wallace-Hadrill, "The Bloodfeud of the Franks," *Bulletin of the John Rylands Library* 41 (1959), repr. in *The Long-Haired Kings* (1962; repr. Toronto: University of Toronto Press, 1982), 121–47.

6. Greta Austin, *Shaping Church Law around the Year 1000: The "Decretum" of Burchard of Worms* (Burlington, VT: Ashgate, 2009), 39.

7. Flodoard of Reims, *Annales*, s.a. 948, 395–98; MGH Conc 6.1, 135–63.

8. Austin, *Shaping Church Law*, 39.

9. Ibid., 39–41.

10. See Regino of Prüm, *Libri duo* 2.80, "De faidis coërcendis," *Libri duo de synodalibus causis et disciplinis ecclesiasticis*, ed. F. G. A. Wasserschleben (Leipzig: Guil. Engelmann, 1840), 245–46.

duced a legislative text intended to govern the peoples under his jurisdiction, the *Lex familiae Wormatensis ecclesiae*.[11]

Burchard of Worms held a dual ecclesiastical role: "Landlord of his dependents, his *familia*, he was in charge of administering justice. But he was also a bishop and a man of God."[12] In the *Lex familiae*, he took the existence of feud and feuding behaviors to be a given of the secular society he governed, and he laid out law to try to control the rampant feuding that was plaguing Worms. To that end, he included in his law text several penalties that had been specified by Henry II in a legislative charter for Worms the year before.[13] While Burchard's law code dealt with the reality of feuding, his canonical works could categorically condemn the practice. As a ruler, he tried to contain or constrain feuding behaviors and the fallout resulting from feuding practices among his people; as a man of God, he could denounce feuding altogether.[14] Burchard went to great effort to balance his role as a clergyman who condemned feud against the more practical (and immediate) needs to control or constrain the feuding behaviors that were an inherent part of the social fabric of his town.

As both a ubiquitous feature of medieval society and a persistent cultural phenomenon, feud was deeply ingrained in the medieval *Weltanschauung*.[15] Recent research has argued, convincingly, that there is a connection between feuding behaviors and legislative activity in medieval England—that is, that one reason for the extraordinarily prolific production of legislation by the Anglo-Saxons was in reaction to their culture of feud. Might the lack of legislation by a society equally steeped in feud culture suggest that there was no need to try to control the waging of feuds because the practice did not threaten regnal authority? Feuding may have been a fact of life in the Ottonian Empire, but its power as an organizing principle for imperial governance stopped short of requiring copious legislative response and a royal monopoly on blood justice.

11. Burchard of Worms, *Lex familiae Wormatensis ecclesiae*, in MGH Const 1, 639–44.

12. Greta Austin, "Vengeance and Law in Eleventh-Century Worms: Burchard and the Canon Law of Feuds," in *Medieval Church Law and the Origins of the Western Legal Tradition*, ed. Wolfgang P. Müller and Mary E. Sommar (Washington, DC: Catholic University of America Press, 2006), 68.

13. DD HII 501.

14. Austin, "Vengeance and Law," 68.

15. Despite (or perhaps because of) its importance and penetration into such a large part of culture and society, even the term *feud* itself is hotly contested. Significant problems inhere in the term, as well as the debates surrounding its legitimacy as a practice, whether it was an institution, and whether Anglo-Saxon *faida* actually can be translated as "feud." Nonetheless, to conform with established conventions, I use *feud* in this chapter to indicate various and overlapping formal and informal obligations that might require those with political affiliations or friendship and kinship ties to use violence on behalf of one another. Paul Hyams has made significant contributions to our understanding of feud: see "Feud and the State in Late Anglo-Saxon England," *Journal of British Studies* 40.1 (2001): 1–43; *Rancor and Reconciliation in Medieval England* (Ithaca, NY: Cornell University Press, 2003).

Feud in Early Medieval Society

Feud was part of an ancient and highly developed system of conflict resolution, a system in which monetary compensation and feud were inextricably linked, and in which the line between the two was unclear at best.[16] This system was complex, involving not only violence and negotiation but also, to varying degrees, the involvement of third parties who could encourage or insist upon arbitration—not to mention the very real element of time, which could be manipulated by both factions of a conflict, as well as by interested third parties, to control the pace of negotiations.[17] Feuding was an ambivalent issue for medieval rulers. Its ubiquity at all levels of medieval political life made it so deeply ingrained within modes of thought and action that there was never any real thought of eradicating it.[18] Yet there was no denying the problems that it could raise with regard to keeping public order. Especially among the ranks of the nobility, there was a high probability that allowing feuds to wage unchecked would not only increase the level of destruction but might also eventually draw the king himself into the conflict. Feuding remained a legitimate way for disputing parties to resolve their differences and "were the expression of a legal consciousness," with participants "behav[ing] in strict accordance with legal procedure,"[19] but we see evidence that kings sought to control how feuding was conducted, or to channel those impulses to their own ends.

The various compensation lists that have survived as parts of Germanic law codes, specifying appropriate compensation for specific acts, not only demonstrate the range of affronts, both major and minor, that might need to be ad-

16. Wallace-Hadrill, "Bloodfeud of the Franks," 146.

17. Peter Sawyer, especially, reacted against Wallace-Hadrill's idea of a "feuding society," stating that it was a gross oversimplification of complex social interactions ("The Bloodfeud in Fact and Fiction," in *Tradition og historieskrivning: Kilderne til Nordens ældst historie*, ed. Kirsten Hastrup and Preben Meulengracht Sørenson. Acta Jutlandica 63.2 [Aarhus: Aarhus University Press, 1987], 27–38). But Sawyer's assertion that the concept of blood feud is merely a literary device is challenged by such studies as the examination of feud culture in medieval Iceland by William Miller, who convincingly demonstrates that Icelandic sagas have much to convey about how feud actually worked in a medieval culture (*Bloodtaking and Peacemaking: Feud, Law, and Society in Saga Iceland* [Chicago: University of Chicago Press, 1990]).

18. We do see public outcry against this kind of activity, which, predictably, largely came from church leaders. But while feuding activity was discouraged and while clergy took an active role in attempting to mediate disputes, the ambivalence that Burchard of Worms expressed in his writings is very likely typical. Burchard pragmatically accepted feud as a social fact in managing his people as a ruler and landlord, and he did what he could to mitigate the scale and consequences of feuding behaviors, as evidenced in his *Lex familiae*. As an ecclesiastical lord, "he could be more ambitious and call for a 'zero tolerance' policy toward feuding. In short, as ruler he would have to compromise, but as a compiler of canons he did not" (Austin, "Vengeance and Law," 68).

19. Brunner, *Land and Lordship*, 14.

dressed but also, in the nature of *lex talionis*, served as ways to limit violence.[20] Nonetheless, the potential for conflict to escalate was recognized. Rothair's Edict of 643 includes a specific clause addressing those who perpetuate a feud after accepting compensation and swearing oaths to avert it.

> Concerning the man who seeks revenge after accepting composition. If a freeman or slave is killed and composition paid for the homicide and oaths offered to avert the feud, and afterwards he who received the composition tries to avenge himself by killing a man belonging to the associates from whom he received the payment, we order that he repay the composition twofold to the relatives of the freeman or to the slave's lord. In like manner concerning him who tries to avenge himself after accepting compensation for blows or injuries, he shall restore that which he accepted in double amount. In addition, he shall pay composition, as provided above, if he has killed the man.[21]

This passage first suggests that the decision to wage feud was a considered one, made by weighing a number of different factors that probably included assessing the strength of the parties on each side, soliciting advice from friends and relatives within the kinship groups who would have had interests in the conflict based on their levels of obligation to the respective parties, and gauging the potential damage the violence might cause. The payment of a composition and swearing of oaths afforded both parties an honorable resolution without their having to resort to bloodshed. This passage also suggests that even if a resolution that did not involve exacting revenge had been agreed on, it was not unusual for emotions to continue to run high. There is nothing here to suggest that feud was considered unlawful, unjustified, or inherently illicit in any way. This edict is concerned with the breaking of a negotiated peace. Once an alter-

20. See, for example, Rothair's Edict and the Laws of King Liutprand in *The Lombard Laws*, ed. and trans. Katherine Fischer Drew (Philadelphia: University of Pennsylvania Press, 1973); The Law of Gundobad in *The Burgundian Code*, ed. and trans. Katherine Fischer Drew (1949; repr., Philadelphia: University of Pennsylvania Press, 1976); *The Laws of the Salian Franks*, ed. and trans. Katherine Fischer Drew (Philadelphia: University of Pennsylvania Press, 1991). The idea of *lex talionis*, the law of revenge, is commonly restated with the biblical phrase "eye for an eye," which is then misinterpreted as extreme justice. Generally misunderstood is how *lex talionis* functioned as a limiting factor to violence. For example, to continue with our biblical context, if someone did, in fact, cause another person to lose an eye, the most that the victim could claim in compensation was the offender's eye. The victim could not turn around and kill the offender or take revenge against the offender's family.

21. *Lombard Laws*, 74–75. See Patrick Wormald, *The Making of English Law: King Alfred to the Twelfth Century*, vol. 1 *Legislation and Its Limits* (Oxford: Basil Blackwell, 1999), 39, regarding how feud was a central part of Rothair's conceptualization of law and order.

native to feud had been mutually agreed on, it was not lawful for the aggrieved party to violate that agreement by using violence to seek further revenge.[22]

The eighth-century laws of Liutprand, king of the Lombards, also recognized how payment of *wergeld*, the compensation value of an assault against another person, could be used to avoid an escalation of conflicts. In the example of an incident where a woman's clothes were stolen while she was bathing, forcing her to return home naked, the likelihood that her kinsmen would kill the perpetrator and that a feud would thus be initiated was high.

> Therefore we decree that the man who presumes to do such an illicit act shall pay his *wergeld* as composition to that woman to whom he did this shameful thing. We say this because if the father or husband or near relatives of the woman had found him, they would have entered into a violent fray (*scandalum*) with him and he who was the stronger would have killed the other man. Therefore, it is better that the culprit, living, should pay his *wergeld* as composition than that a feud develop over a death and produce such deeds that the eventual compensation be greater still.[23]

The violence that might ensue in such a case was not considered illegal or illicit. Though a killing might be honorable in a publicly recognized state of enmity, and the killer might not be considered a criminal, he was still subject to punishment or retribution.[24] Thus, if the woman's kin had confronted the thief (who not only stole her clothes but also caused her public humiliation) and if that confrontation had resulted in a death that precipitated a blood feud, the resolution of the latter conflict would be even more costly. The culprit is enjoined to avert a death, ostensibly his own, by paying the appropriate compensation to the woman he had offended and being done with it.

Late eighth-century and early ninth-century capitularies of the Carolingians strove to constrain feuding behaviors as well. For example, *capitulum* 22 in the *Capitulare Harisallense* of 779 reads,

> Anyone unwilling to accept the price [*wergeld*] paid to buy off vengeance should be sent to us so that we may send him where he can do

22. Analyzing the feud culture of medieval Iceland, William Miller (279–81) points out that a strong impetus against breaking a negotiated peace did not prevent particularly bitter parties from perpetuating hostilities by accusing each other of breaking the settlement or by inventing new grievances to pursue, since hostilities in those veins would be unrelated to the original, settled conflict.

23. *Lombard Laws*, 205.

24. Brunner, *Land and Lordship*, 68.

> the least damage. So that the damage not increase because of a man who is unwilling to submit to justice or pay the price [*wergeld*] paid to buy off vengeance, we likewise wish to send him to such a place.[25]

How enforceable this *capitulum* might have been is unknown, but the exhortation to accept composition instead of furthering hostilities clearly encourages disputants to resolve their conflict without recourse to violence. While the conflict here is unspecified, two later *capitula* from capitularies intended to guide *missi dominici*, envoys of the king, are much more specific. The first, from 802, is clearly intended to prevent an escalation of hostilities in the instance of murder.

> In order that the greatest enmities may not arise among Christians, when by the persuasions of the Devil murders happen, the criminal shall immediately hasten to make amends and with all celerity shall strike an accommodation for the evil done with the relatives of the murdered man. And we forbid firmly, that the relatives of the murdered man shall dare in any way to continue their enmities on account of the evil done, or shall refuse to grant peace to him who asks for it, but having given their pledges they shall receive a suitable accommodation and shall make a perpetual peace; moreover, the guilty one shall not delay to achieve an accommodation.[26]

The second, from 805, suggests that breaking a peace was an infringement of the lord's jurisdiction.

> If one [bearing arms] is involved in a feud, then it should be examined which of the two [enemies] is opposed to reconciliation and they should be compelled to [make] peace, even if they are unwilling. . . . And if anyone after making peace kills the other, he should pay compensation

25. Daniel Lord Smail and Kelly Gibson, eds., *Vengeance in Medieval Europe* (Toronto: University of Toronto Press, 2009), 69; MGH Leges 1, *Capitulare A. 779*, capit. 22, 39: "Si quis pro faida precium recipere non vult, tunc ad nos sit transmissus, et nos eum dirigamus ubi damnum minime facere possit. Simili modo et qui pro faida pretium solvere noluerit nec iustitiam exinde facere, in tali loco eum mittere volumus ut pro eodem maius damnun non crescat."

26. Smail and Gibson, 69; MGH Leges 1, *Capitulare Aquisgranense A. 802*, capit. 32, 95: "Tamen ne etiam peccatum adcrescat, ut inimicitia maxima inter christianos non fiat, ubi suadentes diabulo homicidia contingant, statim reus ad suam emendationem recurrat, totaque celeritate perpetratum malum ad propinquos extincti digna conpositionem emendet. Et hoc firmiter banniamus, ut parentes interfecti nequaquam inimititia super commissum malum adaugere audeant, neque pacem fieri petenti denegare, sed datam fidem paratam compositionem recipere, et pacem perpetuam reddere, reum autem nullam moram compositionis facere."

> for him and lose the hand which he perjured. In addition, he should pay the lord's fine [*bannus*].[27]

This last *capitulum* is interesting in that the lord was not necessarily involved in negotiating a resolution to the conflict, but the breaking of an agreed-on peace was a matter of primary concern to him. Works like these could have encouraged disputants to work out their differences before their feud became disruptive enough to draw the attention of the king. Again, feuding is recognized as a natural course of action; these capitularies do not outlaw feud but, rather, seek to minimize collateral damage and escalation of the conflicts. This impulse drove capitularies issued under Charlemagne's immediate successors as well.[28] Feud itself was not illegal, and perpetuating a feud was not a violation of the peace. One must keep in mind that "it was not the feud itself that marked one as a violator of the peace, but a feud that was unjustified and illegitimate."[29]

We have no way of gauging the success of these early attempts to impose legislation that would regulate feud activities. The activities that these capitularies strove to constrain were, as we have noted, highly ingrained in medieval society. In a letter to Charlemagne in 801, even Alcuin commends a certain Torchmund as one of King Æthelred's loyal men, "a man proven in faithfulness, strenuous in arms, who vigorously avenged the blood of his lord."[30] While in the early Germanic period, as well as in the Middle Ages, there may certainly have been the sense that seeking blood vengeance was a duty and that accepting monetary compensation and renouncing vengeance would result in a loss of honor,[31] there was still the impetus toward settlement, often at the behest of third parties or

27. Smail and Gibson, 70; MGH Leges 1, *Capitulare Duplex in Theodonis Villa Promulgatum*, capit. 5, 133: "De armis infra patria non portandis, id est scutis et lanceis et loricis. Et si faidosus sit, discutiatur tunc quis e duobus contrarius sit ut pacati sint; et distringantur ad pacem, etiamsi noluerint. Et si aliter pacificare nolunt, adducantur in nostram praesentiam. Et si aliquis post pacificationem alterum occiderit, conponat illum, et manum quam periuravit perdat, et insuper bannum dominicum solvat."

28. Louis the Pious, for example, also produced capitularies that contained specific *capitula* referencing feud behaviors. See MGH Leges 1, *Capitula legibus addita recognovimus ope Codicum*, capit. 13, 212: "*De faidis cohercendis.* Si quis aliqua necessitate cogente homicidium conmisit, comes in cuius ministerio res perpetrata est, et conpositionem solvere, et faidam per sacramentum pacificari faciat; MGH Leges 1, *Capitula missorum*, capit. 12, 217: "De nova moneta, et de falsa moneta, et de dispectu litterarum nostrarum, et de latronibus coercendis vel puniendis, et de faidis pacandis, de homicidiis prohibendis, der periuriis et falsis testibus conspescendis, de his omnibus vel caeteris his similibus hoc quod modo constituimus, omnibus adnuntietur et in futurum observetur."

29. Brunner, *Land and Lordship*, 9.

30. MGH Epist 4, *Alcuini Epistolae* 231, 376: ". . . et Torchmundum, Hedilredi regis fidelem famulum, virum in fide probatum, strenuum in armis, qui fortiter sanguinem domini sui vindicavit."

31. Brunner, *Land and Lordship*, 19.

compelled by Christian arguments of magnanimity and forgiveness. But maintaining one's honor might demand the appearance of aggressiveness, even when peace was desired.[32] These capitularies strove against the disruption that the feud could cause and the failure to entertain alternatives to feud when attempts at peacemaking were put forth by one or the other party, not against feuding activity or bloodshed itself. We must remember, too, that kings participated in feud and feud-type activities to as great a degree as their subjects.[33]

The extensive attempts to create legislation to control feuding activities in the Anglo-Saxon kingdoms, a phenomenon that we also saw in the early Germanic kingdoms,[34] is something that we do not see at all under the Ottonians. Otto

32. Miller, 266.

33. Brunner suggests that there was no legal distinction between war and feud, as far as actions within Christendom were concerned (*Land and Lordship*, 33). He notes that even altercations between kings—that is, wars—began with a challenge to feud "not as a mere custom but as a matter of law" (35). Thus, all wars within Christendom were technically feuds in a legal sense. Cnut's laws specify that the protective role of the king with regard to clergy and foreigners included seeking vengeance on their behalf: "40. If a man in holy orders or a foreigner is for any reason defrauded of property or of life, the king shall then be for him in the place of a kinsman and protector, unless he has another. 40.1. And compensation is to be paid to the king, as is fitting, or he is to avenge the deed very severely. 40.2. It belongs very rightly to a Christian king to avenge very zealously offences against God, in proportion to the deed" (*EHD* 1.50, p. 425); II Cn 40.1–2:"[40]Gyf man gehadodne oððe ælþeodigne þurh ænig þinge forӕde ӕt feo oððe ӕt feore, þonne sceal him cinge beon for mæg 7 for mundboran, butan he elles oðerne (hlaford) hæbbe. [40.1] 7 bete man þam cingce, swa hit gebyrige, oððe he ða dæde wrece swiþe deope. [40.2] Cristenan kyningce gebyrað swyðe rihte, þœt he Godes æbylgðe wrece swyðe deope, be ðam þe seo dæd si."

34. The problems of illegitimate feud or feud that was pursued and perpetuated despite overtures to make peace was well known to the Anglo-Saxons. In the description of Grendel in *Beowulf*, the poet emphasizes that the real problem is Grendel's refusal to engage in negotiations for peace, his unjust pursuit of vengeance against people not a part of the blood feud, and, most heinous, his failure to make any reparations (*Beowulf: A New Verse Translation, Bilingual Edition*, trans. Seamus Heaney [New York: Farrar, Straus and Giroux, 2000], 13, lines 151–60). The laws of King Alfred (871–901 CE) show a great deal of concern with feud and vengeance. The laws are quite specific about circumstances in which seeking vengeance is not licit, such as if a man is killed when caught in bed with another man's wife (John Hudson, *The Oxford History of the Laws of England*, vol. 2, *871–1216*, ed. Sir John Baker [Oxford: Oxford University Press, 2012], 173; Dorothy Whitelock, Martin Brett, and Christopher N. L. Brooke, *Councils and Synods, with Other Documents Relating to the English Church, AD 871–1204* [Oxford: Clarendon, 1981], 34). Alfred's laws also present a formal procedure under which a man might seek justified vengeance (Af 42:7). But there is no effort here to eliminate feud; these are largely tactics designed to delay the onset of violence. The laws of Edmund in the mid-tenth century go significantly further in the effort to regulate feud in England, not only by encouraging settlement of disputes by payment of *wergeld* or by arbitration negotiated by community leaders such as the king's council or bishops, much as we saw in the capitularies of Charlemagne, but also by the introduction into royal legislation and laws of the Anglo-Saxon terms *mundbryce* (breach of protection), *hamsocn* (assault on a person in a house), and *forsteal* (obstruction), all "offences that might arise in the pursuit of feuds, the limitation of which was the main concern of the laws referred to as II Edmund" (Hudson, 20). These attempts at regulation did not condemn feud but, rather, outlined appropriate practice of feud under the law. As with the Carolingian and Lombard laws, we cannot know if these laws were successfully enforced or were aspirational in nature. But they speak to the Anglo-Saxon kings' particular concern with managing the feuding behaviors in their realm.

Brunner has argued that "it was futile to prohibit feuds as long as men could not be forced to renounce them in favor of legal institutions backed by the power of the state. Wherever this was not the case, feuds continued."[35] Brunner also observed that "vengeance and reconciliation alike presupposed that the 'state' had no monopoly in the legitimate exercise of force, and that there was such a thing as 'rightful force' below the level of state power. Moreover, the success of a ruler's efforts to impose peace depended upon his power vis-à-vis the nobility. And since the advances in royal power that occurred during the Carolingian period were not sustained after the ninth century, the period from the ninth to the eleventh centuries can be called the 'heyday of the feud.'"[36] While true to a degree, Brunner's statement presupposes a decline in royal or imperial power as a reason for the rampant feuds that took place in the centuries that included the Ottonian and first Salian emperors. Much of the present study argues against that presupposition. Thus, we are left to account for why, as powerful rulers, the Ottonians have left us almost no documents that can be called legislation and little with regard to efforts to regulate feuding specifically. The degree to which they embraced the feud as a matter of course, a standard modus operandi for navigating the social and political landscape, stands in stark contrast to the practices of not only their Carolingian predecessors, whose rule the Ottonians consciously attempted to emulate as a legitimizing strategy for their dynasty, but also the Anglo-Saxons, whose prodigious legislative output dealt extensively with attempts to contain, constrain, and regulate feuding activities.

Brunner asserted a connection between the rise of a centralized or hierarchical legal system and the effective suppression of extralegal dispute resolution.[37] Eliminating a feud culture depended on the development of a highly structured judicial system, which fits with what we know about Anglo-Saxon judicial administration. Unlike the Anglo-Saxons, however, the Ottonians did not develop such a centralized system, instead depending on jurisdictional authority delegated to their magnates and ecclesiastical lords. The Ottonians also did not produce prodigious amounts of legislation, certainly none that can be linked to efforts to control feuding throughout their entire realm.[38] Brunner's assertion suggests that this paucity necessarily indicates a decline in royal

35. Brunner, *Land and Lordship*, 29. Even with the power of the state, feuding behaviors, licit and illicit, persisted well into the early modern era, demonstrating how interwoven these behaviors were within the norms of societal interactions.

36. Ibid., 15.

37. Ibid.

38. Far from trying to control feud, the kings themselves were subject to the same rules and norms of feud, settling their own disputes with their magnates through feud-type conflict resolution (Gerd Althoff and Hagen Keller, *Die Zeit der späten Karolinger und der Ottonen: Krisen und Konsolidierungen 888–1024* [Stuttgart: Klett-Cotta, 2008], 360).

power. Is this the best way to understand feud in Ottonian East Francia, as rampant and uncontrolled—in essence, the "heyday of the feud"? I argue instead for a model of functional feuding, feud that was allowed because it served the interests of peacekeeping in the realm. That tenth-century "peacekeeping" was often overtly violent and destructive should not detract from our understanding of its utility as a method of conflict resolution.

What we see in the Ottonian *Reich* suggests a different kind of power and allocation of resources for governing. The Ottonians did not rely on centralized control in the same way that the Anglo-Saxons did, but the formers' rejection of "centralized control in favor of multiple semi-independent agents"[39] formed a network of jurisdictions with autonomous or semiautonomous authorities responsible for dispute resolution. These operated in concert with the royal courts (where disputes could be brought before the king in a *placitum* or synod) and worked alongside the traditional recourse of waging feuds. The full embracing of these two systems operating in tandem was the foundation of the Ottonian justice system. The Ottonians were shrewd rulers, able to allow nobles and others to work out their own disputes through legitimate feud activity so long as the disruptions did not threaten imperial interests. The armed provincial struggles for precedence among nobles and churchmen were a "harsh but normal manifestation of local political ambition."[40] Occasionally, rulers were able to leverage these disputes to their own advantage. For example, when Duke Giselbert of Lotharingia and Otto I were feuding in 939, the resultant death of Giselbert provided an opportunity for Otto to replace him with his brother Brun, thus assuring that Otto had an ally in a strong position of authority in Lotharingia.[41] In another instance, Otto I granted an episcopal benefice as, in essence, the *wergeld* payment to settle a feud. According to Thietmar of Merseburg,

> The emperor took [Hildeward] by the hand and, with the staff, commended to him the pastoral office with the following words: "Receive this compensation for your father!" The father, Erich, had been beheaded along with Bacco, Herman, Reinward, Wirin, Eserich, and others for having attempted to kill the emperor while he was celebrating the feast of Easter at Quedlinburg.[42]

---

39. Rafe Sagarin, *Learning from the Octopus: How Secrets from Nature Can Help Us Fight Terrorist Attacks, Natural Disasters, and Disease* (New York: Basic Books, 2012), 18.

40. Benjamin Arnold, *Medieval Germany, 500–1300: A Political Interpretation* (Toronto: University of Toronto Press, 1997), 55.

41. Ibid.

42. David A. Warner, ed. and trans., *Ottonian Germany: The* Chronicon *of Theitmar of Merse-*

Consider the circumstances of the *wergeld* obligation here: Otto had Erich killed because Erich had tried to kill him. Even so, that did not free Otto from a blood debt, which he publicly and ceremonially paid by conferment of the bishopric of Halberstadt to Hildeward. Since Hildeward had been the candidate promoted for the position by other bishops anyway, Otto likely took advantage of the opportunity to placate them and relieve himself of the debt in one gesture. As Karl Leyser noted, "The king did not regard himself as exempt from the social obligations which bound his nobles nor is he seen as standing outside the ring of feud and revenge."[43]

We first see attempts to regulate feuding behavior in Germany in the eleventh century. Strikingly, this activity is focused on feuding not between magnates but at lower levels of society. Additionally, the regulations are highly localized. Between 1023 and 1025 CE, Burchard of Worms wrote the *Lex familiae* in an attempt to limit retributive violence in his diocese. He was appalled that thirty-five of his subjects were killed in the course of a single year "because one used to attack another in an insane rage, often for nothing or through drunkenness or for pride."[44] Burchard limited the acceptable homicide to cases of self-defense and the killing of thieves. Otherwise, harsh penalties involving removal of skin and hair, branding, and payment of *wergeld* were prescribed, and the killer was ordered to make peace "in the usual way."[45] But if the victim's family pursued vengeance, those who perpetuated any violence (preparing an ambush, physical attack, killing, even inciting others to get involved in the pursuit of vengeance) were subject to the same harsh penalties and might also face

---

burg (Manchester: Manchester University Press, 2001), 107; Thietmar of Merseburg, *Chronicon* 2.21, in *Thietmari Merseburgensis Episcopi Chronicon*, ed. Robert Holtzmann, MGH SRG 9 (Berlin: Weidmannsche Buchhandlung, 1935), 62–63: "Tali munere inperador arridens per manus suscepit eundem, curamque ei baculo committens pastoralem: 'Accipe,' infit, 'precium patris tui!' Hunc enim, Ericum nomine, cum Baccone, Herimanno, Reinwardo, Wirino, Eserico caeterisque, qui in Quidilingeburg eundem tunc in pascha sollemni occidere conabantur, decollari precepit."

43. Karl Leyser, *Rule and Conflict in an Early Medieval Society: Ottonian Saxony* (Bloomington: Indiana University Press, 1979), 33. The rules of the game with regard to feud and honor in the Ottonian era are discussed at length in Gerd Althoff, *Spielregeln der Politik im Mittelalter: Kommunikation in Frieden und Fehde* (Darmstadt: Wissenschaftliche Buchgesellschaft, 1997), 21–56. The first to refer to feud and social perception specifically as a game of honor, in which honor was not just a socially determined state but an active publicly performed competition, was Miller, in his discussion of feud behavior in medieval Iceland (31–34).

44. Smail and Gibson, 146; Burchard, *Lex familiae*, 643: "Propter homicidia autem, que quasi cottidie fiebant infra familiam sancti Petri more beluino, quia sepe pro nichilo aut per ebrietatem aut per superbiam alter in alterum insana mente ita inseviebat, ut in curriculo unius anni XXXV servi sancti Petri sine culpa ex servis eiusdem ecclesie sint interempti." With *familia*, Burchard was referring to the people under his episcopal jurisdiction.

45. Burchard, *Lex familiae*, 643: "constituimus, ut ei tollantur corium et capilli et in utraque maxilla ferro ad hoc facto comburatur, et weregeldum reddat et cum proximis occisi more solito pacem faciat."

compurgation by boiling water and confiscation of their property. Whether these laws were actually enforced is unknown, but they speak to the frustration that Burchard felt at the ongoing reciprocal violence that seemed endemic among his people.

Henry II had occasion to intervene in the feuding at Worms as well, as recorded in a 1023 charter in which he reprimanded the residents of Worms and Lorsch for the feuding between the two dioceses. The countless murders had finally led to imperial intervention, and Henry, too, prescribed removal of the skin and hair, branding, and monetary compensation for assaulting or killing another person.[46] He also issued a 1024 charter attempting to regulate the feuds between the people belonging to the monasteries of Fulda and Hersfeld, ordering that the advocates and abbots of both monasteries were responsible for making sure those rules were followed.[47]

These examples of attempts to regulate feud were highly localized, intended for implementation in specific communities because of specific circumstances—retributive violence that had gotten out of control. Greta Austin cautions against reading these regulations as evidence of systemic societal breakdown: "That a feud had spiraled out of control does not mean necessarily that the custom of the feud itself was flawed."[48] The possibility of a feud could stimulate negotiation and reconciliation or settlement and was a powerful stimulus to compromise, resulting in what anthropologist Max Gluckman referred to as "the peace in the feud."[49] But allowing feuding as a way to maintain peace required delicate balance, and "once the 'peace in the feud' collapsed, . . . it could be very hard to restore."[50] Preventing feuding behaviors and licit feuding activities from escalating into cycles of retributive violence was a key area of concern for medieval rulers. The breakdown of feuding into chaotic and uncontrolled violence was always a possibility in a system where emotions could run high. If those who were wronged refused to entertain overtures of peace, if those ordered to pay compensations refused to do so, or, worse, if third parties intervened as participants in the feud instead of as peacemakers, the fine balance of the feud as a means for peace could be broken.[51] This fine balance had broken down in Worms in the 1020s.

46. DD HII 501.
47. DD HII 507.
48. Austin, "Vengeance and Law," 67.
49. Max Gluckman, *Custom and Conflict in Africa* (1956; repr., Oxford: Basil Blackwell, 1964), 1–26.
50. Austin, "Vengeance and Law," 68.
51. Ibid., 68. See also Paul Hyams, *Rancor and Reconciliation in Medieval England* (Ithaca, NY: Cornell University Press, 2003), 19–20; Miller, 297–99.

The success of the Ottonian policy of accepting and allowing feud as a normal course of political or legal action among its subjects is attested through the minimal interference required by the king or emperor. The only imperial attempts to regulate feud by the Ottonian *Reich* address small communities with localized problems where feuding activities had gotten out of control. Burchard's episcopal effort at regulating feud in his see supports this assessment as well. These examples also suggest a connection between the production of legislation and the need to limit or control feuding. Other than intervening in periodic specific conflicts that came to their attention, the Ottonians were not compelled to legislate to constrain the feuding activities in their territories. Their reliance on customary self-help methods of dispute resolution, like feud, must have been a successful way to maintain order in their empire.

The one place that the Ottonians did legislate was in Italy, a region that had a violent and disruptive feud culture as well as a reputation for corruption. When he became emperor, Otto I was appealed to almost immediately because of Italy's never-ending land disputes that involved forged documents, false claims, and perjury, and the legislation that was produced there in response to this situation was in the form of capitularies. The first of these were issued in 967 by Otto I, and capitularies continued to be issued in Italy by successive Ottonian emperors.[52] Thus, even in the unlikely event that the Ottonians were completely unfamiliar with the capitularies of their Carolingian predecessors, those they issued in Italy show that the format and purpose was not foreign to them. That the records of the Ottonian court when adjudicating on Italian matters refer more than once to the inherent corruption of the society reinforces the argument that legislation was enacted on an as-needed basis. Italy, with its

52. For examples from Otto I, see *Capitulare Veronense de duello iudiciali*, MGH Const 1, 27–30; *Pactum cum Venetis*, MGH Const 1, 30–36; *Edictum Papiense de duello*, MGH Const 1, 37. Otto II also legislated in Italy (*Pactum cum Venetis*, MGH Const 1, 39–43), as did Otto III (*Praeceptum confirmationis Venetis datum*, MGH Const 1, 45–46; *Capitulare de servis libertatem anhelantibus*, MGH Const 1, 47–48; *Capitulare de iusititio*, MGH Const 1, 48; *Capitulare Ticinense de praediis ecclesiarum neve per libellum neve per emphyteusin alienandis*, MGH Const 1, 49–51). Italy had a long and robust legislative tradition long before the Ottonians arrived, and it is likely that part of the reason for legislation in Italy was that it was a legal idiom well understood by the Italians. Thus, for example, the sole surviving copy of the capitulary for Pavia issued in 971 regarding trial by judicial combat (*Edictum Papiense de Duello*) is preserved in an eleventh-century manuscript of Justinian's *Institutions* (Bamberg D. II. 3 [olim D. nr. 32]). Nonetheless, the reason that the Ottonians needed to legislate was the need for imperial authority in the disputing culture, which had become too disruptive to be allowed to persist. The potential challenge that this kind of conflict and disruption could present to imperial authority is amply demonstrated by the papal fiasco of 963–65 involving Popes John XII, Benedict V, and Leo VIII, when the Romans blatantly challenged Otto I's authority in Roman and papal affairs (Liudprand of Cremona, *Historia Ottonis*, in *Liudprandi Cremonensis Opera Omnia*, ed. Paolo Chiesa, Corpus Christianorum [Turnhout: Brepols, 1998], 167–83. See also Adalbert of Magdeburg, *Continuatio Reginonis*, s.aa. 963–65, in *Reginonis abbatis Prumiensis Chronicon cum continuatione Treverensi*, ed. F. Kurze [Hanover: Hahn, 1890], 172–76).

disruptive and endemic feuding and predilection for forgeries and perjury in lawsuits, necessitated imperial legislative action. Like the out-of-control feuding at Worms, legislation was a necessary tool employed by the crown to solve a problem particular to a specific area. Italy was geographically broader than Worms, and the Ottonians struggled to enforce their supremacy over the region. Inserting themselves into Italian disputing through the use of legislation would have been an attempt to restore a sense of order, an imperial presence, and imperial primacy into the culture of the peninsula. The inability of Italian disputants to resolve their own cases and the chaos that was engendered as a result of illicit methods of dispute resolution, as at Worms, resulted in the issuance of imperial legislation. This situation again suggests a powerful connection between legislation and attempts to control feuding behaviors—that rulers issued legislation as an effort to suppress feud—and reinforces the argument that one reason the Ottonians did not legislate (with the key exceptions noted above) is that reliance on traditional methods of dispute resolution in their realm generally worked. Feud served a functional role, alongside comital or episcopal courts, to facilitate order. The peace that was maintained was good enough, and until that fragile balance was lost, resulting in significant social disruption, the emperor did not need to attempt to control those affairs by issuing legislation.[53]

Royal Feuds

The Saxons in East Francia certainly had their succession crises and contested kingships, and feuds arose in these conflicts at the highest levels of society. According to contemporary chroniclers, Henry the Fowler, the future Henry I, was at the heart of feuding behavior in which the family members of the Saxon kings were direct participants. This feud was a long-standing altercation dating back to the reign of Louis the Child. Widukind of Corvey, in his tenth-century *Res Gestae Saxonicae*, gives a rather dizzying overview of events. Conrad, father of King Conrad, and Adalbert, the nephew of Henry through his sister, were at war with each other. Adalbert's brother was killed. In retribution, Adalbert killed Conrad. As the feud waged on, according to Widukind, "[none] of the

53. The idea of "good enough" derives from biological systems theory and serves to prevent interpretations based on hindsight or a perceived lack of aspirational development. In a "good enough" system, changes are implemented when needed to address a specific threat at a specific point; when a point has been reached where the threat is neutralized, sufficiently reduced, or adapted to in some sort of symbiotic way, change stops.

kings [could] bring to an end the violent warfare between these outstanding men."[54] As a last resort, in 906, Archbishop Hatto of Mainz conspired to capture Adalbert by trickery, and Adalbert was then turned over to King Louis, condemned, and executed. Widukind's remark on this conspiracy is telling: "What is more vile than this act of treachery? But it is true that by cutting off this one head, the heads of many other people were saved. And what is better than advice that resolves conflict and brings peace?"[55] But peace was not to last. Widukind further describes how King Conrad was afraid to grant Henry the Fowler all the same powers that his father, Otto, had as Duke of Saxony, which was perceived as a grave injustice by Henry and the Saxons. Aware of the festering resentment, Conrad decided that his best option was to try to kill Henry by treachery, again with the help of the loyal Bishop Hatto. But the plot unraveled, and Henry gathered an army and began to occupy and seize lands throughout Saxony and Thuringia, seizing any properties that were held by the bishopric and expelling the king's supporters.[56] This approach, as opposed to outright attempts to kill one's enemy, was a common way for a feud to be waged in medieval Germany, and similar descriptions pepper the narrative sources of the tenth and eleventh centuries. Known as *Raub und Brand* (plunder and burning), this method was, according to Brunner, the "main way of waging a feud . . . to 'distress' the opponent by pillage and devastation."[57]

This story of Henry and Conrad is repeated by Thietmar of Merseburg, who hints at widescale disruption when he indicates simply that "it would be tedious for me to relate how many times each [i.e., the king and Duke Henry] was victorious in battle or defeated and how, at the last, the initiative of good men brought about a reconciliation."[58] The story is deliberately downplayed in

54. Widukind of Corvey, *Res gestae Saxonicae* 1.22, in *Widukindi monachi Corbiensis rerum gestarum Saxonicarum libri tres*, ed. Paul Hirsch and H.-E. Lohmann after G. Waitz and K. A. Kehr, MGH SRG 60 [Hanover: Hahn, 1935], 31: "Nec ullus regum tam ingens bellum inter eminentes viros potuit sedare."

55. Widukind of Corvey, *Deeds of the Saxons*, trans. Bernard S. Bachrach and David S. Bachrach (Washington, DC: Catholic University of America Press, 2014), 33–34; Widukind of Corvey, *Res gestae Saxonicae* 1.22, 33: "Hac igitur perfidia quid nequius? Attamen uno capite caeso multorum capita populorum salvantur. Et quid melius eo consilio, quo discordia dissolveretur et pax redderetur?"

56. Thietmar, *Chronicon* 1.7, 12. According to Brunner, this activity would have been seen as an appropriate expression of feuding behavior: "For the feud aimed at retribution and vengeance in order to restore the broken order of Right. It might involve direct acts of retribution, above all in blood vengeance by killing the perpetrator, or 'private acts of distraint'—seizure and sequestration of the enemy's property. Or, less directly, the feud could be pursued by inflicting damages on the opponent in order to compel him to yield to one's demands" (*Land and Lordship*, 28).

57. Brunner, *Land and Lordship*, 69.

58. Warner, *Ottonian Germany*, 72; Thietmar, *Chronicon* 1.7, 12: "Sed mihi ad alia properanti longum est enarrare, quocies congressi mutuo cederent vel vincerent, et quod postremo bonorum instinctu in amiciciam convenirent."

Liudprand of Cremona's tenth-century *Antapodosis*,[59] where the focus of the incident between Bishop Hatto and Adalbert becomes the justice exacted by the king for treason. There are a few other stories about feuding kings and magnates in Liudprand of Cremona's writings. But the bulk of this behavior is pursued in Italy, by Italians, against each other and against the Germanic magnates who are unfortunate enough to get drawn into Italian politics by marriage, conquest, or invitation. Liudprand is explicit that this is not how legitimate kings conduct themselves, and he was expressly attempting to contrast the corrupt and chaotic political situation of Italy with the ordered, consensual and thus legitimate rule of the Ottonians. This agenda most certainly would have caused him to downplay any Ottonian feud-type behaviors.

Regardless of their different approaches to the same events, all three chroniclers emphasize the chaos of retributive violence and the importance of reconciliation. Having rebelled against King Conrad, Henry the Fowler was nonetheless designated by Conrad to be his successor—a good example of how reconciliation could indeed eliminate animosity between parties.[60] But the transition was not smooth; Henry had to deal with Arnulf of Bavaria, who also wanted to be king. They both mustered their armies and rode to confront each other, but they ultimately reached an agreement through negotiation, without engaging in battle.[61] Even in the minority of Otto III, the fourth Saxon king by direct descent in the Ottonian dynasty, the king's safety was threatened when his father died unexpectedly. Young Otto was held hostage by his uncle Henry the Wrangler, who had several attempted coups to his credit by that time and tried to press his advantage after the death of Otto II, until young Otto's safe return was negotiated by his mother and grandmother.[62] Why did Henry not just kill his nephew and be done with it? For some reason, the Ottonians seemed to balk at killing family. They would raise armies against each other, imprison each other, and send recalcitrant sons or brothers into exile, but murdering each other—and even murdering troublesome magnates—did not seem to be within the norms of acceptable political maneuvering. In knightly feuds in Germany "one has the impression that . . . the killing of one's opponent was something rather to be avoided," namely, because a killing of that kind was not exempt from blood vengeance and blood feud and thus had the potential for escalation.[63] This could be one reason for Otto I's lenient treatment of frequent

59. Liudprand of Cremona, *Antapodosis* 2.19, 43.

60. Liudprand of Cremona, *Antapodosis* 2.19 (rebellion), 2.20 (Conrad's exhortation to elect Henry as his successor), 43–44.

61. Liudprand of Cremona, *Antapodosis* 2.21–23, 44–46.

62. Thietmar, *Chronicon* 3.26, 4.1–7, 130–39.

63. Brunner, *Land and Lordship*, 68.

rebellion: even the "fratricidal onslaught" of his brother Henry was tolerated, "almost certainly [because of] the necessity not to impair the royal dignity in his brother, although the latter was not and could not be king."[64] To kill Henry would tarnish Otto's own imperial image.[65] Brunner suggests an additional motivation for the Ottonians' reticence to kill family: "Within the household and the clan, . . . the use of armed force was not considered legitimate. There was no such thing as a just feud between members of a clan, and whoever attacked a fellow member became the enemy of the entire clan. Household and clan were permanent peace associations in which feud was impossible without destroying the association itself."[66]

Feuds and feuding societies depend ultimately on an end to hostilities through a negotiated peace settlement that publicly ends the conflict and restores relationships between the feuding parties.[67] The legislative efforts to control the constant deadly conflict between and among the nobility and the various monarchs in Anglo-Saxon England support the idea that the English worked toward a strong centralized system and legislative tradition, while the Ottonians were happy to delegate jurisdictional authority and allow customary conflict resolution, including feud, to operate alongside more formal legal processes. For them, legislation at the royal or imperial level was not necessary until or unless specific circumstances demanded it.

The intensely violent and endemic feuding culture of the Anglo-Saxon kingdoms was potentially the source of their prolific legislative activity beginning with Alfred in the late ninth century. Paul Hyams has suggested that the centrality of royal authority in Anglo-Saxon England is not incongruous with the existence of a feud mentality. Feud culture, with its inherent violence and potential for political and social disruption, was shared by pre-Alfredian kings

64. K. Leyser, *Rule and Conflict*, 86. Gerd Althoff notes that the one time Otto I had *coniuationes* executed for plotting his murder ended up having negative consequences for him long after (*Family, Friends, and Followers: Political and Social Bonds in Early Medieval Europe*, trans. Christopher Carroll [Cambridge: Cambridge University Press, 2004], 93).

65. The Anglo-Saxons seemed to have no such quibbles about killing family members. See Wangerin, "Royal Feuds."

66. Brunner, *Land and Lordship*, 26.

67. Hyams, *Rancor and Reconciliation*, 12. Hyams's key assertions in *Rancor and Reconciliation* that are relevant for this argument are (1) that feud was "quite central to Anglo-Saxon political culture" (71); (2) that Old English literature establishes the cultural centrality of feud in Anglo-Saxon society (73); and (3) that royal authority is central to Anglo-Saxon England (73). Hyams explains, "The commonsense suspicion that feuds are as likely to involve lords as kinsmen is confirmed for Anglo-Saxon England by the existence of *manbot*, compensation to a lord for the loss of his dependent. . . . No good man, certainly no prudent man, would turn a deaf ear to his lord's appeal that he ride beside him on feud business, or even do the work under his orders but in his absence" (90; primary sources for *manbot* at 90n75).

and their nobility alike.[68] But its potential to undermine royal authority was also recognized. If, indeed, the proliferation of vernacular *leges* proves that, to quote Paul Hyams, "Anglo-Saxon personal vengeance operated in a context that ostentatiously included public, royal courts willing to exert pressure against the private acts they deemed illegitimate,"[69] we have the possibility of drawing some interesting conclusions. From the beginning of the tenth century, royal action against behavior unacceptable to the crown intensified, suggesting, again quoting Hyams, "a new level of royal interest in violence and disorder committed outside the royal circle."[70] This interest in controlling and constraining the most disruptive elements of unrestrained feud coincided with the unification of the Anglo-Saxon kingdoms. Karl Shoemaker has linked the efforts of Anglo-Saxon royal authority to govern sanctuary with law regulating feud, though they achieved mixed results.[71] But the key point is that the laws pertaining to blood feud were indeed the norms, reinforcing the connection between legislation and feud. If the royal *leges* of the Anglo-Saxons were created out of attempts to control a feuding culture, is it possible that we would see less emphasis on legislative activity in a society in which such feuds among the nobility did not cause the same degree of disruption—not to mention outright threats to the crown?

The Ottonians, whose succession crises were far less deadly than those of the Anglo-Saxons and whose nobles were less of a threat to their kingdom as a whole, were able to depend more on traditional feud and negotiation as part of their legal structure, since it was far less disruptive to order in their realm. The almost complete lack of Ottonian legislative activity has long puzzled historians, especially in light of the Ottonians' success as rulers. The smaller principalities and kingdoms that made up the Ottonian Empire were essentially similar to the kingdoms incorporated under Wessex, albeit covering a far larger

68. Hyams, *Rancor and Reconciliation*, 77.

69. Ibid., 73.

70. Ibid., 80. Hyams explains, "The royal leges are the key to the history of feud as a process, for this quintessential testimony to the king's central authority is congruous with the existence of a feud mentality. That is, feud culture was a prime target for much legislative activity" (72). The converse would suggest a key part of my argument, that a lack of feud culture thus would lead to a lack of legislative activity, as with the Ottonians. Hyams continues, "From the reign of Æthelred's successor, Edmund (939–946), comes the central text in the whole argument, the code hailed by scholars as a primary effort to minimize bloodshed and the spread of feud. *II Edmund* was apparently spurred by Archbishop Oda's recent call for 'peace and unanimity,' something with which feud killings were patently incompatible" (82). One needs to study *II Edmund* alongside the contemporaneous text *Wer*, as did tenth- and eleventh-century readers: "This juxtaposition shows that the king intended no outright prohibition of feud [*Wer* 6]" (83). "Not until the reign of Æthelred (978–1016)," notes Hyams, "do the leges assert the existence of bootless offenses, wrongs so serious that redress may no longer be taken by private agreement with the wronged" (84).

71. Karl Shoemaker, *Sanctuary and Crime in the Middle Ages, 400–1500* (New York: Fordham University Press, 2011), 78.

geographic area. But since family feuds were a much more lethal sport among the Anglo-Saxon royal and noble families than among the Ottonians and East Francian magnates, there was no compulsion to create highly centralized, top-down control over minor courts and a highly developed legal ideology around the idea of a king's peace. The few documents that we have that appear to be legislating how feud is conducted are indicative more of correctives to specific and localized issues than of broad legislation intended to address endemic imperial problems. In the Ottonian realm, we see functional feuding: behavior that was allowed because it served the interests of peacekeeping in Ottonian lands. Thus, the persistence of feud and the lack of legislative activity signals a strong and resilient rulership.

If feuding behavior indeed created the need for the written legislation that is such a distinctive feature of Anglo-Saxon law, it is likely that the lack of written legislation by the Ottonian kings is indicative of their reliance on traditional methods of conflict resolution and jurisdictions delegated to local authorities. There was no compulsion to legislate regarding feud throughout the empire, because it was not perceived to be a threat to their realm. When periodic, localized problems involved retributive violence that was perceived to be out of control, the local lord or king would step in and take matters in hand. The one place the Ottonians did legislate on a broader scale, as we saw above, was Italy, where feud remained part of the law for centuries after.[72]

72. Chris Wickham, *Early Medieval Italy: Central Power and Local Society, 400–1000* (1981; repr., Ann Arbor: University of Michigan Press, 1989), 128. See note 52 above for examples of Italian capitularies.

CHAPTER 4

The Idea of Kingship

Ruler Images, Relics, and Rituals

The Ottonian kings and emperors developed a new way of conceptualizing the king's place and role in both the divine and earthly hierarchies, and this idea, sacral kingship, was every bit as important as other institutions of their government, such as the royal *iter*. That the emperor's role was not just to administer justice but to serve as the dispenser of God's justice was vividly displayed through their images and rituals of kingship. This is perhaps nowhere portrayed as clearly as in the ruler portrait of Henry II in the Monte Cassino Gospels (fig. 1).[1] Created in Regensburg in the last years of Henry II's reign, the image fully encapsulates the idea of a sacral king who has been divinely endowed to act as earthly judge.

The figure of Henry II is enthroned in the center of a quatrefoil, flanked by the virtues of wisdom and prudence. The Holy Spirit descends from above to bestow holy wisdom to the ruler. In the corners stand the personifications of justice and piety (*iustitia* and *pietas*) above and law and right (*lex* and *ius*) below. Directly beneath Henry is an executioner standing above a prisoner, who, with raised arms and eyes, beseeches the emperor above him. The legend suggests the gravity of the moment: "Caesaris ad nutum dampnant lex iusque tyranum" (Law and justice condemn the tyrant at the nod of the emperor). John Bernhardt has argued that there is good reason to believe that the figure portrayed represents Pandulf IV of Capua, a prince who was tried and condemned to death, before being saved from execution by order of Henry II.[2] The image

1. "Henry II," Gospel Book of Monte Cassino, ca. 1024, Vatican Library, Codex Ott. Lat. 74, fol. 193v.

2. John W. Bernhardt, "King Henry II of Germany: Royal Self-Representation and Historical Memory," in *Medieval Concepts of the Past: Ritual, Memory, Historiography*, ed. Gerd Althoff, Johannes Fried, and Patrick Geary (Cambridge: Cambridge University Press, 2002), 66–67. Stefan Weinfurter has noted that "Henry appears in God's place as the administrator of the law" ("Authority and Legitimation of Royal Policy and Action: The Case of Henry II," in Althoff, Fried, and Geary, 34).

Fig. 1. "Henry II," Gospel Book of Monte Cassino, ca. 1024, Vatican Library, Codex Ott. Lat. 74, fol. 193v. (PHAS / Universal Images Group / Getty Images.)

projects a strong vision of the emperor as judge, as well as generous and forgiving in his granting of clemency. In the years around 1024, when this codex was produced, the memory of Pandulf's trial and pardon would have been known to many of those who viewed the image. To those unfamiliar with the story and to later generations, the portrait presents the epitome of an imperial ruler, whose power is "ultimately guided by the Holy Spirit of God, sitting as judge of life and death over doers of evil."[3]

This example also demonstrates the end result of the successful transformation of the idea of kingship under the Ottonians. The notion of sacral kingship developed through a careful program of representation over the course of the reigns of Ottos I, II, and III, an ideology of kingship that was further embraced in the iconography of Henry II. This conceptualization is different than anything we see with their predecessors, the Carolingians, or their contemporaries in Anglo-Saxon England or on the Continent. Ottonian ruler images in particular show how their ruling philosophy changed over time and how their idea of sacral kingship was tied to their ideas about the roles of kings and emperors as dispensers of justice.

Ottonian Ruler Images and the Idea of Kingship

The illumination of the Emperor Seated in Majesty from the tenth-century Aachen Gospels is remarkable for a number of reasons, not the least in its artistry.[4] It is a magnificent image (fig. 2). Against a field of gold that fills much of the page, the emperor is portrayed seated on a golden stool with a purple cushion, held aloft by the crouching figure of Tellus, the personification of Earth. On the same plane as Tellus stand two princes, each in a posture of veneration or deference, while two bishops and two warriors stand far below. The lower figures will not concern us at this time, as what appears in the top third of the image is most important to our purpose, the idea of a new conceptualization of kingship. The emperor is surrounded by a golden mandorla, just outside of which are depicted representations of the four Evangelists, looking toward him and bearing a white veil draped in such a way that it bisects him, so the emperor's head and shoulders are seen above the veil, the rest of his body below it. Finally, the cruciform hand of God reaches down from above and touches his head, either placing his crown or bestowing a blessing.

3. Bernhardt, "King Henry II," 69.

4. "The Emperor Otto Seated in Majesty," Aachen Gospels (Liuthar Gospels), ca. 996, Aachen Cathedral Treasury, fol. 16r.

Fig. 2. "The Emperor Otto Seated in Majesty," Aachen Gospels (Liuthar Gospels), ca. 996, Aachen Cathedral Treasury, fol. 16r. (Art Collection 3 / Alamy Stock Photo. All rights reserved.)

While this miniature was originally thought to be a portrayal of Otto II and dated around 975, later scholarship has associated it with Otto III and given it a later date of about 996, coinciding with his imperial coronation.[5] While the gap of twenty years may seem a matter of academic trivia, it is of utmost importance in this particular instance, as it helps demonstrate how, over the course of their dynasty, the Ottonians were reconceptualizing their ideas about rulership. The image does not look strikingly different from illuminations in other Gospel texts by Carolingians or Ottonians, except for one marked change: in other texts, the man inhabiting the mandorla is Christ. Far more than just an artistic innovation to flatter an emperor, this image is a depiction of a new theology of rulership, the culmination of a conscious program that the Ottonians employed to legitimize their rule and that evolved into the idea portrayed in the Aachen Gospels, "liturgical kingship."[6] Not only do the pictorial representations of Ottonian rulers demonstrate how those rulers used images as part of their efforts to legitimize their rule as sacred, but the images also help show the development of Ottonian political philosophy.

The real development of this new way of thinking about kingship lies with the three Ottos. Henry I, the first of the Ottonians, was an effective ruler but was not yet manipulating images to project a specific idea about rule. Henry II, the last of the Ottonians, ably exploited the use of symbols, images, and public display instituted by his predecessors to substantiate his own discourse of legitimacy, but he was building on what was by then past precedent. The real change in a philosophy of rulership came about with the Ottos; while they clearly borrowed rituals and symbols from the later Carolingian rulers, partly out of an effort to ground their legitimacy by linking themselves to the old regime, they ended up creating something new. The Carolingians portrayed themselves as heirs to the great Old Testament kings; the Ottonians ended up portraying themselves as the impersonators of Christ himself, the *christomimetai*.[7] We will better see the dramatic change in direction in which Otto I takes

5. Ernst Kantorowicz uses the earlier dating in his analysis of the image (*The King's Two Bodies: A Study in Mediaeval Political Theology* [1957; repr., Princeton, NJ: Princeton University Press, 1985], 61–78). Percy Ernst Schramm and Florentine Mütherich suggested a date of ca. 990 (*Denkmale der deutschen Könige und Kaiser* [Munich: Prestel Verlag, 1962], 103). More recent studies follow the later dating: see Henry Mayr-Harting, *Ottonian Book Illumination: An Historical Study*, 2 vols. (1991; repr., London: Harvey Miller, 1999), 1:59–60; Christopher de Hamel, *A History of Illuminated Manuscripts* (1986; repr., London: Phaidon, 1994), 60; Eliza Garrison, *Ottonian Imperial Art and Portraiture: The Artistic Patronage of Otto III and Henry II* (Burlington, VT: Ashgate, 2012), 39.

6. Kantorowicz, *King's Two Bodies*, 78. Eliza Garrison (46-60) discusses the political implications of the image specifically with regard to Otto III's coronation.

7. Kantorowicz, *King's Two Bodies*, 65. The timing of this transformation under Otto I coincided with the inauguration of his imperial ambitions and formal anointing as emperor by the

his philosophy of rule, as demonstrated through ruler images, if we first briefly examine the philosophy of his father, Henry I.

According to Widukind of Corvey, when, following the death of Conrad I in 919, Henry was brought the royal insignia and informed that he was king, he was also offered unction and a formal coronation. Henry refused, ostensibly out of humility.[8] Key here is that being anointed and ritually crowned did not seem to matter with regard to his perceived authority, and the ritual itself did not confer that authority. Henry had been nominated by the former king, received the royal regalia, was accepted publicly by the nobility, and thus was the legitimate ruler. Widukind does not seem to find any fault with Henry for declining this ritual display. Henry embodied the medieval incarnations of the older Germanic political structures recorded by Tacitus—that is, networks of kin and close friends. These networks of reciprocal cooperative agreements had proved essential to rulers in Saxony from the mid-ninth century onward, but Henry was especially adroit at constructing and manipulating networks of associates bound by personal loyalties to forge interior stability and exterior security.[9]

With the succession of Otto I (the Great) on the death of Henry I in 936, we begin to see changes in the idea of kingship, although there are still aspects of continuity. For example, Widukind of Corvey provided a quite detailed description of Otto's coronation ceremony but emphasized that it was not that ritual that made him king; rather, he was king *before* the ceremony, because the people had elected him.[10] But we also begin to see how he conceptualized kingship differently than had his father. As soon as he had established his succession to the throne against competing claimants, Otto deliberately began to actively avoid those cooperative bonds that had proved so crucial for his father's suc-

pope. For a discussion of the political implications of this new conceptualization of East Frankish kingship in the larger world, see Wolfgang Huschner, "Kaiser der Franken oder Kaiser der Römer? Die neue imperiale Würde Ottos I. im euromediterranen Raum," in *Otto der Grosse und das Römische Reich: Kaisertum von der Antike zum Mittelalter*, ed. Matthias Puhle and Gabriele Köster (Regensburg: Schnell und Steiner, 2012), 519–27.

8. Widukind of Corvey, *Res gestae Saxonicae* 1.26, in *Widukindi monachi Corbiensis rerum gestarum Saxonicarum libri tres*, ed. Paul Hirsch and H.-E. Lohmann after G. Waitz and K. A. Kehr (Hanover: Hahn, 1935), 39: "Cumque ei offerretur unctio cum diademate a summo pontifice, qui eo tempore Hirigerus erat, non sprevit, nec tamen suscepit: 'Satis', inquiens, 'michi est, ut pre maioribus meis rex dicar et designer, divina annuente gratia ac vestra pietate; penes meliores vero nobis unctio et diadema sit: tanto honore nos indignos arbitramur.'" See also Sverre Bagge, *Kings, Politics, and the Right Order of the World in German Historiography, c. 950–1150* (Leiden: Brill, 2002), 34; Philippe Buc, *The Dangers of Ritual: Between Early Medieval Texts and Social Scientific Theory* (Princeton, NJ: Princeton University Press, 2001), 15–16.

9. Gerd Althoff, *Family, Friends, and Followers: Political and Social Bonds in Early Medieval Europe*, trans. Christopher Carroll (Cambridge: Cambridge University Press, 2004), 84.

10. Widukind, *Res gestae Saxonicae* 2.1, 63–66. Bagge (90) discusses this distinction in detail.

cess.[11] This change was the beginning of a policy that would be continued by Otto I's successors. After him, German kings continued to pointedly avoid entering into any type of bond with their magnates that might be interpreted as an *amicitia*.[12] For Otto, this created serious unrest early in his reign, for while he refused to enter into mutually binding alliances with his own magnates, he did enter into them with foreign kings and foreign magnates. At the same time, he was trying to enforce increased royal demands on his lords. Dissatisfaction with these policies led to revolt by many of his nobles, who felt that these changes would be disadvantageous to their persons and their honor.[13]

While divine unction may have added prestige and perhaps signified divine support, it still was not seen as an essential legitimation of power and did not yet represent the monarchy as an institution as much as the king's personal charisma. It was representative of a personal relationship with God, and the successes of the king were seen as evidence of that divine support.[14] And divine unction was just one of the many ways that the sacralization of the emperor began to take shape under Otto I.[15] He began to reinterpret and practice rites of the late Carolingian rulers and to consciously adopt Byzantine motifs as the foundations for a specific kind of representation of his kingship[16]—for example, adopting a basileus's style for his representation on seals and coins.[17] In trying to legitimize a new and tenuous claim to imperial and dynastic authority, Otto I recognized the ability of symbols to create and perpetuate an image of power and stability. One of the rituals most important to this developing idea of sacrality was being crowned Roman emperor by the pope.[18]

11. Althoff, *Family, Friends, and Followers*, 124.

12. Ibid., 86, 129.

13. Ibid., 85, 129.

14. Bagge, 90–91.

15. The Ottonians also reinforced the idea of sacral kingship through various highly visual symbols of power, such as building churches, the royal itinerary (especially the custom of celebrating certain feast days at the same place each year), attendance at festivals and feasts, public crown wearings, collection and display of relics, sanctification of family members, and, of course, artistic representations of the ruler (Henry Mayr-Harting, *Church and Cosmos in Early Ottonian Germany: The View from Cologne* [Oxford: Oxford University Press, 2007], 4).

16. Jonathan Shepard, "Marriages towards the Millennium," in *Byzantium in the Year 1000*, ed. Paul Magdalino et al. (Leiden: Brill, 2003), 16.

17. Ibid., 12. This was a distinctly different style than that previously seen in the Western Roman Empire, consisting of a full-frontal depiction of the emperor, crowned and holding a cross, orb, and scepter. An exhibit at Magdeburg Cathedral highlighted the changes in the seals of Otto I; for catalog descriptions of several of these seals, see "Kaiserliche Repräsentation in den Siegelbildern Ottos I.," in Puhle and Köster, 572–77. See also Hagen Keller, "Ottonische Herrschersiegel. Beobachtungen und Fragen zu Gestalt und Aussage und zur Funktion im historischen Kontext," in *Ottonische Königsherrschaft: Organisation und Legitimation königlicher Macht* (Darmstadt: Wissenschaftliche Buchgesellschaft, 2002), 132–35.

18. Mayr-Harting, *Church and Cosmos*, 4. Mayr-Harting points out that while past scholars focused on the practical gains for the Ottonians in being emperors, "few historians" today "would rate such practical purposes above those of mystical allure and sacrality."

While we know a little about the rituals of Otto's kingship, few images of him survive, and they are nothing like the luxe miniatures that portray his son and grandson. But the one image that tells us something about this developing idea of sacrality is an ivory plaque of Otto presenting a tiny model of the Cathedral of Magdeburg, which he founded, to Christ (fig. 3).[19] The development of ruler sacrality is still nascent in this image—Otto is the smallest figure on the relief, and he is ushered along by Saint Maurice, patron saint of his empire. Yet it is a pictorial representation of piety and divine favor, not to mention Otto's power and protection of his realm.[20] Saint Maurice was a warrior saint and the patron saint of Magdeburg, where Otto founded his cathedral "as the ecclesiastical focus of his wars against the Slavs," a shrine to which "the military resources of heaven would be harnessed."[21] Additionally, although his insignia are not present here, Saint Maurice is traditionally depicted holding the Holy Lance, another important symbol of the Ottonian court and Ottonian military success over the pagans. Although Otto is the smallest figure on this plaque, it illustrates another key change in how the Saxons were thinking about kingship. Notwithstanding the Germanic idea of the king as *primus inter pares*, which Henry I so embraced and the nobles still clung to, the Ottonian kings were consciously representing themselves as intercessors between heaven and earth, through pictorial imagery as well as the introduction of royal unction and coronation.[22] That relationship is depicted in the ivory plaque discussed here.

There are sixteen extant plaques from the original grouping known collectively as the Magdeburg ivories. Fourteen depict scenes from the life of Christ,

---

19. "Plaque with Otto I Presenting the Cathedral of Magdeburg [Ottonian]," New York, Metropolitan Museum of Art, 41.100.157. For discussion of the plaque, see Mayr-Harting, *Ottonian Book Illumination*, 1:180–81; Schramm and Mütherich, 141–42, 282 (plate 68); Hermann Fillitz, *Die Gruppe der Magdeburger Elfenbeintafeln* (Mainz: Philipp von Zabern, 2001), 29–31. There has been debate over whether this ivory depicts Otto I or Otto II; for an overview of the arguments, as well as further justification for accepting it as a representation of Otto I, see Charles T. Little, "The Magdeburg Ivory Group: A Tenth Century New Testament Narrative Cycle" (PhD diss., New York University, 1977), 111–17. Schramm and Mütherich (141–42) identified it as a depiction of Otto I.

20. Mayr-Harting, *Ottonian Book Illumination*, 1:180. See also Fillitz, 29–31.

21. Mayr-Harting, *Ottonian Book Illumination*, 1:12.

22. Bagge, 90. The imperial crown testifies to this relationship as well. While the ornate cross and arch of the crown as it appears today were later additions (probably from the first quarter of the eleventh century), the original part of the crown dates from somewhere between 960 and 980, in the reign of either Otto I or Otto II. There are eight hinged panels, four of which have enamel plaques depicting biblical scenes. Three Old Testament leaders are depicted (King Solomon, the priest and prophet Ezekiel, and King David), with a fourth plaque depicting Christ in Majesty, flanked by two angels and declaring, "P(ER) ME REGES REGNANT." Thus, the imperial crown asserts the place of the emperor of the West in universal history, part of the succession of great biblical kings, and attests to his special relationship with God and the church. For a detailed catalog description of the crown, see Michael Peter, "Otto der Große und die Erneuerung des Römischen Reiches," in Puhle and Köster, 560–63.

Fig. 3. "Plaque with Otto I Presenting the Cathedral of Magdeburg [Ottonian]," New York, Metropolitan Museum of Art, 41.100.157.

and two portray symbolic scenes with direct significance to the development of Ottonian ruling ideologies. One of these symbolic scenes is on the donation plaque mentioned above. The other is a *traditio legis* (giving of the law) representation, showing Christ's mission to Peter and Paul.[23] The *traditio* plaque takes

23. "Traditio legis et clavium," cover of MS Theol. Lat. fol. 1, Staatsbibliothek zu Berlin; Fillitz, 32–33.

a common Carolingian Old Testament motif—the giving of law[24]—and puts it in a definitively New Testament context that is specifically Ottonian.[25] Indeed, one art historian has noted that there is "no historical evidence to indicate an interest in Old Testament narrative cycles in Ottonian painting,"[26] which suggests that in artistic representation, the Ottonian interest lay decidedly with the New Testament. It also may suggest how the Ottonians saw themselves as being positioned within history: the Carolingians were emperors of the old empire, and the Ottonians were emperors of the new empire, a continuation of the history that began with Christ. Ottonian art yields other similar representations of the *traditio legis* tradition, representations that are closely related to and indeed conceptualize the combined political and ecclesiastical goals of the Ottonians.[27]

Charles Little has observed that dedication plaques in early Christian art "are often composed in much the same way as the *traditio legis et clavum* so that the two images almost become interchangeable both in form and content," but he notes that there are no extant examples in the intervening centuries between the late antique examples he cites and these Ottonian examples that "correspond so exactly."[28] He additionally and tantalizingly suggests that these two Ottonian ivories were carved in a deliberate imitation of the late antique examples, because the image of Christ seated on an orb "preserves and personifies the meaning in precise physical form."[29] This meaning is based on a relationship with the biblical verse from Isaiah 66:1: "Thus saith the Lord, The heaven is my throne, and the earth is my footstool: where is the house that ye build unto me? and where is the place of my rest?"[30] Compare Matthew 5:34–35: "But I say

24. For the importance of Old Testament models in Carolingian ruling philosophy, see Paul Kershaw, *Peaceful Kings: Peace, Power, and the Early Medieval Political Imagination* (Oxford: Oxford University Press, 2011), esp. 137–39. The most obvious literary example of this is, of course, Einhard's comparison of Charlemagne to David throughout his *Vita Caroli Magni*. But the metaphor was used extensively as one of the Old Testament parallels employed by the Carolingians. Mary Garrison notes, "By the 790s, Old Testament comparisons had gained a new prominence and a new public at the Carolingian court. Typology was reified, and the Bible's role as an authoritative text was such that biblical law could be applied to the Franks in the *Admonitio Generalis* and Charlemagne himself could be addressed as David rather than merely compared to him" ("The Franks as the New Israel? Education for an Identity from Pippin to Charlemagne," in *The Uses of the Past in the Early Middle Ages*, ed. Yitzhak Hen and Matthew Innes [Cambridge: Cambridge University Press, 2000], 159).

25. The *traditio legis* motif occurs only rarely in Carolingian art, with only three certain occurrences known (Amy L. Vandersall, "Two Carolingian Ivories from the Morgan Collection in the Metropolitan Museum of Art," *Metropolitan Museum Journal* 6 [1972]: 33). See also Armin F. Bergmeier, "The *Traditio Legis* in Late Antiquity and Its Afterlives in the Middle Ages," *Gesta* 56.1 (Spring 2017), 42–44.

26. Little, 30.

27. Ibid., 104.

28. Ibid., 121–22.

29. Ibid., 122.

30. Isa 66:1, KJV.

unto you, Swear not at all; neither by heaven; for it is God's throne: Nor by the earth; for it is his footstool."[31] As Little points out,

> the sphere-circle motif becomes the perfect means for visualizing this relationship between heaven and earth. Yet the figure of Christ in the Metropolitan Museum [Magdeburg donation] plaque is enthroned upon a garland wreath which decisively departs from the traditional form of the sphere-circle. Nevertheless, the physical and iconographic association between the two forms is close enough to cause no problem. The wreath enriches the meaning because it is a universal sign of the triumph of Christ, His immortality and eternity.[32]

In this case, Little does not take his analysis far enough. The laurel wreath is a sign of triumph but represents both the triumph of Christ and the triumph of Otto. Otto ordered construction to begin on the cathedral at Magdeburg after his success against the Hungarians in 955 but before his coronation as emperor in 962. This construction, designed as a show of Otto's strength and power, was deliberately grand in style, with marble pillars and other building materials imported from Italy, just as Charlemagne had done for his palace at Aachen.[33] It seems reasonable to assume that the wreath on which Christ sits in the dedication ivory is not only Christ's victory wreath but that of Otto as well. The laurel wreath also signified peace, and a peace achieved through a powerful king and his victories would have been an easy association.

Otto II also is displayed in ivories. While the more famous one is the Byzantine plaque commemorating his marriage to the Byzantine princess Theophanu (fig. 4), a more interesting one is held in the collections of the Castello Sforzesco in Milan.[34] On the latter, a Christ in Majesty is flanked by Saint Mary on his left and Saint Maurice on his right. Kneeling at his feet are Otto II, Theophanu, and the young Otto III (fig. 5).[35] The sanctity of the entire family is implied, with

31. Matt 5:34–35, KJV.

32. Little, 107–8. The carving master of the Magdeburg ivories discussed above, representing the *traditio legis* and the Magdeburg Cathedral presentation, has another *Maiestas Domini* ivory attributed to him that depicts Christ in Majesty, seated within an oval-shaped laurel wreath (suggesting both a victory wreath and a mandorla), with the Gospel writers' symbols in the four corners (Fillitz, 23).

33. Little, 198–99.

34. "Otto II and Theophanu Crowned by Christ," ca. 982–83, Paris, Musée de Cluny; "Ivory Plaque with Family of Emperor Otto," ca. 965/983, Collections of the Castello Sforzesco, Milan. Schramm and Mütherich (144) discuss both of these objects.

35. Once thought to portray Otto I and Adelheid, most scholars now consider this ivory to portray Otto II and Theophanu. See Fillitz, 5; Kristen M. Collins, "Visualizing Mary: Innovation and Exegesis in Ottonian Manuscript Illumination" (PhD diss., University of Texas at Austin, 2007),

Fig. 4. "Otto II and Theophanu Crowned by Christ," ca. 982–983, Paris, Musée de Cluny. (Granger / Granger Collection. All rights reserved.)

Fig. 5. "Ivory Plaque with Family of Emperor Otto," ca. 965/983, Collections of the Castello Sforzesco, Milan. (© age fotostock. All rights reserved.)

the special added protection of Mary over the household and of Maurice over the empire, an empire suggested only by the presence of Otto II in conjunction with the empire's patron saint.

With Otto II, we also see our first imperial ruler portrait in a manuscript.[36] This is the first pictorial representation that will lead to the great leap in ideology portrayed in the Aachen Gospels by the miniature depicting Emperor Otto III Seated in Majesty, discussed above. The image of Otto II was a detached miniature included in a copy of the *Registrum Gregorii* donated by Egbert, archbishop of Trier, to Trier Cathedral. It is believed to be a commemorative portrait, as it is accompanied by a poem lamenting Otto II's death in 983.[37] Otto II is seated under a baldachin, wearing his crown and holding the staff and orb of his imperial office (fig. 6).[38] Four women, representing Germania, Francia, Italia, and Alamannia, offer tribute.[39] There is a subtext to the imagery as well. The baldachin has classical columns, with Doric bases and Corinthian capitals, subtly reinforcing Otto's title of Roman emperor. The orb he holds looks very much like a Eucharistic wafer, and in contrast to many images of imperial majesty where the orb is displayed on the palm of the hand, Otto cradles it in his left arm. Otto's connections to God and to Rome, his dominion as emperor and king, and his role as protector of Christendom are all embodied in this image. That it is an image commemorating the death of Otto II might also suggest a more concrete realization of the dual nature of kingship à la Kantorowicz: the body natural may have passed away, but the body politic is eternal and immu-

---

97; Adolph Goldschmidt, *Die Elfenbeinskulpturen aus der Zeit der karolinginschen und sächsischen Kaiser, VIII.-XI. Jahrhundert*, vol. 2 (Berlin, 1918), cat. no. 2; Erich Kubach and Victor H. Elbern, *L'art de l'empire au debut du Moyen Âge: Les arts Carolingien et Ottonien* (Paris: Editions Albin Michel, 1973), 207–8.

36. "Otto II Receiving Homage from Four Provinces of the Empire," ca. 983, Registrum Gergorii, Trier Cathedral, Chantilly, Musée Condé. See Schramm and Mütherich, 147–48. Manuscript production flourished under the Ottos, and it is impossible to know how many manuscripts with ruler portraits have not survived. One lost manuscript we do know about was a luxury volume that Otto II gave to Magdeburg and that had a portrayal of himself and Theophanu worked in gold. Details such as what kind of book the volume was and whether the image appeared on it or in it are unknown (Mayr-Harting, *Ottonian Illumination*, 1:42). The relatively large number of ruler portraits that exist for the Ottonians are striking when compared with the three that are known for the entire Anglo-Saxon period before the Norman Conquest of England. But there was a contemporary development, in both realms, of two other royal iconographic motifs, the crowned Christ and the crowned Magi; see Robert Deshman, "*Christus rex et magi reges*: Kingship and Christology in Ottonian and Anglo-Saxon Art," *Frühmittelalterliche Studien* 10 (1976): 367–405. Deshman argues that these motifs also reflect ruling ideologies, specifically the idea of imperial authority, and that the Anglo-Saxons were equally adept at manipulating images to express a specific idea of regnal power, a "quasi-imperial rulership" (400–401).

37. De Hamel, 58–60.

38. "Otto II Receiving Homage from Four Provinces of the Empire," ca. 983, Registrum Gregorii, Trier Cathedral, Chantilly, Musée Condé, ms. 14bis.

39. De Hamel, 60.

Fig. 6. "Otto II Receiving Homage from Four Provinces of the Empire," ca. 983, Registrum Gregorii, Trier Cathedral, Chantilly, Musée Condé. (© age fotostock. All rights reserved.)

table and continues to exist as the rightful heir to the Roman Empire and the continued protector of Christendom.

With the reign of Otto III, we find large numbers of extant imperial portrayals in manuscripts. While some of the pictures have recognizable precedents (such as the Prayer Book of Otto III, with two facing pages featuring the emperor performing proskynesis, on the left-hand verso, to a Christ in Majesty, on the facing recto—comparable to a similar image in the Prayer Book of Charles the Bald),[40] many, as with the startling image in the Aachen Gospels discussed earlier, suggest new ideas about the nature of the emperor and a changing perception of his relationship to God. Two images with marked similarity to the miniature of Otto II are from the Gospel Book of Otto III and the Bamberg Apocalypse.[41]

The Gospel Book of Otto III is a breathtaking luxury volume that still retains its original jeweled binding. The miniatures include full-page illuminated initials, scenes from the life of Christ, and Evangelist portraits—all of which are to be expected. According to one scholar, "dominating all" of the other miniatures is "a pair of facing paintings showing the peoples of the world adoring Otto" (fig. 7).[42] Otto is enthroned holding the orb and scepter of empire, while the personified Sclavinia, Germania, Gallia, and Roma bear their offerings of tribute and bow before him. While the image is not significantly different in content from the memorial miniature of Otto II, the later portrait's placement as the volume's only portrayal of a person who is not an Evangelist or part of the life of Christ automatically elevates the sacrality of Otto III. He has become an integral part of the story of Christendom.

The imperial portrayal in the Bamberg Apocalypse adds another dimension to the sacrality of the emperor (fig. 8). It shows Otto III seated on an upper plane, the same size and level as Saints Peter and Paul, who together crown him, while personifications of the kingly virtues offer their riches below.[43] Again, Otto III is portrayed as an intimate character in the story of Christendom, receiving his office directly from the representatives of God. The presence of this

40. Gebetbuch Ottos III., ca. 984–85, Mainz Königsgebetbuch München, Bayerische Staatsbibliothek; "Charles in Proskynesis before the Crucifixion," Prayerbook of Charles the Bald, ca. 850–60, Munich, Schloss Nymphenburg, fols. 38v–39r. See Hermann Hauke and Elisabeth Klemm, *Das Gebetbuch Ottos III. Kommentar zur Faksimile-Edition der Handschrift Clm 30111 der Bayerischen Staatsbibliothek München* (Lucerne: Faksimile Verlag, 2008), for extensive commentary on the provenance and unique aspects of this manuscript.

41. "Personifications of Rome and Provinces of the Empire Approaching Otto III" and "Otto III Seated in Majesty," Gospel Book of Otto III, ca. 998–1001, Munich, Bayerische Staatsbibliothek, Clm. 4453, fols. 23v–24r.

42. De Hamel, 60–62. See also Schramm and Mütherich, 155–56.

43. "Otto III Crowned by Saints Peter and Paul and Personifications of the Kingly Virtues," Bamberg Apocalypse, probably 1001–2, Bamberg Staatsbibliothek, Msc. Bibl. 140, fol. 59v.

Fig. 7. "Personifications of Rome and Provinces of the Empire Approaching Otto III" and "Otto III Seated in Majesty," Gospel Book of Otto III, ca. 998–1001, Munich, Bayerische Staatsbibliothek, Clm. 4453, fols. 23v–24r.

Fig. 8. "Otto III Crowned by Saints Peter and Paul and Personifications of the Kingly Virtues," Bamberg Apocalypse, probably 1001–2, Bamberg Staatsbibliothek, Msc. Bibl. 140, fol. 59v. (Photograph by Gerald Raab.)

image in an apocalypse created right at the millennium, combined with his portrayal among the saints, doubtless contributed to a feeling of the emperor's authority transcending ordinary time. A different kind of transcendence is suggested by an image of Otto III being crowned by the Virgin Mary that appears in the Warmund Sacramentary (fig. 9), which also includes a second crowning image and the inclusion of a rare German *ordo*.[44] In addition to the rather obvious suggestion of divine grace in the bestowal of the imperial crown by the Virgin, Robert Deshman has argued that this rather neglected manuscript is actually of paramount significance in its emphasis on the importance of the imperial coronation ritual and that the occurrence of anointing imagery throughout the sacramentary is not a coincidence but relates directly to the liturgical consecration of emperors.[45]

Also from the reign of Otto III, the first page of the book of Matthew in the *Evangelia Ottonis* contains a highly ornate initial page for its *Liber generationis* (fig. 10). The four portraits of Otto III are remarkable, creating the illusion by their placement of the finials on a cross. Each portrait is in a golden medallion, a halo, and has an inscription proclaiming Otto's name and titles.[46] The only other portraits in this text are the four Evangelist symbols, in similar style, on the opening page of Luke. Again, it is difficult to miss the significance of the portraiture and the placement. As part of the *Liber generationis* page, Otto is tied directly to the house of David and the genealogical line of Jesus Christ himself. Otto's halos suggest divinity, and the placement and style beg a direct parallel to the Evangelists depicted in Luke—all four of them. When considered in light of other texts in Matthew, the emperor's picture here, where one would

44. "The Virgin Mary Crowns Otto III," Sacramentary of Bishop Warmund, ca. 1000, Ivrea, Bibl. Capitolare, cod. 86, fol. 160v. Pierre Alain Mariaux argues for a date between 980-996 for the sacramentary ("Warmund d'Ivrée et ses images: Politique et création iconographique autour de l'an mil," [PhD diss., Université de Lausanne, 1997], 248).

45. Robert Deshman. "Otto III and the Warmund Sacramentary: A Study in Political Theology," *Zeitschrift für Kunstgeschichte* 34.1 (1971): 6. Karl Leyser reminds us that "the creation and display of such books partly renewed and partly enlarged upon royal coronation ceremonies as did the crown-wearings on feast days" (*Rule and Conflict in an Early Medieval Society: Ottonian Saxony* [Bloomington: Indiana University Press, 1979], 78). See also Mariaux, 60–68. For an overview of the history and historiography of the Warmund Sacramentary, see Evan A. Gatti, "In a Space Between: Warmund of Ivrea and the Problem of (Italian) Ottonian Art," *Peregrinations: A Journal of Medieval Art and Architecture* 3.1 (2010): 8–48.

46. "Frontispiece to Matthew," *Evangelia Ottonis*, ca. late tenth century, John Rylands University Library, Latin MS 98, fol. 16r. The inscriptions are "ROMANE. R. P. DIVI MEM OTTO IMPER. AVG.," "XPIANE RELIGIONIS ET ROMANE R. P. OTTO IMP. AVG.," "D. CORONATVS ROMANE R. P. OTTO IMPER. AVG.," and "XPIANE RELIGIONIS ET ROMANE. R. P. OTTO IMP." (Montague Rhodes James, *A Descriptive Catalogue of the Latin Manuscripts in the John Rylands Library at Manchester*, vol. 1 [Manchester: Manchester University Press, 1921], 178). Without elaborating or extrapolating, De Hamel (60) notes that the inscriptions proclaim the "name of Otto, emperor of Christian religion and of the Roman people."

Fig. 9. "The Virgin Mary Crowns Otto III," Sacramentary of Bishop Warmund, ca. 1000, Ivrea, Bibl. Capitolare, cod. 86, fol. 160v. (© age fotostock. All rights reserved.)

Fig. 10. "Frontispiece to Matthew," *Evangelia Ottonis*, ca. late tenth century, John Rylands University Library, Latin MS 98, fol. 16r. (Copyright of the University of Manchester.)

expect Evangelist pictures, suggests his intimate inclusion in the story of Christianity. The medallions bear an unmistakable resemblance to Roman coins, on which Carolingian gold coins were modeled; this similarity ties in very neatly with Otto III's desire to portray himself as the progenitor of a Roman *renovatio*[47] and brings us back to the portrayal of Otto III in the Aachen Gospels.

The two decades of difference between Kantorowicz's dating of the miniature to circa 975, early in the rule of Otto I, and later scholars' dating of it to circa 996, coinciding with Otto III's anointing as Roman emperor, makes sense in light of later scholarship about the nature of Ottonian ruling philosophy. The portrayal of Otto III as having been elevated into the realm of heaven and literally in contact with God is described by Kantorowicz as representing "the emperor's two natures, human and divine, or rather, in the language of that age, a ruler 'human by nature and divine by grace.'"[48] The veil is identified as the curtain of the tabernacle that divides the earth from heaven.[49] Here, it also divides the emperor, suggesting that he has entered into heaven—he exists literally in two realms.[50] Whereas the Carolingians conceived of a theocentric emperor modeled on and heir to David, the Ottonians had achieved, in the Aachen representation, the pictorial representation of liturgical kingship, a rule based on the idea of a God-man.[51] This stunning evolution of a philosophy of rule from the consensual kingship of Henry I to a ruler physically embodying the will of God had not yet happened in the reign of Otto I but was pretty well formed in the minds of the Ottonians by the time his grandson was anointed emperor. Otto III consciously tried to emulate both Charlemagne and Constantine I in his rule over the Holy Roman Empire and was characterized by his tutor Gerbert, the future Pope Sylvester II, as a man "Greek by birth, Roman by empire,"

47. Most tenth-century German coins do not have images of the emperor on them, but those that do show a transition from portraying the emperor in profile, under Otto I, to a basileus image, in the coinage of Ottos II and III. In contrast, the Carolingians regularly included ruler images on their coinage between 813 and 818 (Ildar H. Garipzanov, *The Symbolic Language of Authority in the Carolingian World* [Leiden: Brill, 2008], 208). In Carolingian pictorial art, we do not see the direct depiction of rulers until the ninth century (Ibid., 224).

48. Kantorowicz, *King's Two Bodies*, 65.

49. Ibid., 67.

50. Ibid., 67. For further discussion of the implications of this image, see Hagen Keller, "Herrscherbild und Herrschaftslegitimation: Zur Deutung der ottonischen Denkmäler," in *Ottonische Königsherrschaft: Organisation und Legitimation königlicher Macht* (Darmstadt: Wissenschaftliche Buchgesellschaft, 2002), 173–77.

51. Kantorowicz, *King's Two Bodies*, 77–78. Hagen Keller argues that this kind of portraiture was unique to the Ottonians; that the ruler never transcends the threshold between the earthly and heavenly realms in Carolingian art ("Herrscherbild," 173), and that such depiction ended in the late eleventh century, with the Investiture Controversy and a new ideology of kingship ("Grundlagen ottonischer Königsherrschaft," in *Reich und Kirche vor dem Investiturstreit: Vorträge beim wissenschaftlichen Kolloquium aus Anlass des 80. Geburtstags von Gerd Tellenbach*, ed. Karl Schmid [Sigmaringen: Thorbecke, 1985], 30–31, 34).

who sought, "as if by hereditary right," to "recapture for himself the treasures of Greek and Roman wisdom."[52] When one considers additional customs initiated by Otto III, such as feasting alone and apart on a dais,[53] emphasizing his quite literal elevated separation from his magnates, we see how this royal propaganda begun under the reign of Otto I was paying off. "The sacral sphere," as Leyser calls it, had fully enveloped the ruler; we saw the initial stages of this sacrality being formed under Ottos I and II, "beginning with [the emperor's] unction and constantly reaffirmed by crown wearings, festival coronations, and other liturgical honors paid to him, thus help[ing] to set him off against his excluded kin."[54] By the time of Otto III, this "setting off" had become literal, represented by his physical distance at feasts and his sacral distance in the miniature in the Aachen Gospels.

The representation of sacral kingship in Ottonian ruler portraits was used by the last of the Ottonian emperors as well. Henry II continued to utilize ruler images as a way to legitimize his rule and pictorially render the divine nature of his kingship. One coronation image in particular conveys this idea. The Regensburg Sacramentary (also known as the Sacramentary of Henry II) has a magnificent image of Henry II (fig. 11).[55] Henry is standing, not yet enthroned, flanked by two saintly warrior bishops, Emmeram of Regensburg and Ulrich of Augsburg, who support his arms in emulation of Moses versus the Amalekites. Christ, in a mandorla, places the crown on Henry's head, while two angels hand Henry a lance and a sword. Similarly to the image of Otto III in the Aachen Gospels, the head and shoulders of Henry occupies the divine mandorla with Christ, the act of coronation literally elevating Henry above the earthly sphere. Stefan Weinfurter has convincingly argued that this portrait, created at the start of Henry's reign and at a monastery that produced his closest advisors, "reflects the conception of rulership found in the closest circle around Henry II."[56] He further argues that this is the first true coronation portrait, showing the actual moment of king-making. This is an important distinction, connecting this particular image to Henry's program of legitimization. He was not a descendant of the Ottos, and his succession was not uncontested. By suggesting two Old Testament concepts of royal succession—*paterna successio* and *hereditarium ius*—

52. Judith Herrin, *The Formation of Christendom* (Princeton, NJ: Princeton University Press, 1987), 478–49, quoting from H. P. Lattin, *The Letters of Gerbert, with His Papal Privileges as Sylvester II* (New York, 1961), 296–97 (no. 231).

53. Althoff, *Family, Friends, and Followers*, 153.

54. K. Leyser, *Rule and Conflict*, 105; see also Mayr-Harting, *Church and Cosmos*, 4.

55. "Crowning and Investiture of Henry II," Regensburg Sacramentary (Sacramentary of Henry II), Munich, Bayerische Staatsbibliothek, Clm. 4456, fol. 11r.

56. Weinfurter, "Authority and Legitimation," 24.

Fig. 11. "Crowning and Investiture of Henry II," Regensburg Sacramentary (Sacramentary of Henry II), Munich, Bayerische Staatsbibliothek, Clm. 4456, fol. 11r.

and the New Testament idea of sacral kingship, the image demonstrates his legitimacy as the successor to Otto III. *Paterna successio*, succession through the paternal line, is demonstrated by the investiture with the Holy Lance, a symbol of Ottonian kingship.[57] More than just a piece of the royal regalia, the lance was a central identifying symbol of the right to rule. The *hereditarium ius*, the hereditary right to kingship that originates with God, is made explicit through the intercession of Saints Emmeram and Ulrich, who take Henry and guide him to his coronation, performed by Christ as Henry co-inhabits the heavenly sphere.[58]

The coronation image of Henry II appears on the recto side of the folio; the Regensburg Sacramentary is also remarkable for having a second ruler image. On the verso side of the same folio is a picture of Henry II enthroned. This portrait reiterates many of the elements found in a late Carolingian picture of an enthroned Charles the Bald.[59] All of the figures surrounding Henry in this image are earthly subjects, in direct contrast to the saintly and heavenly inhabitants of the coronation picture. In lieu of angels, figures representing the tributary peoples surround him, and his throne is flanked by two attendants in short cloaks.[60] But under the baldachin, the hand of God extends a blessing over the crowned head of the king, with the crown residing in the veil separating heaven from earth. While emphasizing the earthly realm over which Henry rules, the picture reinforces the previous image's portrayal of his kingship as decidedly sacral.

The portraiture of Otto III and Henry II also includes images with less subtle divisions between the heavenly and earthly realms. The illumination of Otto III in the Bamberg Apocalypse, as we have already observed, is horizontally bisected, with the enthroned Otto III in the upper plane.[61] Similarly, a coronation image of Henry II and Cunigund in the Pericopes of Henry II has clearly delineated upper and lower realms (fig. 12).[62] In the upper realm, echoing the ivory commemorating the marriage of Otto II and Theophanu, an elevated Christ places crowns on the heads of the much smaller images of Henry and Cunigund, while Saints Peter and Paul usher them forward. Below, tribute peoples offer gifts, while the feminine personifications of Germania, Roma, and

57. Ibid., 28.

58. Ibid., 26. See also E. Garrison, 138–46, for further discussion of the Regensburg Sacramentary in general and of this sequence specifically.

59. Keller, "Herrscherbild," 177.

60. Ibid.

61. "Otto III Crowned by Saints Peter and Paul and Personifications of the Kingly Virtues," Bamberg Apocalypse, probably 1001–2, Bamberg Staatsbibliothek, Msc. Bibl. 140, fol. 59v.

62. Dedication page, "Henry II and Cunigund Presented to Christ," Pericope Book of Henry II, Munich, Bayerische Staatsbibliothek, Clm. 4452, fol. 2r.

Gallia offer homage.[63] Again, the images of these last two Ottonian rulers quite deliberately portray them as separate and above those they ruled, as inhabiting a sacral sphere that bestowed the legitimacy and authority of kingly power—a physical portrayal of that which cannot be seen, the representation of the divine endowment of sacrality.[64] That portrayals of liturgical kingship or the ideas they convey had become self-conscious by the time of Henry II is suggested by the *arenga*, the preambles, in the diplomas of the last Ottonian king and emperor. John Bernhardt has demonstrated that numerous charters and diplomas issued during the reign of Henry II utilize phrasing in various forms to convey ideas of sacral kingship that adhered to the issuing ruler, suggesting that Henry was sincere about fulfilling the obligations of being endowed with liturgical kingship as he understood them.[65] Henry's additional need to legitimize his right to the throne, emphasized through the coronation image in the Regensburg Sacramentary, was also emphasized in his diplomas. The *narratio* in a charter issued in 1003 for the bishopric of Strasbourg explicitly addresses issues such as his close relationship with and lawful election to succeed Otto III.[66] Weinfurter has argued that this charter outlines the precise way that Henry was creating a legitimizing strategy for his succession, using the coronation *ordo* of Mainz as a source of sacralizing elements, as well as his kinship ties to Otto III (both as his second cousin and his *Königsnähe* to the young king).[67] Weinfurter's argument is important with regard to how we understand these ruler portraits as part of an imperial program. If we assert that the ruler images of Henry II that we have discussed here were the visual articulation of a deliberately conceived agenda, and if we further suggest that these ideas were echoed in contemporary literary works, such as Thietmar of Merseburg's *Chronicon*, we must consider the likelihood that the artistic programs of the Ottos were equally thoughtful, deliberate implementations of how they were reconceptualizing kingship.

63. See E. Garrison, 128–31, for further discussion regarding this miniature.

64. Keller, "Herrscherbild," 168.

65. Bernhardt, "King Henry II," 43.

66. Bernhardt, "King Henry II," 40–41; DD HII 34.

67. Stefan Weinfurter, "Der Anspruch Heinrichs II. auf die Königsherrschaft 1002," in *Papstgeschichte und Landesgeschichte: Festschrift für Hermann Jakobs zum 65. Geburtstag*, ed. Joachim Dahlhaus and Armin Kohnle (Cologne: Böhlau, 1995), 121–34; Stefan Weinfurter, "Sakralkönigtum und Herrschaftsbegründung um die Jahrtausendwende: Die Kaiser Otto III. und Heinrich II. in ihren Bildern," in *Bilder erzählen Geschichte*, Helmut Altrichter, ed. (Freiburg im Breisgau: Rombach Verlag, 1995), 84–87. Weinfurter's thesis is further supported by Eliza Garrison, who argues that Henry II deliberately recontextualized the memorialization of his predecessor by spoliating and redistributing treasures that Otto III had made to Aachen, such as the Gospels of Otto III, which he presented to Bamberg: "Henry II displayed a clear and astute awareness of the representation value of such works and an awareness of the representational value of collections in general" (155, 171).

Fig. 12. Dedication page, "Henry II and Cunigund Presented to Christ," Pericope Book of Henry II, Munich, Bayerische Staatsbibliothek, Clm. 4452, fol. 2r.

While the Ottonians quite deliberately "built up the representation of their kingship as something God-given, sacrosanct and awe-demanding,"[68] that does not mean that this representation was automatically accepted by their magnates, who still felt entitled to the access and privileges they received under the traditional Germanic model of consensual kingship. The feuding that broke out under Otto I when he tried to reassert royal prerogative and avoided *amicitia* agreements has already been noted. Other breaks with tradition, such as Otto III's habit of feasting apart from his men, was also met with grumbling from the nobility. Communal celebrations including eating and drinking together were important medieval rituals that created or solidified bonds between men, and Otto's separation emphasized that the era of rule by *primi inter pares* had truly ended.[69]

Feasting and *Adventus* Rituals

Ruler portraits were not the only means through which the Ottonians promoted and depicted their claim on sacral kingship. While the images painted in manuscripts and carved into ivories would perhaps have been seen by members of and visitors to the imperial court, cathedrals, and royal monasteries, the performance of larger rituals would have conveyed this ideological leap to a larger audience. Many of the rituals that were associated with their rule were highly visual public displays of power that reinforced the idea of sacral kingship, such as the royal *iter*, the *adventus*, feasting, and crown wearings. The *iter*, as a formal assertion of a king's prerogative, was also tied to the liturgical calendar, as the king and his retinue customarily celebrated feasts at specific stops every year. That many of those stops were at royal monasteries further connected the king to the sacral realm. The *adventus*, as a formal entrance of an emperor into a city, was reminiscent of Roman imperial custom, a highly visible and public display of a people's acceptance of their king's supremacy.

The feast, as a political tool, entailed rulers and great men publicly and ritually celebrating alliances and friendships, engaging in gift exchanges, and demonstrating their power and legitimacy.[70] As centers for ritual behavior, feasts

68. K. Leyser, *Rule and Conflict*, 90.

69. Althoff, *Family, Friends, and Followers*, 153. William Miller (*Bloodtaking and Peacemaking: Feud, Law, and Society in Saga Iceland* [Chicago: University of Chicago Press, 1990], 30) gives a compelling description of exactly how important seating arrangements at feasts could be in medieval society, noting that "it is not hard to discern why festive meals are charged with energized significance." Seating arrangements were a public display of men's states of honor, and changes would have been noted as being socially significant.

70. Scholars have noted the importance of feasting as a communal and political event. For

were points where a disruption of that ritual space could symbolize much more than just bad manners.[71] Timothy Reuter once remarked that "the tenth and eleventh centuries were the age of the *convivium*, the ritual banquet."[72] These *convivia*, feasts, were important political events, public demonstrations of relationships, including hierarchies of authority, friendships and alliances, and assertions of consensus.[73]

In the year 936, according to the monk and contemporary chronicler Widukind of Corvey, Otto I was crowned and anointed king at Aachen. After a long and very detailed description of Otto's coronation ceremony, Widukind writes,

> After the praise of the Lord and mass had been solemnly celebrated, the king went down to the palace and took his place at the marble table, ornate with its royal panoply, where he sat with the bishops and all the

---

example, Heinrich Fichtenau noted that banquets (as opposed to daily common meals) were to be an external manifestation of "political potency," an "initiation into a society or the establishment of friendly ties between equals" (*Living in the Tenth Century: Mentalities and Social Orders*, trans. Patrick Geary [Chicago: University of Chicago Press, 1993], 59). Timothy Reuter noted that the ritual of feasting routinely accompanied important events (*Germany in the Early Middle Ages, 800–1056* [New York: Longman, 1991], 228). We see this, for example, when Thietmar of Merseburg entered the religious life and when he was elevated to bishop; both events were celebrated by feasts, the former thrown by his father, the latter by another bishop (Thietmar of Merseburg, *Chronicon* 4.16, 6.40, in *Thietmari Merseburgensis Episcopi Chronicon*, ed. Robert Holtzmann, MGH SRG 9 [Berlin: Weidmannsche Buchhandlung, 1935], 150, 322–25). Althoff, too, has noted the importance of communal eating and drinking in declaring or celebrating personal or communal bonds (Althoff, *Family, Friends, and Followers*, 152–53). Thus, we see feasting as a ritual performance that, through repetition, declared and reinforced the bonds between men or groups. See also Christina Pössel, "The Magic of Early Medieval Ritual," *Early Medieval Europe* 17.2 (2009): 111–25. Attendees at a feast thrown by someone else (e.g., guests at a wedding), might use that neutral location to conduct business (Miller, 105). The people to whom you claimed kinship for the purpose of invitations to feasts might not necessarily be the same members of kinship groups you would rely on for purposes like lawsuits or help in claiming compensation (ibid., 156).

71. Lars Hermanson gestures to the complexity of feasts: comprised of numerous symbolic elements, such as welcomes, toasts, and gift giving, each part of a feast publicly "played a part in communicating, displaying, and confirming power relations" (introduction to *Rituals, Performatives, and Political Order in Northern Europe, c. 650–1350*, ed. Wojtek Jezierski et al. [Turnhout: Brepols, 2015], 23). Vidar Palsson goes one step further, emphasizing the feast itself as "a language of power" ("Power and Political Communication: Feasting and Gift Giving in Medieval Iceland" [PhD diss., University of California, Berkeley, 2010], 44).

72. Reuter, *Germany in the Early Middle Ages*, 228. The ritual of feasting, generally and in the Ottonian court specifically, has been the subject of much study and scholarly dialogue See, for example, Gerd Althoff, "Feste und Bündnis," in *Feste und Feiern im Mittelalter*, ed. Detlef Altenburg, Jörg Jarnut, and Hans-Hugo Steinhoff (Sigmaringen: Thorbecke, 1991), 29–38; Karl Hauck, "Rituelle Speisegemeinschaft im 10. und 11. Jahrhundert," *Studium Generale* 3.11 (1950): 611–21; Detlef Altenburg, Jörg Jarnut, and Hans-Hugo Steinhoff, eds., *Feste und Feiern im Mittelalter: Paderborner Symposion des Mediävistenverbandes* (Sigmaringen: Thorbecke, 1991); Hans-Werner Goetz, "Der 'rechte' Sitz. Die Symbolik von Rang und Herrschaft im hohen Mittelalter im Spiegel der Sitzordnung," in *Symbole des Alltags, Alltag der Symbole: Festschrift für Harry Kühnel zum 65. Geburtstag*, ed. Gertrud Blaschitz et al. (Graz: Akademische Druck- und Verlansanstalt, 1992), 11–47.

73. Hermanson, 5–6, 8.

> people. The dukes served. Duke Giselbert [of Lotharingia], whose authority encompassed this place, obtained all of the supplies. Eberhard [of Swabia] looked after the table. Hermann the Frank [i.e., of Franconia] served as cup-bearer. Arnulf [of Bavaria] was responsible for overseeing the horses [i.e. was marshal] and choosing the place to make camp. . . . After these festivities, the king honored each of the princes with an appropriate gift according to his royal munificence, and then dismissed the great crowd filled completely with joy.[74]

This feast and its symbology, the dukes' service to Otto at table, and the importance of its description of ritual behavior as a way to promote the legitimacy of Otto I have been treated extensively by scholars.[75] Descriptions of feasts, as easily recognizable good or bad rituals, appear within the political culture of contemporary narrative texts as a way for authors to signal a ruler's (or an aspiring ruler's) worthiness or unworthiness to rule.[76] Several elements in Widukind's description of Otto I's coronation feast reflect what one might expect of a good king or lord. For example, it was expected that a feast at a princely court not only be lavish with regard to food and drink but also amply represent the status

74. Widukind of Corvey, *Deeds of the Saxons*, ed. and trans. Bernard S. Bachrach and David S. Bachrach (Washington DC: Catholic University of America Press, 2014), 64–65; Widukind, *Res gestae Saxonicae* 2.2, 66–67: "Divina deinde laude dicta sacrificioque sollempniter celebrato descendebat rex ad palatium, et accedens ad mensam marmoream regio apparatu ornatam resedit cum pontificibus et omni populo; duces vero ministrabant. Lothariorum dux Isilberhtus, ad cuius potestatem locus ille pertinebat, omnia procurabat; Evurhardus mensae preerat, Herimannus Franco pincernis, Arnulfus equestri ordini et eligendis locandisque castris preerat . . . Rex autem post haec unumquemque principum iuxta munificentiam regalem congruenti sibi munere honorans cum omni hilaritate dimisit multitudinem." Bachrach and Bachrach note that the "praise of the Lord and mass" probably refers to the singing of *laudes* (64n14). The importance of Widukind's description itself should not be understated; as with the actual banquet (whatever it may have actually been like), the description by Widukind was intended to demonstrate "an external manifestation of political potency" (Fichtenau, 59).

75. See, for example, John W. Bernhardt, *Itinerant Kingship and Royal Monasteries in Early Medieval Germany, c. 936–1075* (Cambridge: Cambridge University Press, 1993), 5, where Bernhardt notes that Otto I began his reign from a much stronger position than had his father. Althoff has noted that symbolic services, such as service at a banquet, signify the "readiness [of a person] to serve the person to whom the symbolic service was addressed, from then on in real life" (Gerd Althoff, "Symbolic Communication and Medieval Order: Strengths and Weaknesses of Ambiguous Signs," in Jezierski et al., *Rituals, Performatives, and Political Order*, 65; Gerd Althoff and Christiane Witthöft, "Les services symboliques entre dignité et contrainte," *Annales* 58 [2003]: 1293–1318). Widukind's description of the feast exemplifies Althoff's assertion about ritual acts being symbolic of "whole sets of rights and duties"; providing service at table to a king was one way for nobility to publicly proclaim their relationships to their king, as well as their readiness to serve him (Hermanson, 24).

76. This idea is borrowed from Vidar Palsson, who invokes this formula in his treatment of Icelandic sagas ("Power and Political Communication," 41–42). Regarding ritual and performative aspects of feasts, see Hermanson, 4, 6; see also Buc, *Dangers of Ritual*, 4–5, arguing against anthropological readings of rituals described in texts, including feasts.

of that prince or king.[77] The table set for Otto was marble and decorated in a manner befitting a king, as Widukind is careful to point out.

Lest anyone underestimate the importance of these displays of wealth and finery, Liudprand of Cremona relates a tale that speaks to this point. The story concerns two men, Wido, who aspired to be king of the West Franks, and Odo, who the Franks chose to be king instead.

> It is said, however, that the Franks actually did not take Wido as their king on account of this. For when he was coming to the city of Metz, which shines most powerful in the kingdom of Lothar, Wido sent ahead his servant who was to prepare food for him in the royal style. And the bishop of Metz [was propositioned by the servant]: "If you give me at least a horse, I will arrange things [so that] King Wido will be satisfied with a third of all of this once he has feasted." When the bishop heard this, "it is not proper," he said, "for such a king to rule over us, who prepares himself a cheap ten-coin meal." And so it happened that they abandoned Wido and instead elected Odo.[78]

Even though this story is clearly spurious, the sentiment it conveys is not. Kings should promote a certain image and should not be satisfied with cheap meals. There was a definite sense of appropriateness about feasts, judged by the attendees and reflecting, for good or ill, on the host.[79] The eagerness of Wido's servant to get a kickback from the bishop may have signaled not just the servant's untrustworthiness but a lack of generosity of Wido toward his men, his cheapness in general. Feasts such as that at Otto I's coronation provided opportunities to

77. Fichtenau, 58.

78. Paolo Squatriti, ed. and trans., *The Complete Works of Liudprand of Cremona* (Washington, DC: Catholic University of America Press, 2007), 58–59; Liudprand of Cremona, *Antapodosis* 1.16, in *Liudprandi Cremonensis Opera Omnia*, ed. Paolo Chiesa, Corpus Christianorum (Turnhout: Brepols, 1998), 18–19: "Fertur autem hac occasione Francos Widonem regem sibi non adsumpsisse. Nam dum ad Metensem venturus esset urbem, quae potentissima in regno Lotharii claret, praemisit dapiferum suum, qui alimenta illi more regio praepararet. Metensis vero episcopus dum cibaria ei multa secundum Francorum consuetudinem ministraret, huiusmodi a dapifero resposa suscepit: 'Si equum saltem mihi dederis, faciam ut tercia obsonatus huius parte sit rex Wido contentus.' Quod episcopus audiens: 'Non decet—inquit—talem super nos regnare regem, qui decem dragmis vile sibi obsonium praeparat.' Sicque factum est ut Widonem desererent, Oddonem autem eligerent."

79. For example, when Thietmar's father threw a two-day feast for him to celebrate Thietmar's acceptance into the community of Saint Maurice at Magdeburg, he carefully pointed out that the feast was "highly acceptable to all" (David A. Warner, ed. and trans., *Ottonian Germany: The* Chronicon *of Thietmar of Merseburg*, Manchester Medieval Sources (Manchester: Manchester University Press, 2001), 162; Thietmar, *Chronicon* 4.16, 150: "proximaque sancti Andreae natali magnum et valde cunctis acceptabile convivium duos dies peractum est.").

display abundance and wealth, as well as largesse by sharing that abundance with guests. Widukind's story specifies that Otto exhibited his generosity by presenting gifts, before sending people home with a friendly farewell. All of these elements of Widukind's story are familiar attributes of a good feast held by a good king.

Descriptions of good feasts abound throughout Ottonian narrative sources. They are simply what good kings do, and the way that they are incorporated into the narratives reinforces this trope. Ottonian kings were itinerant, but the royal *iter* and the feasts it engendered were purposeful. For example, when the first of the Ottonian kings, Henry I, traveled throughout his realm in 929–30, he visited and feasted at each duchy, in an effort to consolidate his kingship and probably to secure support for the succession of his son Otto.[80] For Henry I's successors, the three Ottos and Henry II, royal itineracy was generally tied to the liturgical calendar, and the kings and their retinue customarily celebrated feasts at specific stops every year. For example, Thietmar mentions, in particular, several of the Easter feasts at Quedlinburg.[81] Feasts also provided opportunities for ambushes and murder, which, from a political perspective, read as public challenges to a ruler's legitimacy. Thietmar notes, in passing, a failed assassination attempt on Otto I's life during an Easter feast at Quedlinburg.[82] Liudprand, whose stories range beyond the bounds of the Ottonian Empire, relates a story about a thwarted assassination plot against Emperor Constantine that was supposed to take place at a feast.[83]

Feasting features prominently in the stories related to succession crises. Shortly after the death of Otto II in 983, three-year-old Otto III was elected king, but his uncle, Henry the Wrangler, tried to assume the kingship for himself, assuming custody of the young king and holding him hostage. Henry first celebrated the feast of Palm Sunday in Magdeburg, asking all the leading men to assemble there and then demanding that they elect him to be king.[84] He then traveled to Quedlinburg to celebrate the royal Easter feast, just as Otto I and Otto II had traditionally done. Thietmar tells us, "During the celebration, the duke's supporters openly greeted him as king and he was honored with

80. Bernhardt, *Itinerant Kingship*, 15; Reuter, *Germany in the Early Middle Ages*, 145. Reuter notes that these *convivia* may have also provided an opportunity to secure support for Otto I's succession.

81. Thietmar, *Chronicon* 4.9, 4.46, 5.31, 140–41, 184–85, 255–56.

82. Thietmar remarks that Otto grants an episcopal benefice as, in essence, the *wergeld* payment to settle a feud that had arisen as a result of an attempted assassination on Otto when celebrating an Easter feast at Quedlinburg (*Chronicon* 2.14, 2.21, 52-55, 62–63).

83. Liudprand of Cremona, *Antapodosis* 5.22, 136–37.

84. Thietmar, *Chronicon* 4.1, 130–33.

divine laudes."[85] But Otto III's mother, Theophanu, had significant support for her claim to oversee the regency of her young son, and she worked tirelessly to secure her son's release into her custody.[86] Ultimately, Henry's attempt to seize the throne failed, and Otto III was returned to his mother. Thietmar reports,

> The king [Otto III] celebrated the next feast of Easter at Quedlinburg where he was ministered to by four dukes: Henry at his table, Conrad as chamberlain, Henry "the Younger"[87] as cellarer, Bernhard as marshal.[88]

The ceremony is described as embodying the same kinds of rituals as Widukind's description of Otto I's coronation feast. Otto III's being waited on at table by Henry signaled that the succession crisis had been resolved, that Henry accepted Otto as the rightful king, and that the king, in turn, had forgiven his uncle and restored Henry's position, a proper kingly thing to do.[89] Additionally, Otto III was reported to have received ambassadors, dispensed gifts, and "taken care of everything." Otto was only four at the time, but it is evident how this good feast, a proper example of kingly feasting and order restored to a kingdom in crisis, was set by Thietmar to contrast with the feasts held a year earlier by Henry the Wrangler, who tried to usurp the throne from its legitimate heir—feasts for which Thietmar fails to mention niceties such as gift giving and pleasant exchanges, feasts that coerced assent from assembled nobles and presumed to co-opt the royal Easter celebration at Quedlinburg. Thus, good and bad feasting in Theitmar's *Chronicon* signals legitimate versus illegitimate kingship.

As with all rituals, the participants in feasts were not compelled to follow a strict script; there were expected elements and variations that could be adopted based on the specific circumstances of each situation.[90] But major changes that were not agreed on by all participants could be problematic, and even good

85. Warner, *Ottonian Germany*, 150; Thietmar, *Chronicon* 4.2, 133–35: "In hac festivitate idem a suis publice rex appellatur laudibusque divinis attollitur."

86. This support extended beyond just the local magnates, including foreign support as well, as evidenced by a letter written by Gerbert of Aurillac to a lady at court soon after Henry the Wrangler seized Otto III:. "Dominam meam Theuphanu imperatricem meo nomine convenite. Reges Francorum [Lothar and Louis V] filio suo [Otto III] favere dicite nichilque aliud conari nisi tyrannide Heinrici velle regem se facere volentis sub nomine advocationis destruere" (Gerbert of Aurillac, Letter to Lady Imiza, January–February 984, in MGH BDKz 2, ep. 22, 45).

87. Henry the Younger was the only surviving son of Duke Berthold of Bavaria.

88. Warner, *Ottonian Germany*, 156; Thietmar, *Chronicon* 4.9, 140–43: "Celebrata est proxima paschalis sollemnitas in Quidelingeburg a rege, ubi quattuor ministrabant duces, Heinricus ad mensam, Conrad ad cameram, Hecil ad cellarium, Bernhardus equis prefuit."

89. For more about this particular episode, see Bernhardt, *Itinerant Kingship*, 141–42; Reuter, *Germany in the Early Middle Ages*, 185; Gerd Althoff, *Otto III*, trans. Phyllis G. Jestice (University Park: Pennsylvania State University Press, 2003), 134.

90. Althoff, "Symbolic Communication," 66.

kings could create disruptions by unilaterally changing the script of a feast. When Otto III, for example, reportedly started dining alone, feasting on a dais apart from his men, it was a development that was met with resistance from the nobility.[91] This change in ritual may have reflected Otto's aspirations for renewal of old Roman imperial traditions, but communal celebrations including eating and drinking together were important medieval rituals that strengthened existing ties or declared new bonds between men.[92] Otto's separation emphasized that the king was no longer a *primus inter pares* but was, quite literally, above and separate from them.

The ritual of *adventus* was closely tied to the royal *iter*. Like feasting, it was a way to publicly put kingship on display and to demonstrate, for all to see, the relationships between a king and the institutions within his realm. A solemn ceremony celebrating the arrival of a king to a city or monastery, the *adventus* was a formal and very public way of communicating the legitimacy of his rule.[93] Barbara Rosenwein has gestured to the *adventus* not only as a way for a ruler to assert his prerogative but also as a way that bishops or monks could exert some form of control over a political event, by choosing to admit or not.[94] These ceremonies not only hearkened back to Roman imperial displays but also were an emulation of Christ's triumphal entry into Jerusalem on Palm Sunday.[95] Thus, the *adventus* had both imperial and sacral associations that contributed to the Ottonian expression of kingship. It is important to note the liturgical aspect of the *adventus* as well. Since the majority of stops on the imperial itinerary were at ecclesiastical institutions—monasteries or episcopal seats—the co-option of the *adventus* ritual by the church was hardly surprising, and this kind of "litur-

---

91. Thietmar, *Chronicon* 4.47, 185: "diversi diverse sentiebat." Althoff, *Otto III*, 139. Althoff suggests that Thietmar's low-key remark should not be dismissed out of hand, that he might be deliberately soft-pedaling an unpopular view, largely because he liked Otto III. For further discussion of Thietmar's remarks about Otto III reviving the Roman custom of feasting alone, see Percy Ernst Schramm, *Kaiser, Rom und Renovatio: Studien zur Geschichte des römischen Erneuerungsgedankens vom Ende des karolingischen Reiches bis zum Investiturstreit* (Darmstadt: Wissenschaftliche Buchsgesellschaft, 1957), 111–12.

92. Fichtenau, 58; Althoff, *Family, Friends, and Followers*, 153–54.

93. See David A. Warner, "Ritual and Memory in the Ottonian *Reich*: The Ceremony of *Adventus*," *Speculum* 76.2 (2001): 257–58; Henry Parkes, *The Making of Liturgy in the Ottonian Church: Books, Music and Ritual in Mainz, 950–1050* (Cambridge: Cambridge University Press, 2015), 4.

94. Barbara Rosenwein, *Negotiating Space: Power, Restraint, and Privileges of Immunity in Early Medieval Europe* (Ithaca, NY: Cornell University Press, 1999), 183.

95. Kantorowicz, "The 'King's Advent' and the Enigmatic Panels in the Doors of Santa Sabina," *Art Bulletin* 26.4 (1944): 210; Kantorowicz, *Laudes Regiae: A Study in Liturgical Acclamations and Medieval Ruler Worship* (Berkeley: University of California Press, 1946), 71–72; Warner, "Ritual and Memory," 255–83; Buc, *Dangers of Ritual*, 39; Peter Brown, *The Cult of the Saints: Its Rise and Function in Latin Christianity* (Chicago: University of Chicago Press, 1982), 98.

gical reception" eventually became "the prerogative of those anointed, bishop and king."[96]

The *adventus* was not the only public processional to display imperial power or connect the emperor to the sacral. Also providing opportunities for a king to publicly connect his earthly rule to the heavenly domain were relic processions and translations, such as the translation of Saint Maurice to Magdeburg in 961. The remains of the Roman martyr and relics of other saints first processed to Otto and were presented to him as part of the Christmas celebrations, then continued on to Magdeburg, where the remains of the saint and his companions were welcomed by a huge crowd, reportedly made up not just of the population of the city but also with throngs who had made their way to Magdeburg specifically for the event.[97] These kinds of formal and public translations of saints, welcoming them into their new communities, were deliberately modeled on the imperial *adventus*. We can imagine that the same curiosity and desire to connect, even at a distance, with the sacred and the ruler would have elicited similar responses to the *adventus* when it was staged for the king. Not only would imperial *adventus* rituals have connected the king with the Roman imperial past and Christian historical precedent, but a translation such as that of Saint Maurice would have given the relics additional immediate parallels for its audience, again connecting the Roman Empire with Christian history and the Ottonians.[98]

The development of the imperial regalia over the course of the tenth century also demonstrates the developing idea of sacrality, as well as providing an example of how that ideology was communicated to the people of the realm. It additionally serves as an example of the overlapping and enmeshed symbols and rituals that together shaped the politico-liturgical world in which the Ot-

96. Kantorowicz, *Laudes Regiae*, 72.

97. Thietmar, *Chronicon* 2.17, 58–59: "Anno dominicae incarnationis DCCCCLXI., regni autem eius vicesimo V°, presentibus cunctis optimatibus, in vigilia nativitatis Domini corpus sancti Mauricii et quorundam sociorum eius cum aliis sanctorum porcionibus Ratisbone sibi allatum est. Quod maximo, ut decuit, honore Parthenopolim transmissum unanimi indigenarum et comprovincialium conventu ibidem susceptum est et ad salutem patriae tocius hactenus veneratum est." For the importance of the actual translation ceremony, see P. Brown, *Cult of Saints*, 92–93 (Brown asserts that it "counted far more than the mere fact of its presence" in a city); Patrick J. Geary, *Furta Sacra: Thefts of Relics in the Central Middle Ages* (Princeton, NJ: Princeton University Press, 1991), 120; Buc, *Dangers of Ritual*, 60.

98. Warner, "Ritual and Memory," 255–83; Buc, *Dangers of Ritual*, 39; P. Brown, *Cult of Saints*, 98. See also Garipzanov, 220, 222, regarding the Carolingian use of Roman imperial symbols on their seals as a way of communicating Carolingian authority. The adoption of Roman imperial symbols and symbolic behaviors as a way of publicly expressing authority would not have been a foreign concept to Ottonian rulers.

tonians operated. One of the key pieces of the imperial regalia was the Holy Lance, a relic closely related to Saint Maurice. In choosing Maurice as an important royal saint by installing him at the new archbishopric of Magdeburg, near the pagan frontiers, Otto was making a statement that he himself, like Saint Maurice, was a warrior for Christ. Maurice's association with the Holy Lance thus made that relic much more polyvalent in its dynastic significance as a part of the imperial regalia,[99] so much that Widukind of Corvey felt compelled to include it in his list of items presented to Henry I on his succession. According to Widukind, the regalia with which Henry I was approached when told he was to be king consisted of a sacred lance, golden bracelets, a chlamys (a short cloak), a sword, and a diadem.[100] Widukind's inclusion of a sacred lance is somewhat puzzling, since the Holy Lance was acquired by Henry I later, after he had become king. It is possible that Widukind is referring to a different (subsequently lost) lance, but it is also possible that the lance was already a famously known element of the regalia by the time he was writing and that its anachronistic inclusion as a legitimizing detail was more important than accuracy. Significant here is that the regalia was a crucial symbol for legitimation of Henry's election as king.[101] This is also emphasized in the successions of both Henry II, the first Ottonian/Liudolfing who was not descended from Otto the Great, and Conrad II, the first of the Salian kings. Henry II, Otto III's second cousin, was at the center of a succession contest when Otto III died without an heir, a contest that initially revolved around the royal regalia. When Henry II, the end of the Liudolfing line, also died heirless, his widow's formal presentation of the royal regalia to Conrad II was the legitimizing act for Conrad's succession.

When Otto III died unexpectedly in Italy in 1002, there reportedly was con-

99. Maurice is depicted with a lance on the mid-ninth-century Flabellum of Tournus, and a mid-eleventh-century relief on the Church of Saint Mauritz in Münster shows Maurice holding a lance and shield (David A. Warner, "The Cult of Saint Maurice: Ritual Politics and Political Symbolism in Ottonian Germany" [PhD diss., University of California, Los Angeles, 1989], 87). A mid-eleventh-century back cover from an evangelary also depicts Saint Maurice holding a lance and shield (Gunther Wolf, "Nochmals zur Geschichte der Heiligen Lanze bis zum Ende des Mittelalters," in *Die Heilige Lanze in Wien: Insignie, Reliquie, "Schickalspeer,"* ed. Franz Kirchweger (Vienna: Skira, 2005), 40, plate 17; Stadtbibliothek Mainz, Hs II 3). Later medieval examples of specifically black Saint Maurice images, most of which bear lances, are cataloged by Gude Suckale-Redlefsen in *Mauritius: Der Heilige Mohr / The Black Saint Maurice* (Houston, TX: Menil Foundation, 1987), 158ff.

100. Widukind, *Res gestae Saxonicae* 1.25, 38: "Sumptis igitur his insigniis, lancea sacra, armillis aureis cum clamide et veterum gladio regum ac diademate, ito ad Heinricum, facito pacem cum eo."

101. It is possible that Widukind was referring to a completely different lance or that the lance was so intricately linked to the Ottonian regalia by the time he was writing that to omit it would have been more noticeable to his audiences than to anachronistically include it. Regarding the Ottonian use of relics as legitimizing objects, as well as the evolution of the symbology of the Holy Lance in particular, see Laura Wangerin, "Holy Relics, Authority, and Legitimacy in Ottonian Germany and Anglo-Saxon England," *Haskins Society Journal* 27 (2015): 15–38.

cern among his people that conflict would arise over who would succeed him. According to Thietmar of Merseburg, his death was kept secret until the army could be recalled and assembled. His body was then escorted, with the army as its guard, to Polling, an estate owned by Bishop Siegfried of Augsburg, where Duke Henry, the future Henry II, met the entourage.

> Duke Henry [the future Henry II] received them and revived their sorrow with his tears. Henry urged each of them, individually, to choose him as their lord and king, and made many promises. He took custody of the emperor's corpse, and also of the imperial insignia, except for the holy lance, which Archbishop Heribert had secretly sent ahead. The archbishop was briefly taken into custody but released, after his brother was left there as a surety, and soon sent back the holy lance. Along with all the others who followed the emperor's corpse, with the exception of Bishop Siegfried, Heribert did not then favour the duke and made no effort to conceal it, but rather declared that he would freely give his assent to whomever the better and greater part of the entire folk inclined.[102]

Thietmar suggests the importance of having the entire insignia in one's possession to enhance a claim to the throne. Archbishop Heribert, who did not support Henry, had secreted away a key part of that insignia, the one that most overtly connected the emperor to God. The Holy Lance, actually a lance head that could be affixed to a shaft for carrying into battle or in processions, was a double relic. This particular lance head, one of several objects being claimed as holy lances in the tenth century, was associated at various times in its history with Constantine, Saint Maurice, and Longinus.[103] The center of the head had been hollowed out to display a Holy Nail, held in place with silver wire, and thus one relic served as a reliquary for the other.

---

102. Warner, *Ottonian Germany*, 187–88; Thietmar, *Chronicon* 4.50, 188–91: "Exin cum ad Pollingun, curtem Sigifridi presulis Augustanae, venirent, ab Heinrico duce suscepti lacrimis eiusdem vehementer iterum commoti sunt. Quos singulatim, ut se in dominum sibi et regem eligere voluissent, multis promissionibus hortatur; et corpus imperatoris cum apparatu imperiali, lancea dumtaxat excepta, quam Heribertus archipresul clam premittens suam sumpsit in potestatem. Archiepiscopus autem custodia parumper detentus, relicto ibi pro vadimonio suimet fratre, cum licentia abiit ac sacram mox lanceam remisit. Is cum omnibus, qui huc inperatoris funus sequebantur, excepto antistite Sigifrido, duci tunc non consenciebat neque omnino denegabat, sed quo melior et maior populi tocius pars se inclinaret, libenter assensurum pronunciabat."

103. Percy Ernst Schramm, "Die 'Heilige Lanze,' Reliquie und Herrschaftszeichen des Reiches und ihre Replik in Krakau. Ein Überblick über die Geschichte der Königslanze," in *Herrschaftszeichen und Staatssymbolik: Beiträge zu ihrer Geschichte vom 3. bis zum 16. Jahrhundert*, vol. 2 (Stuttgart: Anton Hiersemann, 1955), 534–37; Wolf, "Nochmals zur Geschichte der Heiligen Lanze," 23–24.

Liutprand of Cremona's story relating how the Holy Lance came into the possession of Henry I provides a contemporary endorsement of the lance as a relic that legitimized his claim to the throne.[104] As a writer who owed much to the Ottonian court, Liudprand was not unbiased, but his use of the lance story to bolster the rightfulness of the Liudolfing claims to kingship demonstrates its importance. According to Liudprand, Henry I learned that Rudolph of Burgundy had possession of the Holy Lance. When Rudolph was asked by Henry's messengers if he would give it to him, Rudolph's first response was to refuse. But Henry persisted, threatening violence if he was not given the lance. Ultimately, reports Liudprand, "the heart of King Rudolph softened, and he personally handed over what was right to the righteous king who was rightly seeking it."[105] The lance's role as a legitimizing relic is further emphasized in Liudprand's account of the Battle of Birten, the battle fought in 939 when Otto I successfully put down a rebellion staged by his brother, Henry of Bavaria, who was asserting his own claim to the throne. While Widukind of Corvey portrays Otto in emulation of Moses, praying for victory by extending his arms to heaven, Liudprand inserts the Holy Lance into the scene and attributes the success of Otto's army to divine aid, a result of his tearful prayers before the lance.[106] That neither of these versions of the story are strictly factual is obvious. But the deliberate insertion of the Holy Lance into the story of a battle that was ultimately about the rightful heir to Henry I connects the lance with the royal and imperial legitimacy of the Ottonians. Later, at the time of Otto III's death, Duke Henry (the future king and emperor Henry II), a descendant of that same Henry of Bavaria who failed in his attempt to overthrow Otto I, needed the lance to assert his own claims of legitimacy to the Ottonian *Reich*. In these earlier narratives, a royal ideology and the idea of sacral kingship was still nascent, but by the time Thietmar was writing a generation later, the lance had evolved in its symbolism and importance. According to Thietmar, the Holy Lance belonged to the rightful king. Possession of the lance conferred legitimacy on a claim to the throne. Henry II was aware of this symbolic connection and was at great pains to secure that particular piece of the royal regalia.

---

104. Philippe Buc argues that the main purpose of Liudprand of Cremona's writings was to legitimize Otto I's rule over Italy, "the systematic destruction of the dynastic legitimacy of potential contenders for the Italian throne," as well as legitimization of the Ottonian dynasty ("Italian Hussies and German Matrons: Liutprand of Cremona on Dynastic Legitimacy," *Frühmittelalterliche Studien* 29 [1995]: 211, 224). Regarding the lance, see Buc, *Dangers of Ritual*, 44–50.

105. Squatriti, 158; Liudprand of Cremona, *Antapodosis* 4.25, 112: "Quia vero quod petebatur munus erat quo caelestibus terrea Deus coniunxerat, lapis scilicet angularis faciens utraque unum, Rodulfi regis cor emollivit iustoque regi iusta iuste petenti cominus tradidit."

106. Exodus 17:8–13; Widukind, *Res gestae Saxonicae* 2.17, 82; Liudprand of Cremona, *Antapodosis* 4.24, 111. As mentioned above, the coronation portrait of Henry II in the Regensburg Sacramentary (fig. 11) depicts him in the posture of Moses versus the Amalekites, as an angel hands him the Holy Lance.

Henry's enemies knew this, as well, and did their best to prevent Henry from acquiring it. Of course, Henry's situation was not so simple as merely seizing the relic and becoming king. Even having it, Henry spent a tremendous amount of energy securing support for his claim to the throne. But its possession clearly provided an advantage for a person putting forth a claim and was an important enough symbol that it was incorporated into the coronation portrait of Henry II in the Regensburg Sacramentary. When Henry II died in 1024, his widow, Cunigund, personally conveyed the imperial regalia to Conrad II, as the necessary *corroboratio* to confirm his traditional election and confer legitimation on a new dynastic line.[107] Conrad made the Holy Lance an even more visible and public image of imperial legitimacy by commissioning a magnificent gold processional cross, measuring thirty inches tall, as a reliquary to house the lance head and a large piece of the True Cross.[108]

While the Holy Lance with the Holy Nail served as a concrete connection between Christ in heaven and his warriors on earth, the imperial crown, dating to the mid-tenth century, provided a connection to the role of the king as the dispenser of divine justice. Crown wearings were public rituals, and the imperial crown worn by the Ottonians and their successors would have emphasized their developing ideology of themselves as sacral kings. The jeweled panels on the crown are alternated with four panels, three of which are decorated with images connecting the king to biblical lawgivers: King David, King Solomon, and Christ. The fourth panel portrays the prophet Isaiah advising King Hezekiah. In addition to the connection of Isaiah to the *traditio legis* tradition,[109] the story of Isaiah and Hezekiah would have had direct parallels for the Ottonians, who struggled against pagan invaders along their borders. When Hezekiah despaired at receiving a letter in which the king of Assyria described the imminent destruction of Hezekiah's city and lands, he was advised by Isaiah that the Lord's justice would not allow the Assyrians to prevail, and they did not.

> And it came to pass that night, that the angel of the Lord went out, and smote in the camp of the Assyrians an hundred fourscore and five thousand: and when they arose early in the morning, behold, they were all dead corpses. So Sennacherib king of Assyria departed.[110]

107. Wipo, *Gesta Chuonradi II* 2.1, in *Wiponis Opera*, ed. Harry Bresslau, 3rd ed., MGH SRG 61 (Hanover: Hahn, 1915), 19: "Supra dicta imperatrix Chunegunda regalia insignia, quae sibi imperator Heinricus reliquerat, gratanter obtulit et ad regnandum, quantum huius sexus auctoritatis est, illum corroboravit."

108. Herwig Wolfram, *Conrad II, 990–1039: Emperor of Three Kingdoms* (University Park: Pennsylvania State University Press, 2006), 144–46.

109. Bergmeier, 41–42.

110. 2 Kings 19:35–36, KJV.

Thus, the imagery of the crown suggested God's justice, Christ sitting in judgment, and Old Testament law. With imagery that combined the ideas of a tradition of earthly kingship that entailed dispensation of law and justice endorsed by God, as well as the dispensation of divine justice itself, the Ottonians' crown demonstrates one more way that these kings were beginning to conceptualize and portray themselves as sacral.

Like an *adventus*, the occasions at which a king might wear a crown were highly choreographed affairs. Kantorowicz notes that there was some overlap between festival crown wearings and festival coronations; that is, an occasion calling for the former might be preceded by the latter.[111] The king himself no longer placed the crown on his own head. By the tenth century, the ceremonial placement of the crown on the king was reserved to the clergy: "The golden circle in itself had become 'sacramental' and had the character of a quasi-liturgical raiment."[112] The great feasts of the Christian calendar—Christmas, Easter, and Pentecost—had been occasions for crown wearing in Byzantium since antiquity and a tradition of the Carolingian kings in the West. In the Ottonian *Reich*, crown wearings and ceremonial festival crownings increased under Otto I.[113] The adoption of festival crown wearings would have been a tradition echoing the Ottonians' connections and continuities with their Carolingian predecessors and the Byzantines in the East. Festival coronations—the physical reenactment of the coronation of the king—would have been an even more overt assertion of the king's legitimacy and sacrality. The acclamations that accompanied these *coronamenta* would have further emphasized the legitimacy of his claim to rule.

The acclamation is another component of Ottonian kingship that, like crown wearing and the *adventus*, bridged the line between secular and sacred. Serving as both affirmations by the people one ruled and liturgical elements incorporated into festival and Ordinary Masses, acclamations and *laudes* were another important component of the public rituals of kingship and, like the crown wearings and *adventus*, reinforced the ideology of sacral kingship. Hagen Keller has gestured to the importance of continually renewing or augmenting the grace that is bestowed on a king at his coronation, an assurance of his continued sacrality through his inclusion in the liturgy.[114] It is important that

111. Kantorowicz, *Laudes Regiae*, 92; for an overview of the history of festival crown wearings and coronations and their use throughout the Middle Ages, see 85–101.

112. Ibid., 93–94.

113. Ibid., 92, 95.

114. Keller, "Herrscherbild," 183. Eliza Garrison also emphasizes this important role of donations of liturgical books to ecclesiastical foundations, in her discussion of the Pericope of Henry

elements such as *adventus*, crown wearings, and other rituals be considered as a complex of symbolic interactions, as opposed to singular events. An *adventus* was usually accompanied by *laudes hymnidicae*.[115] *Laudes* and liturgical acclamations not only comprised part of the coronation ceremonies but were integrated into every part of the Mass. In early Merovingian contexts, prayer for the king was performed by his favored institutions; by the end of the Carolingian era, prayers for the king had become an expected duty for most Carolingian monasteries and abbeys.[116] Additionally, new liturgical musical forms were developing around the beginning of the tenth century. Two of these new forms, sequences and tropes, had a highly localized flavor. While these forms were associated with a number of monastic centers throughout Europe by the end of the tenth century, the coincidence of their development in East Francia and the rise of the Ottonian dynasty added greatly to the aura of sacral kingship that was forming around the Ottonians.

According to Notker Balbulus (ca. 840–912), a monk at Saint Gall, a sequence was a new kind of Frankish melody, formed by matching syllables of prose to notes in a jubilant addition to the Mass.[117] It was distinctly different from the Gregorian chant that had been imported from Rome and imposed in monastic institutions since the mid-eighth century as part of Carolingian efforts at ecclesiastical reform.[118] Like a hymn, a sequence was a freestanding song that could be inserted into a Mass to prolong it. Even more versatile was the trope, another Frankish innovation; not intended to be a stand-alone song, a trope could be attached to other chants to interpret or augment the meaning of the traditional canonical chants.[119] Together, these new musical forms amplified the solemnity of Frankish Masses, extending their time and (in the case of explanatory tropes) educating the monks in matters of devotion.[120]

An Ottonian book of sequences and tropes that was probably compiled at

---

II, where she notes that "the book's ritual use reified and repeated Henry's donation" and that the inscription on the cover of the book continually recalled the donation ceremony itself (127).

115. Kantorowicz, *Laudes Regiae*, 73.

116. Garipzanov, 45–46: by Charlemagne's time, collective prayer for the king was more significant than merely pious remembrance, and in at least one instance, participation "signaled the acceptance or rejection of royal authority."

117. Notker Balbulus, *Liber ymnorum, latine et theotisce*, ed. Wolfram von der Steinen (Bern: Francke, 1960), 6–7.

118. Richard L. Crocker, *The Early Medieval Sequence* (Berkeley: University of California Press, 1977), 2; Claudio Leonardi, "Intellectual Life," in *NCMH* 3:194; Richard Taruskin, *Music from the Earliest Notations to the Sixteenth Century: The Oxford History of Western Music* (Oxford: Oxford University Press, 2009), 41.

119. Taruskin, 50; Leonardi, 195.

120. Taruskin, 50.

Mainz around 967–72 gives some indication of how the royal or imperial presence was incorporated into the liturgy. BL Add Ms 19768 is a compilation of sequences, processional hymns, Ordinary chants, and litanies, as well as tropes.[121] Many of the sequences are taken from Notker's *Liber ymnorum*, including those with the incipits "Rex regum deum noster colende" and "Tubam bellicosam." But several inclusions are explicitly Ottonian, such as an acclamation hymn that names Adelheid, the second wife of Otto I.[122] Most of the codex is heavily annotated with musical notation, but the page with this hymn has none, perhaps indicating that it was composed as a one-off piece for a specific occasion and that there was no need for current or future monks to mark it for later use. There are also several annotated pages that mention the name *Otto* specifically, and as there were three Ottos in a row, these compositions would have remained current over the course of most of the Ottonian dynasty. Prayers for Otto and his army are mentioned specifically in several litanies and are even more intriguing in that they leave a fill-in-the-blank space for the bishop's name.[123] An Agnus Dei litany also includes a prayer for the king, with a placeholder indicating that his name is to be sung.[124] Even periodic inclusion of the king's name in the singing of the Mass inextricably linked him and his army to the sacred, as a Christian king fighting for Christendom. Given Otto I's struggles on the eastern frontiers and the very real threat of the Magyars, this prayer would not have been idle. To take a bit of an imaginative leap, these *laudes* and tropes were inserted into Masses on specific feast days or at various times, but Otto would have had his name sung even when he was not physically there, augmenting, for those present, his Christian omnipresence with the saints and the popes who were also being named. The sequences included elements such as the two whose incipits are noted above. "Rex regum deum noster colende" and "Tubam bellicosam," while referring to Christ and the armies of the Lord, were sung as part of a set of Mass sequences and tropes that also included *rex nostrum* and *excercitum eius*. Is it possible that, over time, the idea of Christ the king and Otto the king became associated in the minds of the singing monks, where Christ leading his heavenly army was mirrored on earth by the Christian army of Otto I? We can never know that, but we know that in at least one monastery and undoubtedly in more, the name of the king was sung in Mass,

121. See Parkes, *Making of Liturgy in the Ottonian Church*, Part 1, "A Troper," 31–88, for an extended consideration of this manuscript's creation and purpose.

122. BL Add Ms 19768, fol. 58v.

123. BL Add Ms 19768, fol. 54r: "ottonem regem et exercitum"; fol. 54v: "rege nostro ottone et omni excercitu eius."

124. BL Add Ms 19768, fol. 57r.

a legitimizing and sacralizing act that joined his name with the names of saints and that associated his armies with those of Christ.

From Widukind and other contemporary sources, we can see that there was tension between the traditional Germanic emphasis on personal relationships and the new ruler philosophy based on a sacral kingship; not until the chronicles of the Salian kings was the ideology of a Christian doctrine of royal government to whom subjects owed obedience presented in writing as well as in imagery, indicating its full assimilation.[125] But the program of the Ottos put the pieces in place for such a philosophy of rulership to develop. "Impulses that increased the authority of the grounds for royal action at the same time had to work themselves into the received system of rules from the outside," as one historian observed, and many of the systems of ceremony put into place by the Ottos to "present and secure" royal authority were often unable to augment that authority until the new rules and customs became accepted parts of the social order.[126] Still, the foundations for sacral rulership were laid under the auspices of the Ottos, and the evolution of this idea is observable in their portrayals of rulers. The culmination of this new idea of liturgical kingship is the portrayal of Otto III in the Aachen Gospels, as a ruler touching God, transcending the veil that separates heaven from earth, and elevated above mere men. Henry II embraced this conceptualization of sacral kingship and vigorously incorporated it into his own ideology of rulership. Henry's willingness to adapt and modify rituals of his predecessors in the service of his own rule shows, further, how rituals were continually performed and adjusted to communicate new relationships and structures of authority, as well as to reinforce old ones.[127]

The development of sacral kingship was part of a legitimizing program that evolved over time. The portrayals of Ottonian rulers, the inclusion of their names in liturgical contexts, and the use of specific symbols and ritual behaviors in the service of liturgical kingship were reflections of that development of a new ideology. In this new ideology of kingship—this Ottonian ideal of sacral kingship, with the king as a direct mediator of God—we see the most distinct difference between how the Ottonians and the Franks or Anglo-Saxons thought about kingship. David Pratt argues that the tenth-century *Domboc* (Book of Laws), the largest single piece of legislation issued by Alfred the Great (r. 871–99), was modeled on Frankish ideas of peacekeeping but also evoked a

125. Bagge, 93.
126. Weinfurter, "Authority and Legitimation," 22.
127. Bernhardt, "King Henry II," 60.

mental framework that was new, directly related to an Alfredian conception of rulership that had as great an impact on Anglo-Saxon society as the Ottonian transformation had on theirs. At every level, the Alfredian take on peacekeeping "summoned Alfred's own virtual presence, in all manifestations of courtly experience."[128] So where the Anglo-Saxons, via the principles of law expressed and disseminated in the *Domboc*, were experiencing the virtual presence of the king in all legal activity that involved the courts, the Ottonians were the *christomimetai*, imitators of Christ, and through their mediation, as through Christ's, the will of God was conveyed, and God's justice was served. Written law was the extension of the royal presence into the lower courts in England, but the royal presence in Ottonian courts remained at the highest level in the personage of the king, who, as a mediator for God, perhaps did not need to write law. There is likely no better way of understanding how this related to lawgiving and justice than to look, next, at the Ottonian reliance on the bilateral ordeal—judicial duel—as a royal prerogative and method of justice.

128. David Pratt, *The Political Thought of King Alfred the Great* (Cambridge: Cambridge University Press, 2007), 241.

CHAPTER 5

The Dispensation of Justice

The efficacy of the Ottonian system, particularly with regard to the administration of justice, is antithetical to modern sensibilities about what legal systems look like and how they are structured and employed by governments. The idea that strong legislative traditions are representative of strong, progressive rulership suggests, by implication, that kingdoms ruled without legislation are somehow more primitive and less effective.[1] Hagen Keller argues that to try to understand Ottonian justice as an institutionalized administrative jurisprudence system is to miss the point, that the central tenets of Ottonian legal practice were focused on consensus and balance between opposing parties, in

1. James Brundage, for example, fails to mention the Ottonians in his otherwise comprehensive study *The Medieval Origins of the Legal Profession: Canonists, Civilians, and Courts* (Chicago: University of Chicago Press, 2008). Other than remarking on the different ways that evidence and proof were handled under Germanic law versus Roman law and on the reliance of Germanic kings on arbitration, he relegates Germanic law to the period of "law without lawyers," effectively separating its treatment from both canon and Roman law (54–56).

In *Felony and Misdemeanor: A Study in the History of English Criminal Procedure*, vol. 1 (1937; repr., Clark, NJ: Lawbook Exchange, 2006), 35–36, Julius Goebel suggests that there are three stages of judicial activity: in the first, courts have a role mainly as mediators in dispute resolution; in the second, "without dispensing of formal concord, doomsmen and presiding officers enjoin upon the parties the observance of peaceful relations"; and in the last stage, which Goebel argues is a result of the judicial reforms of Charlemagne, peace can be ordered by the court. Goebel is very specific that composition procedure did not equal centralized power and judicial authority over all crimes (38). While he fails to find any evidence of the idea of a king's peace in Frankish law, he is careful to emphasize, "One must not minimize the crown's direct influence in the maintenance of the law. . . . royal authority was used within the folklaw procedural structure modifying the character of the procedure itself without disturbing its premises or purpose" (60).

In *The Making of English Law: King Alfred to the Twelfth Century*, vol. 1, *Legislation and Its Limits* (Oxford: Basil Blackwell, 1999), 108, Patrick Wormald reminds us, "The fact must be faced that strong kings did not *necessarily* make written law, and that those who did were not necessarily stronger in consequence. Neither Edwin of Northumbria (617–33) nor Æthelbald of Mercia (716–57) made written law, though they must have known of Æthelberht. Nor for that matter did Otto the Great (936–73)—except in Italy—though he of course knew of Charlemagne." Nonetheless, Wormald connects written law with Anglo-Saxon governing strength. He is not without his critics in this regard; see Paul Hyams, *Rancor and Reconciliation in Medieval England* (Ithaca, NY: Cornell University Press, 2003), 100–101.

conjunction with peacekeeping.[2] The idea that these kings and emperors were mediators of divine justice is nowhere depicted better than in the image of Henry II in the Monte Cassino Gospels (fig. 1, in the preceding chapter).[3] A "highly political and legal-philosophical picture,"[4] the image of Henry sitting in judgment portrays him as the ultimate arbiter of earthly justice via the divine gift of sacrality. Examining the vertical frames of the quatrefoil, we see first the hand of God bestowing divine wisdom from above to Henry II in the central position, who, in turn, judges the prisoner below him. As Ernst Kantorowicz explains, "In this scene of judgement Henry II clearly functions as mediator between divine Reason and human Law. But, as behooves an Ottonian Prince, the emperor's mediatorship is expressed 'liturgically,' that is, by the *epiklesis* of the Spirit."[5] Thus, the picture defines the role of the king as dispenser of justice as theological; the idea of jurisprudence, or a "spirit of legal science," has not yet developed.[6] If, as John Bernhardt has argued, the judgment in the miniature reflects a historic reality, the treason trial of Prince Pandulf, this liturgical understanding of kingship and law is even more emphatic.[7] With Henry II, we see the promulgation of texts that proclaim him to be the guardian of the law, the author of justice.[8]

In their development of an ideology of sacral kingship, the Ottonians positioned themselves as the imitators of Christ on earth. Not merely kings who promulgated God's law, they were anointed emperors who inhabited the sacral sphere and directly mediated divine will through their judgments. Their version of kingship is articulated in a case-by-case petition-based process, as opposed

2. Hagen Keller, "Die Idee der Gerechtigkeit und die Praxis königlicher Rechtswahrung im Reich der Ottonen," in *Ottonische Königsherrschaft: Organisation und Legitimation königlicher Macht* (Darmstadt: Wissenschaftliche Buchgesellescheft, 2002), 34–50.

3. "Henry II," Gospel Book of Monte Cassino, ca. 1024, Vatican Library, Codex Ottobonianus Lat. 74, fol. 193v.

4. Ernst Kantorowicz, *The King's Two Bodies: A Study in Mediaeval Political Theology* (1957; repr., Princeton, NJ: Princeton University Press, 1985), 114.

5. Ibid., 114–15.

6. Ibid., 115.

7. John Bernhardt, "King Henry II of Germany: Royal Self-Representation and Historical Memory," in *Medieval Concepts of the Past: Ritual, Memory, Historiography*, ed. Gerd Althoff, Johannes Fried, and Patrick J. Geary (Cambridge: Cambridge University Press, 2002), 64–69. Other ruler images of Henry II also indicate his role as the keeper of law. For example, the enthroned picture of Henry in the Regensburg Sacramentary (fol. 11v) proclaims, in a legend, "Nam ditione tua sunt omnia iura subacta" (Stefan Weinfurter, "Authority and Legitimation of Royal Policy and Action: The Case of Henry II," in Althoff, Fried, and Geary, 31). The coronation image on the preceding page also makes an oblique reference to Henry as the keeper of God's law; the budding shaft of the Holy Lance suggests that it is the rod of Aaron, the staff of life, which Moses had been commanded to keep near the Ark of the Covenant. Henry, by being invested with this staff, is thus inaugurated into the catena of kings who are mediators and keepers of God's law.

8. Weinfurter, "Authority and Legitimation," 31.

to a royal legislative program, and reflects some of the distinctive features of governance in the Ottonian Empire. The Ottonian subjects' experience of law differed according to their locale, their lords, and the proximity of the emperor, both geographically and personally. The petition-based nature of imperial law, with its dependence on intercessors, has a certain logic to it when considered in the context of liturgical kingship. After all, the way one communicated with God was by petition and intercession—that is, via prayers and the intercession of priests. It makes sense that a similar process would be required when pleading for justice before the *christomimetai*.

The Ottonian kings' reliance on trial by combat reinforced their ideology of sacral kingship.[9] This kind of ordeal, where accused and accuser fought each other to determine guilt or innocence, provided a judgment ostensibly rendered by God. Karl Leyser once observed that it must have been easier for recalcitrant nobles to submit to a sacral king than to a nonsacral one,[10] and this was surely true regarding the outcome of judicial duels as well. Even when an outcome was unclear or disputed, a duel provided a terminus to a conflict and imposed peace between factions. Like a reliance on feuds, these other elements of Ottonian rulership provided a strong and effective system that did not need to depend on efforts toward legal consistency across the Ottonian realm.[11]

The lack of legislation in the Ottonian Empire reflected a dependence on and the success of feud as a means of peacekeeping in that realm. While the right to dispense justice was controlled by the crown, the Ottonians did not write legislation. Whereas written law in England, especially under the reforms of King Alfred (r. 871–99), served as an extension of the royal presence into all of the courts in England, the royal presence in Ottonian courts remained at the highest level, in the personage of the king, who, as a mediator for God, perhaps did not need to write law.[12]

The Ottonians did not need to control rampant feuding, and they were in an economic position where they could use the revenues of justice as rewards for their counts and as incentives for their magnates. The grants of jurisdiction were a way to allow the stem duchies and major lords, both secular and

---

9. Like the difference between the Anglo-Saxon proliferation of legislation and the nearly complete absence of Ottonian legislation, the frequent use by the Ottonians of trial by combat stands in stark contrast to its complete absence in Anglo-Saxon England.

10. Karl Leyser, *Rule and Conflict in an Early Medieval Society: Ottonian Saxony* (Bloomington: Indiana University Press, 1979), 95.

11. These elements include the development of an ideology of liturgical kingship, the success of their system of delegated jurisdictional authority with a petition-based imperial court, and the use of the bilateral ordeal to help adjudicate certain cases.

12. See Keller, "Die Idee der Gerechtigkeit," regarding the Ottonians' conceptualization of their role as peacemakers in the administration of justice.

ecclesiastical, significant autonomy and independence. At the same time, these grants ensured the magnates' abilities to raise armies, host the royal court on its itinerary, and generally handle matters in their lands without necessitating the constant presence of the king, his justice, or his law to maintain peace and order that was good enough. Peace and order could be maintained in a way that served the immediate needs of the realm without the need for innovative or aspirational governing apparatus; there was no need to devise systems that might be "better" as long as the one that was in use worked.[13]

Delegation and Implementation

The jurisdictional authority of ecclesiastical lords functioned in parallel with the authority of secular lords, and the distribution of lesser jurisdictions that functioned in tandem with the courts of greater lords is equally important with regard to how kings conceived of law and peacekeeping in their realms. For the functioning of secular jurisdictions among the Ottonians, especially at the levels of lesser nobles or landholders, the sources are sparse, and the few that are extant offer tantalizing hints but make broad generalizations difficult. The diplomas of Otto the Great reveal some clues. Of his extant diplomas that mention law in any context, five are grants to secular individuals.[14] In 951, Otto returned to Marquart, a vassal of his brother Henry, land that Otto had earlier confiscated, "with all things by right pertaining to that place."[15] Interesting in this brief document is that the confiscation is signaled as an act not originating from the king alone: "it was taken away by the *iudicio* of the people and was brought back into our power."[16] Unfortunately, there is no specific mention of what pertains to that place by right or to what custom or law *iudicio* specifically refers.

13. That neither the Merovingians or the Carolingians were aspirational in their approach to law is noted by Wormald (*Making of English Law*, 53). Goebel carefully points out that legislation made by both of those dynasties was created to solve problems (62–81); that is, they were creating law to respond to specific issues that arose or needed to be addressed, not for conceptualized problems that might arise. The Ottonians were modeling much of their government on Carolingian precedents, and the Carolingian system would not have served as a potential model for aspirational lawmaking. But it legitimized a method of kingship that would likely have been recognizable—and thus not foreign or suspect—to their magnates. The idea of "good enough" derives from biological systems theory and prevents teleological approaches to understanding an organism's or system's adaptations or evolution (for further elaboration, see note 53 in chap. 3 in the present study).

14. DD OI 135, 201, 220, 330, 371.

15. DD OI 135: "cum omnibus ad eundem locum iure pertinentibus."

16. DD OI 135: "ei iudicio populi fuit ablata in nostramque potestatem redacta."

Confiscated lands were not always returned to the owner, as another diploma of Otto I demonstrates. In 959, Otto gave his own *fidelus*, Rudolf, by perpetual right, along with all that by right there pertained, the lands confiscated from the rebellious Guntram.[17] The language of this document, like that of Marquart's diploma, suggests a broader conceptualization of the king and his people, remarking that Guntram rebelled "contra rem publicam nostrae regiae potestati" (against the realm and our royal power). This could be a conscious invocation of Romanized terminology speaking to the imperial ambitions of Otto, but, at the same time, it suggests the idea of rebellion against the country of the king, not the person of the king—an interesting distinction. A certain Gumbert was also the fortunate recipient of confiscated lands, being granted four manses in 966 by the king. The formula describing the rights is typical of land grants, both Anglo-Saxon and Ottonian, specifying that these manses and their various kinds of land were given to Gumbert as permanent gifts. Gumbert was given all things pertaining by right to the said manses, including, it would appear, returns from the administration of justice.[18]

The texts in these diplomas that make grants of confiscated lands are relatively short. An exception is a diploma from 969 in which Otto I confirms lands held by his *fidelus* Ingo and his sons. The length is partly explained by the large number of properties, many of which were *castri*, castles or other kinds of fortified locales. Additionally, these lands were accompanied by extensive immunities, of a kind more generally seen in diplomas for confirmations and grants conferred to bishoprics and other ecclesiastical lords. The diploma goes on to explain the legal rights of Ingo and, perhaps because Otto was a new ruler in Italy, how documents would be evaluated if any disputes were to arise over the rightful ownership of any of these properties.[19] Of note is the notification

17. DD OI 201: "iure perpetuo," "omnia ibi iure pertinentia." See David S. Bachrach, "Exercise of Royal Power in Early Medieval Europe: The Case of Otto the Great, 936–73," *Early Medieval Europe* 17.4 (2009): 397–403, regarding imperial confiscations and the case of Guntrum in particular. See also Karl Leyser, "The Crisis of Medieval Germany," in *Communications and Power in Medieval Europe: The Gregorian Revolution and Beyond*, ed. Timothy Reuter (London: Hambledon, 1994), 35–45, where Leyser discusses additional examples of punitive land confiscations by Ottonian emperors, in cases related to royal grants made *in proprietatem*.

18. DD OI 330: "cum terris cultis et incultis agris pratis campis vineis pascuis areis viis et inviis exitibus et reditibus quaestis et inquirendis omnibusque rebus ad praefatos mansos iure pertinentibus." I understand "reditibus quaestis et inquirendis" to refer to fees collected in the course of administering the lands granted, including fees related to the administration of justice. DD OI 220, a grant of lands to Duchess Judith of Bavaria, includes a similar formula but without any reference to these kinds of returns: "cum curtilibus agris mancipiis edificiis silvis vineis aquis territoriis pascius omnique usu."

19. DD OI 371: "verum etiam advocatos habere et per inquisitionem res suas defendere et ablatas sibi adquirere et, si monimina chartarum quovis ingenio perdiderint, hac nostri precepti pagina

of the diploma. The formula itself is not unusual until it invokes the laws by which Otto is holding court and dispensing justice, "by all laws of the Italians and Franks and Germans."[20] This invocation suggests that, like his Carolingian predecessors, Otto is conceiving of imperial courts in which the laws of all his peoples can be represented.

From a maximalist point of view, these kinds of documents lead us to not-unlikely assumptions about how local jurisdictional authority functioned. Peacekeeping and the administration of justice at the local level were probably guided by some combination of local customs and law.[21] The revenues from such activities likely went to the local lord, ecclesiastical or secular, and we should probably not assume that if revenues from the administration of local justice are not specifically mentioned, they are not included in the grant. The particular customary rights that attenuated with a landholding would have been known, and which rights went to the local landowner and which to the count or other great lord may not have seemed worth mentioning, falling under the category of "all things pertaining by right to this property." That these are specifically mentioned in some places, such as in Gumbert's grant discussed above, does not mean they were not included in others. That the reference occurs at the end of a formulaic list of a property's features suggests that its inclusion (or not) could be the peculiarity of a particular scribe or that the formula could have been copied verbatim from an earlier document relating to the same property. Things start to become clearer with the land grants that were more involved bequests, such as the extensive properties granted to Ingo. That diploma

corroborati investiti maneant et confirmati nostra largitione abita legaliter defendant et ablata legali examinatione requirant, omnium hominum eradicata controversia." The expansiveness of the document does not derive merely by virtue of it originating in Italy, as the very short document for Marquart's grant (DD OI 135) was produced in Pavia.

20. DD OI 371: "Quocirca noverit omnium sancte dei ecclesie fidelium nostrorumque presentium scilicet et futurorum industria, cum nos in Kalabria residebamus in confine atque planicie que est inter Cassanum et Petram Sanguinariam, ibique nostro imperiali iure nostris fidelibus tam Kalabris quamque omnibus Italicis Francisque atque Teutonicis leges preceptaque ordinatim imponeremus."

21. That there was some sense of formality of law and justice, at least with regard to certain pleas, is demonstrated by Burchard of Worms in his *Lex familia* and by the requests from ecclesiastical lords for copies of Regino of Prüm's *Libri duo* (see chap. 2 in the present study). A secular example of such interest in legal procedure can be found in the person of Eberhard of Friuli, who requested a copy of the *Liber legum* from Wulfstan (also known as Lupus) in the mid-ninth century. That the *Liber legum* was intended, like the *Libri duo*, to be used as a practical reference book by lords deciding cases is indicated by incorporation of the laws of various peoples of the empire and the system of ordering and rubricating implemented by Wulfstan; the addition of later legislation suggests that the book was periodically updated to stay current. See Paul J. E. Kershaw, "Eberhard of Friuli, a Carolingian Lay Intellectual," in *Lay Intellectuals in the Carolingian World*, ed. Patrick Wormald and Janet Nelson (Cambridge: Cambridge University Press, 2007), 85–86; Wormald, *Making of English Law*, 56.

is more similar to an ecclesiastical immunity than to the other secular grants discussed here, and the formulaic invocation of exemption from tolls, taxes, the imposition of laws, and other interference covers every conceivable kind of lord and public functionary. But the freedom from the imposition of laws by outside lords is a clue that some secular lords held not just jurisdictional authority but also legislative authority over their own lands. This authority, unlike local customary law, would need to be specified in a grant, since the county in which the lands lay would otherwise have that right, as well as the right to the revenues it might engender. If we take the broadest leap from this evidence and the local legislative activity we have seen by ecclesiastical lords such as Burchard of Worms, it would appear that great lords in the Ottonian Empire had equally great legislative and jurisdictional autonomy over their realms, that lands within the county or *pagus* that were not their own holdings could have that authority delegated to new owners by order of the king, and that customary law continued to be the main way that disputes were resolved at the local level, until or unless matters escalated to a point at which customary law was no longer sufficient to maintain the peace.[22]

Some great lords in the Ottonian Empire enjoyed exclusive jurisdictional authority over their people. A significant portion of Thietmar of Merseburg's contemporaneous chronicle records events that deal either directly or indirectly with legal activity and justice, much of it by lords. For example, in 973, Duke Henry of Bavaria ordered that the patriarch of Aquileia be castrated and that the archbishop of Salzburg be blinded. Tantalizingly, Thietmar avers from providing the details of their misdeeds: "I do not wish to put forth the reasons [for these mutilations], because I know they are not sufficient to be deserving of them."[23] These men were guilty, but the punishment meted out was, in Thietmar's opinion, too severe. This example indicates that Duke Henry had the prerogative to determine guilt and impose what he believed to be appropriate punishments for those in his demesne who committed wrongdoing. When Henry, on his deathbed, was admonished for these actions by the bishop of Regensburg, the duke admitted to contrition only with regard to the castration, not, as Thietmar carefully points out, in the case of the archbishop. Thietmar's disapproving tone should not be given undue weight; as a church official him-

22. See the discussion of Burchard of Worms in chapter 2 in the present study.

23. Thietmar of Merseburg, *Chronicon*, 2.50, in *Thietmari Merseburgensis Episcopi Chronicon*, ed. Robert Holtzmann, MGH SRG 9 (Berlin: Weidmannsche Buchhandlung, 1935), 88: "Causas preponere nolo, quia ad haec promerenda non esse idoneas in veritate scio." Unfortunately, our other tenth-century chronicles end before 973, and this incident is not mentioned by Richer of Reims, in the MGH DD, or in the RI. It is also not mentioned in other contemporary chronicles or annals in MGH SS 3, *Annales, Chronica et Historiae Aevi Saxonici*.

self, he would not be happy with the idea of the duke's ability to order mutilations for ecclesiastical lords. Regardless of its reliability, Thietmar's account that Henry defended blinding the archbishop as a justifiable act not requiring absolution on his deathbed demonstrates the degree to which dukes could punish those whose actions offended within their realm.[24] Even great ecclesiastical lords were not exempt. If we are to take Thietmar's story at face value, it demonstrates the broad jurisdictional authority that Henry could legitimately employ as duke. If, as is more likely, Thietmar is relating a version of the story that advances his own agenda, it is still remarkable in presenting Henry's punishments of the archbishop and the patriarch as being within his purview. Thietmar is critical of the severity of the punishments Duke Henry ordered, not of the fact that he claimed jurisdictional authority over these ecclesiastical lords.

That a lord had an exclusive right to justice over his own men is evidenced in Thietmar's account of Margrave Ekkehard's men who were caught stealing by villagers: "In the presence of their countrymen, they [the villagers] accused and hanged the perpetrators of this deed, not being aware that they should rightly have notified Margrave Ekkehard."[25] We will never know whether the villagers were actually unaware or got carried away in the heat of the moment, but Ekkehard went with armed men "to extract vengeance." While Thietmar waxes on indignantly about Ekkehard's behavior, it is worth noting that there was no reported bloodshed, just a demonstration of power. Ekkehard's men surrounded the village, led the men of the village off to his fortress, held them there until the villagers paid a fine, and then released them. The issue here is clearly not the punishment imposed on the margrave's men but a contention over jurisdiction. The villagers complained to Thietmar, who expressed outrage that they would not receive any compensation for this offense, but that, again, is likely an expression of the righteous indignation of a bishop. The villagers seemed to have felt justified in accusing and hanging caught thieves. Their complaint to Thietmar means that even after Ekkehard fined them, they still felt justified in their actions. But the guilt or innocence and even the hanging of the margrave's men were not key issues in Thietmar's account of the matter. The villagers' as-

24. Regarding blinding as punishment and how it is entangled with ideas about legitimacy, especially in the West, see Geneviève Bührer-Thierry, "'Just Anger' or 'Vengeful Anger'? The Punishment of Blinding in the Early Medieval West," in *Anger's Past: The Social Uses of an Emotion in the Middle Ages*, ed. Barbara H. Rosenwein, 75–91 (Ithaca, NY: Cornell University Press, 1998).

25. David A. Warner, ed. and trans., *Ottonian Germany: The* Chronicon *of Thietmar of Merseburg*, Manchester Medieval Sources (Manchester: Manchester University Press, 2001), 202; Thietmar, *Chronicon* 4.73, 216: "Namque eos coram suis comprovincialibus accusatos laqueo suspenderunt, quia hoc prefato seniori, ut iustum erat, innotescere non noverunt."

sumption of jurisdiction over the men instead of turning them over to their lord was the issue that most concerned Ekkehard.

The Ottonian Synod

One of a variety of assemblies or councils that a bishop might be involved in, the synod was a prominent feature of Ottonian government and its dispensation of justice. While other assemblies or meetings not designated specifically as synods may have nonetheless been more or less synodal in nature, it is sufficient here to note that assemblies clearly designated as synods were frequent, that they were often convened by the emperor, that they often appear to have been mixed assemblies of nobles and bishops, and that they frequently were attended by other kings. Additionally, synods often occurred in conjunction with *placita*, formal hearings of disputes before the king.[26] Royal justice under the Ottonians, at least for their magnates and bishops, appears to have been fairly accessible.

Contests over the see of Reims attest both to ecclesiasts' engagement in the political arena of the time and to the fact that kings used both bishops and their sees as political currency. For example, in 931, King Raoul (king of France and Duke of Burgundy), with Hugh the Great and others of his men and their armies, first pillaged the *pagus* of Reims and then laid siege to the *urbs*. The city fell three weeks later, and Raoul entered the city and "had ordained as bishop there Artoldus, a monk from the monastery of St-Rémi [Reims] who earlier in the year had deserted [Count] Heribert [who had deserted from Raoul] and

26. *Placita*, both the hearings and the documents produced as a result of them, were an ancient Frankish form of dispensing royal justice, originally exclusively used to resolve disputes over land and to provide written documents attesting to how the dispute was resolved. See Paul Fouracre, "'Placita' and the Settlement of Disputes in Later Merovingian Francia," in *The Settlement of Disputes in Early Medieval Europe*, ed. Wendy Davies and Paul Fouracre (Cambridge: Cambridge University Press, 1986), 23–43. For *placita* in tenth- and eleventh-century Italy, see Hagen Keller, "I placiti nella storiografia degli ultimi cento anni," in *Fonti medioevali e problematica storiografica: Atti del Congresso internazionale tenuto in occasione del 90° Anniversario della fondazione dell'Istituto Storico Italiano 1883–1973, Roma 22–27 ottobre 1973* (Rome: Istituto storico italiano per il Medio Evo, 1976): 41–68; Chris Wickham, "Justice in the Kingdom of Italy in the Eleventh Century," in *La giustizia nell'alto medioevo (Secoli IX-XI) 11–17 aprile 1996*, vol. 1 (Spoleto: Presso la Sede del Centro, 1997), 179–250; Isabella Lazzarini, "La Communication écrite et son rôle dans la société politique de l'Europe méridionale au Moyen Âge," in *Rome et l'état moderne Européen: Collection de l'École française de Rome*, ed. J.-P. Genet (Rome: École française de Rome, 2007), 272–77. The combination of *placita* and synodal hearings to dispense justice seems to have been an Ottonian innovation.

gone over to Hugh."[27] In 940, Reims was besieged again, by Hugh the Great, bishops of Francia and Burgundy, and Count Heribert, who was now allied with his former enemy. The siege was short, according to Flodoard: on the sixth day, Archbishop Artoldus's "entire force of soldiers deserted [him] and joined Heribert," who then was able to enter the city. Artoldus, who had been summoned back to Reims at the behest of both magnates and bishops, "was persuaded to abdicate from the office and power of his see."[28] Heribert's son, Hugh, a deacon, was installed as the new archbishop of Reims in 941.

In 945, King Louis besieged Reims with the forces of several of his magnates, including the former archbishop Artoldus, bolstered by an army of Northmen; Hugh the Great managed to repulse the bulk of the army and sent hostages to the king as a sign of good faith, to arrange a meeting: "Hugh then sent a message to the king at Reims and gave hostages so that Ragenoldus [count of Roucy], representing the king, would come to a meeting with Hugh. When Ragenoldus departed, Hugh treated with him so that the king might accept hostages from [Arch]bishop Hugh and give up the siege at Reims, and so that [Arch]bishop Hugh might go to a *placitum* to provide the king with an explanation for whatever the king asked him." Arrangements were made, and "Duke Hugh and the king participated in a *placitum* through intermediaries, but no sure peace was established." The two sides did agree to a peace for a few months, however.[29]

In 946, Reims again was subjected to a siege, this time by the joined forces of Otto I and King Louis. Otto's involvement in these matters seems to have been at the behest of his sister Queen Gerberga of France, who complained that Louis had been expelled by Hugh the Great and who demanded Otto's help. Flodoard reports, "They surrounded Reims with a siege, enclosing it with a large army. However, [Arch]bishop Hugh saw that he could not break the siege or resist such an immense army and took counsel with some *principes* who

27. Steven Fanning and Bernard S. Bachrach, eds. *The* Annals *of Flodoard of Reims, 919–966* (Toronto: University of Toronto Press, 2008), 20–21; Flodoard of Reims, *Annales*, s.a. 931, in MGH SS 3, 380: "ordinari facit ibi praesulem Artoldum monachum ex coenobio sancti Remigii, qui iam pridem, ipso tamen anno, reliquerat Heribertum et transierat ad Hugonem." For a discussion of Flodoard's presentation of these events, see Jason Glenn, *Politics and History in the Tenth Century: The Work and World of Richer of Reims* (Cambridge: Cambridge University Press, 2004), 215–34.

28. Fanning and Bachrach, 32–33; Flodoard, *Annales*, s.a. 940, 386–87: "sextaque obsidionis die, deserente omni pene militari manu Artoldum archiepiscopum, et ad Heribertum transeunte, idem comes Heribertus ingreditur. Artoldus praesul ad sanctum Remigium evocatione procerum et episcoporum profectus, persuasus est vel conterritus a principibus, episcopii se procuratione vel potestate abdicare."

29. Fanning and Bachrach, 41; Flodoard, *Annales*, s.a. 945, 392: "post haec Remis ad regem mittit, dans obsides, ut Ragenoldus ex parte regis ad colloquium sibi occurrat. Quo abeunte, tracta cum eo, uti rex obsides ab Hugone episcopo accipiat, et ab obsidione Remensi discedat; quatinus idem praesul denominato placito ad reddendam rationem de omnibus, quae rex ab eo quaesierat, accedat."

appeared to be his friends. . . . They advised him to go out with his men and surrender the *urbs* because the kings had decided to expel him completely, and if the *urbs* should be taken by storm, they would not be able to intercede with the kings to prevent his eyes from being torn out." Archbishop Hugh followed this advice and surrendered the city, and the two kings reinstalled Archbishop Artoldus.[30] As might be expected by this point in the story, Hugh the Great and Archbishop Hugh mounted an attack on Reims in the following year, but they withdrew after only eight days. Apparently, the kings felt the matter had gone far enough. Flodoard continues, "At the beginning of August, the kings Louis and Otto celebrated the convening of a *placitum* on the river Chiers. . . . At the court, the bishops heard the dispute between Artoldus and Hugh, the [arch]bishops of the church of Reims. However, because a synod had not been called, the quarrel could not be resolved. A synod was arranged for the middle of November. In the meantime, the see of Reims was conceded to Artoldus, and Hugh, the other bishop, was permitted to stay at Mouzon. King Otto mediated a truce or armistice of the war between King Louis and the *princeps* Hugh [the Great], to last until the meeting of the synod."[31] Two synods were called, both of which Archbishop Hugh refused to attend. At the second synod, however, he sent a letter from Pope Agapetus II, addressed to the bishops and ordering that Hugh be reinstalled. The bishops found this papal order inappropriate and decided that the affair should strictly follow canonical procedure.

> Thus it was ordered that the nineteenth canon of the council of Carthage, concerning the accused and the accuser, be read out. When this was done, it was judged that according to the meaning of this canon, [Arch]bishop Artoldus should retain the communion and the diocese

30. Fanning and Bachrach, 44–45; Flodoard, *Annales*, s.a. 946, 393: "quam cingentes obsidione, ingenti vallarunt exercitu. Videns autem praesul Hugo, obsidionem se tolerare non posse, neque tantae resistere multitudini, locutus est cum quibusdam principibus qui videbantur sibi esse amici, videlicet cum Arnolfo, qui eius sororem, et Uddone, qui amitam ipsius habebat uxorem, sed et cum Hermanno Uddonis fratre; quaesivit ab eis, quid sibi foret agendum. Qui tale consilium dederunt ei, ut egrederetur cum suis et relinqueret urbem, quia id dispositum a regibus erat, ut omnimodis expelleretur, neque intervenire possent apud reges pro ipso, quin eruerentur ei oculi, si urbem vi capi contigisset." For a discussion of the family dynamics operating between the Ottonians and these conflicts in the West Frankish kingdom, see Simon MacLean, *Ottonian Queenship* (Oxford: Oxford University Press, 2017), 60–62.

31. Fanning and Bachrach, 45–46; Flodoard, *Annales*, s.a. 947, 394: "Conventus placiti regum Ludowici et Othonis super Charam fluvium intrante mense Augusto celebratur, . . . ubi res litis inter Artoldum et Hugonem Remensis aecclesiae praesules ab episcopis auditur. Et quia synodus tunc convocata non fuerat, altercatio determinari non potuit. Synodus autem circa medium mensis Novembris habenda denuntiatur. Interim vero sedes Remensis Artoldo conceditur, Hugo alter praesul in Mosomo commorari permittitur. Treugae vel indutiae belli inter regem Ludowicum et Hugonem principem usque ad synodi tempus, Othone rege mediante, disponuntur."

> of Reims (*communio et parrochia*) and Hugh, who had been summoned to two synods but had refused to comply, should abstain from the communion and rule of the diocese of Reims until he should come to a general synod, which was called for 1 August, to purge himself. Next, the bishops had this decision written down in a charter in their presence and they appended their decision to it and dispatched it to this same Hugh. After a day, Hugh sent the charter back to [Arch]bishop Robert [of Trier], saying that he would by no means obey the judgment.[32]

Flodoard provides us with great detail regarding the next synod, including who was in attendance, how affairs proceeded, and how a judgment was determined. King Louis and King Otto were present, and King Louis started off the proceedings by reading off his dispute against Duke Hugh, followed by a recitation by Artoldus naming his complaints against Archbishop Hugh. In the end, former archbishop Hugh was reduced to the office of deacon and sent into exile, and Hugh the Great was excommunicated "until he should do penance and make worthy satisfaction."[33]

This example occupies the intersection of ecclesiastical and secular justice at the highest levels. The continuous attacks on Reims by one faction or the other failed to provide any resolution or to stimulate any imperial interest until it became a family matter, when Queen Gerberga found herself in the middle of the mess and requested Otto's help. Otto used a combination of factors to restore order and provide resolution. First, forcing the usurping archbishop, Hugh, to surrender in a military confrontation, Otto reinstalled Artoldus. Otto then convened a *placitum* with King Louis, but the intricacies of the conflict were found to fall under the purveyance of canon law, so the *placitum* was used to negotiate a temporary peace until the matter could be heard in the appropriate court, a synod. The complaints of both King Louis and Artoldus were heard and dealt

32. Fanning and Bachrach, 47; Flodoard, *Annales*, s.a. 948, 395: "Sicque praeceptum est, ut recitaretur capitulum 19. Cartaginensis concilii de accusato et accusatore. Quo recitato, iudicatum est, secundum diffinitionem ipsius capituli, ut Artoldo praesule retinente communionem et paroechiam Remensem, Hugo, qui ad duas iam synodos evocatus venire contempserat, a communione et regimine Remensis episcopii abstineret, donec ad universalem synodum, quae indicebatur Kalendas Augusti, sese purgaturus occurreret. Ipsumque capitulum mox in carta describi fecerunt episcopi coram se, subnectentes hanc etiam definitionem suam, et eidem Hugoni miserunt. Qui post alteram diem eandem cartam Rotberto praesuli remisit, hoc verbis remandans, quod ipsorum iudicio nequaquam oboediturus esset."

33. Fanning and Bachrach, 49; Flodoard, *Annales*, s.a. 948, 396–97: "donec ad poenitentiam et dignam satisfactionem venire procuret"; MGH Conc 6.2, no. 13 (June 7, 948, Ingelheim). Richer of Reims (*Histories* 2.69–82) also reports extensively on the proceedings at this synod (Richer of Saint-Rémi, *Histories*, trans. Justin Lake [Cambridge, MA: Harvard University Press, 2011], vol. 1, 314–345). See also MGH Const OI, "Synodus Ingelheimensis," 8–12.

with at the synod, resulting in the deposition of Hugh, the former archbishop, and in a public condemnation of the behavior of the prince Hugh toward King Louis. Taking advantage of the convention of bishops, magnates, and kings, "the remaining days of the synod were spent on other important matters," and "many other things were decided."[34] It is worth noting the agency that Flodoard attributes to Otto in guiding the outcome of the synod: "Especially due to the insistence of Liudulfus, King Otto's legate and chaplain, and also because King Otto wished it to happen, Count Hugh [the Great], the enemy of King Louis, was excommunicated because of the evils that he perpetrated."[35]

Despite the dramatic narration of these affairs at Reims, the report deals primarily with local politics. Flodoard provides us this detailed description of events at Reims because of his affiliation with that church; likewise, the great detail regarding episcopal elections in Thietmar's *Chronicon* reflect his specific concerns in his world. Thietmar does not remark at all on these events at Reims, as juicy as they are. In his continuation of the *Chronicle* of Regino of Prüm, Adalbert of Magdeburg relegates the entire affair (to which Flodoard invests pages of explanation and detail) to two short notations. The first is his entry for 946.

> King Louis [IV], having been expelled from the kingdom by his own men, came to King Otto asking for help and got what he wanted. For the king entered Gaul with a strong force and made the towns of Rheims and Laon and many other sturdy and well-defended strongholds return to Louis; and he himself advanced with hostile intent as far as Rouen. From there he returned to the homeland, after almost all of the greater men, with the exception of Robert's son Hugh [the Great], had been subjected to their king.[36]

34. Fanning and Bachrach, 49; Flodoard, *Annales*, s.a. 948, 397: "Ceteris quoque diebus synodi tractata sunt quaedam necessaria . . . . Sed et de aliis aecclesiae Dei utilitatibus tractata sunt et diffinita nonnulla."

35. Fanning and Bachrach, 51; Flodoard, *Annales*, s.a. 948, 398: "insistente praecipue Liuddulfo legato et capellano regis Otthonis, quoniam idem rex id omnino fieri praecipiebat, excommunicatur Hugo comes, inimicus Ludowici regis, pro supra memoratis malis ab ipso perpetratis."

36. Simon MacLean, ed. *History and Politics in Late Carolingian and Ottonian Europe: The* Chronicle *of Regino of Prüm and Adalbert of Magdeburg* (Manchester: Manchester University Press, 2009), 248; Adalbert of Magdeburg, *Continuatio Reginonis*, s.a. 946, in *Reginonis abbatis Prumiensis Chronicon cum continuatione Treverensi*, ed. F. Kurze, MGH SRG 50 (Hanover: Hanh, 1890), 163: "DCCCCXXXXVI. Ludowicus rex a suis regno expulsus auxilium petens regem Ottonem adiit et, ut desideraverat, obtinuit. Nam manu valida rex Galliam intravit et Remensem urbem et Laudunum aliaque castella compluria firma et munitia Ludowico reddi fecit ipseque hostiliter usque Rotomagum pervenit. Inde omnibus pene excepto Hugone Ruodberti filio regni maioribus regi suo subactis in patriam regreditur."

Adalbert's second notation on the affair is in the entry for 948.

> A synod was held by 34 bishops in Ingelheim. It was presided over by Bishop Marinus, legate of the church of Rome, and the renowned kings Otto and Louis were there. Many things of use to the Church were promulgated. The case of Herbert's son Hugh, who had invaded the see of the church of Rheims and expelled Archbishop Artald [Artoldus], was also aired; and he was condemned by the judgment of all the bishops who were there.[37]

Adalbert's short summaries are typical of the annual entries in the *Annals* and reflect his take on which events of each year are worth recording. While their selection would suggest that the affairs at Reims were known throughout the empire, it also suggests that their interest to a contemporary annalist in Saxony lay in their connection to the affairs of the emperor, not in the local dispute over French interests in who was awarded an archbishopric on the fringes of Lotharingia.

Another example of the joining of a *placitum* and synod occurs in the management of a dispute between Archbishop Peter of Ravenna and a certain Rainerius in 967. Pope John XIII and Otto I presided at a *placitum* that was also attended by bishops and archbishops, counts, margraves, dukes, city judges from various Italian cities, and a variety of functionaries, "Romanorum, Francorum, Langobardorum atque Saxorum, Allamanorum."[38] The charges were quite severe, accusing Rainerius, a deacon, of entering the see of Ravenna accompanied by his troops, violating the see, stealing its treasures, and capturing and imprisoning Archbishop Peter. Rainerius had already been judged before three *placita* on the matter, once before Pope John XIII and the Roman clergy, once before a general *placitum* held by the Roman clergy, and then again before the pope. At this fourth hearing, the accused was reportedly summoned by letter but refused to come. Otto and the pope questioned the legal experts present, the judges from Rome and Lombardy, about the legal precedents for a case such as this. The judges responded that refusing to come when summoned "to your synod

37. MacLean, *History and Politics*, 249; Adalbert, *Continuatio*, s.a. 948, 163–64: "DCCCCXXXXVIII. sinodus in Inglenheim a XXXIIII episcopis habetur; cui presidente Marino episcopo, Romanae ecclesiae legato, incliti reges Otto et Ludowicus affuerunt. In qua multis ecclesiasticae utilitatis rebus promulgatis causa quoque Hugonis filii Heriberti, qui Artaldum archiepiscopum expellens sedem ecclesiae Remensis invaserat, ventilatur; et omnium, qui affuerant, iudicio episcoporum dampnatur."

38. DO I 340.

and to your *placitum*" was a crime according to law.[39] There are a number of key things happening here. First, this particular court is specifically referred to as an "imperiali placito" (imperial *placitum*). The pope may have been sitting in judgment with the emperor, but this was an imperial court. Additionally, while reported speech is always problematic, the joining of *synod* and *placitum* as ostensibly interchangeable terms to describe the proceedings occurs twice. Legal experts from Rome and Lombardy are consulted about the law pertaining to the injustice done to Archbishop Peter and about the appropriate punishment for Rainerius. In applying local laws, Otto is largely following the precedent of Charlemagne but is also prudently avoiding possible backlash against his judgment. While the judges advise him as to what is appropriate, it is Otto who renders judgment, even though this judgment involves two members of the ecclesiastical hierarchy. Last, it is notable that in this court, at which a pope is copresiding over a decision pertaining to ecclesiastical conflict, secular law is used to determine the proper course of action.[40]

The mediation of disputes was not always initiated by kings; ecclesiastical lords also were proactive in these kinds of affairs. In 959, Archbishop Brun of Cologne went into Francia to meet with his sister Queen Gerberga and his nephews, who were "all quarreling over some *castra* that King Lothair [Brun's nephew] had captured in Burgundy." After receiving hostages, Brun "arranged a peace . . . until a future *placitum* could be held."[41] The involvement of Archbishop Brun is much like that of Otto in the dispute at Reims. This matter was, in essence, a family dispute. Brun negotiated a peace among the disputants—one of whom was the queen of France—pending a formal hearing of the complaint by the king. These interventions in negotiating peace until *placita* could be arranged were important elements of order in the Ottonian Empire and doubtless prevented reciprocal and escalating violence from spinning out of control. As noted in the introduction to the present study, the Ottonians have often been accused by modern historians of not being aspirational in developing their gov-

39. DO I 340: "Et interrogaverunt predictis iudices et dativi Romani et Longobardi, quit exinde legem fuissent ad fatiendum. Et ipsis iudices et dativi dixerunt: 'Lex iubet, postquam ipso Rainerius diaconus ad vestrum sinodum et a vestrum placitum venire noluit de ipsa crimina que vobis per tantas vices exinde super eum reclamastis, investite istum avocatore domni Petri archiepiscopi de omibus rebus et possessionibus suis.'"

40. This case is mentioned briefly by Maurizio Lupoi as an example of how "it was a guiding principle, resolutely followed, to work towards a 'common' law," when adjudicating a "conflict or choice between two 'laws'" (*The Origins of the European Legal Order* [Cambridge: Cambridge University Press, 1994], 433).

41. Fanning and Bachrach, 63; Flodoard, *Annales*, s.a. 959, 404: "Bruno iterum in Franciam venit, et apud Compendium cum regina sorore ac nepotibus suis discordantibus pro quibusdam castris, quae rex Lotharius ex Burgundia receperat, colloquium habuit; obsidibusque datis, pacem inter ipsos usque ad futurum placitum pepigit."

ernmental systems, particularly the administration of law and order. But one can hardly criticize rulers in hindsight for lacking forward-thinking imagination when what was there worked. The Ottonians were not aspirational, but they were rational. The system they implemented was modeled on a known successful precedent, that of the Carolingians, and was effective enough for them to maintain control and order that was good enough throughout their realm.

The King as Purveyor of Justice

Ottonian kings were dependent on distributed local jurisdictions to maintain order and peace in the realm. The king would often become directly involved in the administration of justice when disputing involved great lords or became disruptive to the peace, or when some appeal was made to him. This is what we see described by Thietmar of Merseburg regarding how plaintiffs or others with business for the Ottonian kings tried to gain a hearing, where the access to the king's court was normally arranged through the use of intercessors.[42]

In the Ottonian assemblies, the advisors and judges adjudicated, but the conceptualization of law and how it worked was substantially different than elsewhere in the tenth-century world.[43] Legislating happened when necessary to enforce the peace but was not an essential component of the workings of justice. In his discussion of some of the legal-philosophical pictorial representations of Henry II, Ernst Kantorowicz perhaps gets at the key essence of Ottonian legal thought. The emperor served as a mediator of divine will. The idea, according to Kantorowicz, is "theological, and not jurisprudential: the emperor is mediator and executor of the divine will through the power of the Holy Spirit,

42. Thietmar, *Chronicon* 3.13. See chapter 3 in the present study, regarding Althoff on the use of intercessors as a normal way of presenting petitions to the Ottonian kings. The use of intercessors is where the idea of *Königsnähe*, discussed in chapter 2, could be so important in gaining access to the king and his court, as it was usually the high-ranking officials of the Ottonian court who served in this regard. For example, the diplomas of Otto I show that archchancellors Frederick of Mainz and Hubert of Parma interceded five times each, and William of Mainz interceded a total of eighteen times in the fourteen years he served as archchancellor. See Sean Gilsdorf, *The Favor of Friends: Intercession and Aristocratic Politics in Carolingian and Ottonian Europe* (Leiden: Brill, 2014), 95n36. Regarding the continuity of personal relationships and intercessors in disputing and conflict resolution throughout the early Middle Ages, see also Warren Brown, "Conflict, Letters, and Personal Relationships in the Carolingian Formula Collections," *Law and History Review* 25.2 (2007): 343–44.

43. Wormald points this out several times in the service of establishing the uniqueness of Anglo-Saxon legal thought, though without elaborating on distinguishing features of Ottonian law (*Making of English Law*, 19, 108).

and not through the secular spirit of legal science."[44] This concept as articulated by Kantorowicz goes far in helping to explain how the Ottonian rulers envisioned their role as dispensers of justice. When the notion of the emperor as heavenly mediator is considered in conjunction with ideas about sacral kingship, discussed below, we can better discern the Ottonians' conceptualizations of rulership, law, and justice.

The importance of the Ottonian king as a direct enforcer of order and peace is referenced several times by Widukind of Corvey. For example, he relates how Henry I intervened in a dispute between two nobles, Eberhard and Bruning. In the course of that feud, Eberhard had burned a city to the ground and killed all of its inhabitants. The king fined Eberhard a hundred talents or that value in horses, and all of the military officers who had participated in the assault had to carry dogs to Magdeburg.[45] This punishment was clearly designed to be a public display of the kind described by Geoffrey Koziol and Gerd Althoff, since the officers received gifts and pardons after their humiliating entrance into the city.[46] Widukind stresses how Henry I and Otto I built networks of loyal men by interceding for them or redirecting their energy, as when he describes how Henry took men convicted of theft and robbery and conscripted them into his army, which, in those years of wars with the Magyars, could be viewed as an astute way to avoid wasting human resources.[47] He notes that Otto I was an avid intercessor for mercy of convicted men and "would believe them guilty of no crime," after which "they would never offend against him again."[48] Widukind further relates that Otto forgave his son and son-in-law upon learning of their

44. Kantorowicz, *King's Two Bodies*, 115.

45. Widukind of Corvey, *Res gestae Saxonicae* 2.6, in *Widukindi monachi Corbiensis rerum gestarum Saxonicarum libri tres*, ed. Paul Hirsch and H.-E. Lohmann after G. Waitz and K. A. Kehr, MGH SRG 60 (Hanover: Hahn, 1935), 72: "Qua presumptione rex audita condempnavit Evurhardum centum talentis aestimatione equorum, omnesque principes militum, qui eum ad hoc facinus adiuvabant, dedecore canum, quos portabant usque ad urbem regiam quam vocitamus Magathaburg." This is an excellent example of the importance the Ottonians placed on maintaining equilibrium through negotiation and the judicious assertion of royal power, their main peacekeeping tools in maintaining the balance of power among their lay and ecclesiastical magnates.

46. Regarding the importance of ritual behaviors in dispute resolution, see Geoffrey Koziol, *Begging Pardon and Favor: Ritual and Political Order in Early Medieval France* (Ithaca, NY: Cornell University Press, 1992); Gerd Althoff, *Spielregeln der Politik im Mittelalter: Kommunikation in Frieden und Fehde* (Darmstadt: Wissenschaftliche Buchgesellschaft, 1997), 21–56. For discussion of other political rituals specific to Ottonian Germany, see Philippe Buc, *The Dangers of Ritual: Between Early Medieval Texts and Social Scientific Theory* (Princeton, NJ: Princeton University Press, 2001), 15–50; David A. Warner, "Ritual and Memory in the Ottonian *Reich*: The Ceremony of *Adventus*," *Speculum* 76.2 (2001): 255–83.

47. Widukind, *Res gestae Saxonicae* 2.3, 69.

48. Widukind, *Res gestae Saxonicae* 2.36, 96: "Nam quosdam audivimus accusatos et peccati manifestos, ipsum eorum advocatum et intercessorem et criminis nullo modo credulum, et ab eo post habitos, tamquam nichil umquam in eum peccassent."

plots against him, despite clear evidence of their guilt.[49] Otto inserted capable agents when circumstances necessitated imperial intervention or oversight; Otto placed his younger brother Brun as Duke of Lotharingia, a region notorious for its difficulty, and Brun "purged the region of robbers, and introduced such discipline in law, that the greatest order and the greatest peace continued in those parts."[50] Widukind's account was intended to glorify his Liudolfing subjects. However, we should not discount the emphasis on the king's role in justice as part of what an ideal king should be doing. Even if this account is exaggerated, it at least suggests the importance attributed to the king in peacekeeping and dispensing justice. Closely related to the idea of sacral kingship, discussed further below, Widukind's portrayal of ideal kingship allows room for mercy, a demonstration of royal power that perhaps made as deep an impression as violence.[51]

The importance of the king as a judicial authority is also evident in contemporary chronicles. His presence at synods and assemblies was seen as an essential aspect of his rule, of which his ability to negotiate peace among his nobles was a key element. Reports of such activities abound. An example is Adalbert of Magdeburg's report of an assembly Otto held at Duisburg in 944 "with the leading men of the Lotharingians and the Franks. There, at the behest of [Duke] Conrad, Archbishop Robert of Trier and Bishop Richar of Tongres[-Liege] were accused of infidelity before the king; but they were quickly absolved of the offences attributed to them."[52] Otto attended a synod at Ingelheim in 948, which Adalbert specifies was presided over by a papal legate. Heard at that synod, in addition to the promulgation of "many things of use to the Church," was the case of Hugh, son of Heribert, who had invaded the see of Reims and expelled Archbishop Artoldus.[53] Otto also convoked a synod in 963, and at his Christmas court in Rome in 967 he ordered the hang-

49. Widukind, *Res gestae Saxonicae* 3.13, 111.

50. Widukind, *Res gestae Saxonicae* 2.36, 97: "regionem a latronibus purgavit et in tantum disciplina legali instruxit, ut summa ratio summaque pax illis in partibus locum tenerent."

51. Widukind's preface to Abbess Mathilda, Otto I's daughter to whom Widukind's work is addressed, stressed the importance of clemency as an attribute of good kingship (and, of course, an attribute of Otto's), a stress repeated later in the work (Widukind, *Res gestae Saxonicae*, praef., 1; 2.29, 91).

52. MacLean, *History and Politics*, 247; Adalbert, *Continuatio*, s.a. 944, 162: "Rex apud Diusburgum in rogationibus placitum cum primoribus Lothariensium et Francorum habuit, ubi factione Cuonradi ducis Ruotbertus archiepiscopus Trevirensis et Richarius Tungrensis episcopus infidelitatis apud regem arguuntur, sed in brevi ab obiecto sibi crimine liberantur."

53. MacLean, *History and Politics*, 249; Adalbert, *Continuatio*, s.a. 948, 163–64: "Sinodus in Inglenheim a XXXIIII episcopis habetur; ciu presidente Marino episcopo, Romanae ecclesiae legato, incliti reges Otto et Ludowicus affuerunt. In qua multis ecclesiasticae utilitatis rebus promulgatis, causa quoque Hugonis filii Heriberti, qui Artaldum archiepiscopum expellens sedem ecclesiae Remensis invaserat, ventilatur."

ing of the Romans who had been the ringleaders in the expulsion of Pope John XIII.[54]

Thietmar, too, reports on the dispensation of justice at these assemblies and synods as an important part of regnal duties. For example, in 977, Duke Henry, Count Ekbert, and Bishop Henry were accused before Otto II of conspiring against him. They were apparently not present to hear the accusation or defend themselves against it and were subsequently captured and sent into exile.[55] At Magdeburg in 995, Otto III held an assembly of his leading men at which "through good counsel, a long-running dispute between [Duke] Henry [of Bavaria] and Gebhard of Regensburg was settled."[56] In addition to numerous such examples, Thietmar gives us a hint of the importance of this idea of justice and law in the idea of kingship when he reports certain events in the course of Henry II's struggle against Duke Herman, another claimant to the right of succession to Otto III, who had died without an heir. At an assembly of both secular and ecclesiastical lords at Merseburg in 1002, "with the consent of all, Duke Bernhard stood before the king and revealed the will of the assembled people, expounding in particular the necessity and law of all, and diligently inquired what he wished from compassion to promise them orally or grant them by deed." The king replied, "I have no desire to pervert your law in any

---

54. Adalbert, *Continuatio*, s.aa. 963, 967. Adalbert specifies that the Romans killed were leading men of the city. There is the possibility that Otto I, in ordering the hanging of these men, was intervening in a feud. Adalbert's description of the papal election of 965 notes that the imperial prerogative of papal selection had been exercised, so John, bishop of Narni, though elected by the Roman people, was an imperial choice. But this Pope John (distinct from Pope John XII who was part of the controversy in 963–65 around Popes Leo, John, and Benedict) "immediately persecuted the greater Romans with a more arrogant spirit than was fitting, and soon he had to endure these men as his greatest and most dangerous enemies" (MacLean, *History and Politics*, 268–69; Adalbert, *Continuatio*, s.a. 965, in *Adalberti Continuatio Regionis*, 176: "Qui statim maiores Romanorum elatiore animo, quam oporteret, insequitur, quos in brevi inimicissimos et infestos patitur." He was captured, run out of Rome, and held captive in Campania. When Pope Leo had been treated similarly and the Romans had been incited to attack Otto, the emperor fought and killed his attackers, but it was described as a battle, not as an imperial order with judicial overtones (Liudprand of Cremona, *Historia Ottonis* §§ 17–18, in *Liudprandi Cremonensis Opera Omnia*, ed. Paolo Chiesa, Corpus Christianorum [Turnhout: Brepols, 1998]). In 966, "the Romans, fearing the emperor's arrival, released Pope John from the captivity in which he had been held," reinstated him, and asked his forgiveness (MacLean, *History and Politics*, 270; Adalbert, *Continuatio*, s.a. 966, 177: "Tunc Romani imperatoris metuentes adventum Rotfredo iam mortuo a custodia, qua tenebatur, Iohannem apostolicum absolvunt et veniam pro malis, quae ei ingesserant, poscentes in locum et sedem suam illum restituunt." Thus, the order to hang the ringleaders would have been a powerful message to the Romans regarding imperial power and imperial jurisdiction, not to mention the limits of internal disorder that would be tolerated without inviting the emperor's direct intervention.

55. Thietmar, *Chronicon* 3.7, 104–5.

56. Warner, *Ottonian Germany*, 165; Thietmar, *Chronicon* 4.20, 155: "Et cum inter hunc et Ratisbonensem episcopum Gebehardum longa contencio haberetur, cum bono consilio ibidem finitur."

way but rather, with life mercifully permitting, to observe it."[57] Thietmar further emphasizes the role of the king in upholding the law when he reports the destruction of the castle of Morsberg: "While the king wished benevolently to give the law [*legem*] to all, whatever their need, Herman and Dietrich, dukes in name alone and not in reality, tried to obstruct him. All was in vain, however, as they soon saw themselves subjected deservedly to the author of justice. For the king, moved by the pressing need of the whole folk, firmly ordered that a certain castle belonging to the duke, called Morsberg, should be destroyed and never rebuilt."[58] In addition to being the instrument of justice, the king was also to preside at court, as when Margrave Henry's men seized the royal treasure and holed up in a burg. Ultimately, the treasure was recovered, but only one man was caught, and he received leniency: "After the captive was presented to the king, the judges sentenced him to death. Nevertheless, through the persistent intercession of Archbishop Willigis of Mainz, the sentence was changed to a payment to be decided by the king."[59] Thietmar's language suggests that while the king had some say in what the commuted sentence would be comprised of, he did not judge at these assemblies; judges judged, ecclesiastical lords interceded for mercy, and the king provided the authority to back these judgments and peacemaking arrangements. But the king was the dispenser of justice, as he often determined the punishment after guilt or innocence was established or after an accommodation between parties was reached. The diplomas that record decisions made at various synods and assemblies support this idea.

Compared to the narrative sources, the diplomas give more formal evidence of the role of Ottonian kings in their roles as dispensers of justice. Several extant Ottonian diplomas relate to the hearing of a complaint or the adjudication of a dispute, but no such documents are extant for Henry I. Several possible explanations present themselves. It could be that Henry was so busy dealing with internal and external conflicts, keeping the nobility in check and defending the

57. Warner, *Ottonian Germany*, 216; Thietmar, *Chronicon* 5.16, 239: "Bernhardus dux cum consensu omnium astante coram rege voluntatem plebis convenientis aperiens omniumque necessitatem ac legem specialiter exponens, quid eis misericordie dictis promittere seu factis vellet impendere, diligenter inquirit. . . . Legem igitur vestram non in aliquo corrumpere, sed vita comite malo clementer in omnibus adimplere et vestre racionabili voluntati, inquantum valeo, ubique animum adhibere."

58. Warner, *Ottonian Germany*, 223–24; Thietmar, *Chronicon* 5.27, 253: "Rege vero, ibidem omnibus aliqua necessitate laborantibus, benigne legem dare cupiente, Heremannus ac Theodericus solo nomine duces, sed non re, temptabant hoc impedire, sed frustra, continuo animadvertentes auctori iusticie se merito succumbere. Nam rex quoddam castellum ducis, Mulsburg dictum, ob instantem tocius populi necessitatem destrui et, ut numquam reedificaretur, firmiter precepit."

59. Warner, *Ottonian Germany*, 228; Thietmar, *Chronicon* 5.34, 260: "presentatoque regi captivo capitalis sententia a iudicibus decernitur, quae Magontinae archipresulis Willigisi intercessione supplici et, quae regi placuit, redemptione amovetur."

frontiers and marches from Magyar attacks, that this particular aspect of formal governance was not feasible and that more direct intervention in conflicts was preferable, as when Eberhard burned down a city as part of a feud. Adalbert of Magdeburg, writing about Otto I in 956, makes a connection between peace and assemblies: "The king, living in peace and great tranquility, held a placitum in a royal assembly of his faithful men at Cologne."[60] Perhaps one of the reasons that Otto was able to convene an assembly is because his time was not consumed mitigating internal or external conflicts. The kind of direct intervention in dispute resolution that Henry engaged in with Eberhard, as opposed to administering justice through use of assemblies, also suggests more of a traditional form of lordship than the image we see later with Otto I, that of an emperor serving as an instrument of God on earth and ruling through consensual kingship. It is possible that assemblies, or *placita*, were just so infrequent under Henry that records did not survive, or perhaps the court had not yet formalized to the point of recording such matters. Since the records we do have are all from Italy, a region that was not consolidated with the empire until the reign of Otto the Great, it is likely that they were the product of a peculiarity of Italian political needs. However, the change in style of governance and rulership that occurred between Henry I and Otto I, usually noted with regard to the different ways they interacted with their *familiares* (Henry as a true *primus inter pares* and Otto beginning to pull away from that model and distance himself from those kinds of close ties and entanglements with his magnates), also signals a change in how they were conceiving of the idea of kingship, its role, and how it should be represented on earth.

Although we have no diplomas recording proceedings and decisions of assemblies under Henry I, we have nine such diplomas extant from Otto I, more than from any of the other Ottonian kings, though they continue to appear throughout the reigns of Otto II, Otto III, and Henry II.[61] These diplomas are interesting on a number of levels. First, although the emperors presided at all the *placita* represented in these diplomas, only two of the documents are actually signed by the emperor himself.[62] Thus, although he convened and presided at *placita* and although the documents promulgated as a result of these

60. Adalbert, *Continuatio*, s.a. 956, 168.

61. DD OI 269, 340, 342, 375, 398–99, 400, 404, 416; DD OII 266, 282, 298, 315; DD OIII 193, 227, 270, 278, 339, 396, 411; DD HII 299, 461, 465, 467.

62. DD OIII 339; DD HII 465. In many instances, the emperor's seal is placed to confirm his authority behind the writ, but he does not sign it, as in DD OI 405: "Quod iuxta sanctissimi imperatoris decretum ante presentiam Pandulfi principis et marchionis et Petri comitis atque Petri cancellarii definitum et determinatum est inter eos, ea ratione ut inviolatum et inconvulsum inter ipsos omni permaneat tempore volumus. Quot ut verius ab omnibus credatur, nostro sigillo sigillari iussimus."

proceedings were in his name, he was not a signatory to them. As most of the diplomas produced by the Ottonian chancery that have survived (mainly concerning gifts, grants, and immunities) do carry the signature of the king, this absence stands out. All these *placita* are presided over by the emperor and the local authority, who might be a bishop, a local prince, a count of the palace, or a pope,[63] plus numerous nobles and others in attendance, both sitting and standing. These were public affairs, intended to be seen, with the results of hearings to be known to all. Several judgments regarding disputes order the lord presiding with Otto at the *placitum* "through his own realm and in all these matters to send his *bannus*."[64] A declaration of the proceedings also often carried with it notice of a financial penalty if anyone were to violate the settlement adjudicated by the *placitum*, with half of the penalty to go to the imperial treasury and half to the aggrieved party. These fines could be quite hefty; in the case of a land dispute recorded on April 17, 967, at Ravenna, the penalty for violation of the settlement was set at two thousand gold mancuses, with half to go to the imperial treasury and half to Archbishop Peter, the plaintiff in the case.[65]

Another way these documents are distinctive is that they were very self-consciously written down. Given the vast output of the Ottonian chancery, this format is surprising. Many of these documents explain that the proceedings are put in writing to preserve what might be lost if only committed to memory.[66] Among the most interesting examples are a pair of documents produced on consecutive days of a *placitum*, the earliest of these types of documents for Otto I, from early in his imperial career. On August 8, 964, at a *placitum* in Lucca, Otto confirmed for Bishop Ermenaldo of Reggio all the rights and lands that had been given to the bishopric by Charlemagne, including a detailed list of

63. For example, DD OI 340 quite specifically references not a synod but a *placita*, with Pope John XIII in attendance: "Dum ressideret in iuditio et imperiali placito domnus Iohannes sanctissimo et coangelico universalis papae una cum domno Otone."

64. DD OI 340: the emperor "iussit . . . ad suprascripto Odbertus marchio et comes palatio, ut in sua vice i[n] ipsis omnibus rebus suos bandum mitere. Que ita fecit suprascripto domnus Odbertus [gloriosus marchio et co]mes palatio, clara voce coram omnibus dixit per verbum, 'Ex iussionem domini mei imp[erator]is ego mitto suo bandum in totia ipsis rebus et posessionibus.'" Sometimes the emperor's own *bannus* is sent, as in DD OI 269: "Insuper miserunt bannum domni imperatori predictis Auberto marchio et comes palacii et Uberto episcopus et missus domni imperatoris super iam dictis omnibus rebus et familiis et in omnia quod in ipsum preceptum legitur in mancosos duo milia, ut nullus quislibet homo magna parvaque persona de omnia quod in ipsum preceptum confirmatum et corroboratum legitur."

65. DD OI 340: "et qui eum disvestire, ut sit compondituros duo milia aureos mancozos, medietatem camare domni imperatoris et medietatem tibi suprascripto domnus Petrus archiepiscopus tuisque subcessoribus."

66. DD OI 340: "Eo quod omnia que gesta esse videntur e prolixis temporibus memoriter retineri non possunt, ideo scripture vinculum roborari cautum est."

regions and boundaries of properties that were confirmed to belong to that diocese.[67] On August 9, 964, Bishop Ermenaldo came before the court again, demanding that the document that he held from the day before be examined by all to confirm that he could have in no way forged or altered it, and that everything declared in the writ to be part of the diocese was conceded and corroborated (suggesting that there were probably some land disputes at stake here).[68] A judge and advocate for the emperor confirmed the authenticity of the document and its contents, but Ermenaldo's overzealousness speaks volumes to one of the main legal problems in Italy that had been appealed to Otto almost immediately when he became emperor, the never-ending land disputes that involved forged documents, false claims, and perjury. By ensuring a second document confirming the authenticity of the first and by having, as a result of his second appearance before Otto's court, the *bannus* announcing his rights and a prohibitive penalty for any who might violate them, Ermenaldo acquired additional protection of his property claims.[69]

That the emperor's role was not just to administer justice but also to serve as the dispenser of God's justice is emphasized in a vignette described by Thietmar and involving Henry II.

> A house in which the king was giving the justice of the law to the populace suddenly collapsed, but only one priest was hurt. He had been living, unjustly and knowingly, with the wife of a man who had been excommunicated. Because of this crime, his guilt exceeded that of all the others and so, with his legs broken, his death served as a punishment for the outrage he had committed.[70]

---

67. DD OI 268.

68. DD OI 269: "Ibique eorum veniens presencia Ermenaldus venerabilis sancte Regiensis ecclesie episcopus una insimul cum Ansprando avocato suo et ipsius episcopii et ostenserunt [preceptum unum]. . . . Prceptum [*sic*] ipsum obstensum et ab ordine relectum fuit. . . . Tunc responderunt iam dicto Ermenaldo episcopus et Asprando avocato eius: 'Vere preceptum istum ibi ostensimus, ut nullus quislibet homo dicere posit quod nos eum occulte aut conludiose abuisemus aut tenuisemus, et nec sciles apareat, et casis omnibus rebus ipsis seu familiis et omnia quod per istum preceptum nobis et pars ipsius episcopii concessum adque corroboratum est, abemus et tenemus ad iure et proprietario ipsius episcopii sancte Regiensis ecclesie."

69. DD OI 269. Hagen Keller and Stefan Ast emphasize the importance of the performative aspect of such *ostensio cartae* ("*Ostensio Cartae*: Italienische Gerichtsurkunden des 10. Jahrhunderts zwischen Schriftlichkeit und Performanz," *Archiv für Diplomatik* 53 [2007]: 99–121). For a discussion of how *placita* from the same period in France demonstrate interactions of orality and textuality in legal procedures, see Patrick J. Geary, "Oblivion between Orality and Textuality in the Tenth Century," in Althoff, Fried, and Geary, 111–22.

70. Warner, *Ottonian Germany*, 244; Thietmar, *Chronicon* 6.9, 285: "Domus, in qua rex populo legis iura dabat, subito cecidit, uni dumtaxat presbitero nocens cum quadam excommunicata

The emperor is active in the distribution of justice, but this story also shows the emperor's court as an extension of God's court, which connects his justice directly with God's justice. As Henry sat in judgment, God's judgment caused the house to collapse and the sinful priest to be killed. This example also demonstrates the end result of the successful transformation of the idea of kingship under the Ottonians. The Carolingians had portrayed themselves as heirs to the Old Testament kings. The Anglo-Saxons situated themselves as heirs to the great tradition of lawgiving kings exemplified by Moses and Christ. The Ottonians went further than that. As we saw in chapter 4, through the development of a program of representation over the course of the reigns of Ottos I, II, and III, the Ottonians instituted the idea of sacral kingship. Their kings were not just the representatives of Christ on earth but were actually the impersonators of Christ himself. Not only was this idea of sacral kingship different than anything in Anglo-Saxon or Carolingian rulership, but the Ottonians' idea of sacral kingship was tied to their conceptions of the roles of kings and emperors as dispensers of justice.

Trial by Bilateral Ordeal

While unilateral trial by ordeal (e.g., by hot iron, cold water, and Eucharist) were prevalent throughout early medieval Europe, Ottonian kings and emperors also exerted their judicial authority by ordering and presiding over judicial duels. Trial by combat was a common feature of Ottonian rule, and it has been noted that providing a forum for trial by combat was an important function of the royal court.[71] The introduction of trial by combat to Italian law by Otto I in 962, in response to complaints about forgery and perjury in property disputes, has also been recognized as an important move in the representation of Ottonian rulership, combining the ideas of the emperor as both dispenser of justice and defender of the church.[72] We can see this kind of divine hand of justice in the duels described in the Ottonian narrative histories.

Liudprand of Cremona's *Antapodosis* portrays the trial by judicial ordeal

domna sepius, quam liceret, commoranti. Ille pre ceteris in hoc reatu culpabilis morte sua cruribus confractis penam luit tanti facinoris."

71. Benjamin Arnold, *Medieval Germany, 500–1300: A Political Interpretation* (Toronto: University of Toronto Press, 1997), 147.

72. David A. Warner, "The Representation of Empire: Otto I at Ravenna," in *Representations of Power in Medieval Germany*, ed. Bjorn Weiler and Simon MacLean (Turnhout: Brepols, 2006), 130–31. Chris Wickham, *Early Medieval Italy: Central Power and Local Society 400-1000* (1981; repr., Ann Arbor: University of Michigan Press, 1989), 128. The capitulary was issued in 967, but the Italian nobility had broached the issue of these property disputes with Otto at his imperial coronation. See MGH Const 1, "Capitulare Veronense de duello iudiciali," 27–30.

as a legitimate form of divinely dispensed judgment and specifically focuses on trial by combat. While the duel, perhaps as a part of feuding behaviors, figures as one way of exacting revenge in *Antapodosis*,[73] Liudprand reports two instances of duels that are distinctly judicial in nature. One is an unfought duel related by Liudprand in such a way as to enhance Henry I's kingly virtues; the other is fought to determine the proof of a fraternal relationship.

In the first instance, after Henry I was elected king following Conrad I's death, the one noble who refused to accept that election was Arnulf. Recently returned to Bavaria from exile in Hungary, Arnulf wanted the crown for himself. When King Henry realized that he had a challenger, he gathered an army and headed for Bavaria; Arnulf, likewise, gathered as many armed men as he could and met Henry halfway. Henry, "a wise and God-fearing man, consider[ed] that irreparable damage could befall either side" if they actually engaged in battle. So he requested a private audience with his challenger.[74] Arnulf showed up alone at the appointed time and place, thinking that he was going to a duel.[75] There was to be no fight, however; Henry persuaded Arnulf of the wisdom of becoming his man, and when Arnulf consulted his followers, they agreed this suggestion was excellent and wise. The point here is that, literary license or no, the duel seemed the most plausible explanation Arnulf could think of for why Henry would want to meet him alone. Liudprand is nonjudgmental about the duel itself. But note this example's emphasis on the possibility of a duel for creating consensus, stressed by Liudprand, first, in Henry's speech to win Arnulf over when he arrives ready to fight and, second, when Arnulf returns to his men (who have expected him to be in a duel as well). Liudprand's story suggests that a duel could stand in as a legitimate substitute for battle. The importance of the consensus that is achieved, even by this duel that failed to be fought, lends credence to the arguments put forth by Rebecca Colman and Peter Brown that the ordeal functioned as a rational part of medieval society, and especially served as a way to resolve disputes and achieve consensus with the least amount of collateral damage.[76]

73. For example, when Liudprand reports that an unfortunate, foolish Bavarian taunted the Italians during a siege and was killed in a duel when an exasperated soldier finally rode out from the city to confront him, the historian casts the event as motivated by revenge (*Antapodosis* 1.2, in *Liudprandi Cremonensis Opera Omnia*, ed. Paolo Chiesa, Corpus Christianorum [Turnhout: Brepols, 1998], 6).

74. Paolo Squatriti, ed. and trans., *The Complete Works of Liudprand of Cremona* (Washington, DC: Catholic University of America Press, 2007), 85; Liudprand of Cremona, *Antapodosis* 2.21, 44: "Cumque in eo esset ut bellum pariter inire deberent, sicut vir sapiens et Dei timens rex damnum accidere, Arnaldo quatinus cum solo solus loquatur, denuntiat."

75. Liudprand of Cremona, *Antapodosis* 2.21, 44: "Putans igitur Arnaldus, quod singulari se acciret certamine, ad condictum locum solus hora statuta pervenit."

76. Rebecca Colman, "Reason and Unreason in Early Medieval Law," *Journal of Interdisciplin-*

It is possible that all of Liudprand's battles in *Antapodosis* are effectively cast as trials by combat, an idea that would make sense within the context of sacral kingship. Philippe Buc suggests as much for the Battle of Birten.[77] Hincmar of Reims had used the story of doubting Saint Thomas to justify trial by ordeal, and Liudprand uses the same passages (John 20:27, 38) to emphasize that Otto I's success at Birten was due to the direct involvement of God. John 20:27 reads, "Then saith he [Jesus] to Thomas, Reach hither thy finger, and behold my hands; and reach hither thy hand and thrust it into my side. And be not faithless, but believing."[78] This is the basis for one of Liudprand's long sermons in *Antapodosis*; the chapter immediately following the description of the battle is essentially a homily about doubting Thomas, about how, when he finally was convinced that he was in the presence of the resurrected Lord, his exclamation "God and Lord!" rendered mute those who had protested, as they recognized the truth of his statement. Thus, according to Liudprand, Thomas's doubt was part of a divine plan. Liudprand then connects this with Otto's victory: "This victory, unexpected because of the fewness of your soldiers, came by the decision of divine Providence, since God wanted to indicate to men how dear to him was one who deserved to obtain such an immense triumph with so few troops, simply by praying."[79] Here, Liudprand is the shouter of truth; readers are to recognize the victory as the just judgment of God. Buc asserts that by using this specific passage, linked by Hincmar specifically to a justification of trial by ordeal, Liudprand clearly identified the Battle of Birten as an ordeal, a trial by combat. This would suggest an endorsement of trial by ordeal as a valid way of determining justice, of allowing God to visibly demonstrate that which is otherwise hidden, the truth in men's hearts: "Just as in touching the visible flesh Thomas had been able to see the invisible divinity in Christ, the ordeal made visible in this carnal world God's eternal justice, the normally invisible justice that would manifest itself fully at the Last Judgment."[80] Given Liudprand's care in making sure that the reader is aware of God's involvement in the outcome of all of the battles related in *Antapodosis*, it is not a large leap to see them all as trials by ordeal.

---

ary History 4.4 (1974): 571–91; Peter Brown, "Society and the Supernatural: A Medieval Change," in *Society and the Holy in Late Antiquity* (Berkeley: University of California Press, 1982), 302–32.

77. Philippe Buc, "Ritual and Interpretation: The Early Medieval Case," *Early Medieval Europe* 9.2 (2000): 192.

78. John 20:27, KJV.

79. Squatriti, 160; Liudprand of Cremona, *Antapodosis* 4.26, 114: "Sic itaque, sic, rex piissime, insperata ob militum paucitatem victoria divinae consilium providentiae fuit, volens mortalibus indicare quam carus Deo esset, qui orando tam inmensum cum paucissimis triumphum optinere promeruit."

80. Buc, "Ritual and Interpretation," 192.

The last duel in *Antapodosis* revolves around contested maternity. Boso, a brother, by the same father, of King Hugh of Italy (r. 924–47), was jealous of Lambert, Margrave of Tuscany, who was ostensibly a brother of King Hugh by the same mother. Wanting to seize the margraveship himself, Boso convinced Hugh that Lambert was not really his brother. When Hugh demanded that Lambert no longer refer to him as brother, Lambert challenged the king to a duel to prove the matter once and for all, publicly: "Lest the king cast doubt on my being his brother, I want to prove in a duel with everyone looking on that we came out into the light of day from one and the same body."[81] The king chose a champion, Teudinus, to fight Lambert in single combat, but "God, however, who is just and whose judgment is fair, in whom there is no iniquity, arranged that Teudinus might fall very quickly and Lambert gain victory, so that ambiguity be shattered and the truth be manifest to all."[82] Again, Liudprand's tone in relating this story is matter-of-fact and mildly approving. While he portrays the duel as a legitimate and fair way to determine truths that there are otherwise no way of knowing for sure, we must remember that one agenda of his writings was to show the evils inherent in Italian politics, and the rest of the story presented Liudprand with a fine example of blatant disregard for the divinely revealed truth of the duel by King Hugh. The denouement to this episode does not go well for Lambert (despite his victory in the duel) and demonstrates some of the problems inherent in Italian family politics. King Hugh, publicly embarrassed, took Lambert into custody, fearing that Lambert would now press his advantage to claim the whole kingdom. Boso ended up with the Tuscan marches after all, and, in a gesture common to Italian and Byzantine political circles when trying to neutralize rivals, Hugh blinded Lambert.[83]

It is interesting that Liudprand endorses judicial combat, being that he is a cleric and is from Italy, a region that did not experience judicial combat until it was introduced by Otto I in 967.[84] His enthusiasm is doubtless an effort to heap praise on Otto, at whose court Liudprand spent his exile and where he was treated extremely well. Liudprand and Hincmar notwithstanding, most clerics objected to the practice. The outcomes of judicial duals were by no means always clear or necessarily accepted as divine judgment, as Hincmar's doubting

81. Squatriti, 136; Liudprand of Cremona, *Antapodosis* 3.47, 93: "Ne inficiari rex possit me fratrem suum esse, nos uno ex corpore eundemque per aditum in lucem prodiisse duello cupio cunctis cernentibus comprobare."

82. Squatriti, 136; Liudprand of Cremona, *Antapodosis* 3.47, 93: "Deus autem, qui iustus est et rectum est iudicium eius, in quo non est iniquitas, ut amphibologiam dirumperet ac veritatem cunctis ostenderet, fecit ut Teudinus citissime caderet et Lampertus victoriam obtineret."

83. Liudprand of Cremona, *Antapodosis* 3.47, 92–93. Lambert was blinded in 931.

84. MGH Const 1, "Capitulare Veronense de Duello Iudiciali," 27–30.

Thomas analogy would have us believe. Robert Bartlett suggests that trial by battle was even more problematic than trial by unilateral ordeal, because the former depended on personal skill in an activity with which most men would have had significant experience. Bloodshed was inevitable, and there was no real opportunity for miraculous influence of the physical elements of fire and water.[85] More important, since the people fighting in these duels knew all of the various criteria that could determine a winner (including physique, arms, and training), putting forth justice as the single determining factor was "not always entirely convincing," and skepticism regarding the outcome had been expressed by kings as well as clerics.[86] Clerical complaints against dueling tended to focus on the shedding of Christian blood, while Liutprand, the eighth-century king of the Lombards, questioned whether it was any use at all in determining truth. Peter Brown gestures to what I believe was the key function of judicial combat in Ottonian society, serving as "an instrument of consensus and as a theatrical device by which to contain disruptive conflict."[87] Whether or not these duels revealed the truth of a matter was not nearly as important as being able to publicly and definitively end a dispute. In this way, the ordeal (unilateral and bilateral) functioned in a manner similar to feud negotiation and resolution, by providing an outcome that, even if it might be the wrong one, was intended to effectively put matters to rest.

Duels are referenced two other times in Liudprand of Cremona's works, once in the *Historia Ottonis* and once in the *Relatio de Legatione Constantinopolitana*.[88] In the *Historia*, Pope John XII accused Otto I of violating his oath of fidelity to the pope and of receiving and harboring the pope's enemies. Otto denied these accusations and sent emissaries to Rome (one of whom was Liudprand) to convince the pope of his innocence. On the off chance that they might prove unsuccessful, the prudent emperor also sent soldiers with the party, "so if the lord pope did not believe it, by a judicial duel they could prove the truth." The pope is portrayed as petulant and stubborn, refusing both the oaths of Otto's innocence and the "proof of the duel."[89] It is interesting that the pope, as a member of the clergy who were immune from the ordeal, would be requested to engage in a trial by combat, even (as we should assume) using a

85. Robert Bartlett, *Trial by Fire and Water: The Medieval Judicial Ordeal* (Oxford: Clarendon, 1986), 116.

86. Ibid., 116–17.

87. P. Brown, "Society and the Supernatural," 311.

88. The *Historia Ottonis* was written around 965, about events occurring between 961 and 964 (Squatriti, 25).

89. Squatriti, 224–25; Liudprand of Cremona, *Historia Ottonis* §7, in *Opera Omnia*, 173: "ut si secus domnus papa non crederet, duello verum esse approbarent."

proxy. We also see an interesting exchange (though if it is reported accurately, it must have been nerve-racking to experience) between Liudprand, as Emperor Otto's ambassador, and the Byzantine emperor Nicephoros, who challenged Liudprand with the accusation that Otto, having unjustly seized Rome and attacked other Italian cities under Byzantine influence, had sent Liudprand to Constantinople as a spy. As proof, Nicephoros offered the testimony of a soldier who defected when his lord became allied with Otto. Liudprand insists both on the veracity of his version of the story of the legitimate conquest of Italy and on his own legitimate mission to Constantinople; when Nicephoros presses, Liudprand states, "If [the soldier] contradicts [my story], one of my soldiers will demonstrate that it *is* so in a duel tomorrow, if you order it."[90] The Byzantine emperor conceded the point. These are two examples of Liudprand himself being involved in potential trials by combat. His report that he himself suggested a duel to resolve an issue shows not only the faith he had (or wants his reader to believe he had) in this method of proving just causes but also his view that there was no impropriety in a cleric being involved in such matters.

It seems as if the threat of losing in judicial combat was a powerful motivating factor to avoid engaging in a duel. Similar to a feud negotiation that, despite the posturing by competing sides, could eventually result in a real (if uneasy) peace, the threat of judicial combat seems a diplomatic tool used successfully by Liudprand in these instances. The soldiers that accompanied Liudprand on these diplomatic missions were intended to be deployed in judicial combat if necessary, and in the first instance, they were sent by Otto deliberately to suggest a duel as a means of proof.[91] The judicial duel was a form of trial common among the Germanic peoples, with the notable exception of the Anglo-Saxons. Its disuse in other regions would have been known to Otto I when he introduced it into Italy in 967, ostensibly because the Italians could not be trusted to present the truth of matters to be judged. It is very likely that the threat of bilateral combat may have convinced disputants that negotiated settlement was a better option than allowing complaints to be heard in Otto's court.

The use of the duel as a means of judicial ordeal in the writings of Liudprand of Cremona is important partly because he presents it as a given, a fact of his culture that needs no explanation or qualification. We know that there was con-

90. Squatriti, 242; Liudprand of Cremona, *Relatio de Legatione Constantinopolitana* §6, in *Opera Omnia*, 190: "Si secus dixerit, meorum aliquis militum, si iubes, cras ita rem esse duello declarabit." Liudprand's intent here is likely not only to emphasize that he is innocent of the accusation but also to contrast the strong German warrior lords of the Western Roman Empire with the soft, pampered emperors of the East.

91. The presence of these soldiers was doubtless also a show of power intended for the protection of his emissary, since the prudent Emperor Otto seemed to have the measure of Pope John.

troversy about the use of ordeal in ecclesiastical circles from at least the ninth century, and two ninth-century popes actually intervened in legal cases to prohibit the use of ordeal: Pope Nicholas I prohibited a judicial duel in 867 in a case involving King Lothair II and Queen Teutberga (the pope did allow an ordeal by hot water instead), and Pope Steven V prohibited unilateral ordeals in cases of infanticide sometime between 886 and 889.[92] There were also writers in defense of the practice, such as Hincmar of Reims, mentioned above. Liudprand, as a member of the church, would likely have been aware of any debates about the efficacy or propriety of ordeals; his position, an unqualified endorsement, is clearly presented.[93] That not everyone was uncritical of ordeals or of judicial combat suggests that this endorsement was intended as well to be praise for the Ottonian court that had received Liudprand in exile and treated him so well.

Judicial duels also figure prominently, if less colorfully, in the works of Thietmar of Merseburg and Adalbert of Magdeburg. While all the duels reported by Thietmar are ordered by the emperor and not spontaneous or local solutions to conflict resolution, they nonetheless follow some of the same patterns as those reported by Liudprand. For 971, Thietmar records, "The emperor [Otto I] learned from an informant that the Slavs at Zwenkau under lord Kuchawiz, whom he had much esteemed, had possession of the duke's armour.[94] With Kuchawiz's aid, a judicial duel was held and the losers were hanged at the emperor's order. . . . I do not know whether they took these things as murderers or, without guilt, discovered the duke's death by chance. In any case, they rightly paid with their lives for having presumed to keep this secret."[95] Thietmar's tone, like Liudprand's, is approving of the punishment and unjudging about the method of determining guilt. A duel Thietmar reported for 973 was ordered

92. John W. Baldwin, "The Intellectual Preparation for the Canon of 1215 against Ordeals," *Speculum* 36.4 (1961): 614n9. The controversy over the use of trial by combat did not prevent its use by ecclesiasts in France, either. For example, in 1098 a land dispute between the monks of Saint Martin of Tours and Holy Cross of Talmont was ordered to be settled by a judicial duel. The case was heard by the count, but the bishop judged that this was the way to resolve the dispute. See Paul Marchegay, "Duel Judiciaire entre des Communautés Religieuses, 1098," *Bibliotheque de l'Ecole des Chartres* 1 (1839–40): 552–64.

93. There is no doubt that Liudprand had at least "a passing aquaintance with both secular and ecclesiastical law" (Jon N. Sutherland, *Liudprand of Cremona, Bishop, Diplomat, Historian: Studies of the Man and His Age* [Spoleto: Centro Italiano di Studi sull'Alto Medioevo, 1988], 41).

94. This would have been the armor of Duke Conrad, who had been killed at the Battle of the Lech.

95. Warner, *Ottonian Germany*, 120; Thietmar, *Chronicon* 2.38, 86: "Post longum tempus imperator ad Merseburg veniens, a quodam proditore com perit exuvias eiusdem a Sclavis in Zuencua sub Cuchavico seniore sibi multum dilecto haberi; et cum auxilio illius hos in singulari prelio devictos suspendi precepit predaeque maximam partem restituit. Sed hoc ignoro, utrum hanc eiusdem interemptores sumpserint, an sic casu accidente, necis eius inculpabiles, invenerint; et quia hoc ullatenus celare presumpserunt, digna morte poenas persolverunt."

by the emperor to resolve an issue regarding the honor of his family, after a man named Cono defamed Otto's daughter Liutgard, claiming she had secretly become his wife.

> Taking this very seriously, the emperor cleared her name in the following way. After all the leading men of the realm had assembled, he first asked them in private whether she was guilty of this thing. Afterwards, when he saw that she had absolved herself by invoking the witness of Christ and by swearing oaths, he announced to all present that anyone of his familiares who wished to defend her in a duel would find in him a firm friend on that day and forever. Hearing this, Count Burchard stepped forward and openly declared that Cono had lied about everything. After swearing that his accusations were true, Cono engaged with Burchard, but lost his false right hand at the first approach. His injustice was revealed by his defeat.[96]

Thietmar also reports a judicial duel that appeared to produce the wrong verdict. "At the instigation of Archbishop Adalbert and Margrave Dietrich," a certain Waldo accused Count Gero of unspecified crimes before the emperor.

> After all the leading men of the realm had convened at Magdeburg, the two men met on a certain island for a judicial duel. Waldo was twice wounded on the neck, but pursued his enemy all the more vigorously, striking him in the head with a strong blow and laying him out. When asked if he could continue fighting, Count Gero was forced to concede that he could not. Waldo then left the place of battle, laid aside his weapons, refreshed himself with water, and fell backwards dead. Then, by the decree of the judges and the emperor's instruction, it was ordered that Gero be beheaded by an executioner on 11 August [979]. This battle pleased no one except Archbishop Adalbert and Margrave Dietrich.

96. Warner, *Ottonian Germany*, 120; Thietmar, *Chronicon* 2.39, 88: "Cesar hoc graviter ferens sic eam expurgavit. Covocatis omnibus regni suimet principibus, primo sevretis allocutionibus eandem, si huius rei culpabilis esset, diligenter inquirit; posteaque cum illam adhibito Christi testimonio et sacramentis se nimis excusare vidisset, presentibus cunctis indixit, si aliquis ex numero sibi familiarium eam armis defendere voluisset, ut se firmum in die hac et in perpetuum acquirere potuisset amicum. Burchardus comes haec audiens in medium prosiliit et Cononem per omnia mentitum fore coram omnibus dixit. Ille autem cum id verum esse sacramentis affirmaret, cum eodem congressus in primo aditu dexteram mendacem perdidit et iniusticiam suimet devictus innotuit; et misericors Dominus a falso crimine hanc eripuit, quam innocencia vitae sibi placere fecit." The text refers to Cono's right hand as "false" because that is the hand used to swear; see *Chronicon* 7.5, where Werner raises his right hand to swear.

> Duke Otto of Bavaria, the son of Liudolf, who arrived on the same day, and Count Berthold, rebuked the emperor for allowing such a great man to be condemned on such a petty charge.[97]

Archbishop Adalbert and Margrave Dietrich's manipulation of a judicial duel to eliminate a political rival, the involvement of judges to evaluate the duel because the outcome was not clear, and the later arrival of the magnates and their rebuke of the emperor for his rendering of an overly harsh punishment speak to the important, public nature of these trials by ordeal, which amounted to a prominent way of serving justice and resolving disputes among the nobility. Thietmar goes on to emphasize that the execution of Count Gero, for whatever "petty charge" he was accused of, was the wrong decision. He describes how Gero's sister and wife established a nunnery in the count's memory, and he reports, "After three years, when his wife was interred by his side, the count's body and even his clothing were found to be uncorrupted."[98] The use of the language of sanctification to make a political statement in protest of an imperial decision was likely an acceptable idiom in which to express dissatisfaction with imperial policy.[99]

Thietmar records another duel in the reign of Henry II. In 1017, Duke Gottfried of Lower Lotharingia and Count Gerhard of Alsace, brother-in-law to Empress Cunigund, arranged a duel to settle a long-standing altercation: "There had long been discord between them. At last, however, a day was set on which they and their supporters were to settle the matter through the unques-

97. Warner, *Ottonian Germany*, 133–34; Thietmar, *Chronicon* 3.9, 107–9: "Accusatus apud imperatorem Gero comes a Waldone et in loco, qui Sumeringe dicitur, hortatu Atelberti archipresulis et Diderici marchionis captus, patri meo patruoque firmiter est commissus. Deinde convocatis ad Magadaburg cunctis regni principibus, congressi sunt hii duo iudicio in insula quadam singulari certamine; vulneratus in cervicem bis Waldo ardencius insequitur hostem percuciensque ictu valido caput prostravit eundem. Interrogatus autem Gero comes ab eodem, si plus potuisset pugnare, coactus est profiteri, quod iam defecisset. Waldo tum egressus aqua refocilatur depositis armis et post tergum mortuus cecedit. Tunc Gero ius sus est decreto iudicum et voce imperatoris a carnifice quodam decollari tercio Idus Augusti. Hec pugna nulli nisi tantum Atelberto archiepiscopo et Diderico marchioni placuit. Correptus est quoque imperator an Ottone Bawariorum duce, Liudolfi filio, eodem die veniente, et a comite Bertoldo, quod ob tam vilem causam tantus vir umquam dampnari debuisset."

98. Warner, *Ottonian Germany*, 135; Thietmar, *Chronicon* 3.10, 109: "Comitis prefati corpus post tres annos, cum iuxta illud contectalis sua poneretur, integrum una cum vestimentis inventum est."

99. This would have been similar to the motives and motifs that surrounded the sanctification of royal murdered/martyred Anglo-Saxon kings and princes. See Laura Wangerin, "Royal Feuds and the Politics of Sanctity in Anglo-Saxon England and Ottonian Saxony," *Mirabilia* 18.1 (2014): 78–94.

tionable judgment of the judicial duel."[100] The opposing forces met in a flowery meadow, where Gerhard's companions lost heart and bolted. Three hundred of them were killed, as opposed to only thirty of Duke Gottfried's men, a clear judgment in Gottfried's favor.

Also in 1017, while Henry II was in Merseburg, Thietmar notes that "many highwaymen were put to death by hanging, after champions had defeated them in single combat."[101] This example is interesting for what it suggests about royal justice. That the men were tried by the emperor instead of by the local jurisdictional authority implies that the king's roads functioned as a separate jurisdictional area. That they were caught, tried, and punished in what might be the most public way possible also gestures to the connection between strong kingship and the prevention of predatory rogue nobility, as suggested by the "feudal revolution" model.[102] Lastly, this example reasserts the importance of the *iter* as an assertive act of the king, claiming both the right to impose the royal presence throughout his realm as well as the right to assure that those essential conduits for royal communication and royal travel were protected.[103]

Adalbert of Magdeburg also reports several trials by ordeal. In 941, Archbishop Frederick exonerated himself in a trial by Eucharist, when he was accused of being part of the conspiracy of Henry, the king's brother.[104] A similar incident to the 973 trial by combat under Otto II that is reported by Thietmar took place in 950, when a niece of the king was slandered by the son of Duke Gebhard, Conrad, who claimed to have slept with her. He was defeated in single combat, "reveal[ing] that he had lied."[105] Ordeals can thus be seen as useful tools in the emperor's administration of justice. They provided opportunities to prove the unprovable, to eliminate doubt as to blame or fault, and to truly provide the last word in difficult disputes, through God's judgment. As in the

---

100. Warner, *Ottonian Germany*, 351; Thietmar, *Chronicon* 7.62, 474: "Illi namque diu invicem discordes certum condixere diem, qua cum suis fautoribus haec certo duelli iudicio discernerent."

101. Warner, *Ottonian Germany*, 343; Thietmar, *Chronicon* 7.51, 460: "Ibi tunc multi latrones a gladiatoribus singulari certamine devicti suspendio perierunt."

102. See Thomas N. Bisson, "The 'Feudal Revolution,'" *Past & Present* 142 (1994): 6–42. On the debate and further theoretical development sparked by Bisson's article, see note 147 in chapter 1 in the present study.

103. Levi Roach, *Kingship and Consent in Anglo-Saxon England, 871–978* (Cambridge: Cambridge University Press, 2013), 46; Karl Leyser, "Ottonian Government," *English Historical Review* 96.381 (1981): 746–47; John W. Bernhardt, *Itinerant Kingship and Royal Monasteries in Early Medieval Germany, c. 936–1075* (Cambridge: Cambridge University Press, 1993), 50–51. 56–57.

104. Adalbert, *Continuatio*, s.a. 941, 162.

105. MacLean, *History and Politics*, 250; Adalbert, *Continuatio*, s.a. 950, 164: "Ibi Cuonradus filius Gebehardi comitis, quoniam cum quadam nepte regis se concubuisse sibi imposcit, a quodam Burchardo Saxone monomachia victus fefellisse patuit."

placita, the emperor awaited judgment, then provided a sentence if one was still necessary, that is, if the combatants had not died. Like a feud, an ordeal effectively ended enmity between men by, in principle, definitively providing a final winner. Trial by combat provided the emperor with an objective forum to resolve accusations intended to dishonor his family, without his becoming personally embroiled in feuds. It allowed the emperor a way to punish counts and dukes, without fear of being labeled a tyrant and without losing that important appearance of consensual kingship. Perhaps most important, it was a public way to connect divine and earthly dispensation of justice and to establish that kings could and should claim a monopoly on blood justice.

The Profits of Justice

The Ottonians' very different approach to maintaining peace and justice (as opposed to that of their continental and insular peers) was largely a matter of royal finances. Royal kingdoms had a variety of sources of income for the crown, in coin and in kind, which, based on other resources that might be available to them, they were able to exploit. For example, the itinerary that the Ottonian kings kept was not just political in nature but also economic.[106] It was far easier for the court to move itself than to transport the food that supported it, and when combined with the ideas of *Königsnähe* and sacrality, hospitality became a privilege as well as an obligation to the king. But the court had to get from place to place, a detail of travel that necessitated a concern with road maintenance. Henry I had prohibited the destruction of bridges in his kingdom, and Otto II reiterated that ban as well as other activities that might affect roads and travel.[107] Brunner noted the concern of the German kings regarding illegitimate feuds waged on the king's roads, the unlawful levying of tolls, and customs duties,[108] and we saw above how Ottonian emperors claimed jurisdictional rights when dealing with highway robbers and bandits on their roads. There was additional revenue to be found in minting, giving special privileges that allowed the striking of coins and sharing in the profits to favored lords,

106. See David S. Bachrach, "Immunities as Tools of Royal Military Policy under the Carolingian and Ottonian Kings," *Zeitschrift der Savigny-Stiftung für Rechtsgeschichte* 130 (2013): esp. 19–22; Bernhardt, *Itinerant Kingship*, 75–87 for a description of the *servitium regis* and overview of the historiography.

107. Arnold, *Medieval Germany*, 150. MGH DD OII 112.

108. Otto Brunner, *Land and Lordship: Structures of Governance in Medieval Austria*, trans. Howard Kaminsky and James van Horn Melton (Philadelphia: University of Pennsylvania Press, 1992), 48–49.

secular and ecclesiastical. There was, of course, the imposition of certain royal dues on landholders, among which was the hospitality to the king noted above. Markets, too, cannot be underestimated in their importance to the royal coffers.

Rampant feuding behavior in England may have contributed to its legislative tradition, providing a way to control feuding and bring it under the legal jurisdiction of the royal courts.[109] One reason the Ottonians did not develop the same kind of legislative tradition is that there was no perceived need to control endemic feuding, which functioned well enough as a means of peacekeeping and extralegal resolution of disputes. Perhaps another reason that they did not feel compelled to legislate is that there was no pressing need for them to collect the revenues of justice for the royal treasury. The Ottonians had access to two great revenue streams that were unavailable to their contemporary rulers on the continent and in England. The first were the great silver veins that were discovered in Eastern Saxony during the reign of Otto I, which produced enough silver that the emperors were able to finance their military campaigns and extravagant lifestyles for the next two hundred years.[110] Additionally, the

---

109. Hyams, *Rancor and Reconciliation*, 73, 77. One of the key areas in which the Ottonians differed from their Anglo-Saxon contemporaries was in the profits to be derived from the administration of justice. While immunities were granted in both realms, the Ottonians used them as a way to delegate authority, rather than simply to keep a hand in local affairs. In Anglo-Saxon England, the bureaucratic network of courts provided the crown with a significant portion of its income. Lords profited from this arrangement as well. See John Hudson, *The Oxford History of the Laws of England*, vol. 2, *871–1216* (Oxford: Oxford University Press, 2012), 60–62; David Pratt, *The Political Thought of King Alfred the Great* (Cambridge: Cambridge University Press, 2007), 31; Patrick Wormald, "Lordship and Justice in the Early English Kingdom: Oswaldslow Revisited," in *Property and Power in the Early Middle Ages*, ed. Wendy Davies and Paul Fouracre (Cambridge: Cambridge University Press, 1995), 114–36.

110. Chris Wickham, *The Inheritance of Rome: A History of Europe from 400 to 1000* (London: Penguin, 2010), 434; Karl Leyser, "The Ascent of Latin Europe," in *Communications and Power in Medieval Europe: The Carolingian and Ottonian Centuries*, ed. Timothy Reuter (London: Hambledon, 1994), 228. Thietmar reports the discovery of a rich vein of silver, noting, "Among us, for the first time, a rich vein of silver was discovered" (Warner, *Ottonian Germany*, 101; Thietmar, *Chronicon* 2.13, 53: "apud nos inventa est primum vena argenti"). Warner notes that while this report was usually taken to reference the silver mines on the Rammelsberg near Goslar, recent archaeological evidence "appear[s] to have completely undermined this assumption" (*Ottonian Germany*, 101n65). Goslar is in the Harz, the mountains where the silver strikes were concentrated. Widukind reports the discovery of veins of silver in Saxony during the reign of Otto I: "terra Saxonia venas argenti aperuit" (*Res gestae Saxonicae* 3.63). In the notes to their edition of Widukind of Corvey's *Res gestae Saxonicae*, Hirsch and Lohmann identify this as a reference to the Rammelsberg mines (*Widukindi monachi Corbiensis rerum gestarum Saxonicarum libri tres*, ed. Paul Hirsch and H.-E. Lohmann after G. Waitz and K. A. Kehr [Hanover: Hahn, 1935], 138n2). Geologists and geochemists date the beginning of mining at Rammelsberg to 968, following Kurt Mohr, *Geologie und Minerallagerstatten des Harzes* (1978; repr., Stuttgart: Schweizerbart, 1993), 388. While Roman and prehistoric mining activities in the Harz are still debated, mining and smelting activities during the early and central Middle Ages is well established, based on geochemical analyses. See Jörg Matschullat et al., "Overbank Sediment Profiles: Evidence of Early Mining and Smelting Activities in the Harz Mountains, Germany," *Applied Geochemistry* 12 (1997): 105–14; F. Monna et al., "Pb Isotopes as a Reliable Marker of Early Mining and Smelting in the Northern Harz Province (Lower

Ottonians had a steady stream of tribute flowing in from conquered areas. Adalbert of Magdeburg notes the subjugation of the Vucrani, a Slavic tribe, by Henry I in 934, when "he invaded and conquered and made [the Vucrani] his tributaries."[111] Thietmar, too, is very aware of the importance of the Saxon tributaries, noting, in a summary of Henry I's accomplishments, that Henry "made the following regions pay tribute: Bohemia, Daleminzia, and the lands of the Abrodites, Wilzi, Hevelii, and Redarii."[112] In a panegyric to Otto I in the prologue to book 2 of the *Chronicon*, Thietmar claims, "Since the death of Charles [the Great] there had been no greater patron, and I believe that the realm will not see a similar pastor again. He established six bishoprics. Conquering Berengar's pride, he forced the Lombards to bend their necks. Rome made the powerful man her emperor, and the distant maritime regions paid tribute."[113] The expansion of empire into Italy is a key accomplishment of Otto's reign that made him great, not just because he conquered Lombardy and became Roman emperor, but also because he was able to extract tribute from the south of Italy: "Imperatorem fecit sibi Roma potentem / Hunc, et maritimi solvunt tributa remoti."[114] The active attempt to transform enemies into imperial tributaries is a concern of the marcher lords as well. Margrave Gero of the eastern march "brought the Lusizi and the Selpuli, and Miesco and his subjects under imperial authority," and Duke Herman "made Selibur and Mistui [Slavic leaders] with their subjects tributaries of the emperor."[115]

In his examination of the immunities for Chur, David Bachrach has gestured to the importance to the Ottonian court of drawing on revenues generated by the grant and expansion of immunities to support the activities of the royal court, including road maintenance and minting as well as comital jurisdictional privileges. While Bachrach is most concerned, in that study, with how immunities contributed to the royal military machine, his thesis makes sense

Saxony, Germany)," *Journal of Geochemical Exploration* 68 (2000): 201–10; H. Kempter and B. Frenzel, "The Impact of Early Mining and Smelting on the Local Tropospheric Aerosol Detected in Ombrotrophic Peat Bogs in the Harz, Germany," *Water, Air, and Soil Pollution* 121 (2000): 93–108.

111. Adalbert, *Continuatio*, s.a. 934, 159: "Eodem anno Sclavos, qui Vucrani vocantur, hostiliter invasit et vicit sibique tributarios fecit."

112. Warner, *Ottonian Germany*, 75; Thietmar, *Chronicon* 1.10, 14: "Has regiones sibi fecit tributarias: Boemiam, Deleminci, Apodritas, Wilti, Hevellun et Redarios."

113. Warner, *Ottonian Germany*, 89; Thietmar, *Chronicon*, prologue to book 2, 37: "Non patronus erat Karoli post funera tantus, Estimo nec simili regnum pastore potiri; Nam senas sedes construxit pontificales. Ipse Beringerum superans virtute superbum, Longobardorum sibi subdit colla furentum. Hunc sibi rectorem prefecit Roma potentem, Vicinique maris sibi vectigalia solvunt."

114. Thietmar, *Chronicon*, prologue to book 2, 36.

115. Warner, *Ottonian Germany*, 102; Thietmar, *Chronicon* 2.14, 54: "Gero Orientalium marchio Lusizi et Selpuli, Miseconem quoque cum sibi subiectis imperiali subdidit dicioni. Herimannus dux Seliburem et Mistui cum suis imperatori tributarios fecit."

with regard to the importance of distributed resources for an itinerant court, as well as the generation of revenues that could—in coin or in kind—serve to enrich both the immunist and the king.[116] John Bernhardt also provides an important assessment of the *servitium regis* of royal monasteries, that is, the payments and services that were due to the king in exchange for royal protection and immunity.[117] The obligations of hospitality and service (hosting the court, providing military support, acting as advisors or *missi* for the court, etc.) were expensive, and among the sources of revenue used to support the court, the itinerary, and its military activities were fees generated through the administration of justice. The delegation of jurisdictional authority saw these fees being collected by immunists, but the royal or imperial court, through the *servitium regis*, ultimately shared in and benefited from these revenues without having to personally administrate a jurisdictional hierarchy throughout their realm; thus, the court had no need to issue legislation.

The Ottonians clearly knew how lucrative the returns of justice could be. The laws of Burchard of Worms specify throughout which fees of justice are to be paid to the bishop. The *placita* discussed above specified significant fines that were designated to the crown if the judgment of the assembly was violated. But the Ottonians were able to delegate and give away immunities and the *bannus*, could reward their magnates with receipts from the courts, and could use the threat of exorbitant fines to assure compliance with royal rulings. It seems plausible that one reason they never developed a complex system of courts, fees, and fines is that they did not need one.[118] The system they had worked well enough to meet the needs of the realm, which included peacekeeping. There was no call to be aspirational in terms of creating a "better" system.

The train of thought regarding the tributaries as such an important revenue source for the Ottonian rulers suggests a different tipping point in their reign. Usually, the key event that sets the Ottonians on the path to success in traditional narratives is the Battle of the Lech in 955, generally presented as the decisive battle that prevented the Hungarians from invading Europe. While

116. D. Bachrach, "Immunities," 19–22.

117. Bernhardt, *Itinerant Kingship*, 75.

118. In comparison, England was a wealthy country, too. But its system of coinage, fees, customs, and taxation formed the foundation of its wealth. Dating from the Anglo-Norman period, the *Dialogue of the Exchequer* "describes the complex system of coinage and taxation which made Henry II (1154–1189) the richest king in Europe" (see Michael T. Clanchy, *From Memory to Written Record: England, 1066–1307*, 3rd ed. [Malden, MA: Wiley-Blackwell, 2013], 26–30). This system of taxation and coinage was already being implemented, if perhaps not exploited to the full extent that the Normans were able, under Anglo-Saxon rule. Much of this revenue derived from the courts and the administration of justice. For revenues of justice, see Wormald, *Making of English Law*, 105, 349, 362. Regarding kings' entitlement to the profits of justice, see ibid., 108.

that was an important moment, I suggest that events of 932 were at least as important to the Saxons, if not to Europe as a whole. In that year, Saxony ceased to be a tribute payer and instead began to become the receiver of tributes.[119] Having earlier established a temporary peace with the Hungarians, Henry I took advantage of the hiatus to train an army on horseback, build up his infantry with conscripted convicts, and fortify the frontiers.[120] According to Widukind, battle with the Hungarians in 932 was preceded by a brave speech from Henry incorporating rhetoric of honor, unity, and the implication that if the Saxons did not take a stand against paying tribute, they would soon have nothing left to give, since despoiling the churches was the only recourse left to them to procure the payments demanded by the Hungarians. Having secured oaths from the people, Henry prevailed. From that point, he became a conqueror intent on subjugating all of the nations around him. In these stories from Widukind, we see the various Germanic nobles uniting in common cause against incursions from Hungarians and Danes, rallying around Henry as their king and military leader while retaining substantial autonomy in their domestic affairs. As the receptor of tribute (in addition to simply retaining revenues and treasures that used to be paid as tribute to foreign kings), Henry I and Saxony began to become wealthy as well as powerful.

The Ottonian development of the ideology of sacral kingship was the result of a specific conception of the ruler as a dispenser of justice. The drive to be a lawgiver—to write law in the manner of the Carolingians or Anglo-Saxons—was not part of their conceptualization of kingship. As discussed in chapter 4, the image of Henry II in the Monte Cassino Gospels conveys the idea of an emperor who holds the power to judge because he is endowed with divine grace. He is guided by the virtues of justice, piety, law, and right, but in the end "all law is subject to his power."[121] Henry, like the Ottos, depended on a personal kind of adjudicating power in petition-based courts. The differing legislative responses that arose as different ideologies of rulership developed in France and England gave rise to different conceptualizations of the role of the ruler in dispensing law. For example, in England, the king established himself as a virtual presence at every level of interaction throughout the kingdom. Especially in the courts, the king was portrayed as the one who conveyed God's justice to

119. Widukind, *Res gestae Saxonicae* 1.38, 55.

120. Widukind, *Res gestae Saxonicae* 1.38, 55–57; 1.35, 48–51; 2.13, 78. Regarding Henry I's military organization, see David S. Bachrach, "Henry I of Germany's 929 Military Campaign in Archaeological Perspective," *Early Medieval Europe* 21.3 (2013): 301–37.

121. Weinfurter, "Authority and Legitimation," 34.

his people, an anointed king in the Old Testament tradition, who brought the will of God to his realm in the form of written law, following the traditions of Christian synods and the kings he succeeded. In comparison, the Ottonians, in their development of an ideology of sacral kingship, presented themselves as the imitators of Christ on earth. Not just the conveyors of God's law, the Ottonian emperors shared the sacral sphere and directly mediated divine will through their judgments.

Even when the outcome was unclear or disputed, a judicial duel provided a terminus to a conflict and imposed peace between factions. Like their reliance on feuds, the other elements of the Ottonians' rulership provided a strong and effective system that did not need to rely on efforts toward legal consistency across their realm. These elements included the development of an ideology of liturgical kingship, the success of their system of delegated jurisdictional authority with a petition-based imperial court, and, when necessary, the use of the bilateral ordeal to help adjudicate certain cases.

Conclusion

That the Ottonians were effective rulers has not been a subject of scholarly contention, but the idea that they had rational approaches to governance and clear ideologies of rulership has been. The Ottonians, heirs to the eastern part of the crumbling Carolingian Empire, have perplexed historians by their success. Even Karl Leyser, a clear admirer of the dynasty, has observed that "the paucity and modesty of central legislative, administrative, and fiscal institutions in the Ottonian *Reich* remain puzzling. Their seeming reluctance to develop in a period of reconstruction, success and rising prosperity confronts the historian with some difficult questions."[1] Key among the puzzles the Ottonians present are what was holding their kingdom and empire together and what gave that empire its longevity, given that it lacked the sophisticated administration of the Carolingians and their court. Challenging some of the traditional ways of looking at government, for example, considering a decentralized government—an administrative structure dependent on delegated or franchised authority, without any implied dilution of regnal power—as a sophisticated ruling apparatus opens the door to a new appreciation of the Ottonians' rule. Leyser was confused about "their seeming reluctance to develop in a period of reconstruction, success and rising prosperity," but the system they had, the apparatuses of government, worked. The Ottonians were not aspirational in trying to "develop," but that is beside the point, and wondering why they failed to create centralized institutions distracts from an understanding and appreciation of the systems they did develop.

The Ottonians created strong and resilient governments that were able to withstand substantial internal and external stresses. Their successes were striking. Their system was substantially different from their contemporaries, as were their ideas and ideologies about rulership and the administration of law and justice. Precisely by examining those differences, we can begin to tease out why

1. Karl Leyser, "Ottonian Government," *English Historical Review* 96.381 (1981): 731.

the Ottonians were successful. In the process, we can see how some of the traditional models for how we understand the early Middle Ages need to be reassessed. The "feudal revolution" was not a ubiquitous European phenomenon, and the Ottonians do not fit neatly within that model. Early medieval Germany was organized in such a way that its ruling structures were able to withstand the rebellions and power struggles that were normal among the medieval nobility. The Ottonians, through a governing system that emphasized the royal *iter*, consensual rule, and delegated authority, created a stable infrastructure of government. Additionally, the manner of landholding in Germany prevented nobles from accumulating large, consolidated estates and ensured that the king had interests throughout the realm. This situation was distinctly different from that in France and is a fundamental reason the "feudal revolution" model is inapplicable to East Francia. The ways in which jurisdictional authority was delegated, as well as how the kings interacted with their magnates, were additional keys to their success in creating a resilient system that could withstand both internal and external pressures.

Another model that this study suggests might bear reexamination concerns the Investiture Controversy of the late eleventh and twelfth centuries. In Germany, ecclesiastical jurisdictions resembled those of great lords in their scope and in their obligations to the emperor. While bishops could operate, like their secular counterparts, with great autonomy in the administration of law and justice over their lands, they were also responsible for duties including military service. The conflicts that would arise later in the eleventh century, as part of the Investiture Controversy, no doubt found their inception in the disputes that arose over episcopal and abbatial elections. The Ottonians tried to place *fideles* in these positions, but bishops in the *Reich* were more like great princes, with substantial revenues and powers. There was still significant fluidity between the concepts of secular and sacred spheres, and episcopal elections could be highly charged events. The effectiveness of the Ottonian system lay largely in its ability to control magnates and command their loyalty, through force if necessary. When the Ottonian dynasty ended, it was perhaps inevitable that great lords, both secular and ecclesiastical, would attempt to assert or expand their influence. The first Salian rulers had to deal with a certain measure of turmoil, reminiscent of the rebellions and struggles with and among their magnates that Henry I and Otto I faced when establishing their dynasty and that challenged Henry II on the sudden death of Otto III. That bishops were among those rebellious magnates should not surprise us. The Investiture Controversy ended up substantially redefining the relationship between the church and the German emperors, but it was not fundamentally a constitutional crisis. The present study suggests that it was, instead, a conflict over patronage and resource allocation, foregrounded in the Ottonians' efforts to create and maintain control over imperial bishoprics and monasteries.

The Ottonians' lack of legislative activity does not signal primitive ideas about kingship or a lack of rationality in a king's approach to law and order. The Ottonians did not legislate because they were not trying to bring feuding behaviors under royal control. They were content to limit their involvement to cases where feuding became too disruptive to ignore. Feud behavior was allowed by the Ottonians because it served their purposes for peacekeeping in the realm. Although they produced almost no legislation of any kind, a few legislative pieces were written by them to address out-of-control feuding activities in specific localities. Attempts to control feud behaviors would have driven legislative activity, as we see under the Anglo-Saxons. To maintain order in the Ottonian realm, its rulers relied on traditional methods of conflict resolution in jurisdictions delegated to local authorities. The Ottonians reconceptualized the idea of what a Christian king looked like. Over the course of their dynastic tenure, they developed an ideology of sacral kingship, presenting themselves as *christomimetai*, who did not just promulgate God's law but directly mediated divine will. This ideology was exemplified by a system of justice based on a case-by-case, petition-based royal process.

When we analyze the Ottonians on their own terms, legislative activity becomes just one of many clues to how they conceived of themselves, as rulers and as purveyors of law and justice. The various "idols" of historical thinking that the chapters of the present study have been trying to challenge in assessing Ottonian rulership, including traditional dichotomies between centralization/decentralization and legal/extralegal, as well as how the relative success of a ruler is judged, have long been a part of our early modern cultural inheritance. But we can attempt to approach our subjects with an appreciation of their differentness from other regimes without suggesting that their approach to rulership was exceptional, on the one hand, or regressive, on the other. Complexity was inherent in the Ottonian system—and it was, indeed, a system. The Ottonians employed the various components of their government intelligently and prudently. Many of these components were inherited or adapted from earlier or existing systems and do not fit the molds of what we moderns consider to be progressive governmental structures. Trying to conceptualize general models that can be applied to the geographic and temporal breadth of the European Middle Ages is a project shot through with problems and distracts us from appreciating how decentralized, extralegal, and sacralized structures worked within the Ottonians' tenth-century world.

That is the distinction that is essential here: the threats and opportunities that presented themselves to the Ottonians were different from those faced by other tenth-century and eleventh-century polities. Other kingdoms had distinctive characteristics of government that arose due to their unique political environments. For the Ottonians, the essential features of rulership and governance—including the royal *iter*, rule by consensus, and delegated authority—were organized around a decentralized, distributed infrastructure. These features served the needs of its kings and emperors, creating stable substructures of government that enabled it to withstand rebellions and power struggles among the nobility. Far from being indicative of a dilution of power or ineffectual kingship, these elements formed the foundation of a highly developed political system.

Bibliography

Printed Primary Sources

Adalbert of Magdeburg. *Continuatio Reginonis*. In *Reginonis abbatis Prumiensis Chronicon cum continuatione Treverensi*, edited by F. Kurze. MGH SRG 50. Hanover: Hahn, 1890, 154–79.

Annales Fuldenses sive Annales Regni Francorum Orientalis. Edited by Friedrich Kurze. MGH SRG 7. Hanover: Hahn, 1891.

Annalista Saxo. Edited by Georg Waitz. MGH SS 6, 542-777. Hanover: Hahn, 1844.

Beowulf: A New Verse Translation, Bilingual Edition. Translated by Seamus Heaney. New York: Farrar, Straus and Giroux, 2000.

Burchard of Worms. *Lex familiae Wormatensis ecclesiae*. Edited by L. Weiland. MGH Leges 4, Const 1. Hanover: Hahn, 1893, 639–44.

Capitularia Regum Francorum. 2 vols. Edited by Alfred Boretius (vols. 1–2) and Victor Krause (vol. 2). MGH Capitularia, Legum Sectio II. Hanover: Hahn, 1883–97.

Codex diplomaticus Langobardiae. Edited by Giulio Porro-Lambertenghi. Historiae patriae monumenta edita jussu regis Caroli Alberti 13, no. 984. Augustae Taurinorum, 1873.

Constitutiones et Acta Publica Imperatorum et Regum. Vol. 1. Edited by L. Weiland. MGH. Hanover: Hahn, 1893.

Die Briefsammlung Gerberts von Reims. Edited by Fritz Weigle. MGH, Die Briefsammlung der deutschen Kaiserzeit 2. Weimar: Hermann Bohlaus Nachfolger, 1966.

Die Konzilien Deutschlands und Reichsitaliens 916–1001. 2 vols. Edited by Ernst-Dieter Hehl. MGH Concilia 6. Hanover: Hahn, 1987.

Diplomata Regum et Imperatorum Germaniae. Vol. 1. MGH. Hanover: Hahn, 1879–84.

Diplomata Regum et Imperatorum Germaniae. Vol. 2. MGH. Hanover: Hahn, 1893.

Diplomata Regum et Imperatorum Germaniae. Vol. 3. MGH. Hanover: Hahn, 1900–1903.

Drew, Katherine Fischer, ed. and trans. *The Burgundian Code*. 1949. Reprint, Philadelphia: University of Pennsylvania Press, 1976.

Drew, Katherine Fischer, ed. and trans. *The Laws of the Salian Franks*. Philadelphia: University of Pennsylvania Press, 1991.

Drew, Katherine Fischer, ed. and trans. *The Lombard Laws*. Philadelphia: University of Pennsylvania Press, 1973.

Ekkehard IV. *Casus Sancti Galli*. Edited by Hans F. Haefele. Ausgewählte Quellen zur deutschen Geschichte des Mittelalters 10. Darmstadt: Wissenschaftliche Buchgesellschaft, 1980.

Epistolae Karolini Aevi. Edited by Ernest Duemmler. MGH. Berlin: Weidmann, 1845.

Fanning, Steven, and Bernard S. Bachrach, eds. and trans. *The* Annals *of Flodoard of Reims, 919–966*. 2004. Reprint, Toronto: University of Toronto Press, 2008.

Flodoard of Reims. *Annales*. Edited by G. H. Pertz. MGH SS 3, 363–407. Hanover: Hahn, 1839.

Gerbert d'Aurillac. *Correspondance*. Translated by P. Riche and J. P. Callu. 2 vols. Paris: Les Belles Lettres, 1993.

Gerhard von Augsburg. *Vita Sancti Uodalrici: Die älteste Lebensbeschreibung des heiligen Ulrich, mit der Kanonisationsurkunde von 993*. Edited by Walter Berschin and Angelika Häse. Heidelburg: Universitätsverlag C. Winter, 1993.

Haddan, Arthur West, and William Stubbs, eds. *Councils and Ecclesiastical Documents Relating to Great Britain and Ireland*. Vol. 3. Oxford: Clarendon, 1871.

Jaffé, Philipp, ed. *Bibliotheca Rerum Germanicarum*. Vol. 3, *Monumenta Moguntina*. Berlin: Weidmann, 1866.

John of Worcester. *The Chronicle of John of Worcester*. Edited and translated by Patrick McGurk. Oxford: Oxford University Press, 1995.

Lattin, Harriet Pratt, ed. and trans. *The Letters of Gerbert, with His Papal Privileges as Sylvester II*. New York: Columbia University Press, 1961.

Liebermann, Felix, ed. *Die Gesetze der Angelsachsen: Herausgegeben im Auftrage der Savigny-Stiftung*. 3 vols. Halle: Max Niemeyer, 1903–12.

Liudprand of Cremona. *Liudprandi Cremonensis Opera Omnia*. Edited by Paolo Chiesa. Corpus Christianorum. Turnhout: Brepols, 1998.

MacLean, Simon, ed. and trans. *History and Politics in Late Carolingian and Ottonian Europe: The* Chronicle *of Regino of Prüm and Adalbert of Magdeburg*. Manchester Medieval Sources. Manchester: Manchester University Press, 2009.

Notker Balbulus. *Liber ymnorum, latine et theotisce*. Edited by Wolfram von der Steinen. Bern: Francke, 1960.

Pertz, G. H., ed. *Legum* 2. MGH. Hanover: Hahn, 1837.

Rather of Verona. *The Complete Works of Rather of Verona*. Translated by Peter L. D. Reid. Binghamton: State University of New York at Binghamton, 1991.

Regino of Prüm. *Reginonis abbatis Prumiensis Chronicon cum continuatione Treverens*. Edited by F. Kurze. MGH SRG 50. Hanover: Hahn, 1890.

Regino of Prüm. *Libri duo*. Edited by F. G. A. Wasserschleben. *Libri duo de synodalibus causis et disciplinis ecclesiasticis*. Leipzig: Guil. Engelmann, 1840.

Reuter, Timothy, ed. *The Annals of Fulda*. Ninth-Century Histories 2. Manchester: Manchester University Press, 1992.

Richer of Saint-Rémi. *Histories*. Translated by Justin Lake. 2 vols. Cambridge, MA: Harvard University Press, 2011.

Robertson, A. J., ed. and trans. *Anglo-Saxon Charters*. 1939. Reprint, Cambridge: Cambridge University Press, 1956.

Ruotger. *Vita Sancti Brunonis, Coloniensis Archiepiscopi*. Edited by G. H. Pertz. MGH SS 4, 252–56. Hanover: Hahn, 1841.

Scriptores. Vol. 3. Edited by G. H. Pertz. MGH. Hanover: Hahn, 1839.

Scriptores. Vol. 4. Edited by G. H. Pertz. MGH. Hanover: Hahn, 1841.

Scriptores. Vol. 6. Edited by G. H. Pertz. MGH. Hanover: Hahn, 1844.

Squatriti, Paolo, ed. and trans. *The Complete Works of Liudprand of Cremona*. Washington, DC: Catholic University of America Press, 2007.

Thietmar of Merseburg. *Thietmari Merseburgensis Episcopi Chronicon*. Edited by Robert Holtzmann. MGH SRG 9. Berlin: Weidmannsche Buchhandlung, 1935.

Die Urkunden Heinrichs II. und Arduins. Edited by H. Bresslau, et. al. MGH Diplomata. Hanover: Hahn, 1900–03.

Die Urkunden Konrad I., Heinrich I., und Otto I. Edited by Theodor von Sickel. MGH Diplomata. Hanover: Hahn, 1879-1884.

Die Urkunden Konrads II. Edited by H. Bresslau. MGH Diplomata. Hanover: Hahn, 1909.

Die Urkunden Otto des II. Edited by Theodor von Sickel. MGH Diplomata. Hanover: Hahn, 1888.

Die Urkunden Otto des III. Edited by Theodor von Sickel. MGH Diplomata. Hanover: Hahn, 1893.

Vita Mahthildis Reginae. Edited by G. H. Pertz. MGH SS 4, 282–302. Hanover: Hahn, 1841.

Warner, David A., ed. and trans. *Ottonian Germany: The* Chronicon *of Thietmar of Merseburg*. Manchester Medieval Sources. Manchester: Manchester University Press, 2001.

Whitelock, Dorothy. *English Historical Documents*. Vol. 1, *500–1042*. 1955. Reprint, London: Routledge, 1979.

Whitelock, Dorothy, Martin Brett, and Christopher N. L. Brooke, eds. *Councils and Synods, with Other Documents Relating to the English Church, AD 871–1204*. Oxford: Clarendon, 1981.

Widukind of Corvey. *Deeds of the Saxons*. Edited and translated by Bernard S. Bachrach and David S. Bachrach. Washington, DC: Catholic University of America Press, 2014.

Widukind of Corvey. *Widukindi monachi Corbiensis rerum gestarum Saxonicarum libri tres*. Edited by Paul Hirsch and H.-E. Lohmann after G. Waitz and K. A. Kehr. MGH SRG 60. Hanover: Hahn, 1935.

Wipo. *Gesta Chuonradi II*. In *Wiponis Opera*, edited by Harry Bresslau. 3rd ed. MGH SRG 61, 1–62. Hanover: Hahn, 1915.

Secondary Sources

Airlie, Stuart. "Talking Heads: Assemblies in Early Medieval Germany." In *Political Assemblies in the Earlier Middle Ages*, edited by P. S. Barnwell and M. Mostert, 29–46. Turnhout: Brepols, 2003.

Altenburg, Detlef, Jörg Jarnut, and Hans-Hugo Steinhoff, eds. *Feste und Feiern im Mittelalter: Paderborner Symposion des Mediävistenverbandes*. Sigmaringen: Thorbecke, 1991.

Althoff, Gerd. *Amicitia und Pacta: Bündnis, Einung, Politik und Gebetsgedenken im beginnenden 10. Jahrhundert*. Hanover: Hahn, 1992.

Althoff, Gerd. *Family, Friends, and Followers: Political and Social Bonds in Early Medieval Europe*. Translated by Christopher Carroll. Cambridge: Cambridge University Press, 2004.

Althoff, Gerd. "Feste und Bündnis." In *Feste und Feiern im Mittelalter*, edited by Detlef Altenburg, Jörg Jarnut, and Hans-Hugo Steinhoff, 29–38. Sigmaringen: Thorbecke, 1991.

Althoff, Gerd. "Der frieden-, bündnis und gemeinschaftstiftende Charakter des Mahles im früheren Mittelalter." In *Essen und Trinken in Mittelalter und Neuzeit: Vorträge eines interdisziplinären Symposions vom 10.–13. Juni 1987 an der Justus-Liebig-Universität Giessen*, edited by Irmgard Bitsch, Rudolf Schulz, Trude Ehlert, Xenja von Ertzdorff, 13–26. Sigmaringen: Thorbecke, 1997.

Althoff, Gerd. "Magdeburg-Halberstadt-Merseburg: Bischöfliche Repräsentation und Interessenvertretung im ottonischen Sachsen." In *Herrschaftsrepräsentation im ottonischen Sachsen*, edited by Gerd Althoff and Ernst Schubert, 267–93. Stuttgart: Thorbecke, 1998.

Althoff, Gerd. *Otto III*. Translated by Phyllis G. Jestice. University Park: Pennsylvania State University Press, 2003.

Althoff, Gerd. *Die Ottonen: Königsherrschaft ohne Staat*. 2nd ed. Stuttgart: W. Kohlhammer, 2005.

Althoff, Gerd. *Spielregeln der Politik im Mittelalter: Kommunikation in Frieden und Fehde*. Darmstadt: Wissenschaftliche Buchgesellschaft, 1997.

Althoff, Gerd. "Symbolic Communication and Medieval Order: Strengths and Weaknesses of Ambiguous Signs." In *Rituals, Performatives, and Political Order in North-*

ern Europe, c. 650–1350, edited by Wojtek Jezierski, Lars Hermanson, Hans Jacob Orning, and Thomas Småberg, 63–75. Turnhout: Brepols, 2015.

Althoff, Gerd. "The Variability of Rituals in the Middle Ages." In *Medieval Concepts of the Past: Ritual, Memory, Historiography*, edited by Gerd Althoff, Johannes Fried, and Patrick J. Geary, 71–87. Cambridge: Cambridge University Press, 2002.

Althoff, Gerd, Johannes Fried, and Patrick J. Geary, eds. *Medieval Concepts of the Past: Ritual, Memory, Historiography*. Cambridge: Cambridge University Press, 2002.

Althoff, Gerd, and Hagen Keller. *Heinrich I. und Otto der Große: Neubeginn und karolingischem Erbe*. Göttingen: Muster-Schmidt, 1985.

Althoff, Gerd, and Hagen Keller. *Die Zeit der späten Karolinger und der Ottonen: Krisen und Konsolidierungen 888–1024*. Stuttgart: Klett-Cotta, 2008.

Althoff, Gerd, and Ernst Schubert, eds. *Herrschaftrepräsentation im ottonischen Sachsen*. Vorträge und Forschungen 46. Stuttgart: Thorbecke, 1998.

Althoff, Gerd, and Christiane Witthöft. "Les services symboliques entre dignité et contrainte." *Annales* 58 (2003): 1293–1318.

Arnold, Benjamin. *Count and Bishop in Medieval Germany: A Study of Regional Power, 1100–1350*. Philadelphia: University of Pennsylvania Press, 1991.

Arnold, Benjamin. "German Bishops and Their Military Retinues in the Medieval Empire." *German History* 7.2 (1989): 161–83.

Arnold, Benjamin. *Medieval Germany, 500–1300: A Political Interpretation*. Toronto: University of Toronto Press, 1997.

Arnold, Benjamin. *Power and Property in Medieval Germany: Economic and Social Change, c. 900–1300*. Oxford: Oxford University Press, 2004.

Arnold, Benjamin. *Princes and Territories in Medieval Germany*. Cambridge: Cambridge University Press, 1991.

Austin, Greta. *Shaping Church Law around the Year 1000: The "Decretum" of Burchard of Worms*. Burlington, VT: Ashgate, 2009.

Austin, Greta. "Vengeance and Law in Eleventh-Century Worms: Burchard and the Canon Law of Feuds." In *Medieval Church Law and the Origins of the Western Legal Tradition*, edited by Wolfgang P. Müller and Mary E. Sommar, 66–76. Washington, DC: Catholic University of America Press, 2006.

Bachrach, Bernard S. *Charlemagne's Early Campaigns (768–777): A Diplomatic and Military Analysis*. Leiden: Brill, 2013.

Bachrach, David S. "Exercise of Royal Power in Early Medieval Europe: The Case of Otto the Great, 936–73." *Early Medieval Europe* 17.4 (2009): 389–419.

Bachrach, David S. "Henry I of Germany's 929 Military Campaign in Archaeological Perspective." *Early Medieval Europe* 21.3 (2013): 301–37.

Bachrach, David S. "Immunities as Tools of Royal Military Policy under the Carolingian and Ottonian Kings." *Zeitschrift der Savigny-Stiftung für Rechtsgeschichte* 130 (2013): 1–36.

Bachrach, David S. "Toward an Appraisal of the Wealth of the Ottonian Kings of Germany, 919–1024." *Viator* 44.2 (2013): 1–28.

Bachrach, David S. *Warfare in Tenth-Century Germany*. Woodbridge, UK: Boydell, 2012.

Bagge, Sverre. *Kings, Politics, and the Right Order of the World in German Historiography, c. 950–1150*. Studies in the History of Christian Thought. Leiden: Brill, 2002.

Baldwin, John W. "The Intellectual Preparation for the Canon of 1215 against Ordeals." *Speculum* 36.4 (1961): 613–36.

Barnwell, P. S., and M. Mostert, eds. *Political Assemblies in the Earlier Middle Ages*. Turnhout: Brepols, 2003.

Barthélemy, Dominique, and Stephen White. "Debate: The 'Feudal Revolution.'" *Past & Present* 152 (1996): 196–223.

Bartlett, Robert. *Trial by Fire and Water: The Medieval Judicial Ordeal*. Oxford: Clarendon, 1986.

Bergmeier, Armin, F. "The *Traditio Legis* in Late Antiquity and Its Afterlives in the Middle Ages," *Gesta* 56.1 (Spring 2017), 27–52.

Berkhofer, Robert, Alan Cooper, and Adam J. Kosto, eds. *The Experience of Power in Medieval Europe, 950–1350*. Burlington, VT: Ashgate, 2005.

Bernhardt, John W. "Concepts and Practice of Empire in Ottonian Germany (950–1024)." In *Representations of Power in Medieval Germany*, edited by Bjorn Weiler and Simon MacLean, 141–63. Turnhout: Brepols, 2006.

Bernhardt, John W. *Itinerant Kingship and Royal Monasteries in Early Medieval Germany, c. 936–1075*. Cambridge: Cambridge University Press, 1993.

Bernhardt, John W. "King Henry II of Germany: Royal Self-Representation and Historical Memory." In *Medieval Concepts of the Past: Ritual, Memory, Historiography*, edited by Gerd Althoff, Johannes Fried, and Patrick Geary, 39–69. Cambridge: Cambridge University Press, 2002.

Bernhardt, John W. "'On the Road Again': Kings, Roads and Accommodation in High Medieval Germany." In *Every Inch a King: Comparative Studies on Kings and Kingship in the Ancient and Medieval Worlds*, edited by Lynette Mitchell and Charles Melville, 303–24. Leiden: Brill, 2013.

Berschin, Walter. "Realistic Writing in the Tenth Century: Gerhard of Augsburg's *Vita S. Uodalrici*." In *Aspects of the Language of the Latin Prose*, edited by Tobias Reinhardt, Michael Lapidge, and J. N. Adams, 377–82. Proceedings of the British Academy 129. Oxford: Oxford University Press, 2005.

Bisson, Thomas. *The Crisis of the Twelfth Century: Power, Lordship, and the Origins of European Government*. Princeton, NJ: Princeton University Press, 2009.

Bisson, Thomas. "The 'Feudal Revolution.'" *Past & Present* 142 (1994): 6–42.

Bisson, Thomas. "The 'Feudal Revolution': Reply." *Past & Present* 155 (1997): 208–25.

Bisson, Thomas. "Medieval Lordship." *Speculum* 70.4 (1995): 743–59.

Blumenthal, Uta-Renate. *The Investiture Controversy: Church and Monarchy from the Ninth to the Twelfth Century*. Philadelphia: University of Pennsylvania Press, 1982.

Blumenthal, Uta-Renate. "The Papacy and Canon Law in the Eleventh-Century Reform." *Catholic Historical Review* 84 (1998): 201–18.

Bouchard, Constance B. "The Geographical, Social and Ecclesiastical Origins of the Bishops of Auxerre and Sens in the Central Middle Ages." *Church History* 46.3 (1977): 277–95.

Bouchard, Constance B. *Strong of Body, Brave and Noble: Chivalry and Society in Medieval France*. Ithaca, NY: Cornell University Press, 1998.

Bougard, François. "La justice dans le royaume d'Italie." In *La giustizia nell'alto medioevo (Secoli IX–XI)*, 1: 133–76. Spoleto: Presso la Sede del Centro, 1997.

Bougard, François. *La justice dans le royaume d'Italie de la fin du VIIIe siècle au début du XIe siècle*. Rome, 1995.

Boussard, Jacques. "Les évêques en Neustrie avant la Réforme grégorienne (950–1050 environ)." *Journal des savants*, 1970, 161–96.

Bowlus, Charles R. "The Early Kaiserreich in Recent German Historiography." *Central European History* 23.4 (1990): 349–67.

Boyce, Helen. *The Mines of the Upper Harz from 1514 to 1589*. Menasha, WI: George Banta, 1920.

Brown, Elizabeth A. R. "The Tyranny of a Construct: Feudalism and Historians of Medieval Europe." *American Historical Review* 79.4 (1974): 1063–88.

Brown, Peter. *The Cult of the Saints: Its Rise and Function in Latin Christianity*. Chicago: University of Chicago Press, 1982.

Brown, Peter. "Society and the Supernatural: A Medieval Change." In *Society and the Holy in Late Antiquity*, 302–32. Berkeley: University of California Press, 1982.

Brown, Warren. "Conflict, Letters, and Personal Relationships in the Carolingian Formula Collections." *Law and History Review* 25.2 (2007): 323–44.

Brown, Warren. *Unjust Seizure: Conflict, Interest, and Authority in an Early Medieval Society*. Ithaca, NY: Cornell University Press, 2001.

Brown, Warren, and Piotr Górecki, eds. *Conflict in Medieval Europe: Changing Perspectives on Society and Culture*. Burlington, VT: Ashgate, 2003.

Brown, Warren, and Piotr Górecki. "What Conflict Means: The Making of Medieval Conflict Studies in the United States, 1970–2000." In *Conflict in Medieval Europe: Changing Perspectives on Society and Culture*, 1–35. Burlington, VT: Ashgate, 2003.

Brühl, Carlrichard. *Fodrum, Gistum, Servitium Regis: Studien zu den wirtschaftlichen Grundlagen des Königtums im Frankenreich und in den fränkischen Nachfolgestaaten*

Deutschland, Frankreich und Italien vom 6. bis zur Mitte des 14. Jahrhunderts, 2 vols. Cologne: Böhlau, 1968.

Brundage, James A. *The Medieval Origins of the Legal Profession: Canonists, Civilians, and Courts*. Chicago: University of Chicago Press, 2008.

Brunner, Otto. *Land and Lordship: Structures of Governance in Medieval Austria*. Translated by Howard Kaminsky and James van Horn Melton. Philadelphia: University of Pennsylvania Press, 1992.

Brunner, Otto. *Land und Herrschaft: Grundfragen der territorialen Verfassungsgeschichte Südostdeutschlands im Mittelalter*. Baden bei Wien: Veröffentlichungen des Instituts für Geschichtsforschung und Archivwissenschaft in Wien, 1939.

Buc, Philippe. *The Dangers of Ritual: Between Early Medieval Texts and Social Scientific Theory*. Princeton, NJ: Princeton University Press, 2001.

Buc, Philippe. "Italian Hussies and German Matrons: Liutprand of Cremona on Dynastic Legitimacy." *Frühmittelalterliche Studien* 29 (1995): 207–25.

Buc, Philippe. "Ritual and Interpretation: The Early Medieval Case." *Early Medieval Europe* 9.2 (2000): 183–210.

Buc, Philippe. "Rituel politique et imaginaire politique au haut Moyen Âge." *Revue Historique* 303.4 (2001): 843–83.

Bührer-Thierry, Geneviève. "'Just Anger' or 'Vengeful Anger'? The Punishment of Blinding in the Early Medieval West." In *Anger's Past: The Social Uses of an Emotion in the Middle Ages*, edited by Barbara H. Rosenwein, 75–91. Ithaca, NY: Cornell University Press, 1998.

Cheyette, Fredric L. "Some Reflections on Violence, Reconciliation, and the 'Feudal Revolution.'" In *Conflict in Medieval Europe: Changing Perspectives on Society and Culture*, edited by Warren Brown and Piotr Górecki, 243–64. Burlington, VT: Ashgate, 2003.

Cheyette, Fredric L. "Suum cuique tribuere." *French Historical Studies* 6.3 (1976): 287–99.

Clanchy, M. T. *From Memory to Written Record: England, 1066–1307*. 3rd ed. Malden, MA: Wiley-Blackwell, 2013.

Clarke, Peter A. *The English Nobility under Edward the Confessor*. Oxford: Clarendon, 1994.

Collins, Kristen M. "Visualizing Mary: Innovation and Exegesis in Ottonian Manuscript Illumination." PhD diss., University of Texas at Austin, 2007.

Colman, Rebecca. "Reason and Unreason in Early Medieval Law." *Journal of Interdisciplinary History* 4.4 (1974): 571–91.

Cowdrey, H. E. J. "The Structure of the Church, 1024–1073." In *NCMH* 4.1, edited by David Luscombe and Jonathan Riley-Smith, 229–67. Cambridge: Cambridge University Press, 2004.

Crocker, Richard L. *The Early Medieval Sequence*. Berkeley: University of California Press, 1977.

Cushing, Kathleen. *Papacy and the Law in the Gregorian Revolution: The Canonistic Work of Anselm of Lucca*. Oxford: Clarendon, 1998.

Cutler, Anthony, and William North. "Word over Image: On the Making, Uses, and Destiny of the Marriage Charter of Otto II and Theophanu." In *Interactions: Artistic Interchange between the Eastern and Western Worlds in the Medieval Period*, edited by Colum Hourihane, 167–87. University Park: Pennsylvania State University Press, 2007.

Davies, Wendy, and Paul Fouracre, eds. *Property and Power in the Early Middle Ages*. Cambridge: Cambridge University Press, 1995.

Davies, Wendy, and Paul Fouracre, eds. *The Settlement of Disputes in Early Medieval Europe*. Cambridge: Cambridge University Press, 1986.

Davis, Jennifer R. *Charlemagne's Practice of Empire*. Cambridge: Cambridge University Press, 2015.

De Hamel, Christopher. *A History of Illuminated Manuscripts*. 1986. Reprint, London: Phaidon, 1994.

De Meulemeester, Johnny, and Kieran O'Conor. "Fortifications." In *The Archaeology of Medieval Europe*, vol. 1, *Eighth to Twelfth Centuries AD*, edited by James Graham-Campbell and Magdalena Valor, 316–41. Aarhus: Aarhus University Press, 2007.

Deshman, Robert. "*Christus rex et magi reges*: Kingship and Christology in Ottonian and Anglo-Saxon Art." *Frühmittelalterliche Studien* 10 (1976): 367–405.

Deshman, Robert. "Otto III and the Warmund Sacramentary: A Study in Political Theology." *Zeitschrift für Kunstgeschichte* 34.1 (1971): 1–20.

Drew, Katherine Fischer. "Public vs. Private Enforcement of the Law in the Early Middle Ages: Fifth to Twelfth Centuries." *Chicago-Kent Law Review* 70 (1994–1995): 1583–92.

Dugan, Máire A. "Coercive Power." *Beyond Intractability*, September 2003. http://www.beyondintractability.org/essay/threats

Ehlers, Caspar. "Bayern und Sachsen im Itinerar Heinrichs II: Ein Beitrag zur Bearbeitung Bayern im Repertorium der deutschen Königspfalzen." *Zeitschrift für bayerische Landesgeschichte* 65.3 (2002): 799–838.

Ehlers, Caspar. "Having the King—Losing the King." *Viator* 33 (2002): 1–42.

Eichert, Stefan. "Early Medieval Fortifications in Carinthia/Austria and Their Historical and Political Background." *Atti della Accademia Roveretana degli Agiati*, 9th ser., 2.262 (2012): 9–31.

Eldevik, John. *Episcopal Power and Ecclesiastical Reform in the German Empire: Tithes, Lordship, and Community, 950–1150*. Cambridge: Cambridge University Press, 2012.

Ewald, William. "Comparative Jurisprudence (I): What Was It Like to Try a Rat?" *University of Pennsylvania Law Review* 143.6 (1995): 1889–2149.

Ewald, William. "Comparative Jurisprudence (II): The Logic of Legal Transplants." *American Journal of Comparative Law* 43 (1995): 489–510.

Ewald, William. "The Jurisprudential Approach to Comparative Law: A Field Guide to 'Rats.'" *American Journal of Comparative Law* 46 (1998): 701–8.

Fehring, Günter P. *The Archaeology of Medieval Germany: An Introduction*. Translated by Ross Samson. New York: Routledge, 1991.

Fichtenau, Heinrich. *Living in the Tenth Century: Mentalities and Social Orders*. Translated by Patrick Geary. Chicago: University of Chicago Press, 1993.

Fillitz, Hermann. *Die Gruppe der Magdeburger Elfenbeintafeln*. Mainz: Philipp von Zabern, 2001.

Fleckenstein, Josef. *Die Hofkapelle der deutschen Könige. Vol. 2, Die Hofkapelle im Rahmen der ottonisch-salischen Reichskirche*. Stuttgart: Anton Hiersemann, 1966.

Fleckenstein, Josef. "Problematik und Gestalt der ottonisch-salischen Reichskirche." In *Reich und Kirche vor dem Investiturstreit*, edited by K. Schmid, 347–74. Sigmaringen: Thorbecke, 1985.

Fleming, Robin. *Kings and Lords in Conquest England*. Cambridge: Cambridge University Press, 2004.

Foucault, Michel. *Power*. Edited by James D. Faubion. 1994. Reprint, New York: New Press, 2000.

Fouracre, Paul. "'Placita' and the Settlement of Disputes in Later Merovingian Francia." In *The Settlement of Disputes in Early Medieval Europe*, edited by Wendy Davies and Paul Fouracre, 23–43. Cambridge: Cambridge University Press, 1986.

France, John. "War and Sanctity: Saints' Lives as Sources for Early Medieval Warfare." *Journal of Medieval Military History* 3 (2005): 14–22.

Ganshof, F. L. *Frankish Institutions under Charlemagne*, trans. Bryce Lyon and Mary Lyon. Providence: Brown University Press, 1968.

Ganshof, F. L. "The Use of the Written Word in Charlemagne's Administration." In *The Carolingians and the Frankish Monarchy*, ed. F. L. Ganshof, 125–42. London: Longman, 1971.

Garipzanov, Ildar H. *The Symbolic Language of Authority in the Carolingian World*. Leiden: Brill, 2008.

Garrison, Eliza. *Ottonian Imperial Art and Portraiture: The Artistic Patronage of Otto III and Henry II*. Burlington, VT: Ashgate, 2012.

Garrison, Mary. "The Franks as the New Israel? Education for an Identity from Pippin to Charlemagne." In *The Uses of the Past in the Early Middle Ages*, edited by Yitzhak Hen and Matthew Innes. Cambridge: Cambridge University Press, 2000, 114–61.

Gatti, Evan A. "In a Space Between: Warmund of Ivrea and the Problem of (Italian) Ottonian Art." *Peregrinations: A Journal of Medieval Art and Architecture* 3.1 (2010): 8–48.

Geary, Patrick J. *Before France and Germany: The Creation and Transformation of the Merovingian World*. Oxford: Oxford University Press, 1988.

Geary, Patrick J. *Furta Sacra: Thefts of Relics in the Central Middle Ages*. Princeton, NJ: Princeton University Press, 1991.

Geary, Patrick J. "Oblivion between Orality and Textuality in the Tenth Century." In *Medieval Concepts of the Past: Ritual, Memory, Historiography*, edited by Gerd Althoff, Johannes Fried, and Patrick J. Geary, 111–22. Cambridge: Cambridge University Press, 2002.

Genicot, Leopold. "Recent Research on the Medieval Nobility." In *The Medieval Nobility: Studies on the Ruling Classes of France and Germany from the Sixth to the Twelfth Century*, edited by Timothy Reuter, 17–35. New York: New Holland, 1979.

Gilchrist, John T. "Canon Law Aspects of the Eleventh Century Gregorian Reform Programme." *Journal of Ecclesiastical History* 13 (1962): 21–38.

Gilsdorf, Sean. *The Favor of Friends: Intercession and Aristocratic Politics in Carolingian and Ottonian Europe*. Leiden: Brill, 2014.

Glenn, Jason. *Politics and History in the Tenth Century: The Work and World of Richer of Reims*. Cambridge: Cambridge University Press, 2004.

Gluckman, Max. *Custom and Conflict in Africa*. 1956. Reprint, Oxford: Basil Blackwell, 1964.

Goebel, Julius, Jr. *Felony and Misdemeanor: A Study in the History of English Criminal Procedure*. Vol. 1. 1937. Reprint, Clark, NJ: Lawbook Exchange, 2006.

Goetz, Hans-Werner. "Der 'rechte' Sitz: Die Symbolik von Rang und Herrschaft im Hohen Mittelalter im Spiegel der Sitzordnung." In *Symbole des Alltags, Alltag der Symbole: Festschrift für Harry Kühnel zum 65. Geburtstag*, edited by Gertrud Blaschitz, Helmut Hundsbichler, Gerhard Jaritz, and Elisabeth Vavra. Graz: Akademische Druck- und Verlansanstalt, 1992, 11–47.

Goldberg, Eric J. *Struggle for Empire: Kingship and Conflict under Louis the German, 817–876*. Ithaca, NY: Cornell University Press, 2006.

Goldschmidt, Adolph. *Die Elfenbeinskulpturen aus der Zeit der karolinginschen und sächsischen Kaiser, VIII.–XI. Jahrhundert*. Berlin, 1918.

Hannig, Jürgen. "Zentral Kontrolle und regionale Machtbalance: Beobachtungen zum System der karolingischen Königsboten am Beispiel des Mittelrheingebietes." *Archiv für Kulturgeschichte* 66 (1984): 1–46.

Hannig, Jürgen. "Zur Funktion der karolingischen 'missi dominici' in Bayern und in den südöstlichen Grenzgebieten." *Zeitschrift der Savigny-Stiftung für Rechtsgeschichte* 101 (1984): 256–300.

Hauck, Karl. "Rituelle Speisegemeinschaft im 10. und 11. Jahrhundert." *Studium Generale* 3.11 (1950): 611–21.

Hauke, Hermann, and Elisabeth Klemm. *Das Gebetbuch Ottos III: Kommentar zur Faksimile-Edition der Handschrift Clm 30111 der Bayerischen Staatsbibliothek München*. Lucerne: Faksimile Verlag, 2008.

Hen, Yitzhak, and Matthew Innes, eds. *The Uses of the Past in the Early Middle Ages*. Cambridge: Cambridge University Press, 2000.

Hermanson, Lars. Introduction to *Rituals, Performatives, and Political Order in Northern Europe, c. 650–1350*, edited by Wojtek Jezierski, Lars Hermanson, Hans Jacob Orning, and Thomas Småberg, 1–40. Turnhout: Brepols, 2015.

Herrin, Judith. *The Formation of Christendom*. Princeton, NJ: Princeton University Press, 1987.

Hill, Boyd. *Medieval Monarchy in Action: The German Empire from Henry I to Henry IV*. New York: Allen and Unwin, 1972.

Hudson, John. *The Oxford History of the Laws of England*. Vol. 2, *871–1216*. Edited by Sir John Baker. Oxford: Oxford University Press, 2012.

Huschner, Wolfgang. "Erzbischof Johannes von Ravenna (983–998), Otto II. und Theophanu." *Quellen und Forschungen aus Italienischen Archiven und Bibliotheken* 83 (2003): 1–40.

Huschner, Wolfgang. "Kaiser der Franken oder Kaiser der Römer? Die neue imperiale Würde Ottos I. im Euromediterranen Raum." In *Otto der Große und das Römische Reich: Kaisertum von der Antike zum Mittelalter*, edited by Matthias Puhle and Gabriele Köster, 519–27. Regensburg: Schnell und Steiner, 2012.

Huschner, Wolfgang. *Transalpine Kommunikation im Mittelalter: Diplomatische, kulturelle und politische Wechselwirkungen zwischen Italien und dem Nordalpinen Reich (9.–11. Jahrhundert)*. 3 vols. MGH Schriften 52. Hanover: Hahnsche Buchhandlung, 2003.

Hyams, Paul. "Feud and the State in Late Anglo-Saxon England." *Journal of British Studies* 40.1 (2001): 1–43.

Hyams, Paul. *Rancor and Reconciliation in Medieval England*. Ithaca, NY: Cornell University Press, 2003.

Innes, Matthew. *State and Society in the Early Middle Ages: The Middle Rhine Valley, 400–1000*. Cambridge: Cambridge University Press, 2000.

Jaeger, C. Stephen. "The Courtier Bishop in *Vitae* from the Tenth to the Twelfth Century." *Speculum* 58.2 (1983): 291–325.

Jaeger, C. Stephen. "Origins of Courtliness after 25 Years." *Haskins Society Journal* 21 (2009): 187–216.

James, Montague Rhodes. *A Descriptive Catalogue of the Latin Manuscripts in the John*

Rylands Library at Manchester. Vol. 1. Manchester: Manchester University Press, 1921.

Jezierski, Wojtek, Lars Hermanson, Hans Jacob Orning, and Thomas Småberg, eds. *Rituals, Performatives, and Political Order in Northern Europe, c. 650–1350*. Turnhout: Brepols, 2015.

Johanek, Peter. "Merchants, Markets and Towns." In *NCMH* 3, edited by Timothy Reuter, 64–94. Cambridge: Cambridge University Press, 1999.

Kaiser, Reinhold. *Churrätien im frühen Mittelalter: End 5. bis mitte 10. Jahrhundert*. Basel: Schwabe, 1998.

Kaiser, Reinhold. "Les évêques de Langres dans leur fonction de 'missi dominici.'" In *Langres et ses évêques, VIIIe–XIe siècle: Aux origines d'une seigneurie ecclésiastique; Actes du colloque Langres-Ellwangen, Langres, 28 Juin 1985*, edited by Josef Semmler, 91–113. Langres: Société historique et archéologique de Langres, 1986.

Kantorowicz, Ernst H. "The 'King's Advent' and the Enigmatic Panels in the Doors of Santa Sabina." *Art Bulletin* 26.4 (1944): 207–31.

Kantorowicz, Ernst H. *The King's Two Bodies: A Study in Mediaeval Political Theology*. 1957. Reprint, Princeton, NJ: Princeton University Press, 1985.

Kantorowicz, Ernst H. *Laudes Regiae: A Study in Liturgical Acclamations and Medieval Ruler Worship*. Berkeley: University of California Press, 1946.

Keller, Hagen. "Die Idee der Gerechtigkeit und die Praxis königlicher Rechtswahrung im Reich der Ottonen." In *Ottonische Königsherrschaft: Organisation und Legitimation königlicher Macht*, 34–50. Darmstadt: Wissenschaftliche Buchgesellschaft, 2002.

Keller, Hagen. "Grundlagen ottonischer Königsherrschaft." In *Reich und Kirche vor dem Investiturstreit: Vorträge beim wissenschaftlichen Kolloquium aus Anlass des 80. Geburtstags von Gerd Tellenbach*, edited by Karl Schmid, 17–34. Sigmaringen: Thorbecke, 1985.

Keller, Hagen. "Herrscherbild und Herrschaftslegitimation: Zur Deutung der ottonischen Denkmäler." In *Ottonische Königsherrschaft*, 167–83. Darmstadt: Wissenschaftliche Buchgesellschaft, 2002.

Keller, Hagen. "Ottonische Herrschersiegel: Beobachtungen und Fragen zu Gestalt und Aussage und zur Funktion im historischen Kontext." In *Ottonische Königsherrschaft: Organisation und Legitimation königlicher Macht*, 131–66. Darmstadt: Wissenschaftliche Buchgesellschaft, 2002.

Keller, Hagen. *Ottonische Königsherrschaft: Organisation und Legitimation königlicher Macht*. Darmstadt: Wissenschaftliche Buchgesellschaft, 2002.

Keller, Hagen. "I placiti nella storiografia degli ultimi cento anni." In *Fonti medioevali e problematica storiografica: Atti del Congresso internazionale tenuto in occasione del*

90° Anniversario della fondazione dell'Istituto Storico Italiano 1883–1973, Roma 22–27 ottobre 1973, 41–68. Rome: Istituto storico italiano per il Medio Evo, 1976.

Keller, Hagen. "Zum Charakter der 'Staatlichkeit' zwischen karolingischer Reichsreform und hochmittelalterlichem Herrschaftsausbau." *Frühmittelalterliche Studien* 23 (1989): 248–64.

Keller, Hagen, and Stefan Ast. "*Ostensio Cartae*: Italienische Gerichtsurkunden des 10. Jahrhunderts zwischen Schriftlichkeit und Performanz." *Archiv für Diplomatik* 53 (2007): 99–121.

Kempter, H., and B. Frenzel. "The Impact of Early Mining and Smelting on the Local Tropospheric Aerosol Detected in Ombrotrophic Peat Bogs in the Harz, Germany." *Water, Air, and Soil Pollution* 121 (2000): 93–108.

Kern, Fritz. *Kingship and Law in the Middle Ages*. Translated by S. B. Chrimes. New York: Frederick A. Praeger, 1956.

Kershaw, Paul J. E. "Eberhard of Friuli, a Carolingian Lay Intellectual." In *Lay Intellectuals in the Carolingian World*, edited by Patrick Wormald and Janet Nelson, 77–105. Cambridge: Cambridge University Press, 2007.

Kershaw, Paul J. E. *Peaceful Kings: Peace, Power, and the Early Medieval Political Imagination*. Oxford: Oxford University Press, 2011.

Kirchweger, Franz, ed. *Die Heilige Lanze in Wien: Insignie, Reliquie, "Schickalspeer."* Vienna: Skira, 2005.

Kleinbauer, W. Eugene. "Charlemagne's Palace Chapel at Aachen and Its Copies." *Gesta* 4 (1965): 2–11.

Körntgen, Ludger, and Dominik Wassenhoven, eds. *Patterns of Episcopal Power: Bishops in Tenth and Eleventh Century Western Europe*. Berlin: De Gruyter, 2011.

Koziol, Geoffrey. *Begging Pardon and Favor: Ritual and Political Order in Early Medieval France*. Ithaca, NY: Cornell University Press, 1992.

Koziol, Geoffrey. "Political Culture." In *France in the Central Middle Ages, 900–1200*, edited by Marcus Bull, 43–76. Oxford: Oxford University Press, 2002.

Kränzle, A. "Der abwesende König: Überlegungen zur ottonischen Königsherrschaft." *Frühmittelalterliche Studien* 31 (1997): 120–57.

Kubach, Erich, and Victor H. Elbern. *L'Art de l'empire au début du Moyen Âge: Les Arts Carolingien et Ottonien*. Paris: Editions Albin Michel, 1973.

Laudage, Johannes. *Otto der Große: Eine Biographie*. Regensburg: Verlag Friedrich Pustet, 2001.

Lazzarini, Isabella. "La Communication écrite et son rôle dans la société politique de l'Europe méridionale au Moyen Âge." In *Rome et l'état moderne Européen: Collection de l'École française de Rome*, edited by J.-P. Genet, 265–85. Rome: École française de Rome, 2007.

Leonardi, Claudio. "Intellectual Life." In *NCMH* 3, edited by Timothy Reuter, 186–211. Cambridge: Cambridge University Press, 1999.

Leyser, Conrad. "Episcopal Office in the Italy of Liudprand of Cremona, c. 890–c. 970." *English Historical Review* 125.515 (2010): 795–817.

Leyser, Karl. "The Ascent of Latin Europe." In *Communications and Power in Medieval Europe: The Carolingian and Ottonian Centuries*, edited by Timothy Reuter, 215–32. London: Hambledon, 1994. Originally published as *The Ascent of Latin Europe: An Inaugural Lecture Delivered before the University of Oxford on 7 November 1984* (Oxford: Clarendon, 1986).

Leyser, Karl. *Communications and Power in Medieval Europe: The Carolingian and Ottonian Centuries*. Edited by Timothy Reuter. London: Hambledon, 1994.

Leyser, Karl. *Communications and Power in Medieval Europe: The Gregorian Revolution and Beyond*. Edited by Timothy Reuter. London: Hambledon, 1994.

Leyser, Karl. "The Crisis of Medieval Germany." In *Communications and Power in Medieval Europe: The Gregorian Revolution and Beyond*, edited by Timothy Reuter, 21–49. London: Hambledon, 1994. Originally published in Proceedings of the British Academy 69 (Oxford: Oxford University Press, 1984), 409–43.

Leyser, Karl. "Ends and Means in Liudprand of Cremona." In *Communications and Power in Medieval Europe: The Carolingian and Ottonian Centuries*, edited by Timothy Reuter, 125–42. London: Hambledon, 1994. Originally published in *Byzantium and the West, c. 850–c. 1200: Proceedings of the XVIII Spring Symposium of Byzantine Studies, Oxford, 30 March–1 April 1984*, edited by J. D. Howard-Johnston (Amsterdam: A. M. Hakkert, 1988), 119–43.

Leyser, Karl. "From Saxon Freedoms to the Freedom of Saxony: The Crisis of the Eleventh Century." In *Communications and Power in Medieval Europe: The Gregorian Revolution and Beyond*, edited by Timothy Reuter, 51–67. London: Hambledon, 1994. Originally published as "Von sächsischen Freiheiten zur Freiheit Sachsens: Die Krise des 11. Jahrhunderts," in *Die abendländische Freiheit vom 10. zum 14. Jahrhundert: Der Wirkungszusammenhang von Idee und Wirklichkeit in europäischen Vergleich*, edited by J. Fried, Vorträge und Forschungen 39 (Sigmaringen: Thorbecke, 1991), 67–83.

Leyser, Karl. "Henry I and the Beginnings of the Saxon Empire." *English Historical Review* 83.326 (1968): 1–32.

Leyser, Karl. "Liudprand of Cremona, Preacher and Homilist." In *The Bible in the Medieval World: Essays in Memory of Beryl Smalley*, edited by Katherine Walsh and Diana Wood, 43–60. Oxford: Basil Blackwell, 1985.

Leyser, Karl. *Medieval Germany and Its Neighbors, 900–1250*. London: Hambledon, 1982.

Leyser, Karl. "Ottonian Government." *English Historical Review* 96.381 (1981): 721–53.

Leyser, Karl. "The Ottonians and Wessex." In *Communications and Power in Medieval Europe: The Carolingian and Ottonian Centuries*, edited by Timothy Reuter, 73–104. London: Hambledon, 1994. Originally published as "Die Ottonen und Wessex," *Frühmittelalterliche Studien* 17 (1983): 73–97.

Leyser, Karl. "Ritual, Ceremony and Gesture: Ottonian Germany." In *Communications and Power in Medieval Europe: The Carolingian and Ottonian Centuries*, edited by Timothy Reuter, 189–213. London: Hambledon, 1994.

Leyser, Karl. *Rule and Conflict in an Early Medieval Society: Ottonian Saxony*. Bloomington: Indiana University Press, 1979.

Linehan, P. and J. Nelson, eds. *The Medieval World*. London: Routledge, 2001.

Little, Charles T. "The Magdeburg Ivory Group: A Tenth Century New Testament Narrative Cycle." PhD diss., New York University, 1977.

Lupoi, Maurizio. *The Origins of the European Legal Order*. Translated by Adrian Belton. Cambridge: Cambridge University Press, 2000.

MacLean, Simon. *Kingship and Politics in the Late Ninth Century: Charles the Fat and the End of the Carolingian Empire*. Cambridge: Cambridge University Press, 2003.

MacLean, Simon. *Ottonian Queenship*. Oxford: Oxford University Press, 2017.

Mann, Michael. *The Sources of Social Power*. 2 vol. 1986. Reprint, New York: Cambridge University Press, 2012.

Marchegay, Paul. "Duel Judiciaire Entre des Communautés Religieuses, 1098." *Bibliotheque de l'Ecole des Chartres* 1 (1839–40): 552–64.

Mariaux, Pierre Alain. "Warmund d'Ivrée et ses images: Politique et création iconographique autour de l'an mil." PhD diss., Université de Lausanne, 1997.

Matschullat, Jörg, Frank Ellminger, Nimet Agdemir, Stefan Cramer, Wilfried Ließmann, and Norbert Niehoff. "Overbank Sediment Profiles: Evidence of Early Mining and Smelting Activities in the Harz Mountains, Germany." *Applied Geochemistry* 12 (1997): 105–14.

Mayr-Harting, Henry. *Church and Cosmos in Early Ottonian Germany: The View from Cologne*. Oxford: Oxford University Press, 2007.

Mayr-Harting, Henry. *Ottonian Book Illumination: An Historical Study*. 2 vols. 1991. Reprint, London: Harvey Miller, 1999.

McKitterick, Rosamond. *The Carolingians and the Written Word*. Cambridge: Cambridge University Press, 1989.

McKitterick, Rosamond. "Charlemagne's *Missi* and Their Books." In *Early Medieval Studies in Memory of Patrick Wormald*, edited by Stephen Baxter, Catherine E. Karkov, Janet Nelson, and David Pelteret, 253–67. Burlington, VT: Ashgate, 2009.

McKitterick, Rosamond. *Charlemagne: The Formation of a European Identity*. Cambridge: Cambridge University Press, 2008.

McKitterick, Rosamond. "The Church." In *NCMH* 3, edited by Timothy Reuter, 130–62. Cambridge: Cambridge University Press, 1999.

McKitterick, Rosamond. *The Frankish Kingdoms under the Carolingians, 651–987*. New York: Longman, 1983.

McKitterick, Rosamond. "Perceptions of Justice in Western Europe in the Ninth and Tenth Centuries." In *La giustizia nell'alto medioevo (Secoli IX–XI)*, 2:1075–1102. Spoleto: Presso la sede del centro, 1997.

Metz, Wolfgang. "Quellenstudien zum Servitium regis (900–1200)." Part 1. *Archiv für Diplomatik* 22 (1976): 187–272.

Miller, William. *Bloodtaking and Peacemaking: Feud, Law, and Society in Saga Iceland*. Chicago: University of Chicago Press, 1990.

Mitchell, Lynette, and Charles Melville. *Every Inch a King: Comparative Studies on Kings and Kingship in the Ancient and Medieval Worlds*. Leiden: Brill, 2013.

Mohr, Kurt. *Geologie und Minerallagerstatten des Harzes*. 1978. Reprint, Stuttgart: Schweizerbart, 1993.

Monna, F., K. Hamer, J. Lévêque, and M. Sauer. "Pb Isotopes as a Reliable Marker of Early Mining and Smelting in the Northern Harz Province (Lower Saxony, Germany)." *Journal of Geochemical Exploration* 68 (2000): 201–10.

Müller, Wolfgang P., and Mary E. Sommar, eds. *Medieval Church Law and the Origins of the Western Legal Tradition*. Washington, DC: Catholic University of America Press, 2006.

Müller-Mertens, Eckhard. *Die Reichsstruktur im Spiegel der Herrschaftspraxis Otto des Großen*. Berlin: Akademie-Verlag, 1980.

Nelson, Janet. "Kingship and Royal Government." In *NCMH* 2, edited by Rosamond McKitterick, 383–430. Cambridge: Cambridge University Press, 1995.

Nelson, Janet. "Literacy in Carolingian Government." In *The Uses of Literacy in Early Medieval Europe*, edited by Rosamond McKitterick, 258–96. Cambridge: Cambridge University Press, 1990.

Nelson, Janet. "Liturgy or Law: Misconceived Alternatives?" In *Early Medieval Studies in Memory of Patrick Wormald*, edited by Stephen Baxter, Catherine E. Karkov, Janet Nelson, and David Pelteret, 433–47. Burlington, VT: Ashgate, 2009.

Nelson, Janet. "Rulers and Government." In *NCMH* 3, edited by Timothy Reuter, 95–129. Cambridge: Cambridge University Press, 1999.

Netterstrøm, Jeppe Büchert. "Introduction: The Study of Feud in Medieval and Early Modern History." In *Feud in Medieval and Early Modern Europe*, edited by Jeppe Büchert Netterstrøm and Bjorn Poulsen, 9–67. Aarhus: Aarhus University Press, 2007.

Netterstrøm, Jeppe Büchert, and Bjorn Poulsen, eds. *Feud in Medieval and Early Modern Europe*. Aarhus: Aarhus University Press, 2007.

Nicholson, Helen. *Medieval Warfare*. New York: Palgrave MacMillan, 2004.

Noble, Thomas F. X. "Secular Sanctity: Forging an Ethos for the Carolingian Nobility." In *Lay Intellectuals in the Carolingian World*, edited by Patrick Wormald and Janet Nelson, 8–36. Cambridge: Cambridge University Press, 2007.

Palsson, Vidar. "Power and Political Communication: Feasting and Gift Giving in Medieval Iceland." PhD diss., University of California, Berkeley, 2010.

Parkes, Henry. *The Making of Liturgy in the Ottonian Church: Books, Music and Ritual in Mainz, 950–1050*. Cambridge: Cambridge University Press, 2015.

Peter, Michael. "Otto Der Große und die Erneuerung des Römischen Reiches." In *Otto der Große und das Römische Reich: Kaisertum von der Antike zum Mittelalter*, edited by Matthias Puhle and Gabriele Köster, 560–63. Regensburg: Schnell und Steiner, 2012.

Peyer, Hans Conrad. *Von der Gastfreundschaft zum Gasthaus: Studien zur Gastlichkeit im Mittelalter*. MGH Schriften 31. Hanover: Hahnsche Buchhandlung, 1987.

Pössel, Christina. "The Magic of Early Medieval Ritual." *Early Medieval Europe* 17.2 (2009): 111–25.

Pratt, David. *The Political Thought of King Alfred the Great*. Cambridge: Cambridge University Press, 2007.

Puhle, Matthias, and Gabriele Köster, eds. *Otto der Große und das Römische Reich: Kaisertum von der Antike zum Mittelalter*. Regensburg: Schnell und Steiner, 2012.

Reuter, Timothy. "A Europe of Bishops: The Age of Wulfstan of York and Burchard of Worms." In *Patterns of Episcopal Power: Bishops in Tenth and Eleventh Century Western Europe*, edited by Ludger Körntgen and Dominik Wassenhoven, 17–38. Berlin: De Gruyter, 2011.

Reuter, Timothy. "Assembly Politics in Western Europe from the Eighth Century to the Twelfth." In *The Medieval World*, edited by P. Linehan and J. Nelson, 432–50. London: Routledge, 2001.

Reuter, Timothy. "*Episcopi cum sua militia*: The Prelate as Warrior in the Early Staufer Era." In *Warriors and Churchmen in the High Middle Ages: Essays Presented to Karl Leyser*, edited by T. Reuter, 79–94. London: Hambledon, 1992.

Reuter, Timothy. *Germany in the Early Middle Ages, 800–1056*. New York: Longman, 1991.

Reuter, Timothy. "The 'Imperial Church System' of the Ottonian and Salian Rulers: A Reconsideration." In *Medieval Polities and Modern Mentalities*, edited by Janet Nelson, 325–54. Cambridge: Cambridge University Press, 2006. Originally published in *Journal of Ecclesiastical History* 33 (1982): 347–74.

Reuter, Timothy. "The Insecurity of Travel in the Early and High Middle Ages: Criminals, Victims, and Their Medieval and Modern Observers." In *Medieval Polities and Modern Mentalities*, edited by Janet Nelson, 38–71. Cambridge: Cambridge University Press, 2006.

Reuter, Timothy. "Introduction: Reading the Tenth Century." In *NCMH* 3, edited by Timothy Reuter, 1–24. Cambridge: Cambridge University Press, 1999.

Reuter, Timothy. "Kings, Nobles, Others: 'Base' and 'Superstructure' in the Ottonian Period." In *Medieval Polities and Modern Mentalities*, edited by Janet Nelson, 300–324. Cambridge: Cambridge University Press, 2006.

Reuter, Timothy. "The Making of England and Germany, 850–1050: Points of Comparison and Difference." In *Medieval Polities and Modern Mentalities*, edited by Janet Nelson, 284–99. Cambridge: Cambridge University Press, 2006.

Reuter, Timothy. *Medieval Polities and Modern Mentalities*. Edited by Janet Nelson. Cambridge: Cambridge University Press, 2006.

Reuter, Timothy. "Peace-Breaking, Feud, Rebellion, Resistance: Violence and Peace in the Politics of the Salian Era." In *Medieval Polities and Modern Mentalities*, edited by Janet Nelson, 355–87. Cambridge: Cambridge University Press, 2006.

Reuter, Timothy. "Property Transactions and Social Relations between Rulers, Bishops, and Nobles in Early Eleventh-Century Saxony: The Evidence of the *Vita Meinwerci*." In *Property and Power in the Early Middle Ages*, edited by Wendy Davies and Paul Fouracre, 164–99. Cambridge: Cambridge University Press, 1995.

Reuter, Timothy, ed. *The Medieval Nobility: Studies on the Ruling Classes of France and Germany from the Sixth to the Twelfth Century*. New York: New Holland, 1979.

Reuter, Timothy, ed. *Warriors and Churchmen in the High Middle Ages: Essays Presented to Karl Leyser*. London: Hambledon, 1992.

Reuter, Timothy, and Chris Wickham. "Debate: The 'Feudal Revolution.'" *Past & Present* 155 (1997): 177–208.

Reynolds, Susan. *Fiefs and Vassals: The Medieval Evidence Reinterpreted*. Oxford: Clarendon, 1994.

Reynolds, Susan. *Kingdoms and Communities in Western Europe, 900–1300*. Oxford: Clarendon, 1984.

Roach, Levi. "Hosting the King: Hospitality and the Royal *Iter* in Tenth-Century England." *Journal of Medieval History* 37 (2011): 34–46.

Roach, Levi. *Kingship and Consent in Anglo-Saxon England, 871–978*. Cambridge: Cambridge University Press, 2013.

Roach, Levi. "Submission and Homage: Feudo-Vassalic Bonds and the Settlement of Disputes in Ottonian Germany." *History* 97.327 (2012): 355–79.

Rollason, David, Conrad Leyser, and Hannah Williams, eds. *England and the Continent in the Tenth Century: Studies in Honor of Wilhelm Levison (1876–1947)*. Turnhout: Brepols, 2010.

Rosenwein, Barbara, ed. *Anger's Past: The Social Uses of an Emotion in the Middle Ages*. Ithaca, NY: Cornell University Press, 1998.

Rosenwein, Barbara, ed. *Negotiating Space: Power, Restraint, and Privileges of Immunity in Early Medieval Europe*. Ithaca, NY: Cornell University Press, 1999.

Sagarin, Rafe. *Learning from the Octopus: How Secrets from Nature Can Help Us Fight Terrorist Attacks, Natural Disasters, and Disease*. New York: Basic Books, 2012.

Sagarin, Rafe. "Natural Security for a Variable and Risk-Filled World." *Homeland Security Affairs* 6.3 (2010): 1–20.

Santifaller, Leo. *Zur Geschichte des ottonisch-salischen Reichskirchensystems*. Ser. Sitzungsberichte der osterreichische Akademie der Wissenschaften, phil. hist. Klasse 229.1. Vienna: Akademie der Wissenschaften, 1964.

Sawyer, Peter. "The Bloodfeud in Fact and Fiction." In *Tradition og historieskrivning: Kilderne til Nordens ældst historie*, edited by Kirsten Hastrup and Preben Meulengracht Sørenson, 27–38. Acta Jutlandica 63.2. Aarhus: Aarhus University Press, 1987.

Sawyer, P. H., and I. N. Wood, eds. *Early Medieval Kingship*. Leeds: University of Leeds, 1977.

Scales, Len. "Beyond the *Regnum Teutonicum*." *German History* 27.1 (2009): 145–49.

Schieffer, Rudolf. "Der ottonische Reichsepiskopat zwishen Königtum und Adel." *Frühmittelalterliche Studien* 23 (1989): 291–301.

Schlesinger, Walter. "Early Medieval Fortifications in Hesse: A General Historical Report." *World Archaeology* 7.3 (1976): 243–60.

Schmid, Karl, ed. *Reich und Kirche vor dem Investiturstreit: Vorträge beim wissenschaftlichen Kolloquium aus Anlass des 80. Geburtstags von Gerd Tellenbach*. Sigmaringen: Thorbecke, 1985.

Schramm, Percy Ernst. "Die 'Heilige Lanze,' Reliquie und Herrschaftszeichen des Reiches und ihre Replik in Krakau: Ein Überblick über die Geschichte der Königslanze." In *Herrschaftszeichen und Staatssymbolik: Beiträge zu ihrer Geschichte vom 3. bis zum 16. Jahrhundert*, 2:492–537. Stuttgart: Anton Hiersemann, 1955.

Schramm, Percy Ernst. *Herrschaftszeichen und Staatssymbolik: Beiträge zu ihrer Geschichte vom 3. bis zum 16. Jahrhundert*. 3 vols. Stuttgart: Anton Hiersemann, 1954–56.

Schramm, Percy Ernst. *Kaiser, Rom und Renovatio: Studien zur Geschichte des römischen Erneuerungsgedankens vom Ende des karolingischen Reiches bis zum Investiturstreit*. Darmstadt: Wissenschaftliche Buchsgesellschaft, 1957.

Schramm, Percy Ernst, and Florentine Mütherich. *Denkmale der deutschen Könige und Kaiser*. Munich: Prestel Verlag, 1962.

Shepard, Jonathan. "Marriages towards the Millennium." In *Byzantium in the Year 1000*, edited by Paul Magdalino, Hugh Kennedy, David Abulafia, Benjamin Arbel, Mark Meyerson, and Larry J. Simon, 1–33. Leiden: Brill, 2003.

Shoemaker, Karl. *Sanctuary and Crime in the Middle Ages, 400–1500*. New York: Fordham University Press, 2011.

Skinner, Patricia, ed. *Challenging the Boundaries of Medieval History: The Legacy of Timothy Reuter*. Turnhout: Brepols, 2009.

Smail, Daniel Lord, and Kelly Gibson. *Vengeance in Medieval Europe*. Toronto: University of Toronto Press, 2009.

Suckale-Redlefsen, Gude. *Mauritius: Der Heilige Mohr / The Black Saint Maurice*. Houston, TX: Menil Foundation, 1987.

Sutherland, Jon N. "The Idea of Revenge in Lombard Society in the Eighth and Tenth Centuries: The Cases of Paul the Deacon and Liudprand of Cremona." *Speculum* 50.3 (1975): 391–410.

Sutherland, Jon N. *Liudprand of Cremona, Bishop, Diplomat, Historian: Studies of the Man and His Age*. Spoleto: Centro Italiano di Studi sull'Alto Medioevo, 1988.

Taleb, Nassim Nicholas. *The Black Swan: The Impact of the Highly Improbable*. New York: Random House, 2007.

Taruskin, Richard. *Music from the Earliest Notations to the Sixteenth Century: The Oxford History of Western Music*. Oxford: Oxford University Press, 2009.

Tellenbach, Gerd. "From the Carolingian Imperial Nobility to the German Estates of Imperial Princes." In *The Medieval Nobility: Studies on the Ruling Classes of France and Germany from the Sixth to the Twelfth Century*, edited by Timothy Reuter, 203–42. New York: New Holland, 1979.

Þorláksson, Helgi. "Feud and Feuding in the Early and High Middle Ages: Working Descriptions and Continuity." In *Feud in Medieval and Early Modern Europe*, edited by Jeppe Buchert Netterstrøm and Bjorn Poulsen, 69–94. Aarhus: Aarhus University Press, 2007.

van Caenegem, R. C. *An Historical Introduction to Private Law*. Translated by D. E. L. Johnston. Cambridge: Cambridge University Press, 1992.

Vandersall, Amy L. "Two Carolingian Ivories from the Morgan Collection in the Metropolitan Museum of Art." *Metropolitan Museum Journal* 6 (1972): 17–57.

Veyne, Paul. *Comment on écrit l'histoire suivi de Foucault révolutionne l'histoire*. 1971. Reprint, Paris: Éditions du Seuil, 1978. Originally published in 1971.

Wagner, Anne. "L'image du pouvoir épiscopal aux Xe–XIe siècle: l'exemple lorrain," in *Hagiographie, idéologie et politique au Moyen Âge en Occident: Actes du colloque international du Centre d'Études supérieures de Civilsation médiévale de Poitiers, 11–14 septembre 2008*, edited by Edina Bozóky, 233–41. Turnhout: Brepols, 2012.

Wallace-Hadrill, J. M. "The Bloodfeud of the Franks." In *The Long-Haired Kings*, 121–47. 1962. Reprint, Toronto: University of Toronto Press, 1982.

Wallace-Hadrill, J. M. *Early Germanic Kingship in England and on the Continent*. Oxford: Clarendon, 1971.

Wangerin, Laura. "The Governance of Ottonian Germany in Historiographical Perspective." *History Compass* 15.1 (2017): e12367. https://doi.org/10.1111/hic3.12367.

Wangerin, Laura. "Holy Relics, Authority, and Legitimacy in Ottonian Germany and Anglo-Saxon England." *Haskins Society Journal* 27 (2015): 15–38.

Wangerin, Laura. "Octopuses and Ottonians: Biological Systems as Models for Decentralized Medieval Government." *Annalen des Naturhistorischen Museums in Wien*, ser. A, 120 (2018): 31–49.

Wangerin, Laura. "Royal Feuds and the Politics of Sanctity in Anglo-Saxon England and Ottonian Saxony." *Mirabilia* 18.1 (2014): 78–94.

Warner, David A. "Comparative Approaches to Anglo-Saxon and Ottonian Coronations." In *England and the Continent in the Tenth Century: Studies in Honour of Wilhelm Levison (1876–1947)*, edited by David Rollason, Conrad Leyser, and Hannah Williams, 275–92. Turnhout: Brepols, 2010.

Warner, David A. "The Cult of Saint Maurice: Ritual Politics and Political Symbolism in Ottonian Germany." PhD diss., University of California, Los Angeles, 1989.

Warner, David A. "Henry II at Magdeburg: Kingship, Ritual and the Cult of Saints." *Early Medieval Europe* 3.2 (1994): 133–66.

Warner, David A. "Reading Ottonian History: The *Sonderweg* and Other Myths." In *Challenging the Boundaries of Medieval History: The Legacy of Timothy Reuter*, edited by Patricia Skinner, 81–114. Turnhout: Brepols, 2009.

Warner, David A. "The Representation of Empire: Otto I at Ravenna." In *Representations of Power in Medieval Germany*, edited by Bjorn Weiler and Simon MacLean, 121–40. Turnhout: Brepols, 2006.

Warner, David A. "Ritual and Memory in the Ottonian *Reich*: The Ceremony of *Adventus*." *Speculum* 76.2 (2001): 255–83.

Warner, David A. "Thietmar of Merseburg: The Image of the Ottonian Bishop." In *The Year 1000: Religious and Social Responses to the Turning of the First Millennium*, edited by Michael Frassetto, 85–110. New York: Palgrave Macmillan, 2002.

Warner, David A. "Thietmar of Merseburg on Rituals of Kingship." *Viator* 26 (1995): 53–76.

Weber, Max. *The Theory of Social and Economic Organization*. Translated by A. M. Henderson and Talcott Parsons. New York: Oxford University Press, 1947.

Weiler, Bjorn, and Simon MacLean, eds. *Representations of Power in Medieval Germany, 800–1500*. Turnhout: Brepols, 2006.

Weinfurter, Stefan. "Authority and Legitimation of Royal Policy and Action: The Case of Henry II." In *Medieval Concepts of the Past: Ritual, Memory, Historiography*, edited by Gerd Althoff, Johannes Fried, and Patrick J. Geary, 19–37. Cambridge: Cambridge University Press, 2002.

Weinfurter, Stefan. "Der Anspruch Heinrichs II. auf die Königsherrschaft 1002." In *Papstgeschichte und Landesgeschichte: Festschrift für Hermann Jakobs zum 65. Geburtstag*, 121–34. Edited by Joachim Dahlhaus and Armin Kohnle. Cologne: Böhlau, 1995.

Weinfurter, Stefan. "Sakralkönigtum und Herrschaftsbegründung um die Jahrtausendwende: Die Kaiser Otto III. und Heinrich II. in ihren Bildern." In *Bilder erzählen Geschichte*, edited by Helmut Altrichter, 47–104. Freiburg im Breisgau: Rombach Verlag, 1995.

Werner, Karl F. "Missus—marchio—comes: Entre l'administration centrale et l'administration locale de l'Empire carolingien." In *Histoire comparée de l'administration (IVe–XVIIIe siècles): Actes du XIVe colloque historique franco-allemand, Tours, 27 mars–1er avril 1977, organisée en collaboration avec le Centre d'Études Supérieurs de la Renaissance par l'Institut Historique Allemand de Paris.* edited by Werner Paravicini and Karl F. Werner, 191–239. BdF 9. Munich: Artemis, 1980.

West, Charles. "Legal Culture in Tenth-Century Lotharingia." In *England and the Continent in the Tenth Century: Studies in Honor of Wilhelm Levison (1876–1947)*, edited by David Rollason, Conrad Leyser, and Hannah Williams, 351–75. Turnhout: Brepols, 2010.

White, Stephen D. "Feuding and Peace-Making in the Touraine around the Year 1100," *Traditio* 42 (1986): 195–263.

Whitelock, Dorothy. *English Historical Documents.* Vol. 1, *500–1042.* 1955. Reprint, London: Routledge, 1979.

Wickham, Chris. *Early Medieval Italy: Central Power and Local Society, 400–1000.* 1981. Reprint, Ann Arbor: University of Michigan Press, 1989.

Wickham, Chris. *The Inheritance of Rome: A History of Europe from 400 to 1000.* London: Penguin, 2010.

Wickham, Chris. "Justice in the Kingdom of Italy in the Eleventh Century." In *La giustizia nell'alto medioevo (Secoli IX–XI)*, 1:179–250. Spoleto: Presso la sede del Centro,1997.

Williams, Ann. "An Outing on the Dee: King Edgar at Chester, AD 973." *Mediaeval Scandinavia* 14 (2004): 229–43.

Wilmes, Peter. *Der Herrscher-"Adventus" im Kloster des Frühmittelalters.* Munich: Wilhelm Fink Verlag, 1976.

Wolf, Gunther. "Das Itinerar der Prinzessin Theophanu / Kaiserin Theophanu 972–991." In *Kaiserin Theophanu, Prinzessin aus der Fremde: Des Westreichs Grosse Kaiserin*, edited by Gunther Wolf, 5–18. Weimar: Böhlau, 1991.

Wolf, Gunther. "Nochmals zur Geschichte der Heiligen Lanze bis zum Ende des Mittelalters." In *Die Heilige Lanze in Wien: Insignie, Reliquie, "Schickalspeer,"* edited by Franz Kirchweger, 22–51. Vienna: Skira, 2005.

Wolfram, Herwig. *Conrad II, 990–1039: Emperor of Three Kingdoms.* University Park: Pennsylvania State University Press, 2006.

Wolter, Heinz. *Die Synoden im Reichsgebiet und in Reichsitalien von 916 bis 1056.* Paderborn: Schöningh, 1988.

Wormald, Patrick. "Lordship and Justice in the Early English Kingdom: Oswaldslow Revisited." In *Property and Power in the Early Middle Ages*, edited by Wendy Davies and Paul Fouracre, 114–36. Cambridge: Cambridge University Press, 1995.

Wormald, Patrick. *The Making of English Law: King Alfred to the Twelfth Century*. Vol. 1, *Legislation and Its Limits*. Oxford: Basil Blackwell, 1999.

Wormald, Patrick, and Janet Nelson, eds. *Lay Intellectuals in the Carolingian World*. Cambridge: Cambridge University Press, 2007.

Ziezulewicz, William. "Abbatial Elections at Saint Florent-de-Saumur (ca. 950–1118)." *Church History* 57.3 (1988): 289–97.

Zotz, Thomas. "Kingship and Palaces in the Ottonian Realm and in the Kingdom of England." In *England and the Continent in the Tenth Century: Studies in Honour of Wilhelm Levison (1876–1947)*, edited by David Rollason, Conrad Leyser, and Hannah Williams, 311-330. Turnhout: Brepols, 2010.

Zotz, Thomas. "Präsenz und Repräsentation: Beobachtungen zur königlichen Herrschaftspraxis im hohen und späten Mittelalter." In *Herrschaft als soziale Praxis: Historische und sozial-anthropologische Studien*, edited by Alf Lüdtke, 168–94. Veröffentlichungen des Max-Planck-Instituts für Geschichte 91. Göttingen: Vandenhoeck und Ruprecht, 1991.

Index

Printed and bound by CPI Group (UK) Ltd, Croydon, CR0 4YY
16/09/2026
14963487-0002